Charles Sweeny,
the Man Who
Inspired Hemingway

Charles Sweeny, the Man Who Inspired Hemingway

CHARLEY ROBERTS *and* CHARLES P. HESS

McFarland & Company, Inc., Publishers
Jefferson, North Carolina

LIBRARY OF CONGRESS CATALOGUING-IN-PUBLICATION DATA

Names: Roberts, Charley, 1948– author. | Hess, Charles P., 1950– author.
Title: Charles Sweeny, the man who inspired Hemingway / Charley Roberts and Charles P. Hess.
Description: Jefferson, North Carolina : McFarland & Company, Inc., Publishers, 2017. | Includes bibliographical references and index.
Identifiers: LCCN 2017038740 | ISBN 9781476669946 (softcover : acid free paper) ∞
Subjects: LCSH: Sweeny, Charles, 1882–1963. | Soldiers of fortune—United States—Biography. | Hemingway, Ernest, 1899–1961—Friends and associates. | United States. Army—Officers—Biography. | Military history, Modern—20th century.
Classification: LCC E748.S928 R63 2017 | DDC 355.3/32092 [B] —dc23
LC record available at https://lccn.loc.gov/2017038740

BRITISH LIBRARY CATALOGUING DATA ARE AVAILABLE

ISBN (print) 978-1-4766-6994-6
ISBN (ebook) 978-1-4766-2884-4

© 2017 Charley Roberts and Charles P. Hess. All rights reserved

No part of this book may be reproduced or transmitted in any form or by any means, electronic or mechanical, including photocopying or recording, or by any information storage and retrieval system, without permission in writing from the publisher.

Front cover image of Charles Sweeny courtesy Georges Rolland

Printed in the United States of America

McFarland & Company, Inc., Publishers
 Box 611, Jefferson, North Carolina 28640
 www.mcfarlandpub.com

To all those who have had the courage
to fight for the cause of liberty
through the ages

Acknowledgments

Any acknowledgment of appreciation for the people and institutions who have aided the authors in the preparation of this book must begin with Colonel Sweeny's grandson, Frank Goodbold. He generously provided us with unfettered access to all of Sweeny's papers in his possession. During a series of interviews, he also shared with us his many personal recollections of his grandfather. Without these contributions, many aspects of this book would not have been possible. We are deeply indebted to him.

We also want to express our special thanks to the following individuals for their able assistance with our research: journalist and author Cheryl Romo for her invaluable research, editing and advice; Georges Rolland of Nice, France, who shared with us the photographs and printed material he purchased at the Sweeny estate sale in Nice after the death of Charles Sweeny, Jr., in 2001; Scott Everson for access to the unpublished autobiography of his father, Kendall Everson; Alicia Mauldin-Ware, curator of special collections; Susan Lintelmann, curator of manuscripts, and Suzanne Christoff, associate director of unique resources, U.S. Military Academy Library; AnnaLee Pauls, reference assistant, and Sandra Calabrese, special collections assistant, Department of Rare Books and Special Collections, Princeton University Library; Theresa Fitzgerald, archivist, National Personnel Records Center, National Archives; Angie Kindig, assistant archivist, Hesburgh Library, University of Notre Dame; Jeanette McDonald Olson, library clerk, the *Spokesman-Review*; Zoltan Balogh, researcher, Bureau des Anciens de la Légion Etrangère; Bruce W. Smith, historian, 80th Division Veterans Association; Peter Kraus, associate librarian, University of Utah; Christel Guezello, Grande Chancellerie de la Légion d'Honneur; the staff of the Bureau Central des Archives Administratives Militaires; and J.C. Garcia, Cimentière Mairie de Saint-Andre de la Roche, Nice, France.

Finally, we want to thank our wives for putting up with our obsession over this project and providing encouragement whenever it was needed.

Table of Contents

Acknowledgments vi
Preface 1
Introduction: Heroes, Role Models and Legends 5

1. Family Influences — 19
2. His Early Years — 37
3. West Point Cadet — 43
4. Revolution in Mexico — 52
5. Venezuela: A Stand Against a Tyrant — 58
6. Nicaragua: Deposing Zelaya — 66
7. Paris, Wife and Children — 73
8. French Foreign Legion in the First World War — 79
9. "Over the Top" with the U.S. Army — 112
10. Polish-Soviet War — 133
11. Greco-Turkish War — 140
12. Morocco and the Rif War — 145
13. Spanish Civil War — 158
14. Dodging the FBI to Recruit Pilots for France — 165
15. The Eagle Squadrons and the Battle of Britain — 178
16. "Wild Bill" Donovan and the Office of Strategic Services — 196
17. *Moment of Truth*, or How Sweeny Would Have Won World War II — 203
18. A Thorn in the Side of Roosevelt — 208

19. 2600 Walker Lane	218
20. Defending Petain	221
21. Blaming FDR for Pearl Harbor	228
22. World Disorder and Revolution	237
23. Sweeny's Last War	241
Chapter Notes	253
Bibliography	271
Index	275

Preface

Charley Roberts: In 1990, I chanced upon a battered, musty 1965 copy of *Register of Graduates and Former Cadets of the Military Academy*. I bought it on a whim. I had no idea that it would lead to an inquiry that became an obsession lasting more than a quarter of a century.

When I later paged through the book, I came across the following entry on page 305 for a cadet from the Class of 1904 who left without graduating but still had quite a career: "*Charles Michael Sweeny, Wash.; Soldier of Fortune; In 7 wars under 5 flags; Pvt. USA SpW; French ForLegion & USA, World War I (Maj.); Polish Ar (Gen) & TurkishAr; French plt in RiffWar; SpCvWar; MG, French ForLegion; CO Eagle Sq. French AF & GpCO RAF, World War II; 3 times wded; D-SL City, Utah, 27 Feb 1963; a-81.*"

Intrigued, I set out to learn what I could about this man. Keep in mind, the Internet was still a few years off in 1990, so research tended to be a labor-intensive and time-consuming process. I found a biography of Sweeny had been published in 1972. However, *One Man's Wars* by British author Donald McCormick raised as many questions in my mind as it answered. I soon began sending Freedom of Information Act requests for records to various federal agencies—the departments of the Army, State and Justice, the Veterans Administration, the National Archives. After weeks or months, back came documents. Some agencies sent a few pages. Some, like the FBI, sent a thick stack. However, large sections of many pages were blacked out, either because the contents might violate some living person's privacy or because the contents were still classified after half a century. The deletions only hardened my resolve to discover the truth.

By early 2015, I had amassed a lot of information from books, newspaper articles, Internet searches and more FOIA requests. I'd also sent letters to French government agencies. (Luckily, I found a resource on the internet, Google Translate, which enabled me to instantly convert English to French.

A translation service wanted $100 a page to do that.) In time, these netted me information on Sweeny's French service record and medals.

Noting how much time and effort I had invested in this inquiry, my wife encouraged me to write a book about Sweeny. However, I felt I still had too many holes in my research. Then I had a brainstorm. I had noticed photos of Sweeny posted on the Internet by a man named Chuck Hess. I guessed (correctly, as it turned out) that he had a family connection to Sweeny. I hoped he might be able to fill in some of those holes. So I located an address for him and mailed him a letter asking if he would be open to discussing Sweeny. I got an immediate affirmative reply. We quickly connected by phone and within a few days decided to join forces. While neither of us had enough material alone, Chuck had the contact information for Sweeny's grandson, Frank Goodbold. After two lengthy phone conversations with Frank, I traveled to his home in Oregon to interview him and ended up taking home boxes of Sweeny's personal papers and photos. Later, I traveled to West Point to review archival material there. Meanwhile, Chuck obtained batches of insightful letters between Sweeny and his editor, Max Perkins, from the Princeton University Library as well as school records and more news accounts. He also uncovered the true story of Sweeny's role in three Latin American revolts. Over the next year, we worked like a pair of madmen, researching and writing, and exchanging drafts and advice on an almost daily basis. It took 25 years to research the book but just 12 months to write it.

Charles P. Hess: I never met Colonel Charles Sweeny. I first heard about him from my wife, Nicole, his granddaughter, in 1972, shortly after we were married. While the stories about him were entertaining I wondered if they were true. Due to tragic events in my wife's life, she lost her mother and brother in a dreadful automobile accident in 1958 and her father in 1965 to a heart attack, she was reluctant to discuss the details of her grandfather's life. The ensuing custody battle after her father's death left my wife with some bitter feelings that she preferred not to dwell on. But still my interest in Colonel Sweeny had been stirred.

A few years later, my brother-in-law, Frank Goodbold, lent me his copy of the book *One Man's Wars*, a biography of Charles Sweeny, by Donald McCormick. While the book answered some questions I had about the Colonel, it left me with an empty feeling inside. Much of the information in the book came from second- or third-hand sources, and many of the events and dates quoted seemed incorrect. I had even more questions after I read the book than before I read it. I became obsessed with finding out who the real Charles Sweeny was. I decided I wanted to write a book giving an accurate account of the Colonel's life.

As the years went by I heard many opinions from the family about the Colonel. At one point, one of my wife's siblings stated that after talking with many people who knew Sweeny, they felt everything written about him was a lie. That didn't deter me in my quest because I realized that any person who obtained notoriety such as the Colonel would have supporters as well as detractors. In the late 1990s I became a family history consultant to help people find out about their ancestry. In learning the job, I decided to use the Sweeny family as a project. The Internet was a tremendous tool that helped me find accurate sources about Sweeny and his family. I found countless newspaper and magazine articles, books, and other material that answered many of the lingering questions I had.

Early in 2015 I felt the time had come to write the book. Within a few days after making that decision I received a letter from Charley Roberts asking me if I would be willing to share the material I had about the Colonel and discuss it with him. I called him immediately and told him I wasn't interested in sharing but I would join forces with him to write the book. He agreed. In Charley, I found a kindred spirit, an experienced writer who was just as passionate and obsessed with this project as I was. If I ran into a problem while writing I would call Charley, and no matter what event or period in Sweeny's life I was inquiring about, he knew exactly what I was talking about and would offer suggestions. I am deeply grateful to Charley for his willingness to help and I'm proud of the results of our collaboration.

Introduction: Heroes, Role Models and Legends

As heir to one of America's great fortunes of the Gilded Age, Charles Michael Sweeny could have been a gentleman of leisure and privilege. Instead, he joined revolutions in Latin America, enlisted in the French Foreign Legion to fight the German kaiser, became the first American to earn France's highest medal for valor in World War I, commanded a U.S. Army battalion in that war, led troops in aerial and ground combat in foreign armies between the world wars, and dodged FBI agents in the United States to recruit pilots to fight the Nazis before America's entry into World War II. For a time, it seemed that wherever there was a war, there was Sweeny.

While these events would have been enough for most mortals, there are many more stories about Sweeny. Among these stories: he ran away from home at 16 to fight in the Spanish-American War, was kicked out of West Point for firing a cannon into the commandant's house as a prank, talked his way out of a firing-squad execution, was offered a harem as a reward for his services by the sultan of Morocco, served as a military advisor to the father of modern Turkey, was a brigadier general in the Polish army, commanded the R.A.F.'s Eagle Squadron in the Battle of Britain, and was a spy for France's intelligence service. Some of these tales are true, some are half-true and some are false, but all are part of the Sweeny legend that made him America's most celebrated soldier of fortune.

Often irascible, frequently irreverent but always irrepressible, Sweeny captured the imagination and admiration of Ernest Hemingway and became one of the author's real-life role models for his fictional manly heroes.

The Ernest Hemingway that Sweeny, then age 40, first met in war-torn Turkey in the fall of 1922 was not yet the famous American novelist. He was a 23-year-old journalist who had been sent to Paris the year before as a foreign correspondent for the *Toronto Star*.

At the time neither man could have imagined the unbreakable bond that would develop between the much older and worldly soldier of fortune, whose exploits had made headlines, and the young, callow writer, whose name was known only to family, friends and colleagues. But over the next four decades they became each other's stalwart booster and trusted confidant. They shared a great deal: adventures and wars, to be sure, but also certain emotional connections. Each man saw in the other some character traits and talents that they envied or wished to emulate. Sweeny was the war hero that Hemingway longed to be, while Hemingway was the acclaimed writer that Sweeny would have liked to be. Sweeny had a knack for dealing with women that Hemingway envied, while Hemingway had a gift for exuberance that Sweeny could only marvel at.[1]

The two men also shared a pattern of behavior that suggests an even deeper emotional link. According to George Seldes, the muck-raking journalist and author who knew both men well in Paris, they each tended to embellish their exploits. "Hemingway created myths and legends about himself and so was forced to live up to them," wrote Seldes in his autobiography.[2] Seldes seemed to hold a similar view of Sweeny, writing that he was "known to all as 'Sweeny of the Legion,' with the reputation of a romantic and dramatic career in the French Foreign Legion, sometimes called 'the greatest soldier of fortune of the century.' He always carried an armful of books, and everyone suspected he was writing his history. Once I asked him. He replied, 'Hell no, I'm writing a life of Jesus.'"[3] Yet, even a famous skeptic like Seldes fell into repeating some of Sweeny's legend. For example, he credited Sweeny, not future Hollywood mogul Merian Cooper, with organizing the Kosciusko Squadron to fight the Russian Bolsheviks in Poland.

Hemingway was born in Oak Park, Illinois, a suburb of Chicago, in 1899. His father was a physician; his mother was a classically trained singer and voice instructor who performed in local concerts. The son was close to his father but frequently in conflict with his domineering mother. In later years as an adult, Hemingway spoke often of how much he detested his

Charles Sweeny with his many military decorations (courtesy Georges Rolland).

mother.⁴ His relationship with his parents was a major factor in shaping Hemingway's personality, just as Sweeny's relationship with his parents had a major impact on him. Hemingway sought to avoid being dominated by women. Sweeny sought to exhibit the kind of raw courage his father had shown in battle and in facing down angry miners.

After a brief stint as a reporter for the *Kansas City Star*, Hemingway became an ambulance driver on the Italian front in June and early July 1918. There he was wounded in the legs and knee by a mortar blast that left him hospitalized for months. He returned to the United States in early 1919, still recuperating from his wounds. In late 1919, he became a freelance writer and then a reporter for the *Toronto Star*. While working in Chicago, and submitting articles to the *Star*, he met Hadley Richardson, who became the first of his four wives, in September 1921. Two months later, he was hired as a foreign correspondent by the *Star* and the couple moved to Paris.

When the Turks launched their offensive against the Greeks toward Smyrna on August 23, 1922, Hemingway's editor in Toronto cabled him to go there to cover the war. After a bitter argument with his wife, who didn't want him to go and refused to speak to him for the three days before he left, Hemingway took the Orient Express to Constantinople.

By the time Hemingway arrived in Constantinople on September 30, the war was essentially over. The Turks had occupied Smyrna on September 9 and a huge fire began on September 13 that swept through the Armenian and Greek quarters of the city. Turkish troops were accused of deliberately starting the fire to make it easier to get the non–Turkish populations to leave. The conflagration was not extinguished until September 22. Estimates of the dead ranged from 10,000 to 100,000. Between 50,000 and 400,000 refugees crowded the waterfront to escape the fire. The refugees spent two weeks on the quay before being evacuated to Greece while Turkish troops and irregulars engaged in looting and murder of civilians during this period.

Peace talks between the Allies and Turkish officials began October 1, Hemingway's second day in Constantinople. The talks took place in Mudanya, on the eastern shore of the Sea of Marmara, about 100 miles by land south of Constantinople. Meanwhile, reporters were confined to the Pera section in Constantinople. Like other journalists, Hemingway was dependent for information on official briefings by British officers and whatever scraps of news he could pick up in the bars.⁵

On October 3, the journalists began to hear stories about the evacuation of refugees from Smyrna. Three days later, the *New York Tribune* amassed enough information to paint a disturbing word picture of the terrible plight of the refugees as they huddled waiting to leave. On October 4, the *Tribune* scooped the competition by gaining entry to the peace talks and reporting that the Greeks and Turks had reached an accord.

By then, Hemingway was sick with fever. On October 6, he began taking quinine for malaria. For the next week he was too sick to even cover the official briefings. He filed stories based on rumors and gossip. On October 13, he was admitted to the British hospital.[6]

Two days earlier, an armistice had been signed. Five days after that, still weak with fever, Hemingway rallied enough to leave Constantinople by train for Adrianople (now Edrine) in eastern Thrace, about 150 miles west of Constantinople and 25 miles from the border with Greece. He spent two days there, during which he witnessed the "silent, ghastly procession" of refugees in the Maritza Valley on the road to Karagatch, part of the quarter-million refugees pouring out of eastern Thrace into western Thrace and Macedonia. He wrote a moving piece about what he saw, including the scene of an old man holding a blanket over a woman giving birth in the rain. Hemingway later drew on this refugee exodus when he described the Italian army's retreat from Caporetto in his 1929 novel *A Farewell to Arms* as well as the Spanish Civil War refugee in his 1938 short story "The Old Man at the Bridge."[7]

Hemingway filed his Greek refugee story and left for Paris by train on October 18. He spent a little less than three weeks covering the Greco-Turkish War, but the time paid him a rich reward. In later years, he was able to use what he did, what he saw and also what he heard from others to make his fiction come alive with true-to-life details.

Hemingway also acquired a real-life model for some of his fictional heroes. Hemingway biographer Carlos Baker wrote that the future novelist pumped a number of soldiers for information about the military situation, but one in particular stood out. "One of the most talkative," wrote Baker, "was a brusk, red-faced soldier of fortune named Colonel Charles Sweeny, who spoke like a man of the world and amazed Ernest with his grasp of military science and tactics."[8]

According to Sweeny biographer Donald McCormick, Sweeny took the young reporter under his wing. When Hemingway was felled by malaria, Sweeny coached him on how to deal with it. When Hemingway lacked sufficient narrative details for one of his deadline dispatches, Sweeny provided the necessary facts.[9]

McCormick speculated that this solicitude might have had something to do with the fact that both men had wives in Paris who were unhappy about their husbands' decision to leave them alone to go off to a war. In McCormick's assessment, "Hemingway saw in Sweeny the kind of man he wished to be, a tough, battle-scarred man of action, a war hero and a romantic soldier of fortune following whichever side captured his imagination and sympathy, an extrovert who enjoyed life and who could hold his own with women."

Hemingway biographer Michael Reynolds provided an excellent series of examples of the novelist's wishfulness about being more of an adventurer like Sweeny and other men of action that Hemingway admired. Among his examples, Reynolds cited Hemingway telling Gustavo Duran that portions of his 1940 novel *For Whom the Bell Tolls* were based on his experiences leading a company for Ataturk in Turkey and participating in revolutionary movements in Cuba, neither of which was true. He also cited Hemingway making up stories about being an Italian army officer with Arditi troops when he had actually been an ambulance driver. There's no shame in that, and Hemingway certainly risked life and limb, but apparently his derring-do just wouldn't do. Hemingway also was "intrigued with revolutions, spies, and clandestine operations through reading, watching, and talking with Charles Sweeny," and longed to be a "revolutionist." And with his deep reading in military history, he hungered to be a military commander.[10] Reynolds' analysis dovetails with McCormick's assessment.

Hemingway's later correspondence also supports McCormick's assessment of the relationship between the two men, in particular Hemingway's appreciation of Sweeny's ability to deal with women.

In a November 16, 1943, letter to Max Perkins, his editor as well as Sweeny's at Charles Scribner's Sons,[11] Hemingway wrote: "So sorry Waldo[12] is having woman trouble. That's one thing you have to hand to Charley Sweeny. He doesn't take nothing from them. If they start to make any trouble with Charley, he gives them that old tone of command. A man who suffers women like Evan[13] say, has a more incurable disease than cancer. And penicillin doesn't cure it."[14]

Professor Rose Marie Burwell has looked closely at Hemingway's relationship with women and concluded that he "believed women were destructive of a man's creative work." She added that Sweeny was "one of three influential males in Hemingway's life, and the only man he ever knew who was able to handle women."[15]

To call the relationship between Hemingway and Sweeny strange doesn't give it justice. How they managed to remain lifelong friends can only be described as bizarre. Both were opinionated, strong-willed men who never backed down from a challenge. They showed each other drafts of their work and then lambasted the other's writing with expletive-filled diatribes. To listen to them, many people thought they were bitter enemies about ready to come to blows or worse. But when they finished, they parted the closest of friends. In some special way, they understood each other and formed a unique kinship.

Hemingway considered Sweeny to be a great military man, but a difficult man to have as a friend. The following account by Hemingway of an incident during the Spanish Civil War offers some insights into their unconventional relationship as well as into Sweeny's personality. In a February 4, 1940, letter to Perkins, Hemingway began by saying Sweeny wanted him for "his staff," which is "a compliment because he is really a very talented soldier." Hemingway was apparently referring to Sweeny's efforts to raise an infantry division of American volunteers to fight the Nazis if they invaded France. Hemingway then described Sweeny's temperament in some detail, noting that he tended to argue with everyone and to berate those around him when things went awry. "He has one of the most brilliant military brains I have ever known and the French General Staff trust and respect him, but I know the sort of thing that will happen when he has a division as he will now, and I could prevent some of it maybe. The kind of thing I mean is that every time Charley gets angry he wants somebody shot."

Hemingway described a terrible row between them during the Spanish Civil War. "We started to argue [me to explain, Sweeny to denounce] at seven a.m. and it went on all over the front all day, in my room until 2 a.m. with Sweeny calling me all sorts of names, continually insulting me, harping on my lack of military education, my abysmal ignorance, my lack of this, my lack of that, balling [sic] me out in front of everybody and everyone there thought we were bitter enemies." Hemingway said those who witnessed the verbal fireworks expected the two men to begin shooting at each other at any moment. Consequently, the witnesses were stunned when the two men referred to each other in affectionate tones as an "old bastard," embraced, kissed each other on both cheeks and parted amicably. "He [Sweeny] is absolutely g__d____ insufferable at times," wrote Hemingway, "but I know he won't shoot me and I'm about the only white man alive that can get along with him all the time."[16]

In the same letter to Perkins, the egotistical Hemingway also expressed admiration of Sweeny's capacity for conceit. "Waldo [Pierce] gets along with him too by taking what no human would take. Ask Waldo about the time he was painting Charley's portrait and Charley finally started painting it himself. Boy, I'd like to have that confidence."

When Sweeny visited Hemingway in Paris in August 1925, Sweeny was on his way to Morocco to get involved in the Rif War there. Sweeny had raised a squadron of American pilots to fight for the French, who were aiding the Spanish, against the Riffian tribes in this colonial war. He invited Hemingway to join him. Hemingway considered the idea but ultimately decided to remain in Paris because going would interrupt his work on *The Sun Also Rises*.[17]

By the fall of 1925, Hemingway had finished the novel and was restless. He wrote to his father that he felt the need to get out of Paris, but wasn't sure where to go. "Will decide tomorrow. John Dos Passos and I may go down to the Rif together," he wrote. His renewed interest in Sweeny's latest military adventure was sparked by a news report the day before that Spanish troops were closing in on the Riffian leader and Sweeny's squadron was garnering plenty of press. In the end, Hemingway left Paris alone, but went only as far as Chartres, a lovely town in the Loire Valley 60 miles southwest of Paris with a cathedral containing the finest stained glass windows anywhere in Europe.[18]

Between the mid-1920s and mid-1930s, Hemingway and Sweeny saw a good deal of each other in Paris. They attended the bicycle races each week for a time until Sweeny learned that the races were "fixed" and refused to go any more.[19] Sometimes they went to Sunday mass together at the Church of St. Sulpice, located in the Latin Quarter near Hemingway's apartment.

During the Spanish Civil War, Hemingway spent a good part of 1937 and parts of 1938 in Spain. Sweeny arrived there in 1937 and, except for a few trips back to France, remained there until the war ended in 1939. Both went there as journalists, although that was primarily a cover for Sweeny.

Hemingway set his 1940 novel *For Whom the Bell Tolls* in Spain during the civil war, and he inscribed several copies of the book for Sweeny. One that was put up for auction in 2010 was inscribed "For Charley with the same affection and the same admiration as always. Ernest." In an article that year about this auction item, Joe Fay wrote that Hemingway and Sweeny were life-long friends, spending time in war zones together, attending sporting events in Paris, going on hunting and fishing trips, exchanging war stories and comparing battle scars. Fay observed, "I doubt there were very many men for whom Hemingway would have had both affection and admiration, much less write down for posterity that fact, which makes this book an even more impressive rarity to me." Fay said Hemingway probably gave the book to Sweeny in Cuba the year it was published. He speculated that Sweeny was in Cuba specifically to see Hemingway, perhaps to go deep-sea fishing or just passing through to yet another war. If Sweeny went to see Hemingway in early 1940, this may be when he asked Hemingway to join "his staff."[20]

Hemingway used Sweeny as one of three models for the central character, Colonel Richard Cantwell, in his 1950 novel *Across the River and Into the Trees*. The other two models were U.S. Army colonel Charles "Buck" Lanham and Hemingway himself as he imagined he might have been if he had been a career soldier instead of a writer. Biographer Carlos Baker cited a letter Hemingway wrote to Lanham to that effect.[21]

Lanham was a 1924 graduate of West Point who retired as a major general. Born in 1902, Lanham was much closer in age to Hemingway than was Sweeny and wrote poetry and short stories. Lanham saw a good deal of Hemingway while leading the 22nd Infantry Regiment through World War II battles in Normandy, northern France and the Hurtgen Forest.[22] Hemingway attached himself to the unit as a self-appointed scout in the approach to Paris and its struggle to break into Germany, which he described in first-hand detail in *War in the Siegfried Line*.

Biographer Michael Reynolds said Hemingway combined the careers of

Sweeny and Lanham to create the character of Colonel Cantwell, who knew too much of war—the misery, waste and blunders. The book was fiction, wrote Reynolds, but the details were fact-based.[23] The fierce, pointless fighting in the Hurtgen Forest "inspired some of Cantwell's most horrific memories in Across the River," wrote biographer Jeffrey Meyers.[24]

Carlos Baker said what Hemingway was trying to achieve was "a picture of a highly intelligent fighting man deeply embittered by experience. The background, as always, was love and death. In the foreground stood the embattled hero, the eternal type of 'one against the world.'"[25] The description is an apt one for both Lanham and Sweeny.

During World War II, Hemingway was induced to edit and write the introduction to an anthology of fiction and non-fiction stories about war. According to biographer Michael Reynolds, what seemed at first a simple task became a complicated undertaking when Sweeny, along with Max Perkins and others, become involved in selecting the stories.[26]

After the war and continuing until Hemingway's death in 1961, Sweeny and Hemingway remained in fairly regular contact through letters and visits. In a letter to his wife in 1945, Hemingway sorted his friends into two categories, his drinking and sporting friends, and his intelligent friends. He listed Sweeny among his intelligent friends, along with the likes of Max Perkins, Evan Shipman and Buck Lanham.[27]

In 1946, Sweeny, accompanied by wealthy Utah socialite Dorothy Bamberger Allen and her brother, Clarence Bamberger, traveled from Salt Lake City to visit Hemingway and his wife, Mary, at their home in Ketchum, Idaho. The occasion was a private screening of the movie *The Killers*, starring Burt Lancaster and Ava Gardner, the first of Hemingway's works on film that he admired. Actor Gary Cooper, who had played Hemingway's hero in the 1943 screen version of *For Whom the Bell Tolls*, and his wife, Rocky (Veronica), were there too.[28] Later that year, Ernest and Mary visited Sweeny and Dorothy Allen in Utah. Hemingway, Cooper and Sweeny also went hunting together during these visits. Over the years, there were more visits back and forth between Idaho and Utah, often to go hunting or fishing together. In addition, Sweeny visited Hemingway in New York in 1950, about the time Hemingway handed his publisher the final chapters of *Across the River and Into the Trees*.[29]

Hemingway as well as the press continued to enhance, if not embellish, the Sweeny legend. In a letter to Lanham, in 1946, Hemingway mentioned Sweeny, "a very old pal and soldier in various armies, Venezuelan against Castro, Mexican with Madero, Foreign Legion, U.S., Morrocan [sic], R.A.F. We were together in Near East and in Spain and he is one of my oldest friends." Hemingway added that Sweeny was staying with Dorothy Allen and her brother, "and they claim to have very high grade shooting with concrete blinds, marsh buggies, motor boats, etc. Sort of thing [I] have never done.

Seems a lot of apparatus to kill the innocent duck but have often found things that sound silly turn out to be practical and fun."[30]

The close personal relationship between Sweeny and Hemingway as well as with his wife, Mary, is demonstrated by the following collection of letters between them in the 1950s. The collection was made available to the authors by Sweeny's grandson, Frank Goodbold.

In a September 3, 1952, letter[31] addressed to "My dear Ernest," Sweeny wrote to offer his thoughts after having just read Hemingway's new novel, *The Old Man and the Sea*.

> I read your story Friday morning. Mary had written me that you were doing something good. In spite of that I was surprised and pleased. It is magnificent.
> I have asked opinions around—largely favorable. Those which were not favorable were enthusiastic.
> I gave it to a boy of fifteen to read. He is in High School, exceptionally bright. I am teaching him French. He curles [sic] up in a chair and read without buding [sic]. When he finished his eyes were full of tears. To comfort him I told him that I would ask you to autograph a copy for him. I sent it to you today. His name is Fred Auerbach. That he cried is a secret between him and me. Children feel deeply and are ashamed....
> Love to Mary. I miss you. Two years is a long time not have news from a friend.
> Affectionately, Charles Sweeny

Hemingway replied in the following three-page handwritten letter dated September 7, 1952, and addressed "Dear Charlie."[32]

> Thank you so much for the cable and for your letter. I'm glad you liked the book. I had a lot of luck with it.
> Tell me, Viejo,[33] what should we have an old man do next? I guess I got tired of reading books by all these despair pussies. Anyway I hope you and Dorothy both liked it.

After writing about fishing conditions, his health and that of Mary and two of their mutual local friends, and the latest doings of his three sons, Hemingway wrote:

> We still talk about the wonderful party and fun in Salt Lake and the fairest daughters of Zion. Wish I was writing a funnier letter.
> We are fonder of you than anybody. I always miss you. Please give our best love to Dorothy and our best to all of our friends out there. Mary sends her love.
> Ernest
> Wish we could get out this fall. There is the biggest current in the gulf stream we [have] ever seen. But the big fish aren't hungry. Yesterday I saw a marlin damned near as big as a gondola. But he just came to the boat and then went down. He would have impressed even you old bastard. Keep well and know we love you. I will look after the book for the boy.

In a September 14, 1952, letter,[34] Sweeny invited the Hemingways to visit and stay "as long as you please" in Dorothy Allen's guest house on her estate outside Salt Lake City.

> There is some good duck and pheasant shooting. Parties would be kept to a minimum. One to get it over with would perhaps be best. I hate 'em as you do. But the public has certain rights.
> What you are going to do now that you are a doddering old man—you speaking—is "doubtless" a tremendous problem. I can picture you doing a bloody thriller, a western or a comic strip tease. Of course you might do a comedy[.] I can imagine you doing a brilliant picaresque novel. There has always been something of the picaresque in all of your works. The subject might be stufft-shirtism in general and the military example in particular. "Over the River" [sic] almost filled the bill. Unfortunately it was a tragedy. My imagination does not go as far as to see Melpomene mistress of a Baladron.[35]

Sweeny then changed the subject to contemporary American politics and the upcoming U.S. presidential election between Republican Dwight Eisenhower and Democrat Adlai Stevenson.

> The two Dromios[36]—Ike and Stevie—disgust me, especially Ike. He does not seem to have even a little bit of character. If there is any good in the spectle [sic] it is to see the much propagandized military leaders shown up for the poor fish they are. I shall not vote or I shall vote for [the Progressive Party's Vincent] Hallinan. He at least stands for something. In 1948 I voted, my first essay, for Thurman [the Dixiecrats' Strom Thurmond]. He also stood for something.

Sweeny signed off with love to Mary and the hope that if Hemingway came to visit he would bring her along. "If you leave her at home I shall [be] much disappointed."

Sweeny's votes in these elections were apparently protests against the establishment party candidates because the views of Hallinan and Thurmond were at opposite ends of the political spectrum. Hallinan was a liberal California lawyer who battled powerful business interests and defended union leader Harry Bridges in his 1949 trial for perjury for denying he was a communist. Thurmond was a conservative South Carolina governor and U.S. senator who fought to preserve racial segregation. According to his biographers, Hemingway respected Sweeny but did not share his political views.

On October 25, 1952, Sweeny wrote again.[37] This time he mentioned that he planned to be in New York and Europe soon and wondered if they might be there at the same time and could get together. "As soon as I get this damned book out of my system I shall be on my way to Europe to live out my few remaining years," wrote Sweeny.

Mary Hemingway replied on October 30, 1952,[38] that they had no definite plans yet. "Ernest's idea is to go to Paris via the Isle de France or the Liberte, with minimum time in New York [and unadvertised] in time to finish up the jumping-racing season there; then in whatever way is most comfortable to go down to Kenya and Tanganyika to help some of his old friends attend to the Mau-Maus.[39] Back here in April." She suggested Sweeny let them know when he would be in Paris and how to reach him there so a meeting might be arranged. She said they hoped to avoid the press and fans on this trip. "Dear Charles," she added, "could we possibly go for another hour around the Louvre together? And let us go also to that restaurant where we eat the 'truffle au cinders.' And let us walk, walk, walk around that lovely town—if I can keep up with you. Dear Charles, you have, in the below-signed, a constant and fervent admirer."

The last part of the letter raises questions about the nature of the relationship between Mary and Sweeny. This letter, taken together with later letters below and one other clue, hint at a possible affair at some point, although it might simply have been an especially close friendship or a harmless flirtation. That other clue is a book of love poems, *Sonnets from the Portuguese*, signed by Mary that Sweeny's grandson, Frank Goodbold, found when he opened Sweeny's safe deposit box after his death. When he showed the book to Dorothy Allen, with whom Sweeny lived for the last 16 years of his life, he said she reacted "like someone had slapped her" and denied anything went on between Sweeny and Mary Hemingway.[40] However, putting a book in a safe deposit box implies it held special significance for Sweeny, but one which he wanted kept hidden, while Dorothy's reaction strongly suggests she also saw the book and its location as evidence of an affair.[41]

In any event, Sweeny replied to Mary on November 7, 1952[42]:

> Your problem of anonymity is a tough one. If you stay in New York the vultures will hunt you out. You might go to Philadelphia. Could pass a hundred years there without ever being aroused from your somnolence. Brooklyn might have the same effect but if you need a rest there is nothing like good old Virginia. I can recommend highly the John Marshall Hotel or the Jefferson [both in Richmond]. They are both so classical. After one hour under this influence Papa would write Georgian English a la Churchill—the meticulous absurdity of the Right Honorable Gentleman's pronouncements will go down through the ages side by side with those of Catilina when, in reply to Cicero, he postulated "quod erat Demonstradam."[43]
>
> I am not hoping to see Europe before the last days of winter or the first of spring. I am for California to work on this damned book. But if, a mournful if, we are ever again together in Paris, I shall be your faithful and devoted Cicerone.[44]

Many of the letters between Sweeny and the Hemingways concerned the respective health of the correspondents. Neither Sweeny nor Hemingway apparently accepted limitations to their previous robust lifestyle with anything resembling good grace. Sweeny had serious health problems in the early 1950s from which he only slowly and partly recovered.

In a May 14, 1957, letter, Mary Hemingway wrote to Sweeny[45]: "We are both delighted and relieved that the medicos cracked down on you in 1954—even wild boys like you and Ernest must pay some attention to your poor defenseless bodies—and it is marvelous that this last check-up of yours showed you in such good shape. But don't please—for all of us—now go jumping fences or working too long or too hard on the]Empire of Oil.] No single critique is so important to us, no matter how important to the oil fellows, as you are." After assuring Sweeny that she would see to it that Hemingway inscribed some books for Sweeny, Mary Hemingway added:

> We had a fine time in Spain last fall and I missed you furiously in Paris—the Louvre had all the best old things and some fine temporary exhibits on which I yearned for your comments and criticisms.
> Dearest Charles, we think and speak of you so often, and I miss your devil face. Best love to you and Dorothy—and best health and best luck.
> Your devoted Mary

In early 1959, Sweeny visited the Hemingways in Ketchum, Idaho. Shortly after his return to Salt Lake City, Sweeny telephoned Hemingway to say that he had had another stroke, which left him slightly paralyzed on one side. Coming on the heels of the loss of a close friend there in Ketchum, Hemingway, apparently feeling his own mortality, reportedly remarked, "I have very little depth on the bench in friends."[46]

In a March 3, 1959, letter to Sweeny, Mary Hemingway wrote[47]:

> What a man you are, to save us the bad news and go it alone. I wish I believed in prayer, or rather the power of same, because I'd pray for that wise doctor of yours, as well as for you. I pray for you sometimes and will continue to do so because I like doing anything that might pass as an attempt at some kind of return for all the enlightenment and stimulation and entertainment you've given me; but I have little faith in the praying (mantis) routine—it's just a gesture for you, or maybe a hedge in case I'm betting on the wrong horse. Though I couldn't do that for your doctor, tell him sometime for us how really grateful we both are that he has looked after you so well....
>
> Like a drop of water meandering through a swamp, I've been concerned lately in my head with this f—ing business of growing old. (This was caused partly by the sudden death two weeks ago of our good friend, Taylor Williams, who was a fishing and hunting guide here for many years and came each spring to fish the Gulf Stream with us in Cuba.... It was a body blow to us, and I was appalled by all the people here who said, "Well, maybe it was for the better—he was failing, you know," thus insuring themselves from having to come to grips with any strong, uncomfortable grief. He hadn't been failing—he'd been doing fine with his head sharp and sound and his body strong enough to work a full day every day.)
>
> I've been thinking that courage comes easier when you're young (you are the exception to this theory). You wear it, when young, like a feather in your hat and it is easy because you're dealing with chance and external hazards; but it's more difficult when you're old because you're forced to look inward—what goes into the damn body and what comes out of it. The area allotted to the exercise of courage narrows down, it becomes less fun, and so it's harder. (I mentioned this one time to Papa while we were in Escorial and he disagreed, but I can't remember why. Maybe he was thinking of you—and maybe it is just that you would never consider that it's harder now than it used to be.)
>
> Papa once said to me he had never given his body any quarter, and I think that's the way to do it; but I don't blame the Milquetoasts with their built-in cautions. I don't

think they have the blood to help it, unlike your Italian grandmother. Papa would run through half a dozen bodies in a couple of years."

After briefly describing their daily routine in Ketchum and their plans to go to Cuba and then on to Spain in mid-May, she signed it, "You always have my greatest admiration and devotion and a big kiss. Mary." Ernest Hemingway penned a brief postscript to the letter: "Best love and luck, Charlie, Much, EH."

The love continued but the luck they each had enjoyed through numerous adventures finally ran out for Hemingway on July 2, 1961, when he committed suicide with his favorite shotgun in the foyer of his home in Ketchum. As an indicator of how important Sweeny was in the famed novelist's life, he was one of 17 honorary pallbearers at the funeral in Ketchum. It was an eclectic group. It included well-known persons such as Buck Lanham, publisher Charles Scribner IV, author A.E. Hotchner, Spanish bullfighter Antonio Ordonez, *New York Post* syndicated columnist Leonard Lyons, New York restaurateur Toots Shor, and U.S. diplomat David K.E. Bruce as well as little-known local friends from Cuba, Florida and Idaho.[48]

A final indicator of Sweeny's importance was revealed in a 1963 article in *Esquire* magazine about Hemingway's home, Finca Vigia, outside Havana, Cuba. Surveying the contents of Hemingway's office, the author noted that alongside a framed wedding portrait of a son in uniform, photos of his two other sons and a grandchild, there was a photo of Sweeny. Photos of "various wives, Gary Cooper and Ingrid Bergman, atrocity pictures from the Spanish Civil War, Antonio Ordonez and African safari scenes" were put away, stuffed into drawers.[49]

Chapter 1

Family Influences

Any story of Charles Michael Sweeny has to begin with his family. If it wasn't for his father's (Charles Sweeny, Sr.) fanatical, almost maniacal, rise to fame and fortune, the son would not have had the financial means to become a crusader. If it wasn't for his loving mother, Emeline, who interceded on his behalf with his father, who became angry and disgusted with his son's "lavish bohemian" lifestyle, he would have been cut off from his family's fortune. If it wasn't for his brothers' and sisters' willingness to share the family fortune, he would not have been able to make his stand against the tyrants of the world.

Charles Sweeny, Sr., was cunning and ruthless. He was fearless, calculating, boastful, contentious, daring and let nothing stand in his way on his pathway to fortune. His enemies called him a fraud, a calculating schemer with no ethics, morals, or conscience. He was opportunistic and could recognize moneymaking opportunities where others couldn't. Yet first impressions of him were that he was confident, well-spoken, charming, "but above all, he was a promoter, a ballyhooer whose words, it was said, could charm the birds from the trees."[1] His amazing power of speech served him well in amassing his fortune. At his death, his countless acts of kindness, generosity, and charity became well known. He was a man of immense contradictions. He gained, lost, and regained his fortune many times over his lifetime.

He was born in New York City on January 20, 1849. His father, John, was an Irish immigrant from County Armagh; his mother, Mary, was from Manchester, England. Charles was the second child in the family; he had an older sister, Sarah Ann. John was a tailor who had "a limitless capacity for going into debt."[2] When Charles was three, his family moved to Paterson, New Jersey. There, his father became a merchant tailor with James A. Fleming. Over the following nine years, three more Sweeny children were born. Young Charles, age 12, attended public schools and worked at clerical jobs to contribute to the family finances. In 1863, another brother, Nicholas, was born, which added even more financial pressure on the family budget. Whether Charles tired of the burden of being the oldest son and supporting the family, or the glamour of the Civil War became too enticing, at age 15 he ran off to join the Union army. He was sent home because he was considered too young. Five days later, on January 29, 1864, he went to Trenton, New Jersey, and enlisted for a $300 bounty in Company F, Third New Jersey Calvary. He used a phony name, James McNulty, and lied about his age. This time he was accepted.[3]

The Third New Jersey was outfitted with Spencer repeating rifles that gave them a tremendous rate-of-fire advantage, 20 to 30 per minute, over Confederate muzzle loaders, two to three per minute. They also received new uniforms that were designed to be a recruiting tool to attract new recruits. The pants were sky-blue with yellow stripes. The jackets were dark blue with yellow cords across the front. On the front of the collar there was an orange-colored background. The regiment added a row of polished metal buttons on either side of the row of buttons on a standard cavalry jacket and connected them with yellow braid. Because of these ornate uniforms, they became known as the Butterfly Boys.[4]

The Third New Jersey was assigned to the Army of the Potomac, as a unit of the Third Division commanded by Major General Philip H. Sheridan.

In his service record, McNulty-Sweeny recorded that he saw action in the battles of the Wilderness, Spotsylvania Courthouse, Cold Harbor, and the early days of the siege of Petersburg. He also had the opportunity to serve under George Armstrong Custer when Sheridan promoted Custer and put the third New Jersey under his command.

When the war ended, McNulty-Sweeny was mustered out of the army on August 1, 1865.[5] The Third New Jersey had lost three officers and 47 enlisted men killed or mortally wounded in battle. However, the regiment lost two officers and 105 enlisted men, or twice the battle death toll, to disease. In considering total losses on both sides during the war, three of every five Union soldiers who died did so by disease, or about 224,000. For the Confederacy, two of every three deaths resulted from disease, or about 164,000. More Civil War Soldiers died from disease than in battle. McNulty-Sweeny was lucky to be alive at war's end.

Sweeny returned home a 16-year-old battle-tested veteran. He regaled his family with tales of glorious battles. However, life at home was boring and mundane when compared to the life of a soldier. He considered himself a man and decided to strike out on his own to seek his own destiny. Within weeks, he had enlisted in one of the thrown-together companies of Union and Confederate veterans to fight Maximilian, the Austrian royal installed by Napoleon as emperor of Mexico in 1864. Hundreds signed up. Sweeny's unit was called an American Legion. They boarded a ship and sailed to Acapulco but were prevented from landing by a force of United States Marines, who had been sent there to enforce U.S. neutrality. Thwarted, the Legion sailed on to southern California, disembarked and dispersed.

Sweeny made his way up the coast to San Francisco, arriving there in June of 1866 to visit his cousin, Peter Donahue, one of the founders of the Union Iron Works and Brass Foundry. Donahue gave Sweeny a place to sleep and a job as an apprentice bookkeeper. At night, he went to school and studied to become an accountant. In 1868, Charles moved into his own quarters at 570 Howard Street, completed his courses, and found another job moonlighting as a bookkeeper at boilermaker McAlpin, Spiers and Company. On April 20, 1869, Charles married Margaret Swords, a 17-year-old dressmaker who went by the name of Maggie.

About this time, his father, John, and his family, along with his grandfather, Paul, and his wife, Sarah, moved from Paterson, New Jersey, to San Francisco, and moved in with Charles and Maggie. John and his wife, Mary, now had six children, and Mary was pregnant again. Over the next three years, John and Mary would add another son and daughter to their family. Maggie Swords was pregnant too. When Charles and Maggie's daughter, Lillian, was born, she was about the same age as her youngest aunt. Living in a teeming household with so many Sweenys—six adults and nine children—under the same roof proved to be too much Sweeny for Maggie.[6] She left Charles and he divorced her on August 23, 1871.[7] Now Charles found himself a divorced man with a daughter to provide child support. He also was the main breadwinner for his grandparents and his father's enormous family. Lillian lived with her mother Maggie until April 20, 1896, when Maggie passed away.[8]

The next two years were monumental for Charles. He met two people who would change his life. First, he met Emeline Agnes O'Neil, whom he married on February 12, 1873, in St. John's Church, Oakland. The story of their wedding is amusing. Four months after the marriage he was behind bars, according to the *Territorial Enterprise*. "In Oakland, California, Charles Sweeny has been indicted by the Grand Jury for the crime of perjury. On the 12th of February, Sweeny applied to the County Clerk for a license to marry Emeline O'Neil, a minor, whose parents were averse to the suit. Charles swore her age up to the regulation standard and pines in a dungeon for his liberty and his Emeline. He will be tried in County Court on the 22nd instand [sic]." His new in-laws intervened and he was let off lightly.[9] Emeline's love and devotion to Sweeny and their marriage was remarkable. For the rest of her days she lived the life of a gypsy, following her husband on his quest for riches.

Charles Sweeny, Sr., family, 1898. From left, Emeline (wife), Francis Rockwood, Mary Gertrude, Sarsfield, Charles Michael, Lillian, Robert, Charles Sr., Emeline (courtesy Heritage University).

Second, he met John W. Mackay, an Irish Immigrant who got caught up in the gold rush and went to California in 1851 to seek his fortune. After prospecting for several years in the Sierra Nevada foothills, he went to the Comstock Lode in northern Nevada near Virginia City. He became a mining contractor, digging tunnels and constructing timbering for the local mines, accepting mining shares for payment. When the value of these shares soared, he decided there was more money to be made by processing ore than by digging for it. Using his mining shares to fund the project, he built one of the largest mills on the Comstock. In the 1860s, he formed a partnership with James C. Flood, William O'Brien, and James C. Fair, and they gained control of most of the valuable properties on the Comstock. Their business savvy paid off in 1873 when they struck the Big Bonanza, a vein of ore that produced more than $100 million in gold and silver. Mackay spent much of his time conducting business in San Francisco, frequenting gambling halls and boxing clubs. Charles' employer, the Union Ironworks, was rushed with orders for mine machinery. Sweeny met Mackay who told him to go east a matter of 300 miles to Virginia City to make his fortune. Miners there earned four dollars a day (a considerable amount at that time) for each eight-hour shift. That advice sent Charles into mining, with tremendous results, for it gave him the entry into a field where his daring, courage and sagacity had limitless potential.[10]

Charles resigned his bookkeeping job, moved his father's family to Oakland, and he and Emeline headed to Virginia City. It was a dirty, crowded, and busy town of about 20,000. It also was a place where a man could get rich or die young. In an average month, 15 men died in mining accidents. The miners still mourned the 49 who died underground in the 1869 fire in the Yellow Jacket, Crown Point, and Kentucky mines, one of the worst fires in mining history. Emeline hated the place on sight with its steep streets and crude homes scattered up the mountainside. The mills were almost within city limits and ran continuously; the loud noise they produced was annoying, to say the least.

Charles went to work in the Belcher Mine, one of the camp's major producers. "I worked at everything in mining—sinking shafts, running drifts, stopes—up to shaft boss [foreman]," he later said. He gained experience in timbering, the reinforcement of mineshafts with timber to prevent cave-ins as the miners dug deeper in the mountain. Sweeny claimed that one day he met up with Mackay, who offered him a job in the Consolidated Virginia. "We are having trouble on the 1600 foot level," Sweeny said MacKay told him. "Nobody seems to be able to get square sits [timbering] to hold up under the pressure at that depth. If you pull it through I'll give you a thousand dollars." That mine was truly a Hell on Earth. The mine at that depth was dangerous; the ground was unstable and porous, with streams of hot water that created clouds of choking steam. Powerful blowers could not ventilate it adequately at that depth. Under those conditions, men could only work for a few minutes each hour. To help cope with the conditions, each man was allotted as much as 95 pounds of ice to chew in a shift. Despite the hazards, Sweeny took on the challenge. Where others had failed, he succeeded. In fact, his timbering of the mine was so effective, MacKay kept him on the job for months as superintendent of timbering operations.[11]

At the conclusion of the timbering job, Sweeny returned to the Belcher Mine. The change nearly cost him his life. The lower levels were so hot that the regular shift had to be shortened in some of the drifts (tunnels) to four hours or less. Even then miners had to be sent out at regular intervals to recuperate. On October 30, 1874, the mine's steam whistle blared out a warning that the Belcher was on fire. Fortunately, the miners were lifted to safety without any loss of life, with only one serious injury. Sweeny was not on shift at the time, but hearing of the fire he volunteered to go back into the mine with 17 other men to seal the tunnels so the fire couldn't spread. The volunteers were naked from the waist up and wore cotton overalls on their legs. "Minutes after they began closing the bottom of the air shaft," according to one account, "a cave-in sucked the fire directly onto them. All were painfully burned and were lifted to the surface for treatment."[12] Charles had severe burns on his hands and face. When the doctors got through with him, he was a huge bundle of oiled cotton. Emeline, insisting on tending him alone, but during the night when she tried to shift his bandages, her dripping candle set the oiled cotton afire. Within a moment, Charles was a human torch. Although near death, he leaped from his bed, gathered the blankets around him and smothered the flames. It was weeks before he was able to leave his bed.[13]

Emeline had had enough of Virginia City and the Comstock. She insisted that they leave. With San Francisco in economic straits and the anti-Chinese rioting going on there, they decided to go to Portland, Oregon instead. Charles got a job as a sawyer in a little lumber mill on the Willamette River at $60 a month. That kept him busy for ten hours a day, but this employment was just a starter for his daytime activities. Before breakfast, he ran the company's store. At noon, he looked after shipping orders. In the evening, he relaxed by selling goods in the store and keeping its books. Feeling that there was no future in being a sawyer, and feeling overworked and misused by the company, he quit in disgust. The couple returned to Portland using a small stake they had accumulated.

At Portland, he found a job bookkeeping for Knapp-Burrell Company and branched out from that into general expert bookkeeping. It was not long before he recognized the need for a Merchants Exchange in Portland, so he went into a partnership with John McCracken, P. Wasserman, Williams Wadhams, D.J. Malarkey, M.S. Burrell, D.P. Thompson, James Steel, D.F. Leahy, and W.S. Ladd. Together they formed the Exchange in December 1879. Capitalized for $50,000, they sold shares for $50. Many of the subscribers represented the grain dealers and millers of the Willamette Valley, where much of the Pacific Northwest's exportable wheat was grown. At that time, wheat prices were controlled by buyers for the great English exporting offices. These buyers would get daily cables from London and Liverpool showing current prices of grain, and then go out to buy from the local farmers and dealers who had no idea of the market value of their products. The buyers were masters of negotiating prices way below the market value in order to turn a larger profit. Sweeny secured a cable service to give him a daily report on English markets and arranged with Western Union for special rates on brief coded messages to each of his subscribers, putting them on equal terms with the buyers.[14] Sweeny was the secretary of the exchange so he managed the office, sent market reports on a daily basis in code to the subscribers and members, sold stock and subscriptions, and maintained the accounts.

After the exchange had been running for a short time, Charles came up with a scheme that he thought would make him wealthy. Waterfront properties in Portland and Seattle were selling for absurdly low prices. So he resigned from the Knapp-Burrell Company, sold all of his shares in the Exchange totaling $18,000, and took out options on open waterfront property in both cities, in hopes of selling them to oil tycoon John D. Rockefeller. Traveling by ship and train, he journeyed to New York City, and by using his superior power of persuasion, he obtained an audience with Rockefeller. Although Rockefeller was impressed by his presentation, he failed to see the potential of the proposal. Sweeny wasn't able to convince him to invest in the property of two such obscure western terminals. With his money lost when the options expired, he gave up hope of turning the deal and worked his way back to Portland taking odd jobs as he went.

About this time, Emeline and Charles were blessed with a son. Charles Michael Sweeny was born January 26, 1882. Charles had an older sister, Mary Gertrude, who was born in January 1880, and apparently Emeline took her and went to San Francisco to be with her parents when Charles Jr. was born. This was probably due to the fact her husband was away from home trying to earn his fortune. Over the years the Sweenys would have a total of 12 children. Six of the children—Emeline, Sheridan, Richard, and the triplets Louis, Florence and Sarah—died as infants, and six survived. A second son, Robert, born in 1884, gained notoriety during the 1920s as a talented amateur golfer. Frank Rockwood, born in 1886, was the only one of the sons who eventually worked in his father's business. The fourth and youngest son, Joseph Sarsfield, born in 1895, was killed during World War I, serving as a captain in the artillery. The final surviving child, a daughter named Emeline Agnes, was born in 1889.

During his adventure to New York City, Sweeny was gone for almost a year. When he finally arrived back in Portland, he took a job as a special solicitor for the Pacific Mutual Insurance Company. He and Emeline were living in a hotel, the Clarendon. When his brother, Nicholas, a tailor like his father, came to Portland from Oakland, they all moved into a house together.

Although Charles Sr.'s mission to New York had failed, the failure didn't quench his ambition. His driving inner voice was telling him there were better ways to earn a living and he wanted to work for himself. Finally, in January of 1883, he quit his job, and with very little money in his pocket took the Northern Pacific eastward to Spokane Falls, arriving on January 19, 1883. Spokane at the time was nothing more than a railroad town. Sweeny later recalled, "The night I got there the town burned down—most of it, that is. Practically all the business part of the town was in the block between Front and Main Avenues on Howard Street. Fire that night ... swept the row of buildings on the east side of Howard Street in that block, including the store of Frank Moore and Goldsmith on the Front Street corner, opposite the California house." Where most people saw a disaster, the shrewd and clever Sweeny saw opportunity, and used his bravado to strike a bargain. "The next day I bought the stock Moore and Goldsmith had saved from the fire, $16,000 worth of it, for $10,000 [which he did not have but promised to pay] and set up business in a little shack further west on the river bank."[15] Charles Sweeny the wandering opportunist became a merchant almost overnight.

He took a partner, Robert J. Linden, and they started selling their fire-damaged goods and put the following ad in the *Spokane Falls Review* on May 19, 1883:

> To Be Cleaned Out at Any Price
> Having Bought this stock at 40 percent less than
> Any wholesale merchant could buy it, we to give our
> Customers the benefit thereof.
> We are bound to do the business
> If we don't make a cent.
> Call & See Us & Satisfy Yourselves!
> Sweeny, Linden & Co (successors to F.R. Moore & Co)
> Dealer in General Merchandise

Soon Sweeny bought out Linden and took full control of the store. "Not long afterwards Johnny Kreinbuhl built me a new store building next to Ziegler's hardware store on Howard Street north of Riverside Ave."[16] Sweeny advertised frequently in the newspaper but by October he demonstrated his ballyhooing skills by placing this ad: "This space reserved for Chas. Sweeny & Co.—who is so rushed with customers as to be unable to write out this advertisement."

In April, several men wandered into his store. According to Sweeny, "A gang of 26 men came in one day to figure on supplies. I had been around mining camps enough in my life to know they were miners in search of an outfit. A.M. Cannon was running a store on Riverside Ave. about Mill Street and I sent them over there to get figures from him. They got his prices and then come back to me and bought a bill of $3,000 of goods, all put up in 50 pound packs—flour, bacon, picks and a great quantity of other goods."

"That was the first outfit to start for the Coeur d'Alene placer diggings," Sweeny later recalled. "They were led by a man named [Willard O.] Endicott and the entire party was from Santa Rosa, Cal. Endicott had a letter from [Andrew J.] Pritchard, after whom Pritchard creek was named, telling of the discovery of placer gold, and the party was on its way into Pritchard's diggings." Pritchard had served with Endicott's father in the Civil War. After prospecting in several states, he had made his way to the mountains of northern Idaho in 1878. As he panned the streams feeding into the north fork of the Coeur d'Alene River, Pritchard concluded that the area had huge deposits of gold. He decided that he wanted to establish a religious colony supported by the gold found in the nearby creeks. He wrote letters to the people he knew urging them to come to Idaho promising them that the area could support employment of 15,000 to 20,000 men. This is what brought Endicott and his men to the Coeur d'Alenes. Sweeny recalled: "I didn't know this at the time and didn't find out about it till some time later. I was anxious to know where the men were bound for, and so I sent a man after them along the trail to bring me back word. They caught my man following them and threatened his life, so that he was glad to give up the chase and came back."

More determined than ever, on the fourth of July Sweeny set out on a "Fishing Trip" to find out where Endicott and his men went and met up with a man named George Ives. "Doc Allison, my wife and myself were up on Coeur d'Alene Lake fishing, when George Ives came into our camp," Sweeny recalled. "He had come down the North Fork and was on his way into Coeur d'Alene City for supplies. I rode in with him and he told me about the new diggings and it was then I found out where the Santa Rosa Bunch had gone. I went back with Ives and Sam Hayes to Pritchard Creek in August. Sam Hays located the site of Eagle City, where Pritchard creek empties into Eagle Creek. I bought the place off him, built a cabin and opened a store with supplies I brought in by pack train."[17]

"The first real discovery of gold was not made by Pritchard at all, but by George Ives," Sweeny said. "Pritchard had found nothing but flake gold. When Endicott and his bunch found that the old man had got them there without having anything to show, they were much disgusted. They threatened to hang Pritchard after they had worked for some weeks without result and were about to do it on the very day that Ives got down to bedrock and hit real pay dirt."[18]

Sweeny became active in buying and selling property in Coeur d'Alenes. By the end of 1891, when he had been active in the Idaho mines for seven years, Sweeny had been partner or agent for no less than 30 men from Salt Lake, San Francisco, and Portland. By himself or with others he had controlled as many as 60 mining claims. Some of these claims he sold within days, some he held for years. He was not unwary of a quick profit, as in the case of the Homestake, which he bought in the morning for $1,500, and sold in the afternoon for $2,000. Among those to whom he sold property were Wyatt and James C. Earp. They had paid $132 for the site of their saloon, the White Elephant. The Earps got into a heated dispute with a man by the name of Bill Buzzard over another piece of land. Sweeny and his friend, Volney Williamson, were on their way back up a gulch after a trip to Sweeny's store when the trouble started. "All of a sudden they started blazing away back and forth at each other across the gulch" recalled Sweeny. "One of them yelled to us, 'get down behind that log if you don't want to get killed.' Every time one of us would stick up his head to see if the way was clear to make a run for it, somebody would shout, 'get down d__n you, and keep down.'"

At this point Sweeny showed his courage and audacity. "Well, I went up there and stopped the fight. The row was over ownership of a lot and they agreed to leave it to me [to decide the issue]. Old Man Buzzard, who claimed the lot, had been shot in the thigh as he lay in his tent. We all went down to the store and after I heard all the argument I gave the lot to Buzzard. That made the Earps sore and they talked about getting me." Sweeny looked over his shoulder many days in fear of retaliation from the Earps.[19]

Placer mining in Eagle City petered out in 1884, so the miners moved on to Murray City and then on to Wardner on the south fork of the Coeur d'Alene River, where the Bunker Hill and Sullivan mines had been discovered. Sweeny went with them. This area became one of the major producers of silver and lead in the nation. With John Burke and other associates Sweeny bought an interest in the Tyler and the Emma mines, and later the Last Chance Mines. Their claims were neighboring to the Bunker Hill and Sullivan mines and others on the same mountainside. The years 1885 to 1893 were busy ones for Sweeny and his partners; they developed their mines as fast as possible by borrowing huge amounts capital to finance their operations, and were at the point of making them profitable. They faced serious obstacles as they developed their claims. The mines at Wardner required experienced, skilled miners who were paid $3.50 a day wages. When the Bunker Hill and Sullivan Mines were sold to new owners in 1897, they lowered the wage to $2.50 to $3.00, depending on the skill of the miners. The Sweeny group followed suit. This angered the miners, who immediately called a strike to have the previous wage restored. As a compromise to the miners, the company changed the rate to $3.00 and $3.50, depending on the experience of the miners, and work resumed. However, the miners, alarmed by the arbitrary wage reduction, formed the Wardner Miners' Union in November 1887, and unionism spread throughout the Coeur d'Alenes. This started a bitter dispute between labor and management that affected all of the mines in Wardner and other cities for the next 12 years. Strikes and violence were commonplace during this time.

To understand why the miners were so upset about what seems as an insignificant amount, it is necessary to consider that a dollar was worth a lot more in 1899. According to the Federal Reserve's inflation calculator, $3.50 in 1899 is the equivalent of $86.10 today. So a reduction of $1.00 in pay was actually a loss equaling $26.10 in daily purchasing power to the miners. The miners also found it unfair that they had to shop at the company stores and live in company boarding houses, with the prices and rents controlled by the mine owners, who earned a tidy profit on this arrangement. The miners felt they were in servitude to the mines.

Management formed a Mine Owners Association (MOA), whose sole purpose was to break the unions. The MOA tried to break the union by bringing in non-union miners from outside the area, going as far as Michigan to hire non-union workers. The union used threats and violence to intimidate the imported miners who they called scabs. Sweeny, a member of the MOA, was chosen to escort the Michigan miners to Burke, Idaho. He and 54 guards armed with Winchester and Marlin rifles met the imported miners as their train pulled into Helena, Montana. All along the rail route, union men threatened and reminded them that they were strikebreakers. When they arrived at Burke on May 14, 1892, an angry crowd of union miners formed a human barricade on the train platform hell bent on stopping the strikebreakers form exiting the train. But the iron-willed Sweeny refused to be intimidated. He led his 54 guards and the Michigan miners through the crowd, into town and up the hillside to the Union Mine.[20]

An uneasy peace settled in over the whole mining district for the next several years. There were frequent strikes, beatings, threats and murders, as non-union miners were physically run out of town. The unions tried to impose their will against the MOA. Several times the union tactics shut down the Sweeny Group's mines and brought them to the brink of financial disaster, but each time, using his commanding negotiating skills, Sweeny was able to survive. The unions committed acts of terrorism that resulted in the dynamiting of the Bunker Hill mill and other properties. Twice, in 1887 and 1899, the area fell under martial law and federal troops had to be sent in to restore order.

Sweeny had to overcome a succession of obstacles—unionism, excessive railroad rates, and finding an adequate power supply for his mines. By using his power of persuasion, he was able to overcome and put them behind him. It seemed that his problems were over. But his biggest problem was already looming on the horizon.

As the miners of the Sweeny Group dug deeper into the mountainside in Wardner, they made a startling discovery: they were mining the same vein of galena (ore) as all of the other mines. When men from the Tyler mine followed the foot wall of their vein downward into Last Chance ground, Last Chance miners listened in the earth to the Tyler digging closer and closer. When the Tyler broke through, there occurred a brief, belowground fight with fists and shovels in the flickering light of miner's candles. The apex law of the day stated that mine owners had the extralateral right to follow a vein of ore outside the boundaries of their claim as long as they were working a separate vein of ore. When they staked their claims, the mine owners failed to recognize that they were all working the same vein. Now the litigation began over who had the rights to the single vein of ore.[21] What resulted were countless lawsuits spanning several years. In one year alone, Sweeny was a party to more than 36 lawsuits with three decided in the Supreme Court in one day.[22]

Initially, the owners of the Sullivan and Bunker Hill mines sued the Sweeny Group and won a federal injunction against the Sweeny Group preventing them from operating their mines. Of course, they appealed. But with their mines shut down during the appeal, Sweeny's financial condition was desperate. He was deeply in debt to the bank, and he needed money to continue the appeal in federal court. He also needed money to provide for his family.

To add to his challenges, there was a national economic crisis, the Panic of 1893 going on, and there were thousands of men out of work. Jobs were scarce. A man by the name of Jacob S. Coxey of Massillon, Ohio, started a grassroots movement across the country encouraging a national road improvement program to create jobs. He organized the Good Roads Army of the Commonweal to march on Washington, D.C., and lobby for change. All over the nation, jobless men began forming companies to join Coxey's army. Sweeny got a job as a federal marshal and was put in charge of a force of 50 deputies to insure the peace in the Pacific Northwest and make sure that Coxey army recruits obeyed the law. By June 1894 the movement was over so he collected $600 in pay and began to look for other endeavors.

With the federal injunction still in place against the Sweeny Group, and awaiting a decision on their appeal, their mines were still idle, producing no income. Sweeny had no choice but to move his family from Wardner to Coeur d'Alene, where he owned a small house. He heard that there was new mining activity going on in the Rossland, British Columbia, area of Canada, and that meant there was an opportunity to make some money. He had two $20 gold pieces to his name. So he gave Emeline one, kept the other, and hopped on a railcar on a train headed north out of town. At Marcus, Washington, he hopped off the railcar and was ferried across the Columbia River by a local Native American. He then hiked into Rossland camp with his $20 gold piece still in his pocket.[23] The Le Roi mine was just coming into its own, as a major gold producer, and soon eastern Canada was in the middle of a major gold rush.

Charles Sweeny began to work his magic with words, just as had done in Spokane when he started his store. With nothing more than a $20 gold piece in his pocket, and his commanding personality, be began taking out mining options and buying claims, promising future payment. He began turning over his interests and within a year he formed the Silverene Gold Mining Company in October of 1895. It was formed to promote a gold-silver property in the Rossland area. The company was capitalized at $500,000 and his stock was printed at one dollar par value, and rose to 11 cents a share in 1896, its highest. The Silverene was one of dozens of Rossland companies with extravagant capitalization selling penny shares. In November of 1896, he sold a bloc of Silverene Stock that netted him $20,000. In later years he claimed this was a turning point in his career. Upon receiving payment, he recalled saying, "When I got that money, I actually bit it to see if it was real!" Like many mines of its day, it eventually became defunct.

While in Rossland, Sweeny got good news. He received word from Washington that his group had won its appeal in the Supreme Court and the injunction against them was lifted, so the Sweeny Group could resume their mining activities at Wardner, Idaho. He returned to Idaho with cash in hand and renewed ambition.

In 1900, he helped form the Empire State-Idaho Mining and Smelting Company to take over various holdings. He also formed the Buffalo Hump Companies to develop immense low-grade gold properties in central Idaho. After forming Buffalo Hump, he discovered its mines could not be run at a profit because of the high cost of transporting low-grade ore to smelters for processing. So he closed down the mines while the while the company's treasury was still full of cash from the proceeds of stock sales. He secretly used this money to buy the productive Tiger-Poorman mine, which was a masterstroke, acquiring productive property for a worthless one. Ever the promoter, Sweeny later sold the Buffalo Hump property to the Guggenheims for $3,000,000, convincing them to build a railroad to the area to transport the ore.[24]

About this time, Sweeny went into the banking business when he bought control of the Exchange National Bank. But the vexatious lawsuits continued. Claim after counter-claim continued, costing Sweeny and his partners a considerable fortune to defend themselves. Between 1900 and 1903, Sweeny made a monumental decision. It solved two problems: one, curbing the number (but not eliminating) the lawsuits against him; and two, addressing the monopoly the American Smelting and Mining Company held on lead production. American was owned by the Guggenheim family, and with their smelters they controlled most of the lead ore reduction of the Coeur d'Alene mines and they were players in the national market. They used a quota system and refused to buy all of the ore the mines could produce, thus limiting production, and controlling the price of lead. As a result, the Coeur d'Alene mines were not operating at full capacity, and that was cutting into their profits.

To overcome the Guggenheim monopoly, Sweeny made the decision to buy all of the mines at Wardner and put them under the control of one entity, the Federal Mining and Smelting Company. Henceforth, they would either acquire or build their own smelters, and go into direct competition with the Guggenheim's American Smelting and Mining Company. Sweeny and his representatives approached the mine owners at Wardner, and at first they were all excited and agreeable to the proposition. They could make a considerable profit selling their mines, and Federal could operate the mines at full capacity. As time went by, however, the owners of the Bunker Hill and Sullivan mines refused to sell, but they still liked the idea of forming Federal.

In order to make the merger work, Sweeny needed capital, considerably more, than that he and his partners would be able to raise. He moved to New York City and turned to John D. Rockefeller, Jr., of the Standard Oil Company for financial backing. He was the son the man who many years before refused to buy the Portland and Seattle real estate options from Sweeny. Whether it was Sweeny's powerful personality, or the idea of being in competition with the Guggenheims, Rockefeller and his people bought into the plan. With their backing, Federal was formed with Sweeny as president at an annual salary of $25,000. He received several thousand shares and a considerable amount of cash in the transaction. As Federal commenced business, the competition that Federal posed was too big a threat to American. The Guggenheims approached Rockefeller and Sweeny with a generous offer and bought out Federal in March of 1905. They left Sweeny in charge at $50,000 a year. Sweeny told newspapermen that the sale of Federal brought him $2,660,000, although that was probably a low estimate. In later statements under oath, he indicated that he received $1,014,000 for his common stock alone, but still held his preferred stock that was worth more millions. The *Spokesman-Review* estimated that "it would take three boxcars loaded to their limits to bring Mr. Sweeny's $2,660,000 back to Spokane should it be dished out to him in silver." In today's dollars, Sweeny's $2,660,000 would be worth more than $68,000,000.[25]

Charles Sweeny had political aspirations as early as 1902. But the merger of the Coeur d'Alene mines had been foremost on his mind. When he was asked by the Republicans in Washington State to run for Congress, he took a few hours to think about it. He then issued this statement: "I have never had any notion of becoming a candidate for senator and could not entertain the proposition made to me today. My business interests are so great that they are almost too much for me to attend to as it is. My refusal is final and absolute."[26] Although he refused at the time, the seed had been planted for him to make a run later. By 1905, he was a millionaire and the president of a major corporation with influential friends. He had all of the makings of a viable political candidate. Even though he had been investing in real estate for years, he returned to Spokane and immediately began to invest further by buying the Rookery and Riverside Buildings at the corner of Howard and Riverside.

After he had been in Spokane for a few days, he went to Portland, Oregon. Portland had been in the throes of an economic depression for several years, and the people of Portland were discouraged and had lost faith in the future of their city. Once again, he saw opportunity in a dire situation. Within 24 hours of arriving Sweeny invested around $1,250,000 in cash for several real estate holdings around the city. This would be the equivalent of more than $30,000,000 in today's money. The influx of cash seemed to stimulate the economy and revitalize the faith of the people. What followed was an economic boom in Portland that lasted for years. The publicity Sweeny received in the press was invaluable as his popularity soared. By his large investment in Spokane, Portland and other cities the people saw him as a man of vision who saw an unlimited future for the Northwest. Sweeny was rewarded for his vision, within a few years; he sold the real estate holdings he had bought at distressed prices for a hefty profit.[27] His wife, Emeline, became a proficient real estate appraiser and developer in her own right and made several shrewd purchases along with her husband.

He was now ready to run for Congress, but many of his opponents feared he would use his great wealth to buy his seat in the Senate. While he spent his money freely to set up and publicize his campaign, he didn't indulge in the political graft of buying votes. The Republican Party at the time supported the creation of a railroad commission to regulate the rates and practices of the railroad. But the mine owners opposed the commission because officials of the Northern Pacific had previously visited Spokane and made an under the table deal promising to build a second track into the Coeur d'Alenes and ship ore at lower rates in exchange for their support. But Sweeny showed his political savvy by siding with the party in favor of the commission. This was probably motivated by the fact that when Federal was sold to the Guggenheims he signed a non-compete agreement to cease all activities in the Coeur d'Alene area. Also on his agenda was support for Theodore Roosevelt's proposal to enlarge the Interstate Commerce Commission.

In addition to Sweeny, there were several other men in the running for the seat. The incumbent was Addison C. Foster of Tacoma, former senator John L. Wilson, and a young man from Kentucky Samuel H. Piles. These men became the front-runners in the race. In 1905, the Washington State Legislature, meeting in Olympia, elected the state's U.S. senators,[28] and the nomination required a majority of 69 votes to win. The voting commenced on January 17, 1905. On the first ballot, Foster garnered 43, Piles 32, Sweeny 27, Wilson 15, with the rest scattered among men who would soon drop out. Over the next six days there would be 12 voting sessions with no clear winner. By the 12th vote Foster had picked up 54 votes; he was within 14 of winning the election. With Foster gaining support and Sweeny stalled at 27, it was time to compromise. Fearing another vote would elect Foster; Sweeny went to see Sam Piles, finding him depressed. Piles told him, "he could see no chance for a poor man to be elected Senator, unless you help me."[29] Piles story was inspiring. He had once put $10,000 into a Yukon expedition, and then came to the northwest to check on its progress. His investment had vanished and he was financially devastated, forced to stay in the Pacific Northwest taking odd jobs to survive. He then opened a law office and slept on the floor, eating only one meager meal a day. Piles then entered the King's County Prosecutors Office without pay, and campaigned for Republican candidates throughout western Washington. He went into a law partnership with Prosecutor J.T. Ronald, who almost immediately dissolved the partnership to become mayor of Seattle. Having survived several setbacks, Piles had won a reputation for party loyalty. His characterization of himself as being a poor man may have struck a sympathetic chord with Sweeny. He could be charitable as well as callous. Sweeny as always saw an opportunity in the face of defeat. As a price for his support, Sweeny procured a written promise from Piles that he would support a state railroad commission, support Roosevelt's proposal to enlarge the Interstate Commerce Commission, advocate a separate federal judicial district for eastern Washington, and a port of entry for Spokane.

Sweeny returned to his campaign headquarters with Piles' promises in his pocket. Foster's people called and offered to pay for his campaign expenses in exchange for his endorsement. Sweeny felt he had struck a better deal with Piles so he sent word back to them, "he was able to pay his own bills, and at this session, a poor man will be elected Senator."[30]

Sweeny then called his backers together, told them of his decision, and then went to the floor of the legislature to formally withdraw. When he entered the chambers, the senators rose to cheer him. He then delivered his support to Piles who won the election with 125 votes. The *Spokesman-Review* reported, "The history of Samuel H. Piles' election to the United States Senate may be summarized in a single sentence—Charles Sweeny refused to be held up." The newspaper reported that five of six men who had been at Sweeny's side during the early balloting demanded money to keep their votes from Foster. When Sweeny turned them down, his managers recognized that he had forfeited the election.[31] The *Spokane Daily Chronicle* on January 27, 1905, declared "Charles Sweeny Hero of the Hour" and the big man of the Republican Party.

Returning to Spokane, Sweeny offered the following explanation: "I know there were a good many Spokane people who had a wrong opinion of me. They thought I went down there to get the election, regardless of means. Well, now my campaign is over, and I left politics of the state purer than they've been for a long time.... Some of the grafters went down to Olympia expecting that they would go home with enough money to start national banks." This ended Charles Sweeny's political aspirations. But in the press, his popularity soared. On January 6, 1906, the *Spokane Daily Chronicle* printed this article:

GIFT OF TWENTY THOUSAND DOLLARS FROM CHARLES SWEENY:
"Charles Sweeny, the Spokane Capitalist, presented Bishop O'Dea with a check for $20,000 last Thursday to be used in the constructing of a Catholic Cathedral now being built in Seattle," so states a report received from Seattle today. This is the largest individual gift to the cathedral fund. The new edifice will be completed within 12 months. "Mr. Sweeny has contributed nearly $500,000 to Catholic Churches and institutions in Spokane," states the Seattle report. "By turning his support in the last legislature to Piles, he made the latter's election to the United States Senate possible."[32]

He traveled to New York and resumed his role as president of Federal. He always said that he would retire at age 60, so on January 29, 1909, Sweeny resigned as president of the Federal Mining and Smelting Company, nine days past his 60th birthday. Sweeny spent his retirement years speculating in the stock market and oil properties and signed occasional depositions for long-standing lawsuits. He spent a great deal of his time reminiscing with old cronies about his glorious past victories. Even before his retirement he was taking highly questionable risks in the stock market. Just as he had done all of his life when he acquired great wealth, he would make a Custer-like charge into an investment without considered the consequences. His friend, John D. Rockefeller, Jr., disapproved when he said that speculating in stock, "a pastime in which a man who has no scruples against gambling may indulge with funds he does not need." As early as 1907 Rockefeller had warned Sweeny to get out of the market before prices fell, and in mid–March, he did, and avoided the losses. Then the market rallied and Sweeny, assuming the financial crisis was over, jumped in with both feet and invested freely. When the Panic of 1907 happened a short time later, which caused the suspension of the Knickerbocker Trust Company[33] on November 4, the nation fell into a widespread panic. Sweeny probably lost at least half of his fortune, but he never revealed how much the panic cost him. The shock ruined his health and a few years later he recalled that period as "when things were worst on earth!" Rockefeller bought 500 shares of Federal from Sweeny to keep him afloat financially.[34] Emeline insisted that he take life easier, suggesting a cruise around the world to take his mind off his terrible losses. With that in mind, he bought a yacht, the Czarina, and presented it to Emeline. It was re-christened the Emeline in her honor. It was a 206-ton, two-masted, steam-screw ship. A short time later, Sweeny became interested in larger ship, the Katomba, and bought it. It was a two-deck, twin-screw, schooner-rigged ship, 196 feet long. Sweeny re-christened it the Emeline as well

As business rallied, Sweeny the optimist returned to the market. He purchased 25,000 shares of the Rock Island Railroad at $35 and realized a quick profit when the stock jumped 31 points in one day. Sweeny never quite recovered fully from the Panic of 1907, but made reasonable gains in the market. No matter how unpredictable his investments he tried to provide his wife and family with the funds to live a lifestyle to which they were now accustomed. He and Emeline formed the Sweeny Investment Company to manage their assets. Six of the children of Charles and Emeline had died as infants; there were four living sons and two daughters. He established a trust in which his wife Emeline was to acquire 7,500 shares in the Sweeny Investment Company, his son Charles 2,500, and his son-in-law Francis Finucane 2,499.[35] That represented one share less than 50 percent of the total shares of the Sweeny Investment Company, with the rest to be divided among his remaining children, Robert, Frank, Sarsfield, Gertrude, Emeline, and Lillian, his daughter with Maggie Swords.

In 1914, his health started to fail and he was hospitalized frequently. He continued to play the stock market from his bed, investing the same $10,000 several times. He would buy in stocks he had a hunch would make quick gains and quickly sold them when they did. Late in 1915, Sweeny went to Portland and checked into the Portland Surgical Hospital. He was released but suffered a stroke and returned to the hospital on February 1, 1916. Emeline rushed to Portland to be with him. He recovered slightly but then his strength faded and on May 30, 1916, Charles Sweeny died with Emeline, daughter Gertrude and son Frank at his side.[36]

The funeral services for Sweeny were held June 2, 1916, at Our Lady of the Lourdes in Spokane. The Reverent Father A. Verhagen, assisted by the Reverent Father James Mackin, conducted the service of low mass. After the mass, Bishop Edward O'Day of Seattle gave a eulogy and in part made the following remarks. "In closing I'm going to ask you relatives, you friends, you members of this congregation, you of this city and country to reverence and remember Mr. Sweeny and to pray for the repose of his soul. To the members of this congregation in particular I say you would be very ungrateful should you forget him. He was your best friend. To him more than any other benefactor you owe this beautiful church in which you and your children worship. Not only did he help to build this church but he gave liberally of his wealth to help me build the beautiful cathedral in Seattle."[37]

Charles and Emeline were more than generous to the charities they felt strongly about. Father Mackin recalled several contributions stating, "He used to come and give to the poor although he lived in another parish." Mackin recalled that Sweeny was one of four men who paid a $3,000 debt when a damaged Hillyard Church was remodeled as St. Patrick's Church. It was Mackin's goal to build an adequate orphanage in Spokane. After 11 years of fundraising, he had raised enough money to start the project. Not only did Emeline and Charles provide the chapel, but when construction bills totaling $38,000 went unpaid, they wrote a check for the entire amount. Father Mackin wanted to start a home and school for wayward girls to be staffed by Sisters of the Good Shepherd. The Sisters had been operating temporarily in a rented house. The priest struggled to raise $6,500 for the price of a desirable 40-acre site but only came up with $1,500. The Sweenys not only offered $5,500 but also included the deed to the desired property that was made out to Emeline, and she signed it over to the Home of the Good Shepherd. Other charities they contributed to were the Sacred Heart Hospital and Gonzaga University for an Infirmary.[38] The total amount of their contribution is not known but estimates were in excess of $500,000.[39]

It is fitting to note that when Charles Sweeny was taken to his final resting place, one of the honorary pallbearers was Samuel H. Piles, the poor man he sent to Congress. It is ironic that just a few years earlier, Sweeny's opinions were front-page news across the country, but upon his death, he was more famous for being the father of a dashing, fierce-looking young man in a French uniform, his son Charles Michael Sweeny.

Chapter 2

His Early Years

In the spring of 1881, Emeline and Charles Sweeny were overjoyed when she discovered she was pregnant with their second child. Her husband, true to his relentless quest for fame and fortune, gave her enough money to sustain her and their daughter, Mary Gertrude, and then left them to seek their family fortune. This was probably when he went to New York City to sell the land options he took in Portland and Seattle to John D. Rockefeller of Standard Oil. As the time neared for her to deliver, she went to San Francisco to be with her parents and family so they could help her after the baby was born. On January 26, 1882, she delivered a healthy baby boy and named him Charles Michael Sweeny.[1] Over the years, he would also go by Charles Sweeny, Jr.

When his father returned to Portland from New York, he got a job with Pacific Mutual Life Insurance Company as a special solicitor. The family lived in Clarendon Hotel for a short time until Nicholas Sweeny, brother of his father, moved to Portland and they moved into a house together. For the rest of Charles Jr.'s childhood, his father probably seemed like a heroic figure who appeared and then disappeared in his life frequently. Most of the responsibility for the upbringing of young Charles and his siblings fell on the shoulders of his mother. Emeline was a remarkable woman. When she married at age 15 she had wisdom beyond her years. She also had great courage to endure the times she was left to her own devices to raise her family while her husband was gone for extended periods of time seeking their fortune. The nomadic lifestyle caused great sorrow. Out of the 12 children she bore, only six survived to adulthood.

In January 1883, Charles Sr. became restless; his overpowering desire for fame and adventure took control of him. He quit his job, and with little money in his pocket, got on a Northern Pacific train and headed east out of town. As previously stated, he ended up in Spokane Falls, Washington on January 19, 1883, shortly after the business district of Spokane had suffered a devastating fire. He purchased the goods of burned out merchants and set up shop in a shack a little further west on the river. Overnight the Sweenys became merchants. Young Charles was just a year old when his family moved to Spokane.

In April 1883, Sweeny Sr. sold supplies to a group of 26 miners. After learning the location of their diggings, in what became Eagle City, Idaho, he returned there in August, bought a parcel of land, built a cabin and opened a store with supplies he brought in by pack train. He also moved his family there.

Eagle City was a typical mining camp with its usual vices, saloons and brothels. Obviously, Eagle City was a terrible place to raise a family and Emeline did her best to shield her young children from the common vices of the miners. It also was a dangerous place, as illustrated by one of the true legends that became family lore: their father's previously mentioned run in with the Earp Brothers and the shoot-out that ensued.

By 1884, placer mining had run its course around Eagle City and the miners moved on to Murray City and then on to Wardner, on the south fork of the Coeur d'Alene River, where the Bunker Hill and Sullivan mines had been discovered. Sweeny went with them. The Wardner area became one of the major producers of silver and lead in the nation. About this time another son was born to the Sweenys. They named him Frank Rockwood.

In 1891, the Sweenys became concerned about the education of young Charles, as the schools in Wardner were of poor quality. Emeline had done her best to home school her children, but seeing the necessity for better schooling, the Sweenys sent young Charles to the Jesuit school at Gonzaga College in Spokane.[2] Gonzaga had originally been proposed as a school to teach Indian boys from the various Pacific Northwest Jesuit Missions. However, when Gonzaga opened in the fall of 1887, it accepted only white boys. It was named after Italian Aloysius Gonzaga, the patron saint of youth.

The curriculum was typical for the day. In the years that young Charles attended there, Gonzaga had three types of schools: college, high school, and elementary. It included a commercial course, the classics, the elementary course, literature, philosophy, theology, and the natural sciences. To be admitted, "applicants must be able to read and write, and not under ten years of age." Young Charles was going to turn ten during the school year so he was accepted for admission. School went from early September through late June. Tuition was $250 for the 10-month session. No student advanced unless he passed an exam at the end of the year.

While at Gonzaga, young Sweeny lived the life of a monk. There was a regimented schedule for the day, started at 5:30 a.m. with wake up and ended at 8:30 p.m. with prayers and bedtime six days a week. On Sunday, students attended two masses and other religious activities instead of classes. Extracurricular activities included sodality, debate, drama, band, choir, orchestra, and athletics.[3] Years later, Charles Jr. gave credit to the Jesuits for teaching him discipline, and helping him understand what law, order, and justice meant. "It was the Jesuits who taught me self-discipline and that's the only discipline worth having in the long run. If you're in a tough spot, it's self-discipline which will see you through, not the discipline of the parade ground."[4] Young Sweeny was bright and intelligent and learned French from the Jesuits to the point he could converse reasonably well. He was fond of books and had a remarkably retentive memory. He read studiously whenever he could get a hold of something to read. One biographer claims that Emeline had brought her children up as strict Catholics and had made up her mind that these qualities would make Charles a fine priest.[5]

The years 1885 to 1893 were busy ones for Sweeny Sr. and his partners, they developed their mines as fast as possible by borrowing huge amounts of capital to finance their operations, and were at the point of making them profitable. While young Charles was at Gonzaga, his father had to deal with unionism. Sweeny Sr.'s courage in the face of rowdy groups of miners made a lasting impression on young Charles.

A bigger problem arose while Charles Jr. was attending Gonzaga that almost destroyed the Sweenys' finances. This was the previously mentioned long, complex legal battles when it was discovered all of the mines in Wardner were mining the same vein of ore.

In 1896, the 14-year-old Charles Jr. went to the Rossland, British Columbia, mining camp to live with his father to learn the mining trade. There he witnessed first-hand his father in action. Although he admired his father for his bravery and ingenuity, he felt his father's ethics were questionable. As time went by, a rift between father and son widened. The Rossland experience also proved another pivotal point in the younger Sweeny's life. It happened that the house where they lived had a set of volumes on the history of the Civil War. Young Charles read them all and with his exceptional memory had an encyclopedic knowledge of that war. With that knowledge and the stories his father told him about his own war experiences, young Charles began to aspire to be a soldier.[6]

While in Rossland, the Sweenys got good news. They received word from Washington that the Sweeny Group had won their appeal in the Supreme Court and the injunction against them was lifted, so they could resume their mining activities at Wardner. Sweeny Sr. and his son returned to Idaho with cash in hand and renewed ambition.

Upon their return, his father sent him to work in the Wardner mines. His father's advice was "to learn how to work hard first, then if you have time, you can study afterwards."[7] The son spent long hours underground learning the lingo of the miners, their vices as well as their good points. This experience gave him a practical education while on the job. He gained knowledge of mining and engineering and also the self confidence to stand up and fend for himself.[8] In fact, he may have gained too much bravado for his own good. One of the legends of Sweeny Jr. is that when he was 15, he was lured into an infamous, seedy night haunt by some of his cronies. According to biographer Donald McCormick, the place was called the Golden Wheel and someone challenged the boy to make a "date" with Tiger Lil, the Golden Wheel's main lady of the evening. She also was the mistress of one of the meanest and toughest prospectors in the area. Never one to back down, Sweeny asked her to have a drink, and was led to her room in the back of the club. Their encounter was soon interrupted by Lil's prospector, who picked up Sweeny and tossed him out on the street with his trousers around his ankles. Enraged, Sweeny pulled up his pants, went back into the Golden Wheel and inflicted a bloody nose on the prospector, but was knocked unconscious and thrown out on the street again. When his father heard about this brawl, he was furious, but the Golden Wheel incident was a result of his own insistence of having his son work with lawless, brutal, and immoral miners. This incident ended his mother's hope that her son would become a priest. His mother had erroneously thought that his quick mind and fondness of books suggested a priestly calling.[9] Charles Jr. was becoming an argumentative, rebellious, and freethinking man, much to the displeasure of his father.

During the years 1897 and 1898, Charles Jr. was enrolled again at Gonzaga College along with his brother Robert.[10] In April 1898, tensions between the United States and Spain erupted into war following an explosion that sank the U.S. battleship Maine in Havana Harbor, Cuba. Charles, like his father during the Civil War, reportedly ran off to join the U.S. Army. He was 16. Many years later, newspaper accounts of Charles Jr.'s life reported that he served in the U.S. Army in the Spanish-American War. *The Register of Graduates and Cadets at the U.S. Military Academy*, where he later was enrolled, states it too. However, the wording of some of the entries, including Sweeny's, suggests the information is not necessarily based on official records. Some later newspaper accounts even reported that he saw action in that war.

However, it's improbable that he saw any action because this war was over so quickly. Admiral George Dewey destroyed Spain's Pacific Fleet in Manila Bay, the Philippines, on May 1, just six days after the war began. Two months later, U.S. troops captured San Juan Hill, overlooking Santiago Harbor, Cuba. This forced Spain's Caribbean Squadron out of the harbor and into the waiting guns of Admiral William Sampson's fleet, which, like Dewey's, quickly sank the Spanish ships. The war ended August 12, less than 16 weeks after it began.

The Gonzaga spring term ended in late June of 1898 and the fall term began in early September of that year. So there was a small window of time, in July of 1898, when he could have enlisted. If he did so, no record of it has been found. There also is no record of Sweeny receiving a pension for his service in the Spanish-American War, although he did ask for and receive a pension for service in the Philippine Insurrection, which overlapped his years as a West Point cadet. Therefore, it seems likely that, if he requested a pension for his time as a cadet, he also would have requested a pension for serving in the Spanish-American War if he had served. The best available evidence suggests he did not serve.

A probable explanation is that, if he ran off to enlist, the authorities discovered his real age and sent him home. His own son, the third Charles Sweeny in three generations, told biographer Donald McCormick that his father ran away from home at age 16 to fight in the war with Spain. It was his understanding that when he returned home his grandfather "kicked him down the steps."[11]

Through these ups and downs, the Sweeny family remained loyal to Gonzaga. In 1900, Charles Sr. and Emeline donated the medal for Rhetoric.[12] In 1903, Charles Jr. donated the Gold Medal for the top student of the Junior Class.[13]

Young Charles was becoming more and more suspect of his father's ruthless, unethical business practices. One of the more infamous cases against his father was *Kennedy J. Hanley vs. Charles Sweeny, F. Lewis Clark, and the Empire State Mining and Development Company*. In 1897, Sweeny and Clark wanted to purchase the Skookum, Chemung, and other mining claims from Hanley. In order to do so, they were to purchase 125,000 shares of the Chemung and two deeds, one for one-third of a McKelvey claim, and one for one-eighth of the Skookum claim. The agreed upon price was $28,000. The transaction was to be handled in three different transactions. First, they met at Sweeny's bank, the Exchange National Bank in Spokane, and made a $2,000 down payment. Hanley showed them two envelopes, one containing the 125,000 shares of the Chemung, the other containing the two deeds, all to be deposited in escrow until Hanley had received full payment. Sweeny had Hanley mysteriously called to a different part of the bank on another matter. While Hanley was gone, Sweeny took the deed to the Skookum claim and secretly put it in the envelope with the Chemung shares. On September 1, Clark paid more than $16,000, enough to release the stock envelope, so he withdrew the stock envelope containing the stocks and the deed to one-eighth of the Skookum mine. Of course Hanley thought the envelope only contained the stocks. Sweeny and Clark were no longer interested in the other claims and refused to pay Hanley the rest of the money. Hanley sued repeatedly, winning repeated judgments against them, but Sweeny always appealed and Hanley never received his money.[14] The litigation lasted 12 years and included eight appeals to the federal court of appeals and three to the U.S. Supreme Court. It finally ended when Hanley had to sell what property he still owned to pay the debts he had run up fighting to get what the courts said was rightly his but never got.

Appealing court decisions until the other party gave up was a standard operating procedure for Sweeny Sr. In 1903, the First National Bank of Spokane was considering suing Sweeny for the losses they took when the bank failed in 1893 when Sweeny didn't repay his loans. He argued that he would appeal in court and it would cost the bank far more in attorney fees and court costs than they would ever recover. They didn't pursue the case.[15] Charles Jr. had no patience with hypocrisy; however, it didn't stop him from taking money from his father and family.

When young Charles returned home from his Spanish-American War adventure, his mother was anxious to have him straighten out and go into the family business. However, his father had another idea. If his son was determined to follow a military career, he should attend West Point, the United States Military Academy. Secretly he probably hoped that the academy would break his son's rebellious spirit and teach him respect for others. His mother argued successfully that their son didn't have the sufficient education to compete successfully at West Point. The academic requirements were beyond his capabilities. So, on September 7, 1898, Charles Jr. enrolled at Notre Dame University. The archives at Notre Dame show that Charles M. Sweeny, Jr., son of Charles Sweeny of 2017 Pacific Avenue, Spokane, Washington, entered Notre Dame on September 7, 1898. He was a 17-year-old Catholic. He attended Notre Dame only for one academic year—1898-99. He lived in Brownson Hall and studied the following subjects: Christian Doctrine, Algebra, Arithmetic, Grammar, History, Geography, French, German, Spanish, Geometry and Composition. He also participated in Gymnastics. While he did not graduate from Notre Dame, he did receive awards (premiums) for doing well in his classes. He is listed in the *ND Scholastic* under Brownson Hall for receiving a 1st Premium in 2nd German and 3rd Algebra, a 3rd in Christian Doctrine and a Mention in Special Orthography (the system for writing a language, including spelling, capitalization, emphasis and punctuation). The students received these awards at commencement, which was held June 11–15, 1899.[16]

Sweeny felt he was now ready for the academic challenges at West Point. On his application, he listed that he had received his education at three years at public schools, three years at private schools, and five years of college education.[17] It is unclear how Sweeny arrived at five years of college on his application after only one year at Notre Dame's college prep school and one year at Gonzaga College. In any event, he entered the military academy on June 19, 1900.

Chapter 3

West Point Cadet

After young Sweeny completed his year at Notre Dame University, he and his family felt he was ready for the rigors of West Point. So Sweeny Sr. contacted U.S. representative Wesley L. Jones of Yakima about getting his son appointed to the United States Military Academy at West Point. Congressional appointment was one of the methods of gaining admittance to the academy. Jones and Sweeny Sr. had been active in Republican Party politics in the state of Washington for several years. On May 24, 1899, Jones announced in the *Seattle Post-Intelligencer* that he had nominated Charles Sweeny, Jr., of Spokane as a cadet to West Point. The article described young Sweeny as 18 years old (although he was really only 17 in 1899), 6-feet-1-inch tall and weighing about 180 pounds. The announcement included a picture of him.[1]

The older Sweeny's prominence and political connections almost certainly influenced the congressman's choice of an appointee. Representative Jones was first elected to Congress in November 1898, and took office March 4, 1899, less than three months before he made Sweeny's appointment. At the time of his election, Jones was a lawyer practicing in North Yakima. A Republican, he was elected at-large, meaning statewide, and defeated an incumbent from Sweeny's domicile, Spokane. The fact that Jones made Junior his first West Point appointee suggests that Senior supported him in the election. It's doubtful a new congressman would have done such a favor for an adversary.[2]

On March 1, 1900, Sweeny traveled to West Point and took the entrance exams. Although he didn't achieve a perfect score, he did reasonably well. In writing and orthography, he scored 87 out of 100 possible points, 86 in arithmetic, 92.4 in grammar, 88.7 in geography, and 97 in history.[3] With these results on March 16, he was officially appointed as a cadet to begin his education at the academy in June.

Charles Michael Sweeny arrived at West Point on June 19, 1900, as a member of the class that would graduate in 1904.[4] When Sweeny enrolled at West Point, it was Sweeny's father's hope that the military discipline at West Point would teach his son something he had failed to achieve—respect and self-control. But the hazing from other cadets and the rigorous regimentation at the academy proved to be a shock to young Sweeny's sensibilities. He hated being treated by the other cadets as somewhat backward and the pampered son of a rich industrialist. After all, hadn't he already proved he could make a living and survive on his own as a miner? Sweeny was looked upon as being pig-headed, self-opinionated, and hating regimentation. He soon proved to be a disciplinary problem and a less than enthusiastic student as well.[5]

The hazing and training at West Point was focused on taming the ego of cadets from wealthy families or famous people, and smoothing out the rough edges of cadets coming from rural areas of America.[6] It was thought that once the cadets' individual traits were removed, they could be molded into the arch-typical West Point graduate, ready to lead men into battle. To show initiative was looked upon as disobeying the textbook, and to take charge of fellow cadets and organize them in ways that differed from the textbook was looked upon with disdain and a sign of arrogance and rebellion.[7]

The methods of command taught at the academy during the period Sweeny was there were outdated. Most of the professors and instructors had been there a long time, some more than 35 years. Stephen E. Ambrose in his book *Duty, Honor, Country: A History of West Point* wrote: "They used the same text books and methods their mentors had employed and for all intents and purposes the graduate of 1898 knew no more and no less than the graduate of 1848." Sweeny complained bitterly about his French instructor at West Point. The lessons he taught were "utterly useless and not to be compared to the lessons I had from the Jesuits" at Gonzaga. The instructor taught only grammar and made no effort to teach the cadets to speak the language. "He couldn't even speak it himself," Sweeny said.[8]

Charles Sweeny's West Point appointment announcement from the *Seattle-Post Intelligencer*, May 24, 1899.

3. West Point Cadet

Fill Out and Return at once to the Adjutant, United States Military Academy, West Point, N. Y., in the Enclosed Envelope.

INSTRUCTIONS.

Read the whole sheet over carefully several times before attempting to fill it out.
The name of the Candidate must be written in full, viz.: John William James Smith, not John W. J. Smith.
The legal residence of a Candidate (except appointments "At Large") must be within the Congressional District from which he is appointed.
If the residence of the parent or guardian is in a city, the street and number must also be given.
[This INFORMATION IS STRICTLY CONFIDENTIAL.]

State appointed from: **Washington** No. of Congressional District **At large**
Candidate's signature: **Charles Michael Sweeny**
Candidate's legal residence: Town **Spokane** County **Spokane** State **Washington**
Candidate's date of birth: **January 26, 1882**
Candidate's place of birth: Town **San Francisco** County **San Francisco** State **California**
Name of parent or guardian: **Charles Sweeny**
Address of parent or guardian: Town **Spokane** County **Spokane** State **Washington**
Date of appointment (letter from War Department): **March 16, 1900**

TIME OF ATTENDANCE AT:

Public school: common **3** years ____ months; high school ____ years ____ months;
Private school: common **3** years ____ months; high school ____ years ____ months;
Normal school or Academy, or school of like grade: ____ years ____ months;
University or College, **5** years ____ months.

TIME EMPLOYED IN:

Teaching school (if any) ____ years ____ months; In private study (with or without a teacher) ____ years ____ months; Special preparation for examination for admission to U. S. Military Academy ____ years **6** months; If tutored at home, give time: ____ years ____ months.

Is your father living? **Yes** Is your mother living? **Yes**
Occupation or profession of parent: Is or was **Miner**
Note: If mechanic, state what kind; if merchant, state dealer in what.
Does your parent or guardian reside in the country ____ in town ____ in city **Yes**
Nationality of father **American** Nationality of mother **American**
Did you have a competitive examination? yes or no **No**; How many competitors including yourself? ____ Do you use tobacco in any form? yes or no **No**; For how long a time have you used tobacco? ____ Ever at the Military Academy as a Candidate or Cadet? yes or no ~~No~~ When? **March 1, 1900 as a Candidate to take examination**

Charles Sweeny's West Point personal information form.

Even though he hated the teaching methods at West Point, he developed an eagerness for soldiering. It was this enthusiasm that touched off a spirit of revolt in him, and he would argue back if he saw a simpler way of accomplishing a task that was not in a textbook. "I knew I wanted to be a soldier and that I could be a good one but West Point was only holding me back. Its attitude to war, after all, was pre–Civil War," he later said. "The whole business was mere playing at soldiers. I wanted to learn to be a practical soldier in actual fighting, not on the parade ground. I have always thought it was bloody nonsense to say that battles are won on parade grounds." Instead of focusing on his studies, he began to read extensively about military history, particularly the tactics of famous generals in the classic battles of the past, with an emphasis on the American Civil War. The Civil War was studied intently at West Point, and when Sweeny's reading led him to conclusions at odds with those of his instructors, he did not hesitate to challenge them. This tendency marked him as a rebel in an institution that prized conformity. According to one story, Sweeny wrote an essay that stated, "if Napoleon had been at West Point, he never would have made himself master of Europe. Napoleon was the perfect general because he learned his soldiering as an ordinary soldier and not through text books."[9]

In time, Sweeny's instructors began to suggest that perhaps the wayward cadet might be better suited to a career other than soldiering. If this was intended to induce him to quit, it seemed to have the opposite effect. Instead of giving up, he became ever more committed to graduating from the academy and pursuing a career as a soldier. He ended his first year in June of 1901, ranked 112th out of 141 cadets in his class. While low, his marks were not disqualifying. He ranked 91st in mathematics, 94th in English, 109th in French, and 91st in drill regulations.

But discipline was an issue. Any infraction of the very strict and detailed regulations governing cadets could earn a cadet demerits. The number of demerits for each infraction depends on the seriousness of that violation. The highest number of demerits for any single incident was 10. Offenses earning ten demerits included absence from post, breach of arrest, asleep while serving as sentinel, corporal of the guard or officer of the guard; assaulting or attempting to assault a cadet officer, abuse of authority, criminal carelessness, disrespectful conduct to superiors (including making ungentlemanly or disrespectful comments about an officer passing him) careless use of fire in the vicinity of explosives, hazing a fourth classman, gambling, insubordination, intoxication, mutinous conduct and neglect of duty (such as failing to exercise authority or failing to report to an officer in charge that a serious disturbance had taken place).[10]

Sweeny never earned more than five demerits for any of his acts of misconduct. Most were for relatively minor things such as buttons not buttoned, late at parade, late for breakfast, late for guard duty, long hair, absent from formation, hair-oil on gun, dirt on clothes, contraband goods, etc. But academy records show that he earned demerits on almost a daily basis, often for misconduct he had already been warned about. His behavior smacks of teenage rebellion by a spoiled child. It appears Sweeny either wanted to get kicked out or he wanted to harass and annoy his superiors without regard to the consequences.

His most serious offense involved "hazing" a fourth classman during the summer of 1901 when Sweeny had become a third classman. Although he was initially placed under arrest for this, the fact that he received only five demerits, not the full 10, for this breach suggests the form of hazing involved was of a mild variety, such as shouting at the cadet instead of using a normal tone of voice.[11]

At the end of his first year, Sweeny ranked only 77th in conduct out of 141 in his class, but he had garnered a total of 136 demerits, 11 over the maximum allowed of 125. He was given the opportunity to make up the demerits by walking punishment tours[12] but by October 1901 he still had 127, two over the limit. On October 18, 1901, he was discharged for excessive demerits. His discharge is recorded as Special Order Number 202 in the *Orders Received from Commandant of Cadets, 1901, Adjutant's Office, USMA*. It states: "Sweeny, Third Class, recommended [by] Academic board for discharge on account of deficiency in conduct is, in accordance with paragraph 13, Special Order 238, discharged from the service of the United States. He will settle his accounts with the Treasurer and proceed to his home."

Wesley Jones, the congressman who appointed Sweeny to West Point, wrote a letter on October 30 to the superintendent, Colonel Albert L. Mills,[13] inquiring why Sweeny was dismissed. In a return letter dated October 31, Colonel Mills stated that Sweeny was deficient in discipline with more than 125 demerits between June 1 and Dec. 31, inclusive, having had 127 demerits recorded against him between June and October 4, 1901. "In connection with his case, I beg to assure you that Cadet Sweeny's demerits arose mainly from carelessness and continued disregard of regulations. There is nothing against his moral character, and the most serious of his offenses was a violation during the summer of the regulation adopted to prevent hazing."[14]

As time went by, a different story developed as to why Sweeny was dismissed in 1901. The story became part of the Sweeny legend. According to the legend, Sweeny was discharged for tethering a goat to the roof of the chaplain's house as a prank, and later pleading Fifth Amendment protection against self-incrimination when asked about it.[15] However, a thorough search by the authors of all available records in the academy archives in 2015 failed to find any evidence of any such incident by Sweeny or any other cadets during his time at West Point.

When Sweeny returned home his father was infuriated by his son's dismissal from West Point and grumbled about his lack of character. His mother worried about what was going to become of him. Sweeny realized that while he had shortcomings, he did not lack for character and will-power to succeed. After enduring the criticism of his father, he decided he would apply to West Point for re-admittance. In what McCormick described as a relentless effort of writing letters of appeal, by sending Colonel Mills a logical and impassioned thesis on why he could become a competent officer, and seeking the help from Congressman Jones, he was able to secure re-appointment to the academy.[16]

On August 28, 1902, Sweeny was re-admitted to West Point by Special Order 167, issued by Colonel Mills. While being re-admitted is not an everyday occurrence, it is not without ample precedent. In fact, another cadet in Sweeny's class, Torrey Borden Maghee, was re-admitted on the same day as Sweeny.[17] Both returned as third-classmen, part of the class of 1905.[18]

Sweeny completed the 1902-03 school year, but roughly halfway through the 1903-04 school year, he resigned on December 24, 1903. The cause this time was a deficiency in Philosophy.[19] Academy records show he earlier had been deficient in Drawing[20] and had made up that deficiency. But he failed to make up the subsequent deficiency in Philosophy within the time allotted and resigned.[21]

Once again, however, an alternate story later developed to explain his resignation. It, too, became part of the Sweeny legend. According to the legend, "he was asked to resign to cover up a scandalous prank, which might have made the academy a laughing stock of the nation."[22] The legend is that Sweeny had been the ringleader of a group of cadets that had seized the Reveille Gun from its place on Trophy Point, overlooking the Hudson River, and hauled it some 200 yards across the parade grounds to the commandant's house. There they had used it to blow a hole in the roof of the house. No one was injured, according to the legend, but Sweeny was arrested and put under close confinement. There was no special reason for this prank other than the fact that Sweeny didn't like the commandant. According to the legend, the authorities decided that it would be better for Sweeny to quietly resign rather than punishing him and risk national publicity.

The real cannon incident is just as interesting as the legend. When Sweeny enrolled at West Point, the academy was embroiled in a national controversy over hazing. The time-honored tradition of hazing was designed to put all cadets on equal terms so they could be molded into ideal officers. The sons of the wealthy or famous, as well as those with perceived weaknesses, received especially intense treatment. Hazing was supposed to make the cadets mentally tough. The methods of hazing the upper classmen inflicted on the plebes (new inductees) were in some cases both brutal and atrocious.

Cadet Phillip H. Sheridan was forced to ride a wooden broomstick up and down the company street mimicking his father's command at the battle of Winchester to "turn men turn." General Sheridan rode 20 miles to Winchester during the Civil War to rally his retreating troops to turn and fight the confederates. Young Sheridan was also forced to repeat the poem "Sheridan's Ride" several times while riding his broomstick. Other forms of intense physical hazing included "eagling," which required standing on toes, squatting, and jumping up and down flapping arms like an eagle. This was done to the point of exhaustion. Cadet Ulysses S. Grant III, the grandson of general and later president Grant, was severely hazed and required to do eagling and football dips and exercises to the point of exhaustion. Other forms of hazing took the form of forcing the plebes to drink pitcher after pitcher of milk until they threw up. Many were forced to swallow several drops of especially hot Tabasco Sauce. Others were forced to sit on the floor facing each other blindfolded to have a molasses race, feeding each other to see who could eat more than 50 prunes and a bowl of molasses the fastest.[23] The upper classmen thought the after-effects of the digestive distress and diarrhea suffered by the plebes the next day was funny. Another favorite activity was to pour hot candle wax on the bodies and feet of sleeping cadets. Other hazing tactics included bracing (marching in a constrained posture), standing at attention for extended periods of time, and holding rifles at arm's length until exhausted.

The hazing controversy started when a cadet by the name of Oscar L. Booz entered West Point on June 10, 1898. Soon after, he sent letters telling his parents and siblings the details of the hazing he had received. The boy's mother and sister received letters stating that he had hot candle wax poured on him while in bed. He also had hot Tabasco sauce poured down his throat, both in camp and at the dining table. He was perceived weaker than the other cadets and was forced to fight a fellow cadet to toughen him up. During the fight, both of his eyes were blackened and he gave up when he became tired. On other occasions, he was told he was a coward and a disgrace to the corps. When the boy's father complained to a Lieutenant Blakely at the academy about the treatment of his son, Blakely said the hazing would stop once the cadets got back to the barracks. But it didn't, so Booz resigned from West Point and returned home in August 1898, broken in health.[24] He died December 6, 1900, of tuberculosis of the throat. When the Booz family complained to the Army, the national press picked up on the story and hazing at West Point became a national scandal.

Two investigations were conducted into the hazing of Booz, one by a military court and the other by a congressional committee. William H. Booz, the boy's father, testified that during the fight, not only did his son receive two black eyes, but several teeth were loosened and he suffered intense pain from a blow over the heart that he received during the fight. He also spoke of his son being dosed with Tabasco sauce. When young Booz returned home, his throat was so sore he couldn't swallow the juice of an orange. When he was taken to the family doctor, he recommended that he see Dr. S. Cohen of Philadelphia, a throat specialist. Dr. Cohen was called to testify at the hearing and stated that Booz suffered from tuberculosis of the throat and "a spoonful of Tabasco sauce would likely scald the throat and produce the lesions that were found." A quote from one of Booz's letters was read, "The upper classmen are tyrants, brutes, and bullies, and they have an eager desire to injure and pain someone."[25] Several cadets, including future general of the Army Douglas MacArthur, Class of 1903, who was severely hazed as the son of a general in the summer of 1899, were called to testify. While they confirmed that hazing took place, they refused to name those who were the culprits, saying they couldn't remember.

After both hearings, it was determined that hazing at the U.S. Military Academy must be stopped. Colonel Mills, as superintendent, called the upper classmen together and they came to a formal agreement that hazing would end. However, the cadets got the impression that informally Mills would look the other way when certain hazing practices, such as bracing, happened. After all, they reasoned, hazing was a time-honored tradition at West Point and necessary to the training of fourth-classmen. The stated intent of hazing was to deflate the egos of cadets from prominent families by showing the new cadets that they were no better than anyone else at the academy. The Army has its own class system based on military rank, not the social register.

When Mills punished some cadet leaders for bracing fourth-classmen, some of the upperclassmen were angered and organized a protest to show their displeasure. They felt Mills had not kept faith with them. Although there is no evidence that Sweeny was involved, on April 16, 1901, more than 80 cadets[26] went to the parade grounds after supper, took the Reveille Gun that was fired each day when the flag was raised and lowered at the beginning and end of the day, and moved it about 200 yards to a point across the roadway from Mills' residence. The cannon was pointed at his front door to intimidate Mills, who was home at the time with his family. But, unlike in the Sweeny legend, the cannon was not fired. The cadets gave disparaging yells aimed at Mills and then dispersed to their barracks for the night without further incident.

Mills was outraged, calling the act a "mutinous demonstration." The next day, he appointed three officers on the West Point faculty as a board of inquiry to "determine who instigated the demonstration and those taking part in it."[27] The board began taking testimony from cadets the following day. One by one, the panel interrogated more than 30 cadets. It quickly became apparent that while the cadets all had witnessed some or all of the events, most of them claimed they could not recall the names of any cadet engaged in the demonstration. When some of them were told to leave the room and think about their responsibility to testify honestly under the cadet honor code, many of them recalled a few names. The board concluded the "mutinous demonstration" was a direct reaction to the superintendent's crackdown on hazing in the wake of the Booz scandal and the disciplining of two cadet leaders, one for bracing fourth-classmen, and the other for failing to stop a food fight at his table in the mess hall or report the miscreants to the officer of the day.

On May 7, 1901, the findings were announced. Five cadets were singled out as the ringleaders: Birchie Oliver Mahaffey (president of the class of 1902), Henry Lee Bowlby, John Abell Cleveland, Traugett Frank Keller (who had been Booz's boxing opponent), and Raymond Aaron Linton. All five were immediately dismissed. Mahaffey complained that none of the cadets were shown the testimony used to expel them or given a chance to refute it.[28] Seven other cadets were suspended from the academy for a year. In addition, the cadet battalion commander, the cadet company commanders, and several other cadet leaders were stripped of all rank. All cadets judged to have been active participants or aiders and abettors were confined to the barracks, except for classes, for several months and given many hours of punishment tours to walk off.[29]

However, only the five named as ringleaders were expelled from the academy. All five went public with their story, writing letters of protest to their congressmen, and the press again picked up on the story, which became national news. Retired major general Francis V. Greene, an 1870 West Point graduate, and his partner, Avery D. Andrews, who were principal officers at the New York and Bermudez Asphalt Company, were sympathetic to the cadets' cause. They offered them jobs with the company to go to Venezuela and other Latin American countries to head their security forces at the company's holdings in those countries.[30] They were offered the employment on the condition that they drop their petition to be reinstated to the academy.[31] The national press had picked up on the story and the publicity was an embarrassment to West Point. Mahaffey, Linton, and Keller took them up on their offer.[32]

While it appears Sweeny was not the ringleader or even an active participant in the cannon incident as his legend claims, the outcome for the expelled cadets would soon play an important part in his own future.

Chapter 4

Revolution in Mexico

The details of Sweeny's life between the time he left West Point in 1903 and the year 1910 were somewhat of a mystery for years. For reasons that will become apparent, Sweeny was entirely silent about this period in his life. By piecing together clues from newspapers articles, published interviews with friends and acquaintances, and second- and third-hand stories collected over the years, a picture has emerged of some of Sweeny's activities during this time.

When Sweeny returned home from West Point the second time, his father sent him to Mexico to report back on mining possibilities there. To do a proper evaluation, he took a job with another mining company to scout out their claims and mining procedures. The working conditions he found there were appalling. Years later, Sweeny described what he witnessed:

> When I arrived in Mexico to work for an American company, it was like stepping back into the Middle Ages, into a civilization of masters and slaves. The company was supreme. Its concession, about three miles square, was completely surrounded by barb wire fence twelve feet high. The workmen, even including the American staff, worked twelve hours a day, seven days a week. Standard wage for gringos was a dollar a day gold, including board and lodging fees. The greasers, usually called pelados (natives), got 80 cents a day, about thirty-five cents gold. The pelados once in the concession could not leave except to be buried or to go to prison. They were treated like savage beasts and supposed to be dangerous. Every gringo was advised to carry a pair of forty-five revolvers conspicuously, and use them at the slightest suspicion of violence.[1]

This exploitation of the pelados opened Sweeny's eyes to the brutal human rights violations that existed in the under-developed countries of Mexico and Latin America. Not only were the dictators of these countries brutal and inhumane, but the policies of foreign companies who operated within their boundaries were just as ruthless and vicious.

The president of Mexico at the time was José de la Cruz Porfirio Díaz

Mori (known as Diaz). He ruled Mexico with an iron fist and surrounded himself with rich advisors, called the científicos, who dominated Mexico as a privileged upper class. Diaz is credited with the creation of the "rurales," bandits that the president heavily armed so that they could carry out his programs. He suppressed all opponents by violence and intimidation with this band of thugs. The poor people of Mexico suffered immensely under the dictatorship of Diaz.[2] Their lands were taken away and they were forced into a system akin to slavery. Freedom of speech was not tolerated. Díaz distanced himself from his own Mexican heritage, and was so infatuated with Europeans, that he would occasionally paint his face to make it look whiter than it actually was.[3]

As money flowed into the coffers of Díaz and his cronies, one by one, they sold their rights to foreign companies so those interests could exploit Mexican natural resources. These companies paid top dollar to buy oil fields, establish copper mines, and build extensive railroad systems that traversed the country. U.S. and British investors owned the railroads, as well as vast oil reserves. French investors built several textile mills around Veracruz.

In the meantime, power was maintained by terrifying the lower classes and maintaining a stranglehold over the local state governments by Diaz appointing his own men as governors. The científicos felt that the only problem keeping Mexico from being as prosperous as any European country was that it had too many poor people.[4] Millions were suffering under the rule of Diaz. The wealthy became strong supporters of Diaz because they were prospering under his rule.

Diaz and his advisors felt the best way to develop their country's economy was to enforce laws and regulations that ensured economic development no matter the cost in human suffering. This program provided justification for the harsh measures used by Diaz, who believed that only when economic stability is achieved could social progress be made. Under the reign of Diaz, Mexico modernized under his regime and entered into an age where electricity was brought to the cities and thousands of miles of railroad tracks were laid. Factories were opened and the national debt was paid in full. However, the social atrocities committed on the poor in order to implement these achievements created a political firestorm that could not be put out. The cry for revolution could be heard throughout the country. Conditions were ripe for rebellion and fit right in with Sweeny's creed to fight for the cause of freedom and honor wherever those things were threatened. This would be the first of several revolutions in which Sweeny would take part in opposition to despicable oppressive dictatorships.

It was about this time Sweeny most likely met and became friends with Francisco I. Madero.[5] Madero was from one of the wealthiest families in northern Mexico. Among its holdings, the family owned the largest smelter in Mexico. Sweeny was interested in finding out about the Madero smelter because it was a competitor of the Federal Mining and Smelting Co. that Sweeny's father was president.

Francisco and his brother Gustavo A. Madero were educated at the Jesuit college in Saltillo. However, he experienced a religious conversion when he discovered his father's subscription to the magazine *Revue Spirite*, which turned his interests to Spiritism,[6] an outgrowth of Spiritualism. As a teenager, Madero was sent for advanced studies to the famed École des Hautes Études Commerciales de Paris (HEC). While there, Madero visited the tomb in Paris of Allan Kardec, the author of Spiritism, and became converted to its precepts. In fact, he soon came to believe he was a psychic and a medium.[7] Next, he was sent to the Culver Academies, a college preparatory boarding school in Culver, Indiana. From there he was sent to the University of California at Berkeley to study agriculture and to improve his command of the English language. During his time there, he was influenced by the Theosophist ideas[8] of Annie Besant,[9] and felt he was developing a deep spiritual insight that would help him solve problems that would arise in his life.

In 1893, the 20-year-old Madero returned to his Mexico to take charge of the family hacienda at San Pedro, Coahuila. He began putting into practice what he had learned in his studies and travels. He installed a new irrigation system, imported and planted American cotton in his fields, built a soap factory and an ice factory. He followed his spiritual beliefs and began supporting charitable groups. He treated his employees well, with good pay and regular medical exams. He also sought to improve life in the local communities by constructing schools, hospitals, and community kitchens to feed the poor. In addition, he set aside funds to aid orphans and deserving students. He taught himself homeopathic medicine and offered medical advice and treatments to his employees. Madero became increasingly involved with spiritualism and in 1901 was sure that the spirit of his brother, Raúl, who died at age four, was in some way communicating with him, advising him to practice self-discipline and work for the benefit of others. Madero became a vegetarian, quit smoking, and became a teetotaler.[10]

By the time he met Sweeny, Madero was well known for his progressive social ideals and fair treatment to the lower classes. Sweeny was impressed by his ideals and sincerity and that he actually used some of his profits to benefit his workers.[11]

Sweeny and Madero each became involved with the PLM (Partido Liberal Mexicano) and the Mexican Liberal Party. Madero financed the PLM newspaper *Regeneracion*. Initially, the goal of the PLM was social reform for the entire country. On July 1, 1906, the PLM published a manifesto calling for an eight-hour workday, a ban on child labor, a minimum wage, employer compensation for accidents, and free compulsory secular education. But as time progressed the PLM became more radical and called for the overthrow of the corrupt Diaz government. Madero was more of a moderate and turned away from the more violent faction of the movement.[12]

In September of 1906, Madero declared, "I never would lend aid to make a revolution, for I have a veritable horror of bloodshed."[13] But Sweeny was a firebrand who favored violence and revolution to effect change. Porfirio Aguilar, the grandson of one of the PLM revolutionaries, said about Sweeny's demeanor, "I recall my grandfather speaking of Charles Sweeny as a good friend of the Mexican people who risked the disfavor of his family by aiding our cause. My grandfather always said that Madero was much less of a revolutionary leader than Sweeny. It was Sweeny who wanted to raise his own rebel army of volunteers to launch the revolution."[14] Sweeny and Madero remained friends even though their philosophies differed. PLM cells were being formed all over Mexico to start a revolution and effect change. Sweeny felt there was an urgent need for cells outside of Mexico to be created to supply reinforcements in the event of an open revolt and to provide intelligence and send arms and supplies to the revolutionaries. As a result he agreed to help form cells in Texas and Arizona.[15]

One of the legends about Charles Sweeny is that about the time he met Madero he also met a beautiful 24-year-old Mexican revolutionary who went by the name of Capitano Juanita. The legend credits her along with Madero with helping convert Sweeny to the revolutionary cause. According to Porfirio Aguilar, "she claimed to be Mexican but my grandfather swore she was Spanish, the illegitimate daughter of some Spanish grandee. Perhaps she had a Mexican mother. Anyhow, no matter, you may be wondering why she was called Capitano, she was, believe it or not, a soldier of Fortune." According to the legend, she was the leader of a militant revolutionary cell dedicated to acts of sabotage and she was a crack shot with a rifle and revolver. During this period, Sweeny and Juanita often disappeared together for weeks on end. Sometimes they went to Texas to hold talks with Mexican revolutionaries in exile.[16]

Much as the American Revolution began with the "shot heard round the world" at Lexington and Concord, the Mexican Revolution of 1910 actually got its start with a violent incident in 1906. It occurred at Cananea, Sonora, 23 miles south of the Arizona border, on June 1, 1906. Led by PLM members,[17] 3,500 workers at William C. Greene's Cananea Consolidated Copper Company went on strike. The strikers objected to the American workers receiving a pay hike that was denied to the Mexicans. They demanded equal pay, access to American-held jobs, an eight-hour workday and dismissal of two abusive foremen. The strike turned violent when two American workers fired on the strikers, killing three Mexicans. The strikers then killed the two Americans by setting them on fire. Greene telephoned the governor of Sonora for help and the governor, in turn, called in 275 armed American "volunteers" led by a captain of the Arizona Rangers, the territorial police force.[18]

Neither the governor of Arizona nor the U.S. government heard about any of this until after the volunteers had crossed the border into Mexico. The American volunteers returned to Arizona when 2,000 Mexican troops arrived and put down the strike. Twenty miners and six company men died in the strike.

The U.S. intervention fanned the flames of Mexican nationalism and boosted the PLM's cause. Sweeny was angered when he learned that U.S. secretary of state Elihu Root had telegraphed the U.S. ambassador to find out if the Mexican government wanted help from U.S. troops to restore order. Sweeny considered this a shameful interference in Mexican domestic affairs aimed at suppressing the rights of Mexican workers and poor peasants.[19]

What further infuriated Sweeny was the U, S. government's growing complicity in supporting the Diaz government. The Mexican ambassador to the United States, Enrique Creel, provided Secretary of State Root with the names of members of the Mexican Liberal Party within the United States and requested their arrest for violating U.S. neutrality laws. Root, who wanted to maintain the close relationship that had developed between the United States and the Diaz regime (probably to protect the U.S. business interests in Mexico), asked U.S. attorney general Charles Bonaparte to take appropriate action. A network of agents was eventually created from U.S. Customs, the Immigration and Naturalization Service, the Marshals Service, the Secret Service, the Postal Inspection Service, the State Department, Army Intelligence, and the Bureau of Investigation, to investigate and enforce U.S. neutrality law violations.[20]

One of Sweeny's tactics in support of the revolt was to organize and arm workers by getting them to steal arms from Greene's guards at the Cananea Consolidated Copper Company. By September 1906, the revolutionaries were ready to act. Their plans had been upset partially by Arizona Rangers raiding the homes of PLM members in that state. On September 26, Sweeny participated in the first armed rebellion against Diaz. He, reportedly joined by Capitano Juanita, led a guerrilla force across the border from Texas at night, gathering supporters along the way. He joined forces with Juan Jose Arredondo y de Leon Barra and together with 60 men seized the main plaza of Jiminez, Coahuila, a mile from the Rio Grande River and the Texas border. Juanita cut the telegraph wires[21] as the rebels sacked the town treasury, and for a brief time it looked like the revolutionaries might succeed. But Mexican federal troops arrived before the rebels could fortify their position and they were driven off. Sweeny was slightly wounded during the skirmish and went into hiding. United States officers sprang into action to find both Mexicans and Americans involved with the Jimenez Raid. They arrested three Mexican newspaper men—Pedro N. Gonzales, Demetrio Castro, and S.V. Marquez—and six Americans, and took them to San Antonio, Texas to charge them with involvement in the September 26 raid.[22] Sweeny fortuitously avoided being arrested. This wouldn't be the last time in his career that he would run afoul of U.S. neutrality laws and be pursued by federal officers.

The PLM launched two other attacks soon after at Vera Cruz and Carmargo. Sweeny took part in the firefight at Carmargo and narrowly escaped capture again. However, this ended Sweeny's involvement with Mexican revolutionaries. Possibly he lost confidence in Madero as a leader but more likely some of the people taking charge of the revolutionary cells were just as corrupt as Diaz.[23] According to the legend, another factor may have been that Juanita left the country too. So Sweeny moved on to Venezuela and Nicaragua.

In November 1911 Madero and his followers were able to overthrow the Diaz Government. Madero was able to stay in power for only 15 months. In February 1913, his government was toppled by Felix Diaz, the nephew of Porfirio Diaz. Madero and his vice president Jose Pino Suarez were arrested and on the way to prison were ambushed and murdered by henchmen of Diaz. Of course, the official government position was they were killed "while trying to escape." Newspaper reporters saw the murder for what it was, a bloody political assassination, and sent out news stories worldwide to that effect.[24]

Chapter 5

Venezuela: A Stand Against a Tyrant

When Sweeny left Mexico he was looking for a "just cause" to take part in. From his West Point days, he remembered Birchie O. Mahaffey, John A Cleveland, and Raymond A. Linton, three of the cadets who were expelled from the academy as a result of the "mutinous demonstration" in 1901. They had been hired by the New York and Bermudez Company to take command of the company's armed forces in Venezuela and other Latin American countries to protect company assets there.[1] Sweeny may have contacted one of dismissed cadets.

In *One Man's Wars*, McCormick states that Sweeny contacted a friend who suggested that he should go to Venezuela, for the cause was just, and besides, he could make some money at the same time.[2] The company at the time of Sweeny's inquiry was having a major quarrel with Venezuelan dictator Cipriano Castro. Castro had nationalized the property of the New York and Bermudez Company and was trying to force it out of the country. To describe Cipriano Castro as a dictator was perhaps too kind a description. He was a tyrant who seized power in a coup and held on to it through brutality, intimidation and corruption.

Castro was born October 12, 1858, at Capacho, in the Venezuelan state of Tachira, on the slopes of the Andes, near the border with Colombia. In his boyhood, he tended cattle and later ran a country store with cattle trading and rustling as a sideline. When Venezuelan tax collectors came around to collect, he would drive his cattle over the Colombian border and when the Colombians attempted to collect taxes, he would move his cattle back to the Venezuelan side. He turned to politics when the tax collectors from both Venezuela and Colombia joined forces and showed up at the same time and confiscated all of his cattle. He felt this unfair and in a rage raised a small force to support the cause of the Tachira state president who was seeking re-election despite constitutional restrictions.³ This proved to be a losing cause so Castro fled to Colombia where he stayed for a few years. He then reappeared in Caracas as a member of the national legislature from his native state of Tachira, nominated by Venezuelan president Ignacio Andrade. People from Tachira were considered backward, uncivilized, and uncouth. No one from that area wore boots, including Castro, but as a legislator in Caracas he was expected to wear them. He found them tight and uncomfortable, so upon entering the Chamber of Deputies he would remove them and put them on his desk in front of him. The habit earned him jeers and ridicule from his colleagues in the Assembly who treated him with disrespect, scorn, and indifference. Castro left in disgrace with a deep hatred of the government.⁴

In 1899, because of the mistreatment he received in Caracas, he decided to start a revolution to overthrow President Andrade. The Venezuelan public was in a panic because the economy was in shambles due to the worldwide drop in coffee prices and the huge debts owed to foreign countries for past loans, which frequently went to enrich whoever held the presidency. President Andrade had been a tyrannical leader whose iron-fisted tactics antagonized the Venezuelan people.⁵ At the start of Castro's revolt, Andrade had 500 of his opponents jailed, charged with political offences.⁶

Starting with a force of no more than 60 men, Castro marched 500 miles across Venezuela, from Tachira to Caracas, capturing towns and cities and garnering support and recruits as he went.⁷ As he neared Caracas, his force had grown to more than 2,000 but he was still outnumbered three to one by government forces. Later, he was asked by a reporter, "How was it that you conquered in the battle of La Victoria, the turning point of the revolution? By all means you should have been easily beaten." Castro replied, "I won because the gods of battles fought upon my side and because my opponents were damn fools." He paused for a moment, thinking about the battle, and then went on: "I never could have won if my enemies had possessed the least of military ability. They outnumbered my troops more than three to one and were much better supplied with ammunition than I was." They could have surrounded him and defeated him easily, he said. "Instead of doing that they wasted their energy and men by making stupid frontal attacks on my strong positions. They fired away all of their ammunition uselessly, and then when my fresh supplies came I simply led my men right at their center and there was nothing they could do but retreat as quickly as possible."⁸

Having bested the government forces in battle, Castro assumed the presidency of Venezuela in October 1899 with Juan Vicente Gomez as his vice-president.⁹ Gomez became a friend of Castro when he was exiled in Colombia, and was one of the first to join his rebel forces. Castro soon assumed the mantle of a vicious dictator, either jailing or killing his political enemies and critics.¹⁰

When Castro took over, Venezuela was still in the midst of an economic crisis, world coffee prices were still at a low level and the country was deeply in debt to Germany, Italy, and Great Britain. In the ensuing years, Venezuela also became indebted to France, the Netherlands, and the United States. Castro felt the debts claimed by the debtor countries were grossly inflated and were crippling the Venezuelan economy. When he refused to pay, it angered the debtor countries that formed naval blockades and fired upon important ports and naval vessels.[11] As the conflict intensified, it alarmed the United States public, who felt it could draw America into an unwanted war if it enforced the Monroe Doctrine, which declared that any European efforts to interfere in the affairs of Central or South American nations would be regarded as an act of aggression against the United States.[12] To calm the fears of the public, President Theodore Roosevelt announced the Roosevelt Corollary.

The Roosevelt Corollary of December 1904 stated that the United States would intervene as a last resort to ensure that other nations in the Western Hemisphere fulfilled their obligations to international creditors and did not violate the rights of the United States or invite "foreign aggression to the detriment of the entire body of American nations."[13]

The United States, in creating a commission in 1904, became the arbitrator for all parties that were owed money by Venezuela. The amount agreed upon as being owed was Bs35,575,154. To service the debt, 30 percent of revenues from the two principle ports of La Guayra and Puerto Cabello were pledged. In 1905, the Castro government was required to enter into a new agreement consolidating the debt owed to British bondholders and to Diskonto Gesellschaft of Berlin totaling an additional Bs132,049,925. To pay the additional debt, another 25 percent of revenue was pledged for a total of 55 percent of the revenue of the two major ports.[14] (The monetary term Bs stands for Venezuelan Bolivars. One boliver was equal to about 42 cents in U.S. money at the time.) To enforce Roosevelt's policy of "speak softly and carry a big stick," the United States sent warships under the command of Admiral George Dewey to patrol the waters off Venezuela to make the U.S. presence visible.[15]

Castro not only made enemies of the European powers, he also angered American business interests. Several American companies were interested in the oil reserves of Venezuela. One of those companies was the New York and Bermudez Company (NY&BC), a subsidiary of the National Asphalt Company of Philadelphia. Together, the two companies became known internationally as the Asphalt Trust and had a virtual monopoly of the asphalt business in the United States. In 1885, they had purchased a 25-year lease from its original owner, Horatio R. Hamilton, for the rights to collect and transport the asphalt base from Lake Bermudez to the United States.[16]

The locals knew it as Lake Guanoco. The *Deseret Evening News* described the asphalt in the lake "as queer stuff that has come into such general use as paving material during the past few years. In Trinidad and Bermudez it is found in 'great lakes' which look as though they were nothing but masses of black mud. The surface is fairly firm, and a curious thing about the lakes is that the quantity always remains the same no matter how many thousands of tons are taken out. As the stuff is dug out, more of it oozes up, and in a very short time the holes fill up and the surface of the lake becomes smooth again. As it is taken out it looks like coal, and when refined it becomes like coal tar. For use in paving it is mixed with sand, carbonate of lime, and other substances."[17]

NY&BC had spent millions building its refinery and railroad at the lake.[18] In order to protect its interests, the company kept 1,000 armed employees at the location to run the operation and insure its security.[19]

When Castro came into power in 1899, he saw an opportunity to impose higher taxes on NY&BC and other American companies. Most of the revenue generated went to line the pockets of Castro and his cronies.

In May of 1900, two men, Charles M. Warner and P.R. Quinlan, bought part of the lake from some native Venezuelans who claimed title to the property. Warner and Quinlan thought that the property was outside the boundaries of the NY&BC claim and commenced to mine and ship asphalt. This sent the officials of NY&BC into a panic because the company had just begun to realize profit from its operations after years of huge capital investments. NY&BC immediately took the case to court at Cumana, Venezuela, claiming that its lease gave it exclusive rights to the whole lake. Castro favored Warner and Quinlan, thinking more exports would generate more revenue for the country.[20] The company, in desperation, sent its manager on the company's steamer, the Viking, to Cumana with $10,000 in gold on board to bribe the judges involved. There were three judges involved in the case and one of them contacted the central government in Caracas. Castro summarily dismissed the court and had the case transferred to the court in Caracas. The irony of this episode is that the court in Caracas ruled in favor of NY&BC.[21]

Because Castro had been so decisive in dismissing a court that could be bribed, the company came to the conclusion that Castro was hostile to its interest.[22] So it backed a coup, led by General Manuel Matos, in 1901. This was the beginning of the "Asphalt War" that would last several years to the end of Castro's administration. When Matos was defeated, and Castro learned that NY&BC had backed Matos, Castro had the operation at Lake Guanoco nationalized and the company fined $5,000,000.[23] The company refused to pay and chose to fight it out in lengthy court battles in the Venezuelan court system, while at the same time secretly sponsoring covert operations to overthrow Castro. The U.S. government turned a blind eye to the intrigue, secretly hoping the revolts would succeed.²⁴ U.S. government officials felt that Castro had caused enough trouble in the region. President Roosevelt called Castro "an unspeakably villainous Monkey."²⁵

It was at this point that Sweeny got involved. At the recommendation of his cadet friend, Sweeny went to Philadelphia to the offices of the New York and Bermudez Company, and offered his services, pointing out that he had West Point experience like Mahaffey, Cleveland, and Linton. He was immediately hired as a military trainer. He learned that the company had secretly opened negotiations with Juan Vicente Gomez, Castro's vice president, for the overthrow of the Castro regime. Gomez agreed, in return for a bribe, to turn a blind eye if the company wanted to take independent action to overthrow Castro. The company further promised to support Gomez in a bid to replace Castro as president when and if Castro was removed from office.²⁶

Sweeny was told by the company to contact General Antonio Paredes. General Paredes had been a senior officer in the Venezuelan army and had been the last holdout against Castro in his revolution against President Andrade in 1899. Paredes was captured by Castro's rebel forces at that time and thrown into jail at Maracaibo for three years before being released by Castro under an act of amnesty.²⁷ He was bitterly opposed to Castro's regime. Paredes was organizing a coup to overthrow Castro and had been in New York City to garner support and purchase arms and supplies. He had chartered a steam yacht and loaded it with 15,000 Mauser rifles and several million rounds of ammunition.²⁸

Sweeny needed a convincing cover story for his involvement with the Paredes revolt in case Castro discovered his mission. The brutality of Castro was well known and life expectancy among his opponents was very short. He sought out a friend in New York who was a newspaperman who set him up with a press card and credential as an accredited news correspondent in Latin America. Sweeny enthusiastically agreed to be a reporter and promised to send the newspaper reports of the excesses and corruption of the Castro government and of the expected coup when it occurred. This was his first assignment as reporter; there were many more to come.²⁹

Although Gomez wanted the coup to overthrow Castro to succeed, he wasn't ready to run the deadly risk of being found in rebellion against him if the coup failed.³⁰ He would offer no support to the Paredes revolt. Castro was an archetypical dictator, suspicious of everyone around him, living in fear that his associates and advisors were constantly plotting to depose him. Gomez didn't have the courage to publicly oppose him.

Paredes and his forces landed in Venezuela in early February 1907 at Pedernales. He chose Pedernales because the nearby Orinoco River is the great doorway to the interior of Venezuela and the rest of the coastline is protected by a rampart of mountain ranges that keep out invaders. Gomez's fear of Castro proved to be well founded. When Castro heard of Paredes' landing, he immediately had Gomez's home searched for arms and ammunition. Gomez wouldn't leave his home because he feared retribution from Castro and stayed there until the crisis ended. Castro also ordered the wholesale arrest of at least 50 revolutionary suspects whose only offense was that they were friends of Gomez.[31]

Paredes printed and distributed a passionate plea for his fellow countrymen to join forces with him to restore liberty and justice to Venezuela.[32] His plan was to advance to the interior of the country, recruit a force of 5,000 to 8,000 men and march on to take control of Caracas.[33] In *One Man's Wars*, McCormick said Sweeny was dubious of this plan and quoted him as telling a friend: "It was one occasion in my life when I actually felt I was marching to my doom. Talk about the Charge of the Light Brigade: that was at least spectacular and daring. But this march to the coast was just a slow procession to certain death. If I had refused to carry on, I should have been called a coward and at worst liquidated. So I just kept going and hoped for a miracle."

Before they had progressed very far they encountered Venezuelan troops equipped with machine guns and were quickly defeated. Sweeny's horse was shot out from under him and he suffered a concussion and lost consciousness when he fell. When he came to he found that he had been taken prisoner along with others of Paredes' little army and that they were en route to Caracas.[34]

Castro sent a telegram with orders to execute Paredes and his officers, of which Sweeny was one.[35] There was contention between the officers ordered to carry out the execution because capital punishment had been outlawed in Venezuela 30 years previous. General Penalosa and Colonel Benavides refused to carry out the order. Sweeny overheard their conversation about the execution and had the presence of mind to produce his passport and press credentials, insisting he was merely a newspaperman embedded with the rebels to send their story to the New York newspapers. He demanded an interview with Castro, saying that he was sure the president would be extremely angry if a foreign newspaperman was shot and that any such action would bring the United States fleet to Venezuela. Since there were American gunboats patrolling the waters off Venezuela, his bluff worked, and he was sent to Caracas to meet with Castro. Unfortunately for Paredes and 17 of his other men, General Jesus Garcia carried out the execution order. The condemned men were taken to a sandbank along the river and shot to death, and their bodies were thrown into the river. Among the dead were John Godskin and Thomas Lovelace, American citizens. Since capital punishment was against the law, the Castro government's official version, of course, was that the prisoners were "shot while trying to escape."[36]

McCormick's description of Sweeny's encounter with Castro in Caracas seems surreal. Castro had been extremely ill during the Paredes revolt. According to McCormick, when Sweeny was taken to Caracas, he was thrown into prison. Castro was being cautious because of the American warships in the vicinity, so he visited Sweeny in prison. As the story goes, Castro spent the better part of a week playing chess with Sweeny. At the end of that time, Sweeny was released and ordered to leave the country immediately. He took a ship back to the United States and called on the asphalt company to collect his pay. He had been promised something like $50 a week—a considerable amount in those days. But the president of the company indignantly declared that he had never heard of Sweeny or any revolution plan and had him thrown out of the offices.[37] It is likely this action was taken because the New York and Bermudez Company and the Asphalt War had become a hot political controversy nationally.[38]

In *One Man's Wars*, McCormick states that Sweeny had an interview with Theodore Roosevelt soon after he returned from Venezuela. Such a meeting could have happened because of Roosevelt's interest in the overthrow of Castro. The story of this encounter demonstrates Sweeny's impertinence. Hanging on the wall of Roosevelt's office was a painting of Roosevelt charging up San Juan Hill in Cuba. According to McCormick, Sweeny asked, "Why do you have that picture? You weren't even there." "I know," said the president, "but the damn fools like it."[39] If the meeting occurred, it is hard to imagine Roosevelt disavowing his most famous moment, especially since he really was there. The historical record is clear: Roosevelt and his Rough Riders charged up Kettle Hill and then joined the charge up nearby San Juan Hill.

By mid–1908, another crisis arose in Venezuela. Relations with Curacao had been strained for some time because it had been a haven for political refugees from Venezuela. Curacao was a small island some 40 miles off the Venezuelan coast, and it was a Dutch possession. Its ports were used to ship goods to Venezuela. On May 7, 1908, Castro issued a decree cutting off its trade with his country on which Curacao's economy largely depended. This caused loud demonstrations against Venezuela in Curacao and as a result the Dutch minister was expelled from Caracas. In November, the Dutch retaliated; Holland would no longer honor the Treaty of 1904. The treaty prohibited the use of Curacao as headquarters for revolutionary movements against Venezuela. As a result, rebel forces were free to ship arms and supplies to their ports. This naturally angered Castro, who announced that his country was in "a state of defense." Holland dispatched three naval vessels, the warship *Jacob Van Heemskerk*, and two cruisers, the Gelderland and Friesland, to Venezuelan waters. Hostilities began when the Gelderland captured the Venezuelan coast guard ship *Alix* and put its crew ashore and then towed it to Willemstad, Curacao. A short time later another small vessel, *23 De Mayo*, was captured by the *Jacob Van Heemskerk*. The Dutch authorities announced that Holland didn't consider itself to be at war with Venezuela, but the capture of the two vessels was only to enforce a blockade until matters could be resolved. Venezuela didn't strike back but relations between the two countries remained tense.[40]

While the trouble with the Dutch was being played out, Castro left the country for Europe to receive treatment of his long-term kidney disease and other ailments. When he left, his vice-president, Juan Vincente Gomez, saw his opportunity and seized control of the government, appointing himself president. He became just as ruthless a dictator as Castro, but relations with Holland, America, and the other foreign powers improved.[41] He returned the Bermudez Lake to the New York and Bermudez Company.

Castro became a man without a country. As his boat approached France, he was notified he wasn't welcome there. He was, however, permitted to land and go to Paris. After a few days he went to Berlin and put himself under the care of a Berlin specialist.[42] After a few more days he was asked to leave. He then gained admittance to the United States but wasn't allowed to stay because he was under indictment in Venezuela for the murder of Paredes and his men.[43] He eventually spent the rest of his life in exile in Puerto Rico. He died in 1924. His successor continued to rule the country until his own death in 1935.

Chapter 6

Nicaragua: Deposing Zelaya

The next just cause that Charles Sweeny took on actually found him in a most unusual way. According to McCormick in *One Man's Wars*, after Sweeny returned from his adventure in Venezuela, he found a job as a reporter for a newspaper in New Orleans. While the excitement and danger of being a soldier still appealed to him, what he experienced in Venezuela as a journalist made journalism his second choice as a vocation. In fact, in his later years, after World War II, he would insist that he was "just a plain, g—d— reporter."[1]

While working for the New Orleans paper, he indulged in a youthful indiscretion. Instead of doing his job as a reporter, he joined in the Mardi Gras celebration. Since Mardi Gras is set to occur 46 days before Easter each year, this probably happened early in 1909. He got carried away with his celebrating and ended up falling asleep on a park bench in a drunken stupor. As he lay there asleep on the bench, he was awakened by a policeman bringing him a message from the chief of police: he had been fired from his newspaper job. But the chief of police knew of a job for him. Undoubtedly hung over but always up for a challenge, he followed the officer's instructions to "go across the river to meet ———." Sweeny went and met with a man who offered him a commission of captain in a rebel army at a salary of $200 a month. The mission was to invade Nicaragua and overthrow its ruthless dictator, Jose Santos Zelaya.[2]

At first, reading this story seems far-fetched. It raises some rhetorical questions. Why would the police chief wake up a young man sleeping off a hangover on a park bench to tell him he was fired from his job and then direct him to a job as a mercenary? Why was care taken, in telling the story, not to reveal the name of Sweeny's contact who offered him the job? Why would Sweeny risk his life for $200 a month? After extensive research, the following appears to answer to these questions: His work as a reporter had enabled him to become friends with the police and they had probably heard about his dismissal from the newspaper before he did.[3] Because of Sweeny's penchant for embellishing stories, he had probably regaled them with tales of his adventures in Mexico and Venezuela. And this, together with his West Point training, led the police to see him as an ideal candidate for Nicaragua. The man that Sweeny met, who offered him the job, was Juan Jose Estrada or one of his senior officers. Care was probably taken not to mention Estrada's name because the United States was secretly helping him with his plan. Estrada was organizing a force to overthrow Zelaya, whose extreme human rights violations were well publicized and his actions toward neighboring nations were causing political upheaval in the region.[4] New Orleans was Estrada's base for supplies and recruits for his rebel army. American mercenaries were hired to train recruits in the use of modern weapons and to command the rebel troops in combat.[5] The police were aware of Estrada's mission and had referred Sweeny to him. As for the pay, $200 a month was the equivalent of more than $4,000 in today's money.

Zelaya came to power in Nicaragua in 1893 during a period of political chaos. Conservatives had held on to power for the previous 30 years. Former president Joaquin Zavala, who was upset with conditions in his country, led an internal revolt against President Roberto Sacasa. The turmoil resulted in Nicaragua having three different presidents that year. The last of the three was Zelaya, the leader of Partido Liberal (Liberal Party), who was able to seize control of the government and install himself as president/dictator. He immediately abolished the conservative Constitution of 1858 and initiated a reign of terror. He instituted a new constitution that called for the separation of church and state, and nationalized and confiscated the property of churches, victimized the clergy, and defiled houses of worship.[6]

The new constitution called for many reforms that were popular with the young. Though the reforms were appealing in concept, Zelaya had no intention of putting them fully into effect. He simply used them as propaganda to popularize his government. He felt Nicaragua should be under his personal control. Conservatives were persecuted, their property confiscated, and their homes desecrated by the military. He established instruments of torture for punishment of political opponents. Whipping posts, feet-shackles, handcuffs, and iron collars were put into use, and scores died. According to one historian, there wasn't a citizen of prominence whose body didn't show signs of torture from Zelaya's police and military. The public jails were filled with citizens whose only offense was to protest the excesses of the government.[7]

Zelaya had no respect for women and was a licentious predator. As he traveled throughout the country, if he saw a pretty girl that appealed to him, he would order her brought to him at his palace. If the parents of the girl objected to the impending rape of their daughter, they were arrested and put in jail or sent to a convict labor camp. Zelaya acknowledged the paternity of 45 children from this deplorable practice. No woman who was a Nicaraguan citizen was safe from him.[8]

He was re-elected in 1902 and 1906. He had a creative way to assure his re-election so he didn't have to use military force to stay in power. In many of the districts in Nicaragua, the natives were hot-headed and lovers of bombastic rhetoric. Three candidates were presented to them for their consideration, Jose and Santos and Zelaya. Their platforms were presented and the natives would hotly debate for the candidate of their choice. Those who supported Jose would denounce Santos, those who favored Santos denounced Zelaya, and Zelaya followers would denounce the other two and so on. But always in the end Zelaya would win and the other two would retire from public life. It was only in the capital that the president was known as Jose Santos Zelaya. In later years, he tired of this system and had the constitution changed so that he was elected by the legislature, and he owned the legislature by virtue of owning the army.[9]

For years, two canal projects were considered to cross the isthmus of Central America so ships would not have to travel around Cape Horn to get from the Caribbean Sea to the Pacific Ocean. One project called for a canal in Nicaragua and the other one in Panama. The proposed route for the Nicaraguan Canal was from Greytown on the Caribbean side, up the Rio San Juan River that coursed through a natural depression that was 31 miles wide and only 165 feet above sea level, and connected with Lake Nicaragua. Once a vessel got to the lake, it could steam across the lake to a point near Rivas where a short canal could be dug to Brito on the Pacific coast. Although this route was longer than the canal proposed in Panama, it was more convenient to the Gulf of Mexico, and made the trip from New York to San Francisco shorter and two days faster.[10] But when the French project to build the Panama Canal failed due to disease and financial collapse, the United States' interest shifted to Panama. When Panama won its independence from Colombia in 1903, with the help of the United States, Panama awarded America a renewable lease, sometimes incorrectly referred to as a 99-year lease, and the right to finish the canal.[11] In 1904, America bought the uncompleted canal project from the French for 40 million U.S. dollars and completed its construction by 1914. In 1909, Zelaya didn't endear himself to the U.S. by continuing to search for funding for the Nicaraguan Canal from Japan, Germany, and England. He wanted the economic growth that a canal would bring to his country.[12] The United States didn't want the competition. They interpreted his action as anti–American and a European-owned canal would threaten U.S. political dominance of Central America.

A canal of his own was only part of Zelaya's grand plans. He wanted to unify the countries of Honduras, Costa Rica, Salvador, and Guatemala with Nicaragua. His idea of unification was to conquer and dominate his neighbors with himself as supreme dictator.[13] Either through his direct invasion or his sponsoring of revolutions, Central America was constantly in turmoil. In December 1907, the United States hosted a peace conference where a treaty was signed by the five countries. The treaty stipulated that the parties "shall not recognize any other Government which came into power in any of the five republics as the consequence of a *coup d'etat*, or of a revolution against the recognized government, so long as the freely elected representatives of the people thereof have not constitutionally reorganized the country."[14] Although Nicaragua signed the Washington Treaty of 1907, Zelaya still continued with threats and rhetoric against his neighboring countries that made U.S. business interests nervous.

In 1895, Nicaragua had annexed the Mosquito Coast that ran along its eastern border. There were many American companies heavily invested in the area, including the United Fruit Company, which owned the Bluefields area that included ten banana plantations and the Bluefields Steamship Company. There were 100 American residents at Bluefields and to make it as much like home as possible, the company built Small Town, USA, in the style of an American city. They even imported lumber to do the construction to make it look realistic.[15] One of the other U.S. companies in the area was the La Luz y Los Angeles Mining Company, whose manager was Adolfo Diaz. Upon annexation of the Mosquito Coast, Zelaya immediately raised taxes on the American businesses at Bluefields. By the summer of 1909, rumors were spreading that he was going to resume his expansionist activities, which included invading El Salvador and possibly Costa Rica again. He had crossed people who were tired of his brutal tactics, his human rights violations, and the danger he posed to the survival of U.S. companies.

It was against this backdrop that General Juan Jose Estrada, governor of the east coast of Nicaragua, started a revolution to remove Zelaya and make himself president of Nicaragua. His revolution was financed by Adolfo Diaz, who, despite an annual salary of only $1,000 a year and no other income, was able to provide Estrada with $600,000. How was that possible? The answer may be found with the company he worked for, the La Luz y Los Angeles Mining Company. It was owned by shareholders of the Pittsburgh-based Riter-Conley Company (a builder of steel mills and foundries) and the Carnegie Steel Company, who were protective of their assets at Bluefields. The owners also had close ties to Philander Knox, the U.S. secretary of state.[16] Estrada also had support from the Conservative Party, Manuel Cabrera, ruler of Guatemala, and the American consul at Bluefields, Thomas C. Moffat. In fact, on October 7, 1909, Moffat informed Washington of the revolt and proposed the United States recognize Estrada as soon as possible.[17]

Hostilities between Estrada and Zelaya began when two American mercenaries, Leroy Cannon and Leonard Groce, were sent into Nicaragua to do advanced reconnaissance for the rebel army. They were captured, tortured, and then executed by firing squad at the order of Zelaya. The U.S. government saw this as a violation of the 1907 peace treaty and as justification of American support of Estrada.[18] Estrada's army, of which Sweeny was now a member, was transported from New Orleans to Bluefields, Nicaragua, by U.S. warships.[19] There were several hundred U.S. Marines on board in case the rebels needed back up. At first landing the rebel force was met by fierce resistance from Zelaya's army, and was forced to withdraw with the American warships providing covering fire while they re-embarked.[20] American newspapers reported the incident nationally.[21] The ships sailed along the coast until they found an undefended landing area and Estrada's force went in. This time there was no opposition and the landing went smoothly. Sweeny was put in command of the advance guard.

While Sweeny was no doubt pleased to be given command of this important unit, he was unhappy with his status in the rebel army as a whole. He held the rank of captain but Estrada had handed out commissions to every American volunteer as a recruitment tool and a captain, it turned out, ranked fairly low overall.

According to John F. Wells, one of the other American volunteers, "Sweeny was especially chewed up about this." He made successive demands for promotion. After the first day's march, he demanded to be made a major. Sweeny's argument was that he should outrank those he was leading. After another day's march, he demanded promotion to colonel. This time the commander refused, ridiculing the idea of such rapid promotion. Sweeny's argument this time was that he needed the higher rank to deal with the prisoners that he expected to capture.[22]

The next day, 200 prisoners were taken.[23] Sweeny later told a friend, Francis D. Wormuth, a professor at the University of Utah, that he captured 23 of them and the next day received his promotion to colonel.[24] Zelaya's army soon ran out of supplies and the rout was on.[25] Again according to Sweeny, his advance party marched across the country, defeating any of Zelaya's forces they encountered, and occupied the city of Granada on the shore of Lake Nicaragua. The final step was to capture the capital, Managua, so Estrada could take control of the government.

However, Sweeny was not present for the final victory. A friend in Estrada's army, wise to the ways of Central American revolutions, warned him that now might be a good time for Sweeny to disappear. Once the revolution is over, the friend told Sweeny, "they will be anxious to get rid of the

American volunteers. They won't want an American who has managed to acquaint himself with all the police and having access to their files to go free. My guess is the president will have you shot because it will be cheaper than paying you off."[26] Sweeny reluctantly realized there was some truth to what he was saying. In Central America at the time human life was held cheaply and the friend's counsel was a wise assessment of the situation. Sweeny decided that it was better to escape with his life than to wait to be paid and be killed.[27]

Sweeny quickly "borrowed" a horse and quietly rode out of Granada, giving up on being involved with the capture of Managua. He made his way through Honduras and El Salvador to Guatemala, where he was arrested and taken by the police chief to Estrada Cabrera, the president of Guatemala. Sweeny told Wormuth what happened next. "At the door of the Presidential Office a sentry stood with two forty-fives [pistols] drawn and cocked. After another sentry had examined me thoroughly he ordered me to enter the office with my hands clasped on top of my head and to walk slowly towards the table just in front of the door. Only then was I ordered to lower my hands and arms and place them on the table until I was ordered to leave. When I was told to leave I must place my hands on my head again and walk backwards out of the room." The situation seemed fraught with peril, but Cabrera merely questioned him about events in Nicaragua and then released him.[28]

With his forces in headlong retreat, Zelaya made a hasty exit from Nicaragua in December 1909.[29]

After Sweeny's departure, the Nicaraguan legislature elected Jose Madriz, a man hand-picked by Zelaya, as president. Washington recognized him as a provisional or temporary president because he wasn't duly elected by a majority vote of the people of his country.[30] Madriz inherited a country in chaos. There were no funds left to run the country and European creditors were demanding payment for their bonds. The U.S. government intervened, mainly at the request of the Nicaraguan conservatives and the rebel forces, and sent Thomas C. Dawson to Granada as an advisor. To bail out of the government, New York banks made fresh loans secured by a controlling interest in the National Bank and the State Railways.[31]

On August 23, 1910, Madriz vacated his office under pressure from Dawson and fled the country. Jose Dolores Estrada, a member of the legislature and brother of Juan Jose Estrada, the leader of the revolution, took temporary control of the government and secured the appointment of his brother, the rebel leader, as president.[32] One of the first things Estrada did was to restore religious freedom to his country.[33] Although Estrada lived until 1967, his presidency lasted only eight months. On May 9, 1911, he was replaced as president by Adolfo Diaz, the Nicaraguan executive of the American mining company who had provided funds to Estrada to launch the revolution. Diaz soon had to call on U.S. Marines, who were bivouacked at Bluefields, to put down a Liberal revolt. The Marines occupied Nicaragua from 1912 to 1933.

While Sweeny retained his love of soldiering and adventure after Nicaragua, some of colleagues there came away with quite a different view of war.

One of the men Sweeny served with in the invasion of Nicaragua was Marine Corps General Smedley Darlington Butler, a two-time Medal of Honor winner. He was born into a Quaker family and became famous as the Fighting Quaker. During his career, he served three different tours in Nicaragua, carrying out U.S. government policies. On a fourth tour, the overthrow of Zelaya, having fulfilled his initial mission, he set up a local militia, the *Guardia Nacionale*, to protect the rights and demands of international trade. At the head of this National Guard he placed Anastasio Somoza as its commander.[34] For the next 20 years, American and Nicaraguan businesses made vast fortunes at the expense of the common people of Nicaragua. After 33 years and four months in the Marine Corps, Butler retired and became a critic of U.S. military interventions.[35] He wrote books and gave speeches on the subject, calling war a racket. Here are some excerpts of a speech that Butler gave in 1933:

> I wouldn't go to war again as I have done to protect some lousy investment of the bankers. There are only two things we should fight for. One is the defense of our homes and the other is the Bill of Rights. War for any other reason is simply a racket.

> * * *

> I served in all commissioned ranks from Second Lieutenant to Major-General. And during that period, I spent most of my time being a high-class muscle-man for Big Business, for Wall Street and for the Bankers. In short, I was a racketeer, a gangster for capitalism.

> * * *

> I helped make Mexico, especially Tampico, safe for American oil interests in 1914. I helped make Haiti and Cuba a decent place for the National City Bank boys to collect revenues in. I helped in the raping of half a dozen Central American republics for the benefits of Wall Street. The record of racketeering is long. I helped purify Nicaragua for the international banking house of Brown Brothers in 1909–1912 (where have I heard that name before?). I brought light to the Dominican Republic for American sugar interests in 1916. In China I helped to see to it that Standard Oil went its way unmolested.[36]

Sometimes the line between a righteous intervention and the overthrow of a government to further U.S. business interests becomes murky.

The overthrow of Zelaya marked the end of Sweeny's Latin American adventures. He returned home and his mother immediately took him to Paris, France, in hopes she could monitor his activities and keep him out of harm's way.

Chapter 7

Paris, Wife and Children

When Sweeny returned home from his Latin America escapades, he was almost out of money. Because he had not been paid for his participation in the revolutions in Venezuela and Nicaragua, he was financially devastated. His mother, Emeline, worried about his lack of focus. He had a tendency to drift from job to job. Since leaving West Point, he had worked for mining companies in Mexico, the New York and Bermudez Company in Venezuela, and as a newspaper reporter in New Orleans. Yet he didn't hesitate to give up work to take up what he thought was a just cause whenever the opportunity presented itself.

His mother had lost several children over the years and was worried about his safety. She didn't want to lose Charles while he was off fighting in some wild crusade. So, she convinced him to accompany her on a trip to France. Francisco Madero had told Sweeny about his time in Paris while a student at the École des Hautes Études Commerciales de Paris (HEC). Based on Madero's description, Sweeny imagined Paris as the most glamorous, exciting, and desirable city in the world.[1] When they arrived there he was not disappointed. He immediately became captivated by France, its people, and was thoroughly impressed by Paris. Sweeny and his mother checked into the Hotel Majestic in Paris with Mrs. Jacob Vanderbilt and some members of the Jacob E. Bamberger family.

The Bambergers were a wealthy Jewish family that had immigrated to the United States from Germany. Jacob was born in Germany on March 7, 1852, and came to the United States when he was 13 years old. He and his brothers, Simon and Herman, first located at Pleasant Hill, Missouri, and engaged in the mercantile business. Jacob left there in 1873. He followed the Union Pacific rail line westward, setting up several mercantile businesses as he went. In 1875, he arrived in Salt Lake City, Utah. He worked at the Post Office as a clerk for a short time, but soon his efforts turned to mining and he was able to develop several mining companies that he later sold. He then bought, along with partners, the Silver King and Daly-West mines in Park City, Utah, one of the top producers of silver and lead in the country.[2] Charles Sweeny, Sr., young Sweeny's father, had met Jacob in 1903 while he was negotiating with Bamberger, on behalf of the Federal Mining and Smelting Company, for the purchase of the Park City mines.[3] Although the negotiations failed to produce a sale, the two families became acquainted. This relationship, as it will be seen, became an important part of young Sweeny's life in his the final years.

Soon Sweeny was studying at the Sorbonne and met Pierre Paul Leroy-Beaulieu,[4] whose theories were a major influence on Sweeny's later views of world events. Leroy-Beaulieu was a French economist and a promoter of French imperial expansionism who publicized his ideas in newspaper articles and books. He was especially concerned about Algeria and the nations of Islam. He thought that colonization was an activity limited to civilized peoples, and he compared the relationship between the colonial power and the colony to that between parent and child. He referred to colonies as societies "in a state of childhood" and France as "the adult society." Colonizers would place "the young society it gave birth to" in a position to develop its abilities. By infantilizing colonial peoples, he argued that the potential development of colonies applied only to those "in their first two ages, childhood and adolescence." He warned that the parent society had to accept the prospect that the colonies would eventually become "adults" and claim their independence. The parent also should realize that the child would be badly behaved, suspicious, cantankerous, and insolent. It would be foolish to expect gratitude or respect.[5] The child society would be resentful of the democratic principles forced upon them. Sweeny bought into Leroy-Beaulieu's ideas. He would later say, "I found that the French had brought an astonishing system of law and order to the Barbarian nations of Islam."[6]

More and more Sweeny wanted to be identified with the people of France. He would later learn first-hand, however, how much the Islamic tribes of Morocco despised French and Spanish colonial rule. Even today, nations of the free world and the United States in particular, are making many of the same assumptions about Muslim nations as Sweeny did a century ago. They ignore centuries of Middle Eastern religion, culture and customs and assume that the nations of Islam would be better off with governments based on the Western principles of democracy and freedom. However, what many Muslims demand is a theocracy based on the Koran. They look on America with distain and label it the Great Satan and most Americans as infidels or unbelievers. They look at the fair treatment of women in American society as an abomination. Their society is based on the total domination of women. Men control the clothing their women wear, when they can leave their homes, who they can associate with, and how much education they can receive. There is little tolerance for other religions aside from Islam. The more democracy is forced on these nations, the more they object and turn to violence and terrorism to make their point. Honor killings and punishment are handed out when their people break the moral and loyalty codes of Islam. In the most extreme cases, anyone who is not a follower of Islam is singled out for death.

While Sweeny was staying with his mother at the Hotel Majestic, he noticed an attractive young woman who had come

Charles Sweeny (courtesy Georges Rolland).

to the hotel several times. After making a few inquiries, he learned that she had been born in Brussels, Belgium but raised in France, she was three years his junior in age, she made hats for Mrs. Vanderbilt, and her name was Eva Felicianne Vons. For Sweeny, it was love at first sight. One day, while she was at the hotel, he pointed her out and said, "That is the girl I am going to marry." The remark was typical Sweeny—impulsive, dramatic and self-confident. He hardly knew Eva. In fact, he hadn't even asked her out on a date yet, let alone asked her to marry him. He introduced himself that same day and asked her to walk with him in the Luxembourg Gardens. During the walk, he told her he would like to call on her family.[7] They had a whirlwind courtship and fell passionately in love. There is evidence that his family objected to the romance because of Eva's lower social standing compared to the wealthy Sweenys and their friends. About this time he rented an apartment that he shared with Mrs. Vanderbilt's son, Clarence, near the Luxembourg Gardens. It provided a secret rendezvous place for Eva and Charles. Faced with the unpleasant situation of parental disapproval, they eloped to England and on August 12, 1911, they were secretly married in Christchurch, a small town on the south coast of England just east of the port city of Bournemouth. Just four months later, on December 20, 1911, their son, Charles Francis Sweeny, was born.[8] He was the third Charles Sweeny in as many generations.

For some time after their marriage they lived in the small Vons family home at 16 Avenue Savoye, Bois-Colombes, a suburb of northwest Paris. They also spent part of each winter in another house owned by the Vons family in

Nice. In the early days of their marriage, Charles and Eva were rapturously happy, with Charles describing the time to a friend as "an idyll that was born in the Gardens of Luxembourg ... just living in France is like a prolonged honeymoon, with wine when you want it, a lovely girl to share it with, sitting out at pavement cafes, lunching at bistros, going to concerts and just having non-stop fun. In this wonderful country there is everything I ever dreamed of, so many splendid things to see and do."[9]

Sweeny had yet to graduate from any college, but he took this opportunity to continue his education. He studied law and attended lectures at the School of Political Science at the Ecole de Guerre. He wanted to better understand the causes of revolution and unrest, and the origins of political systems. He felt he could do this better in France than in the United States.[10]

Two more children were born to the Sweenys during the next few years. A daughter, Emeline Sophia Sweeny, was born January 29, 1914, and a son, Patrick O'Neil Sweeny, was born May 9, 1917. Sadly, Patrick was born with physical and mental infirmities that required constant care.[11]

In early 1913, Sweeny became bored with his studies and was struck with the wanderlust again. He and Eva took trips to various parts of France and occasionally to Italy, Germany, and Belgium. Once the children arrived, however, he tended to travel by himself. He loved Italy and went there often. He also visited Germany occasionally but he found it ominous and disconcerting. "I admire their military bands and their great feeling for music," he said, "but I find a bloodthirsty spirit in the kind of music they like best. The whole nation stinks of war." His intuition served him well and his statement proved to be prophetic as world events progressed. Later he traveled to Palestine, Egypt, Tunisia, Algeria, and Morocco. "He knew Egypt better than almost any guide," said his son. "When he visited a country he read everything about if that he could lay his hands on. He had a remarkable memory. Once he read something he would never forget it."[12]

Morocco became his favorite nation in North Africa. He explored Tangier and Fez, and ventured into the dangerous Berber territory of southern Morocco and the Atlas Mountains. In Tangier, Sweeny became friends with Walter Burton Harris, the *Times* correspondent in Morocco. Harris, a wealthy socialite and writer as well as a journalist, had built a house in the Moorish style in the Kasbah. At this point the legend of Capitano Juanita popped up again. Harris used to tell the story of Sweeny's search for a long lost love in the Rif country of Spanish Morocco. His description of the woman was similar to that of Juanita, but he could not remember her name. Harris recalled that the woman was a soldier of fortune who wore a kepi,[13] and had fought in Latin American revolts before her arrival in Morocco. According to Harris, Sweeny was told that she had been captured by tribesmen and had probably been sold into slavery in a harem. "Sweeny wanted to organize a party to rescue her, but we persuaded him that unless he knew exactly where she was not even his gallantry could save her. This story was later distorted into a report that he had actually rescued her from the desert. In fact, years later he heard that she had died in Malaga through a relative having returned a ring he had given to this female soldier of fortune." There also is a yarn that he had flowers delivered to her grave in Spain every year on her birthday until World War II stopped him.[14]

Sweeny soon came to the conclusion that France was an example of justice, tolerance, and culture to the world, although his reasoning in this instance seems a classic case of upside-down logic. To him, the Alfred Dreyfus affair demonstrated a perfect example of French justice. Dreyfus was a French army captain and a Jew wrongly convicted of selling military secrets to the Germans in 1894. When the true culprit was unmasked, the army engaged in an elaborate cover-up. To many, however, the Dreyfus case exemplified how corruption can cause a miscarriage of justice, and made the French wonder how this could happen in their country. It was Sweeny's opinion that the French would not tolerate an injustice indefinitely as, in his view, the Dreyfus case demonstrated: "In what other country of the world would people fight for justice to be done for so long?"[15]

While Sweeny had great respect for the French colonial system of government, he still admired revolutionaries. In Paris before World War I, Sweeny met

Charles Sweeny, his wife, Eva, and their children, Charles Jr. and Emeline, in 1916 (courtesy Mark Trapp).

many Russian revolutionaries in exile and, according to biographer McCormick, even played chess with Leon Trotsky on a number of occasions. In his conversations with Trotsky, Sweeny proved to be well informed and was convinced of the inevitability of world war before the end of 1913. He reportedly told his wife, "[France] is a country worth dying for because the ordinary people believe in it. The *poilus* literally die with the cry 'Vive la France' and a smile on their lips. I cannot imagine that happening anywhere else in the world." He also said, "it was impossible not to feel what the French people were feeling, impossible not to want to be on their side, impossible not to want to fight for *La Belle France*."[16]

Chapter 8

French Foreign Legion in the First World War

While the Sweenys were busy starting a family, Europe had become a political tinder box that could ignite at any moment. Nationalist rhetoric and rancor had inflamed already simmering tensions between ethnic, religious and economic rivals throughout the continent. Over the decades leading up to this point, the great powers of Europe had entered into a series of alliances and mutual defense agreements that pitted Austria-Hungary and Germany against Russia, France and Great Britain. If one of the partners was attacked, the others were obligated to join the fight. As a result, a regional dispute could be transformed into a much wider conflict. All that was required to turn this kindling of grievances, competition and pacts into a conflagration was a spark that would plunge the countries of Europe into a costly and bloody conflict. When that spark occurred, it drew the entire world into "the war to end all wars."[1]

On June 28, 1914, a band of Serbian and Bosnian nationalists lit the fuse when they assassinated Archduke Franz Ferdinand, the heir to the sprawling Austro-Hungarian Empire, during a state visit to the Bosnian capital, Sarajevo. Over the next three weeks, as Austria-Hungary made demands on Serbia aimed at punishing it, Russia offered its protection to the little Slavic state. Austria-Hungary and Russia also began mobilizing their armed forces. The militaries of each of the great powers knew precisely, to the hour, how long it would take their forces, and those of their rivals, to become fully capable of launching an offensive. If any nation delayed its mobilization to await a diplomatic solution, it could find itself at a significant disadvantage; it could be attacked while it was still mobilizing.

On July 28, 1914, a month after the assassination, the pressures created by the competing mobilizations reached the breaking point and Austria-

Hungary declared war on Russia. One by one, in the days that followed, the great powers were dragged into war by their mutual defense pacts and the need to mobilize against a potential foe. On June 29, Russia declared war on Austria-Hungary and the next day it ordered a general mobilization aimed at Germany. Germany responded by declaring war on Russia. On August 2, expecting France to come to Russia's aid, Germany crossed into neutral Luxembourg en route France and on August 3 declared war on France. On August 4, after neutral Belgium refused to let German troops cross its border to outflank the French Army, Germany declared war on Belgium. That same day, Great Britain—as France's treaty partner and a defender of Belgium's neutrality—declared war on Germany. Thus, in the span of just eight days, the mightiest nations in Europe had been swept headlong into a continental conflict that would quickly become global.

The German invasion plan was a classic flanking maneuver aimed at moving quickly through Luxembourg and Belgium to the English Channel before turning south and then east below Paris to encircle the French forces from the front, side and rear. By marching through the neutral nations, Germany could avoid the fortifications and rough terrain of France's border with Germany and arrive on its lightly defended northern border. To do this, Germany concentrated the bulk of its army on the northern wing. The smaller southern wing would first attack through the provinces of Alsace and Lorraine to draw France into committing its forces there. Then Germany's northern wing would pivot around the fortress city of Metz in a giant right hook to close the trap.

France's strategy anticipated launching offensives north and east into Germany from around Metz, thereby threatening the German homeland and giving the French army the initiative. France's strategists considered an attack through Belgium possible but underestimated the strength Germany was able to commit to it. When the attack came, France's forces on the northern border were too weak to stop it.

Young Charles Sweeny of the Foreign Legion with the Legion of Honor and Croix de Guerre, with palm and stars (courtesy Nicole Hess).

Germany's rapid advance through Belgium had assumed Belgium would stand aside so the troops could pass or else be quickly subdued. Neither assumption proved to be accurate. The Belgian army fought back, delaying the German advance, giving the French time to prepare to meet the attack from the north. The sheer weight of the German advance, however, pushed the French back, farther and farther, in the Battle of the Frontiers. In early September, the German high command changed the plan from swinging west around Paris to driving due south, just east of Paris, to try a double envelopment of the French forces This allowed the British Expeditionary Force, which was northwest of Paris, to move against the German flank while the French counterattacked northward. The German offensive was halted on the Marne River on September 9. More attacks and counterattacks followed but by September 18, the battle stalled out. Unsuccessful attempts to outflank each other led to a line of trenches from the English Channel to the Swiss border. In November, winter and stalemate set in.

Sweeny, who was a voracious reader of history and a keen follower of world affairs, had concluded months before that a European war was inevitable. When news of Germany's invasion reached him on August 4, he was vacationing with his family at Sables d'Olonnes, a resort town on the Atlantic coast about 285 miles southwest of Paris. His reaction was classic Sweeny. While lying on a beach with his wife, he simply informed her he was leaving, and without further explanation he took a train to Paris.[2]

Once back in the French capital, Sweeny sought out his close friend, George Casmeze. Born in London to French parents in 1878, Casmeze had become a naturalized U.S. citizen in New York City in 1895. By 1912, he was working in Paris as a sales representative of an American vacuum-cleaner company.[3]

Casmeze and Sweeny shared a love of France and a desire to help defend her and the ideals associated with the French Revolution. They were not alone. There were thousands of Americans living in France at the time. Many of them shared the same affection for France and felt the same impulse to take a stand against Prussian aggression. Between August 1 and August 5, ads appeared in the Paris newspapers urging Americans and other nationalities residing in France to volunteer to fight for her.

One of those ads was placed by Casmeze in the *New York Herald*'s European edition,[4] which was widely read by American expatriates. It stated:

> In the war of Despotism versus Equality, Justice, Liberty and Fraternity, which France and her Allies have undertaken to defend, I am prepared, like a true-spirited American, to offer myself as a volunteer and to abide by any orders the Ministry of War may give me.
>
> Surely there will be other Americans who share my sentiments—Americans who, apart from considering France a second motherland, have for years enjoyed the great

freedom and hospitality of this glorious Republic. Able-bodied American citizens residing in France, who desire to manifest their brotherly feeling towards the citizens of France, should not hesitate to enlist as volunteers.

The response to these ads was immediate and overwhelming. Thousands of would-be volunteers rushed forward. The French authorities were unprepared for such a flood of volunteers.[5] They also were in a bit of a quandary. French law did not permit foreigners to join the French Army. There also was the matter of America being a neutral country.

The answer to both issues turned out to be the French Foreign Legion. King Louis Philippe created the Legion in 1831 with the goal of removing foreign fighters who had fled there after the 1830 uprisings in neighboring countries and posed a danger to civil order in France. Legionaries served under French officers but were separate from the regular army and, most importantly, they could only serve outside of France. Prior to 1914, the Legion was deployed to expand and defend France's colonial empire.[6]

Charles Sweeny, Foreign Legion photograph (courtesy Nicole Hess).

While French law permitted foreigners to join the Legion, it required them to enlist for a term of five years. No one conceived of the lengthy war that lay ahead, so a five-year commitment was seen as an impediment by volunteers. Facing a dire emergency, the French government quickly waived this requirement in favor of an enlistment for "the duration of the war." It also waived the restrictions on the Legion serving in France.

The issue of American neutrality was more difficult and multi-faceted. Seeking a solution, one small group of Americans paid a visit to the U.S. ambassador to France, Myron T. Herrick. As recounted in his biography of Herrick, Colonel T. Bentley Mott wrote: "These first volunteers came mostly from students and other American residents who, when they saw their comrades going off to the front, were stirred by a desire to enlist in the army and strike a blow for France and civilization. But they first wanted to know whether they had a right to go and a group of them decided to consult their ambassador. Mr. Herrick could never speak of this visit without a flash of emotion."[7]

Herrick was sympathetic to the group's desire to enlist and reviewed the relevant U.S. and international laws with the group. A prime impediment was the U.S. Neutrality Act of 1794, which was enacted during George Washington's presidency to prevent adventurers from drawing the United States into foreign wars. Violators were subject to imprisonment for up to three years and a fine of $3,000. In addition, the current president, Woodrow Wilson, was determined to keep the nation out of the war, and in a public appeal declared that the country "must be neutral in fact as well as in name." So, prosecution of Americans who joined a foreign army to fight in this war seemed a strong possibility.

Herrick advised them that the laws seemed to leave little room for maneuver. But he could not stop himself from encouraging the young Americans to follow their passion. "I brought my fist down on the table saying, 'That is the law, boys, but if I was young and stood in your shoes, by God I know mightily what I would do.' At this they set up a regular shout, each gripped me by the hand, and then they went rushing down the stairs as though every minute was now too precious to be lost. They all proceeded straight to the Rue de Grenelle [Hotel of the Invalides] and took service in the Foreign Legion."[8]

The "loophole," as one writer has called it, that allowed Americans to use the Legion to skirt the neutrality laws, was as brilliant in its simplicity as it was in its sophistry. The reasoning went like this: Service in the Foreign Legion, unlike enlistment in the French Army, did not require swearing allegiance to France. Legionnaires only had to swear an oath to the Legion's flag.[9]

The American volunteers adopted this legal fig leaf to excuse their enlistment. But they did so nervously. Over the next three years, Americans in the Legion continued to make private inquiries back home about whether they would face the loss of their U.S. citizenship and/or prison.[10]

With the question of how to join in the defense of France seemingly resolved, a call went out for recruits to join an American Volunteer Corps. Exactly who the organizers were seems to be somewhat in dispute. According to Legionaire Paul Ayers Rockwell,[11] three Americans living in Paris—Rene Phelizot of Chicago, William Thaw of Pittsburgh and James Stewart Carstairs of Philadelphia—"summoned their countrymen to muster." A competing claim was made by Legionaire Bert Hall.[12] He said the "movement was started by George Casmeze, who had lived in France for some years. Rene Phelezot, Charles Sweeney [sic] and I were the committee chosen to get volunteers. We received permission from the government to train in the grounds of the Palais Royale. Sweeney, being a West Pointer, was later one of our most valuable instructors."

In any event, Casmeze opened an office to promote the cause. It was located at 11 Rue de Valois.¹³ A quick look at a map of Paris indicates its central location—across the street from the garden of the Palais Royal, two blocks north of the Louvre Museum, and, conveniently, just one block west of Casmeze's apartment at 26 Rue Croix des Petite.

The history of the Palais Royal made it an auspicious place to muster volunteers. It was here in 1789, in what had been a royal residence and later a den of aristocratic decadence and dissent, that "Camille Desmoulins jumped on a chair and made the speech that started the French Revolution." His call-to-arms spurred a Paris mob to storm the Bastille, which led to the dethroning of the French monarchy. Similarly, the clarion call in Paris of 1914 drew volunteers to battle a new set of hereditary rulers. So it was appropriate, wrote Legionnaire John Bowe, that "these latter day revolters against the 'Divine Right of Kings' and absolute monarchism began the greatest adventure the world has ever known" from the Palais Royal.¹⁴

Although the American volunteers were eager to get into the fight, the French military delayed their enlistment until after August 20 to avoid overwhelming the already crowded trains and training camps clogged with Frenchmen responding to the mobilization. During the two weeks after the appeal was published, volunteers arrived at Casmeze's office, filled out forms that he and Sweeny had created and then returned each day to drill in the gardens of the Palais Royal with Sweeny as their drill instructor.

About 150 American volunteers had signed up by the time the French authorities were ready to begin processing them, according to Hall. However, when the recruits assembled at the Hotel des Invalides on Friday, August 21, only 43 Americans showed up to sign their enlistment contracts and be sworn into the Legion. The other recruits' zeal to fight for France had apparently waned.

Foreign Legion comrades. Back row, from left: George Casmeze, Charles Sweeny, J.J. Casey, M. Badall. Front row: J. Stewart Carstairs, William Thaw, J.J. Bach (courtesy Georges Rolland).

The Hotel des Invalides is an imposing structure, located about midway between the Louvre and Eiffel Tower, on the opposite side of the River Seine from the Palais Royal. It was built in the 1670s by King Louis XIV as a hospital and home for wounded and homeless veterans. In the center of this complex, in what was once the ornate private church of the Sun King, is the tomb of Napoleon Bonaparte, and in one wing of the Invalides is the Musee de l'Armee (Army Museum). The swearing-in ceremony for the volunteers was held in the courtyard and took on a festive air despite dismal news from the front lines where French forces were being pushed back in the Battle of the Frontiers. When the ceremony concluded, the assembled recruits signed their enlistment papers and received medical exams.

The following Tuesday, August 25, the recruits assembled at 11 Rue de Valois "and had breakfast through the courtesy of George Casmeze at the Café de law Regence."[15] They then crossed the street to the Palais Royal where Sweeny called the roll. Their journey from civilian to combatant was about to begin, and it started with an impromptu parade.

At 8:45 a.m., Sweeny blew his whistle and the recruits fell into ranks for the one-mile march to the Gare St. Lazare train station. Then Sweeny gave the order, "Forward march!" Alan Seeger, a Harvard-educated poet, and Rene Phelizot, a big-game hunter, led the way, each man carrying a large American flag with Sweeny calling cadence. Word quickly spread that the Americans were coming, and Parisians hurried to watch. Recalled Rockwell, one of the 43 volunteers: "Huge crowds cheering wildly lined the Avenue de l'Opera, the Place de l'Opera, the Rue Auber, and other streets through which the volunteers passed. The men were dressed in their oldest civilian clothes, and wore almost every shape of straw, felt, and derby hats; most of them carried bundles or small valises. They had been instructed to encumber themselves as little as possible, and to take with them only their least valued possessions. The very unmilitary aspect of the group added, if anything, to the enthusiasm of the throngs wishing them Godspeed."[16]

At the station, they took a train to Rouen, a port city on the River Seine, 80 miles northwest of Paris in Normandy. Rouen was a fitting place for the volunteers to train to repel the German invasion. It was in Rouen, in 1431, that the English burned Joan of Arc at the stake, an act that inspired the French to drive out these earlier invaders.

The 43 Americans were Jules James Bach of New York City and France; Charles Beaumont and Charles Boismaure of New York City; Edgar John Bouligny of New Orleans; Ferdinand Capdevielle of New York City; James Stewart Carstairs of Philadelphia; John Jacob Casey of San Francisco; brothers John and Louis Charton of New York City; Herman Chatkoff of Brooklyn; Harry C. Collins of Boston; George Delpeuch of New York City; Dennis Dowd of New York City; Emil Dufour of Butler, Pennsylvania; Joseph W. Ganson of New York City; Theodore Haas of Cleveland, Ohio; Louis Haeffle of Buffalo, New York; Bert Hall of Higginsville, Missouri; Charles Hoffecker of San Francisco; David King of Providence, Rhode Island; Nick Karayinis of New York City; Fred Landreaux of New Orleans; Edward Morlae of San Francisco; Thomas F. McAllister of Grand Rapids, Michigan; Jack Noe of Glendale, Long Island; Siegfried Narvitz of New York City; Achilles Olinger of New York City; Robert Percy of New Orleans; Tony Paullet of New York City; Rene Phelizot of Chicago; brothers Kiffin Yates and Paul Ayres Rockwell of Asheville, North Carolina; Bob Scanlon of Mobile, Alabama; Alan Seeger of New York City; Robert Soubiran of New York City and France; Edward Mandell Stone of Chicago and New Bedford, Massachusetts; Charles M. Sweeny of Spokane and Paris; William Thaw of Pittsburgh; brothers Bertrand and Ellingwood Towle of Larchmount, New York; Charles Trinkard of Brooklyn; Rupert Van Vorst of Cincinnati, Ohio; and Frederick W. Zinn of Battle Creek, Michigan.

They were an odd assortment of men indeed, thrown together by desperate times and a common objective—to get into the war as soon as possible—if not a common motive. Some were idealists, like Seeger and Casmeze; some were rich adventurers, like Thaw and the Rockwell brothers; and some were experienced soldiers, like Bouligny and Morlae. Sweeny was all three.

In the first in a series of six articles for the *Evening Star* in Washington, D.C., published on June 29, 1917, after the United States had entered the war, Sweeny described the volunteers' early days in the Legion, starting with the training camp.[17]

We met in Rouen August 26, 1914, we recruits for the Foreign Legion. It seemed to me the veterans of the old legion who had been given the task of breaking us in wore an air of dejection. Certainly no crowd ever looked less soldierly than we did. There were a dozen nationalities and as many tongues. Rich men. dandies, poor men, toughs, of all heights, complexions,

From left: William Thaw, Charles Sweeny, J. Stewart Carstairs (courtesy Georges Rolland).

ideals, clothes and morals stood in a disorderly group. We were alike in but one thing. We meant to fight for France. We loved France. Something in each of us, voiceless and confused as we were, told us that the world would be the gainer if France won and immeasurably the loser if France were crushed. I do not know that many of us carried the argument further. The officers hurriedly sorted us into groups by nationalities. I was sent to the English group. Not many of us had had any previous military experience. We seemed hopelessly amateurish in our stained "cit" clothes. Most of us slouched. We were to get rid of that fault.

"Fall in." We straggled down Rouen's streets in a disorderly column of fours. That night we slept in straw under the benches of a school. Next day uniforms were issued to us and we embarked upon the course of training which in six weeks made us over into the raw material for soldiering. No other nation than the French ever attempted such a thing in so short a time, but France was driven by necessity. At the end of our six weeks we were sent into the trenches; we completed our training under fire. At 5 o'clock each morning at Rouen we heard the reveille. At first we stumbled out of the school. As the days went on we emerged from our straw more alertly, for our physical condition was bettering. The first task before our instructors was to make us fit men for the hard work ahead. We used to walk five to ten miles out in the country and back again each day. No bands for us in those days. There was no time for bands. We whistled "Soldiers of the King" and "Tlpperary" and kept step to the tunes. Our noncommissioned officers were all old Legionaries from Algiers.

Shown No Pity.—"Left, right, left, right"—Aching muscles and stiff joints and swollen eyes were the rule those days. The old legionaries had no pity on us. We thought they were iron men, but by and by we became iron men, too. We had got as far as "about face" in our instruction when one night we were loaded on cattle cars and taken to Toulouse. Forty men to the car, not enough room to lie down or even to sit up in. No straw. An agony of fatigue.

On September 1, the German juggernaut threatened Rouen, so the 2,000 recruits of all nationalities were moved by train 500 miles south. After four days and nights of discomfort riding in cattle cars, they arrived at a barracks on the outskirts of Toulouse, a large city in southwest France within sight of the Pyrenees Mountains that separate France from Spain.

At Toulouse, the recruits marched 20 to 30 miles a day. They trained in squad and company formation. The effects of the physical conditioning became apparent. "Fat fell away fell away from us," Sweeny wrote in the June 29 article. "Our faces grew lean and hard and eager."

On September 6, the recruits finally exchanged their civilian clothes for coarse white military fatigue uniforms. Up to that point, the only military gear they had been issued was a canteen on a sling. They also received rifles, bayonets and other equipment. The issuance of this gear coincided with the arrival from North Africa of veteran legionnaires. The regiments were reorganized and the veterans mixed in with the recruits. The early American volunteers became part of the 1,000-man Second Marching Regiment of the Second Foreign Regiment, Battalion C. The drilling intensified.[18]

On September 12, less than a month after joining the Legion, the Americans volunteered for front-line duty in response to an appeal for recruits with prior military experience to accompany veteran legionnaires who were moving up. This was three days after the Germans had been halted on the Marne River and the French were scrambling to find enough troops to support an offensive. Paul Rockwell said that those who lacked prior military experience quickly invented some in order to be sent along. One inventive recruit claimed his prior experience was in the Salvation Army. The non-commissioned officer taking down the information was not familiar with the organization and accepted the recruit's cheeky ruse without further examination.

Five days later the volunteers were issued the Model 1877 dark blue overcoat, Model 1897 red trousers and Model 1884 kepi.[19] They would not receive the more modern horizon-blue uniforms for another year, just before the Champagne battle. Continuing his description, Sweeny wrote:

> On to Mailly [500 miles north of Toulouse and 200 miles southeast of Paris] for company and battalion formations. "What is that?" It was the sound of the guns. It was the first time most of us had heard them. But from that time on we were never out of hearing. We were being made into soldiers in the atmosphere of war, in the practical French way. Every day we saw the wounded on their way to the rear. The smells of the hospital became familiar to us on the streets. Our minds grew used to the thought of wounds and death. We were hardening to our work, although we did not know it. One afternoon the word came that we were to leave for the front that night. Perhaps 25 percent of us were veterans of the Moroccan wars. The rest were raw recruits, but strong and fit. In six weeks' time we had been made fit for trench warfare.

As the Battle of the Frontiers gave way to a stabilizing of the battle lines all across France, the armies dug in. The American legionnaires arrived in the war zone at Mailly on October 2, entered the trenches October 18, and came under fire for the first time at Verzenay, near Rheims, 80 northeast of Paris.[20] Sweeny described the experience in his June 29, 1917, article for the *Evening Star*[21]:

> **First Day Under Fire.** "One battalion for the front at once." We had reached Verzenay after several days' march. My battalion was chosen and we started for the front in a soaking rain. Underfoot the fields were marshy, so that we sank mid leg deep in the mud. For the first time that day I came under fire. I had been made orderly, and as we did not know the road to the trenches I had been sent from Verzenay to find Col Glaudel, a veteran of the Moroccan wars. I came out of the street to overlook the plain which leads to Rheims when the shrapnel began to fall about me. I felt funny. That is the only word for it—funny. We went on to Beaumont [40 miles north of Rheims]. A broken village, a battered, crushed, ruined little town. Walls, houses, church all beaten down. It was the first time our men had seen anything of war. They looked at these things stupefied, amazed, a little frightened. It was hard to comprehend. It was foreign to all our previous experience. The Germans were shelling it with what seemed a brutal persistence. We stood in the ranks, silent, flinching, angered by this danger to which there was no reply and for which it seemed there was no need. Lips trembled. Yet our men were not cowards. It was only that this was new. We were ordered back to the

banks of the canal. We shuffled back through the dust and the shreds of pottery and the broken masonry of the walls!

Frightened of course. The scream of the shells overhead seemed incessant. They exploded everywhere amid those broken houses and in the little gardens which were persistently green in spite of war. So we got to the canal, 100 yards from the very center of the bombardment, a clear stream of brown water, bordered by little bushes, with here and there the platforms on which the country women kneel to wash their clothes in the stream. It seemed almost familiar to us. This scene, for there were men kneeling on those little stages, washing their clothes, bathing in the stream, sitting on the banks, sewing kits in hand, playing cards, gossiping. It was quiet and homely and peaceful, in spite of the shells that burst such a little distance away. These men were veterans and that bombardment that had so shaken us was merely an Incident of the day to them. We began to comprehend. Here we had open order drill every day. We went out five or six miles and worked out battle and assault problems on the way back. They seemed real to us now with the guns sounding in our ears and the planes flying overhead.

It was at Mailly that the story of the flag that the Americans had marched behind in Paris took on special significance. Before going up to the front, the officers had ordered all national flags to be turned in. The Americans, however, held on to their banner. At Mailly, the Americans used an indelible pencil to write their names on the flag. It was then entrusted to Phelizot, who wore it around his middle, under his coat. In February 1915, while the unit was in reserve behind the lines, the story of the flag took a tragic turn, as recounted in the *Sun*[22]:

> A stupid quarrel arose one evening when the men were at repose billeted back of the front line. One of the old time legionaries began criticizing the Americans as the original legionaries were fond of doing to the young volunteers and a fight began. It became a general scrimmage between factions and during it one of the old legionary hit Phelizot over the head with a metal bucket. The injury did not seem grave for the day but later Phelizot was found insensible on the road and Phelizot was sent to the hospital at Fismes. Tetanus, one of the scourges of the first year of the war, set in and he died. He had the American flag around his waist and he clung to it, waving it around in his last minutes. Sergt. Morlae, who went to see him but found him dead, took charge of the flag and as soon as possible deposited it with Miss Margaret A. Stevens, an American resident In Paris, who had always taken a great Interest In the welfare of the American volunteers, being untiring in her efforts to supply them with cigarettes, chocolate, books, magazines and all sorts of comforts to cheer their life In the trenches In winter. He asked Miss Stevens to try to have the flag placed In the Museum of the Invalides as token that some Americans had at once remembered the debt of their country to that of Lafayette. The flag, after Phelizot's death, had to be disinfected and the names Inscribed upon it have thus become somewhat hard to decipher. Two of them seem to have been blotted out on purpose, for reasons unknown. Thirty-one can still be made out. Seven of these are dead and a dozen are still in the service of France. Several could not stand the training, their will to serve being stronger than their powers, and so did not reach the front. Their record as whole is one that their country can be proud of.

The flag's significance increased in the summer of 1917 when France installed it in the Musee de'Armee at the Hotel des Invalides with great ceremony. The attendees included the president of France, the minister of war, the American ambassador, the president of the Chamber of Deputies, the president of the Senate, Marshal Joseph Joffre, and Generals Ferdinand Foch, Henri-Philippe Petain and John J. Pershing, the newly arrived commander of the American Expeditionary Force. A century later, it is still prominently displayed there and visitors to the Invalides can still make out the names, Sweeny's included, though faded and smudged.

As the battle lines hardened in late 1914 and winter ended major offensive action until spring, the Americans moved into trenches in front of Craonne, a village between Soissons and Rheims facing a 12-mile-long ridge rising 200 feet above a level plain. The Germans had turned the tunnels and caves created by centuries of quarrying into a fortress studded with machineguns, backed up by artillery.

Sweeny provided a detailed description of the Americans' first tour of duty in the trenches in his second of six articles for the *Evening Star*, published July 1, 1917.[23]

> No soldier ever forgets his first march forward to the trenches. There is something definite about it—decisive. The things of peace have finally been put aside and he has entered into the war. Once I lay with a green battalion near Cuiry-les-Chandardes, on the Aisne. We waited to be sent to the trenches near Craonne, in front of the plateau of Craonne and just below the Chemin-des-Dames which figured in the last assault. These were bad days for us. The buildings of the abandoned farm where we were billeted had been torn to pieces by a bombardment. Three times in three days the German airplanes circled overhead and dropped bombs on us. We ran to cover, clrcling [sic], confused, like frightened chickens. Reason told us we had little chance to dodge an air bomb, but we dodged anyhow. At night we slept badly. Men were forever sitting up in their blankets, rolling cigarettes, talking In low tones. We were being hardened for what was to come. At last the word was passed to us: "Tonight we go to the trenches."
>
> As orderly I was told to accompany the captain and the lieutenant to the front in order to acquaint ourselves with the route and the location. It was a miserable, rainy, dark day. Our march was a long wallow through the mire. The Germans were shelling the roads, so that we were forced to take to the fields. This is a sugar beet country and the farmers had not had any opportunity to harvest their crops. We squashed through the mud mid-leg deep, slipping on the beet roots, splashing each other with the half-fluid mud, soaked through by the falling rain, perspiring at every pore. After seven miles of this going we came to a little wood which ran up a gentle hill. A sentry halted us: "Your positions are at the other edge of the wood."
>
> We crept up the hill through the slender trees. The rain dripped endlessly through the branches. At the top of the hill we saw the French trenches in the open, perhaps fifty yards from the grove. The Germans were 200 yards away, across a shallow valley. We were standing there, examining the position through our glasses, arranging for the night's disposition of the troops. "One platoon there," said the captain. "Another here." There was a nasty, venomous scream in the air. A shell burst almost under our feet, it

seemed at the time. You should have seen the three of us dive into a shell hole. We laughed nervously and glanced at each other. Then we sneaked through the wood again downhill, our tails between our legs. We felt cheap, humiliated. It was as though we were doing an unsoldierly thing. Later we learned taking cover is good common sense.

Back to the village—another seven miles of glue and puddle and splash—arriving well after dark of an October night. It took us three hours to do the seven miles. An hour or so for rest and then the company was formed up. "Forward march." It was impossibly dark. One could not see one's hand before one's eyes, and it rained dismally, persistently. The columns lost each other and doubled up and strangled and the sous-officers kept thrusting the men back in line by that extra sense which an old non-commissioned officer develops in handling green troops. The sense of humor deserted us, so that we did not laugh or joke. We were only conscious of the frightful discomfort of that progress through the sticking mud of the battlefields. At last my company got up to the wood, and I told the platoon commanders which path to take.

First Sight of Blood. The moon had come out—a watery, faint, pallid moon—across which rain clouds drifted. The men stumbled forward into the black wood and passed through. Just at the far edge of the wood, five freshly killed men were lying. The Germans had bombarded the trenches after seeing us that afternoon, and these were the victims. It was the first that most of our men had seen of men killed in war. Some of them had hardly seen dead men before in all their lives. They went by in hushed silence in Indian file, glancing out of the corners of their eyes at the five dead, covered by their overcoats. They had not known before how quiet the dead lie. It was their introduction to the life of the trench.

We took up our positions, slithering into the soaked and muddy trenches, ourselves soaked and muddy. The moon disappeared. We sent out the listening posts and settled down to our first night in the trenches. Nothing happened, but few slept, for all knew the Germans were just a little distance away. Our men whispered to each other and shuffled uneasily in the slime and were very cold. The dugouts were only pools of mud under the dripping arch of the earth roof. Next morning the faces of the men had changed. They had begun to realize. They were sober and drawn and a little pale. That morning we buried the five dead men who had kept silent watch behind us. Over their graves we erected little crosses and hung their kepis on them. In the crossbars of the crosses we wrote the soldier's epitaph: "To Our Comrades of the Forty-ninth of the Line, From the Soldiers of the Legion."

Monotony and vermin and mud and cold and thrills and dulling work and hunger and that gambler's happiness which only the soldier knows in its fullest perfection—all these things enter into life in the trenches. During the day a front trench is somnolent, grouchy, dull. Only the sentinels are awake. They do their two-hour guards, watching against a possible surprise by the enemy. The other men of the company lie in their dugouts. While they can they sleep. They eat at the ordained intervals. They grease their boots and patch their clothes, and sometimes try to make themselves clean. If they are very lucky there is water enough so they can wash their faces. It matters very little. In the front trench one rarely is able to shave anyhow. The morning toilet is merely the rubbing of red eyes with grubby fingers and stretching muscles kinked by the cold and growling at the comrade. It is at night that one is alive. Then the trench is lined with active figures. The night is noisy and furious.

Six Days In and Six Days Out. But let us consider trench routine as the soldier knows it. Sometimes the company spends six days in and six days out. Sometimes it does six days in the front trench, six in the intermediate and six in what the army ironists call "repose." In the rear. There is little danger of surprise by day in the front trench. An enemy must be mad to try to penetrate then that tangle of rusty wires which lie at the eye-level as you glance out through the trench ports. The sentinels are posted and the men who have been awake all night sleep in their dugouts, of which the openings are barely above the level of the trench floor. Before turning in they do the "first fatigue duty," which is the cleaning up of trenches and dugouts. Coffee and bread are brought in by fatigue parties from the kitchens back of the lines. After breakfast they go to sleep. The sentinels stand at their posts, delighting in the warmth of the sun upon their backs after the chill of the night. Each has a sector of the trench opposite to watch. One gets a bug's-eye view of the terrain because one is hardly above the level of the earth. New hands find a difficulty sometimes in adjusting themselves to this change of status. Things which would be easily recognizable if they might stand on the trench parapet become puzzling, although easily seen. As the sun rises a certain uneasiness penetrates their minds. They begin to wonder how soon the enemy artillery will begin to register on their trench.

Each morning the artillery fires a few shots at the position opposite, searching for "probable error." Yesterday they had the range exactly, perhaps, but today the atmospheric conditions have altered. It is warmer or colder or mistier than the day before, and even the slightest change means the range must be adjusted. After the first registering shots there is peace, unless the day turns briskly warm. Then the "probable error" is corrected again. In the afternoon there are a few more sighting shots. This is merely preparedness. The artillery must be ready for anything at any time. The sentinels watch the wires and the brown ground of No Man's Land and the thin line of faded, upturned earth which marks the enemy trench through their periscopes. In front of each is a plan of the German trench opposite, with every turn and angle set out. Whatever may be seen across the way is set down on this plan: "Man smoking here at 10 o'clock." "Working party here at 11 o'clock." "Men cooked breakfast here," are sample notations. When the sentries are relieved at the end of their two hours' guard these annotated maps are placed before the officer in command. After a few days' observation he is able to tell with accuracy what Is going on in the other trench. He knows where the officers' dugout is, and where the Place d'Armes is where the men met to eat and gossip, and where the machine guns are located.

Between times the sentries watch for the trench mortar bombs, for some times the minenwerfers are pneumatic, and one cannot hear the "sough" of the discharge, though one can always see the missile tumbling slowly across the sky. If anything seems worth the officer's attention he is signaled by a bell system to his dugout. At 10 o'clock the men all wake up and crawl out of their dugouts to take the sun and make what passes for a toilet in the trench and smoke a cigarette. A fatigue party goes out for the midday soup, and after it is served at 11 o'clock the men meet in the Place d'Armes to hear the news of the day. The sous-officers read the orders and the morning communiqué and any papers that may have found their way into the trenches. Then the men go back to the undergrounds, where they are required to stay as much as possible, because of the danger which always threatens in the open trench. Four o'clock comes, and more soup and bread and coffee. Then the men are selected for the night outpost duty, and as soon as darkness falls they squirm over the parapet and wriggle across the open ground to the places where they must lie that night to guard against surprise.

On October 25, 1914, Sweeny was awarded the Croix de Guerre (War Cross), the second highest French military decoration for heroism after the Medallo Militaire (Military Medal). His service record does not contain a description of the actions that resulted in the medal.[24]

This was the first of several awards of the Croix de Guerre to Sweeny during the war. An article in the *Sun* shortly after the war said Sweeny's decorations included the Croix de Guerre with two palms and two stars.[25] Each star or palm represents a mention in dispatches resulting in an award of the medal by a commanding officer of at least a regiment. A bronze star denotes an award by a regiment or brigade commander; a silver star represents an award by a division commander; a silver gilt star stands for a mention at corps level; a bronze palm denotes a mention at the army level; and a silver palm represents five bronze stars. It appears from Sweeny's stars and palms that he was twice cited at the regiment, brigade or division level and twice at the army level for a total of four awards of the Croix de Guerre while serving in the Foreign Legion.[26]

In December 1914, the first promotions were issued. Bouligny, Morlae and Sweeny became corporals.[27] Each spoke French and had prior military experience. Bouligny had served two enlistments in the U.S. Army. Morlae had served in the U.S. Army in the Philippines and reportedly in the Mexican revolution. In addition, Bach, Capdevielle, Phelizot and Thaw were promoted to privates first class.[28]

Later that month, Corporals Sweeny and Edward Morlae were selected to take a course of instruction in French military science, an indication of future promotion.

The Americans passed the winter of 1914-15 in these trenches. "War was not proving exactly what these volunteers expected," the *Sun* reported.[29] "They never fired their rifles, as they never saw an enemy. Digging trenches and placing barbed wire were their chief pursuits. Their lines were bombarded from time to time and men were wounded or killed from time to time but the Americans lost none of their number" to an enemy attack.

During this period, Sweeny's fluency in French led to his being assigned as the "colonel's cyclist," carrying messages between battalion headquarters and the front line. While the job sounds benign, it was hazardous. Instead of the relative safety of the dugouts, Sweeny dodged German shells as he crisscrossed the area behind the lines.

The Americans continued to dodge death, but casualties began to mount. Bouligny became the first, hit by a shell fragment in the leg while on outpost duty November 17. By the end of the first winter of the war, wounds, illness and transfers had cut into the ranks of the Americans who had marched behind the flag in Paris. Some of the wounded returned to the regiment. Others were invalided out of the Legion and returned to the United States. Paul Rockwell was given a medical discharge but chose to stay in France to be near his brother. He became an ambulance driver. While still others in the unit were transferred to other duties, including James Bach, Bert Hall and William Thaw to aviation.

In January 1915, Sweeny witnessed what he later described in an article in the *Evening Star* as "a magnificent example of heroism" in the face of certain death[30]:

> It was during a German attack upon a French position on the Aisne that I was privileged to witness the most sublime example of military courage I have ever known. This was in the earlier part of the war, before the heavy artillery had begun to play the all-Important part it does nowadays. Then neither side had many guns. The Germans still maintained their theory of mass attacks. The bombardment preliminaries to an attack were usually short and of little weight by comparison. When the attacking forces moved forward, the defenders held their positions by rifle fire, hand grenades, and in the final rush by butt and bayonet and knife. "Make your way to the hill at our left and find out what is happening," the battalion commander ordered me. This was in January 1915, when I was still a cyclist orderly. An infantry regiment from the south of France held this little hill and had been severely attacked. We had few guns then and almost no ammunition for them. Nor were our machine guns numerous or well provisioned. We were accustomed to rely on rifle fire for the most part to hold our positions. I reached the hill just at dusk on the evening of January 18, if my memory serves me well. I remember that I could just make out objects which were at a distance of sixty or seventy-five yards. Beyond that distance all blended into a common background. They are coming, some man said next to me in the trench.
>
> **The Hymn of Death.** The French line was at the top of this little hill. I could see at the bottom a gray mass moving forward slowly, with something to the effect of a retarded but irrestible [*sic*] wave. The Germans were still too far away to permit me to pick out individuals. I only saw a gray-green thickening in the increasing dusk. Then we began to hear their voices. The Germans were singing the "Lorelei." It is a sad and yet a very beautiful air, that "Lorelei," the story of the young man who was lured to his doom by the mermaid's song as she combed her golden hair. It especially lends itself to the needs of a male chorus. The great volume of sound surged up the hill toward us, waiting in the French trenches, with an effect that is difficult for me to describe. It was overpoweringly masculine and yet it was almost theatric in its appeal. Perhaps it was because we knew most of the singers were going to their deaths that we found something ineffably sad in the intoning of the mournful air. "Poor devils," I heard the men whisper on either side of me. It was sheer pity plus that magnificent chivalry of the Frenchman that I led the men from the south to withhold their fire until that solid wall of Germans was within fifty yards. It seemed as though we could not fire upon those magnificent young men, marching knowingly upon a sure fate. The song rose higher as they came nearer our trench, for they could see our heads over the parapet and the rifles held in rest and they knew that any second death might spurt in their faces.
>
> **Then the Bullets.** It reached a magnificent crescendo at last: "*Ich welss nlcht was soll es bedeuten Das Ich so traurlg bin.*" ["I know not if there is a reason why I am so sad at heart."] Then the captains nodded and the rifles began to crackle all along that line.

The first rank dropped, and the second rank moved on across their writhing bodies, still singing. There came a rift in the clouds so that the last pale rays of a wintry sun shone down upon the scene. The cries of the wounded rose until a tragic undertone mingled with the mournful rhythm. Some of the advancing men were screaming in a German rage—the furor Teutonicus—and others were grunting in a sort of battle delirium. Over all rang that wonderful male chorus, however, and so they sang, and so they marched on and so they died, until in the end they crowded us out by sheer weight of numbers and took the trench. Toward the last the advancing men literally crawled over a hedge of bodies to get at us. I know that one often reads of such a thing, but it is not often witnessed. The men who die that way are the bravest of foes. No more magnificent example of heroism has been seen in this war, I am sure. I have fought the German from the beginning of the war because I felt it to be my duty. I have no kindly feeling for the race or for the individuals that compose it. But I would be the last to decry the personal courage of the German. The men who can do a thing like that—who can sing in the face of certain death and keep on singing and dying—whatever else they may be, they are not cowards.

In February 1915, Edgar Bouligny, Edward Morlae and Sweeny were promoted to sergeant.[31] They were reportedly the first Americans to attain that rank in the war.

The (New York) *Sun*'s correspondent in Paris, an Englishman named Francis Bernard Grundy, closely followed the activities of the Americans in the Legion for his paper if for no other reason than the number of New Yorkers among the volunteers made for high reader interest. Sweeny was a frequent topic. In a June 6, 1915, round-up of recent events, he recounted a story told to him by fellow Legionnaire Jack Casey on April 25.[32] It seems that while on a midnight reconnaissance in No Man's Land, Sweeny and his men had penetrated the German wire. Sweeny became nervous when the patrol failed to encounter any enemy fire. He began to suspect he had crawled into a trap, and he and his men began to work their way back to their own lines. As he did so, he noticed a German helmet appear about a dozen yards away. Then another one poked up nearby. As Sweeny lay on the ground under a small tree, he noticed a basket hanging from a branch above his head. He lifted it down and inside he found a bottle of beer, some tobacco, a box of cigarettes and three sandwiches. Sweeny told Casey he was puzzled until he suddenly concluded that the basket had been left there by the Germans for him to find. "With the basket under my arm, I got up, bowed low to the round hats, and walked back to our trench without ever being fired on." Inside the basket were "two sandwiches of white bread and the other of the famous KK bread. One had very fine quality fresh butter and honey, the second butter and roast veal, and the third Westphalian ham." There also was a note written in perfect French, said Casey. The note read:

> To our comrades of the French army: We have been here all the winter and feel as If we are friends, although we have not seen each other except at the distance of a bullet.

> We see that the papers you kindly left for us state that we are hungry and starving, therefore we have left this basket that you may know what we receive each day. We hope that the war will end soon so that you, our comrades, may go back to your families as well as we.
>
> We are sorry that the war arose. We Germans have always looked upon you French as our comrades and friends. England is the enemy. She it is who is the real cause of the war, to save her commerce. We hope the French will make peace and then form an alliance to war on the common enemy, England. Hoping for the end of the war, we are "Your comrades of the German Army."

According to Casey, some Americans had left a bundle of American and English newspapers for the Germans where Sweeny had found the basket. The papers were marked to highlight reports that the Germans were starving. The basket was the Germans' offer of proof to the contrary. Casey said the captain of Sweeny's company let him keep the cigarette box, which had been made in Dresden, as a souvenir.

With the arrival of spring 1915, the French and British began a series of offensives aimed at breaking through the center of the German western wall. The British achieved surprise with a small-scale attack at Neuve Chapelle south of Lille in March, only to be halted by communications failures. The French suffered a bloody failure trying to eliminate the St. Mihiel Salient in April. A joint British and French offensive—the Second Battle of Artois—suffered heavy losses. And the French launched the Champagne offensive, between Rheims and Verdun, in September, again with heavy losses. The goal was to break through the German trench system and either force a general withdrawal or open a war of maneuver. But the result was continued deadlock. "Barbed wire, machine guns, entrenchments and supporting artillery could form a barrier that massed bayonets and human courage could not breach."[33] The Germans spent 1915 on defense in the West in order to shift troops to major offensives against the Russians.

In early May, the First Foreign Regiment, into which some of the original group of Americans had been assigned, fought in the Second Battle of Artois, north of Paris.

The main French attack was directed at seizing Vimy Ridge, a key piece of high ground. A thunderous French barrage preceded the attack but when the French troops reached the German entanglements, they found the shelling had failed to cut the wire. As they worked furiously to carve pathways through it with wire-cutters, they were raked by German machinegun fire. Those who made it through moved on and took the objectives. But the Germans recaptured these positions before French reserves could reach the advance units.[34]

The First Foreign Regiment seized Hill 140, a shoulder of the vital Vimy Ridge, but when reinforcements did not arrive the unit was finally driven back by a powerful German counterattack.[35] The First Foreign Regiment earned glory for itself in this battle but paid for it in heavy casualties, including most of its senior officers killed or wounded. "The losses of the Legion were tremendous," wrote Kiffin Rockwell from his hospital bed on May 15. "Of the four thousand men who went into the attack, some seventeen hundred came through unscathed. Of the company in which was the American squad, fifty-five men out of the two hundred and fifty who climbed out of the trenches on the morning of May 9 answered the roll-call, when the regiment was drawn out of the firing line."

The Second Foreign Regiment was envious of its brother regiment's new stature, but it would have its own opportunity for bloody glory soon enough. In late May, it was moved from the Aisne sector, where it had spent the past several months, to the Champagne sector, a mostly featureless chalk plateau east of Rheims. The area was ideal for a war of maneuver if the French could first break through the triple layer of German trenches. The French army knew the area well. It had held large-scale maneuver tactics over this same ground in the years before the war. But the Germans had a year to fortify this area and they knew it was the likely avenue of the next attack. Surprise was impossible.

While the Legionnaires prepared for the Champagne offensive, the *Sun* reported on June 6, 1915, that Sergeant Sweeny was to be sent to an officer's school in a month's time to be prepared for promotion to lieutenant. Said the *Sun*[36]:

> All the boys are delighted at Sweeny being in line for promotion. He comes from Spokane, Wash., and was at West Point from 1900 to 1904. It is a great compliment to him, as the rule is that a man must become a Frenchman before receiving a commission. One of Sweeny's latest exploits was to take a corporal who understood German and creep within the German lines and listen to the conversation, thus obtaining valuable Information. It took them three hours to crawl 200 feet. If Sweeny is promoted to be lieutenant it will be a sort of recognition of the American volunteers' services. We started about forty strong and now number seventeen here. Thaw is an aviator, Bach and Hall are trying to become the same, Rockwell is in the First regiment and the rest are at the rear trying to get well. We feel as if someone ought to be rewarded and Sweeny is certainly the best man.

Sweeny received his promotion to second lieutenant on July 11 for the duration of the war.[37] According to Rockwell[38] as well as an article in the *Sun*,[39] Sweeny was the first American volunteer of 1914 to become an officer. The *Sun* article noted, "The Sun's correspondent with the Foreign Legion has mentioned him frequently for his constant display of great pluck, and has always spoken of him as a favorite with the men.... The fact that he has been made a commissioned officer is, in a way, a compliment to all the Americans in the Legion, for it is a rule that only Frenchmen may hold commissions."

In anticipation of the upcoming Champagne offensive, the Second

Foreign Regiment was pulled out of the front line to prepare them for the attack. Sweeny later described the special training that "shock troops" receive before they "go over the top" in another in the series of articles for Washington, D.C., *Evening Star*[40]:

> Soldiers are trained for the "attack" just as athletes are. I do not mean that they undergo the same sort of training that a pugilist does. As the end is different, so the means are different. The aim is to supply them, physically and mentally, so that when the supreme moment comes and they "go over the top" they will be literally "fit to fight for their lives." Tomorrow we start for the rear, we were told in August 1915. We are to be made ready for an offensive. The weeks that followed rest in my memory as among the happiest of my life as a soldier. We had been undergoing the usual grueling at the front. Suddenly we were transplanted from this life of mud and discomfort and danger to the region north of Belfort. The boche had never occupied this territory. The little towns were as peaceful in the sunlight as though war was not raging a few miles farther on. The quaint cobbled streets between the stone walls which are a feature of the villages of France rang with the laughter of children. Men and women went quietly about their business. A little time before soldiering had seemed the normal manner of life. Now the horizon blue of the uniform seemed out of place in these charming streets.
>
> **Fed Up to Kill.** Six weeks we spent there. A cynic might say that we were being fed up for killing. So we were, in a way, but we were also being given a glimpse of happiness. We bathed when we would. Our meals were perhaps no better than they had been, but we were in the midst of a civilian population and were able to add to the daily menu. Pretty girls went by. Dogs wagged about us and birds sang in the rose bushes, and we slept in real beds. After a time at the front a fragrant hayloft seems a luxury. There were cows everywhere. Did it ever occur to you that the cow is the emblem of true peace? Cows in the countryside means that war is afar off. All this time we worked hard. We rose at 5 o'clock every morning to drill until 10 or 11 o'clock. It was a pleasure this drill, our arms springy and sinews elastic after the repose the night before, our nerves freed from the constant strain of the front. For an hour or so each afternoon we likewise drilled, but each day we had many hours to ourselves. The usual tasks of soldiering were made light to us. We were a "corps du shoc" and the efforts of the officers were directed to making us 100 per cent perfect physically. In the trenches we had grown stale.
>
> **They Don't Know Defeat.** The corps du shoc is a military institution, if not peculiar to France, is at least an integral part of the French military system. It is a body of the best troops obtainable, who are retained for that moment when the enemy's position is to be carried by assault. Age does not matter. Even physical condition sometimes does not matter in the individual. The corps du shoc is built upon spirit—elan—the espirit de corps. Such men are irresistible. They do not know defeat. They tear through an enemy's lines without recognizing the cost. It was the famous 20th Corps that saved the day on the Couronne de Nancy. The Germans had been hammering the French troops back until the 20th Corps came up and were hurled against their lines. No statement of their losses has ever been published, but the German rush stopped. They saved that part of France.
>
> **Hurled Into Verdun Breach.** It was the same corps under Gen. Petain that was hurled into the breach at Verdun, when it seemed the Germans were about to break through. It has been publicly stated that some regiments of the 20th Corps have had

16,000 names on their rolls since the war began. That means the regiment has been replaced four times over. When we marched out of the region of Belfort to enter the battle of Champagne in the pink of condition, it was a pleasure to see the men march. They were on their toes like dancing masters. They sang the songs of the army as they took the route. Their eyes were bright and they played like children—or like young animals—when the regiments halted for rest. The French theory of physical training had been proven out again. When our corps went forward in the battle of the Champagne no men we could reach stood against us.

In the next article in the series for the *Evening Star*, Sweeny focused on the final hours of his regiment's wait to serve as shock troops in the Champagne offensive[41]:

Somehow there was a curious air of peace in the company that night. The hard work was over. The strain of preparation was over. We had "made our [haver]sacks," and the officers had packed their trunks. That day we had bathed and put on fresh underwear, to lessen the danger of Infection if we were wounded the next day. It had been bright and sunny and pleasant, and we had written our last letters to the folks at home, and told our comrades what bits of our kit they were to have if anything happened. There was nothing else to do. When dusk came most of the men laid down in the trenches and slept....

Preparing for Attack. The preparation for an attack is a work of infinite detail. Roads are built—wagon roads, railroads, little De Cauvllle tram roads, pack roads—any sort of a road over which a wheeled vehicle can be pulled or pushed. The artillery is brought up. Some of the guns fire daily, and others are silent until the moment comes when the full chorus of cannon Is to open on the enemy. The men of the *corps de shoc* have been resting in pretty little villages, far from the scene of action. Shortly before the day set for the battle they are brought up by train and sent to their new billets. Preparing for a battle is the most complex bit of business there is in modern business life. The new arrivals are kept hidden In woods and villages by day. At night they are marched forward toward the front. They build trenches for the stretcher bearers and trenches to be used by troops going: up to the attack, and circulating trenches, and every other sort of trench the occasion demands. They see all the paraphernalia being prepared for the event. Temporary hospitals and clearing stations are put up and narrow gauge roads built over which the shell trains are rushed.

Last Day of Getting Ready. Before the fight of Champagne we were billeted near the little town of Suippe, in a little wood. The town had been badly knocked about by the crown prince in his retreat. We worked hard, but not so hard as to take the spring out of us. By night we dug trenches and by day we practiced bombing drill, bayonet drill, every sort of drill. Now and then general orders were read to us. We were kept acquainted, in a general way, with the progress of the war. Orders plus communiques plus gossip kept us in touch with what was going on immediately in front of us. Then the last day came. I have glanced at what we did on that day. There was no work for us, for our trenches were dug and everything was in readiness. The previous day the corps commanders had read the orders to us. We knew who was in front of us, what we were to do. How we were to do it. We studied the terrain that we were to cross as closely as was possible—we could see little of it through the port in a trench parapet—and talked to each other of our plans. On the last night the soup came up early, and after disposing of it most of us laid down to sleep. It was real sleep, too. The healthy snores were in evidence. At last 9:16 a.m. came, and we stepped drowsily into line and began the march for the foremost trenches. It was from these trenches that the attack was to be launched the next day. The charge proved to be rather unfortunate for me. A rifle ball passed through my lung and liver.

On September 25, 1915, the French launched their Champagne offensive with 20 divisions on a 20-mile-wide front, supported by artillery and a cloud of chlorine gas. In his final article in the *Evening Star* series, Sweeny described the moment of attack[42]:

The climacteric moment of a soldier's life is the attack upon the enemy's trench. Yet it is not at all like the charge that artists picture. The men go forward at a walk. By and by they walk a little faster. In the last moments they may strike up a little dog trot. Never do they rush forward cheering, the officers waving swords, banners fluttering. That is romantic, but it isn't business—and war is the grimmest of businesses. Usually the attack comes at 6 o'clock in the morning. The men have been marched up the night before through communicating trenches. On reaching the place nearest the enemy, where they are to be held until the moment of the charge arrives, they lie down and go to sleep. Not all, perhaps. Nevertheless most of them do. By and by an officer from headquarters comes through. He bears the official time, and the watch of every officer in the trench is set by his timepiece. His coming has been a momentary diversion. The men lie down and go to sleep again. A quarter of an hour before the time fixed for the charge they are wakened up. They stand in the trenches, rubbing their eyes and growling. Some nod in spite of themselves.

When "Drum Fire" Comes. The bombardment has been growing in intensity. Finally the sleepy men in the trenches recognize the "drum fire" that precedes the final burst. The guns are being fired so rapidly that it really sounds as though some Titan were tapping upon a super-earthly drum. The men are no longer sleepy. They speak to each other nervously. They laugh and joke. The officers have a hard time keeping them in the trenches. They are impatient for the start. It was at such a moment that I witnessed one of the most ludicrous incidents of the war. I was holding my company in one of the trenches leading up to the foremost trench. A Y trench led off from our position, so that an island of land was created between the three trenches. On this a rabbit had made its bed. The men talking in the trenches on each side awakened it, and it sat up and looked at us in the pale dawn, its long ears tilted forward as it peered at these strange beings in gray blue. The temptation was too much for two of the legionnaires. They scrambled out of the trench and on the island. "He is mine!" each shouted. So the two wild men chased it about the little island, throwing clods and bits of stone at him while they and the rabbit were impartially pelted by the shouting men in the trenches. Half were for the rabbit and half for the men. They jeered each other and threw their caps in the air and fairly howled with laughter. The scene only ended when one of the men caught the beast and thrust it in his haversack. "He'll do for supper tonight," said the winner. Two minutes before the time ordered for the charge the section officers nod to their men. They brace themselves against the sides of the trenches ready for the move. A minute passes. He nods again. Then that moment comes which was determined weeks ago, perhaps, by a council of officers, at headquarters, and the officer leaps forward, his men at his heels. They go forward at a slow walk. Then comes the prettiest bit in the whole machine of war, as it seems to me the perfect coordination between the charging men and the artillerymen hidden miles away, unable to see a foot of the ground on which their shells are hailing.

Under Curtain of Steel. The artillerymen have been showering the enemy trench with their deadly missiles. Their purpose is threefold: to destroy the trench, to keep the enemy under cover for the leisurely trapping to come, and to keep the enemy from resisting the attack. At a given moment, marked by rigid instructions, the "barrage" or curtain of fire is lifted fifty yards nearer the enemy. The men break into a little faster walk. The barrage lifts again. Behind that curtain of breaking steel and thunderous explosives and darting fire the men walk in safety. At last the barrage lifts beyond the German trenches. If they are lucky the charging men get to the enemy trench before the Germans have realized the significance of that last "lift" of the curtain and come growling out of their dugouts to man their machine guns. If they are lucky, the first wave of men goes right over the trenches. On the other side they reform, and still following that pillar of fire that leads them to victory, they make for the second line of trenches. Behind them come the "trench cleaners." It is their job to make sure of the enemy in the trench that has been crossed. They hurl bombs in the undergrounds and shoot down the late comers who crawl bewilderedly to the air. Far ahead the charging wave is walking, just behind the barrage. They know their limit of safety almost to a meter, and keep just beyond the radius of the bursting shells. When they reach their objective—the distant trench they have been ordered to take—they "turn it around," and begin to make themselves comfortable. After the roar and turmoil of the day a cigarette and a pull at the canteen seem doubly welcome. Each man feels he has played a soldier's part that day.

Two French armies were committed to the offensive. On the day of the attack, an early morning fog and heavy rain reduced visibility but did nothing to dampen the spirits of the French troops, who were anxious to break the stalemate and escape the trenches.

The main axis of attack was due north, straight up the road (D977 today) from Souain-Perthes les Herles (30 miles east of Rheims) in the direction of a local crossroads at Sommepy-Tahure. The left wing's attack bent left toward a wooded area, the right wing angled right toward the Butte of Souain, and the center took aim at Navarin Farm, the key German strongpoint. Navarin Farm stood atop the lip of a large bowl, about two miles north of Souain, the village at the bottom of the bowl where only a few roofless walls remained.[43]

Battalion C was positioned with its left flank on the road and its rank flank about 800 yards to the east. Its objective was Navarin Farm. Owing to his recent promotion, Sweeny was assigned as a "supernumerary" in the Third Company, according to Sergeant Edward Morlae, who was in the First Company.[44]

While some of the American legionnaires had grown war-weary, others went into this fight eagerly. In a letter home on the eve of the battle, Alan Seeger, the Harvard-educated poet expressed such a sentiment: "I expect to march right up the Aisne borne on an irresistible elan. It will be the greatest moment of my life." Fellow Legionaire Edmund Genet, a great-great-grandson of Citizen Genet, the French representative to America after the French Revolution, was far less enthusiastic. In a letter to his parents that same day, he wrote about the "ghastly condition" of the German prisoners, some "mere boys," that he passed as he moved up to the front. "Bleeding, clothing torn to shreds, wounded by ball, shell and bayonet, they were pitiable sights." It is not hard to read between the lines that Genet could see a similar fate for himself.

Whatever their private hopes and fears, the troops went "over the top" at 9:15 a.m. They advanced in seven waves, each soldier about two yards from the one to his right or left, with each successive wave about 100 yards behind the one in front of it. Sweeny's regiment was in the second wave, behind the Colonials and Moroccans.

Morlae provided a vivid personal narration of the start of the attack: "The world became a roaring hell. Shell after shell burst near us, sometimes right among us; and, as we moved forward at the double-quick, men fell right and left. We could hear the subdued rattling of the mitrailleuses [machine-guns] and the roar of volley fire, but, above it all, I could hear with almost startling distinctness the words of the captain, shouting in his clear, high voice, 'En avant! Vive la France.'"[45]

The shell bursts were coming from French 75-millimeter guns providing a "fire curtain" in front of the regiment as it moved through the wire entanglements toward the German trenches, recalled Morlae. When the curtain lifted to fire on the next line of German trenches, the legionnaires rushed forward. Most of the German defenders were killed or demoralized. The few who resisted were bayoneted before the legionnaires resumed their advance to the next trench, which was being pummeled by the French 75s. "I remember now how the men looked. Their eyes had a wild, unseeing look in them. Everybody was gazing ahead, trying to pierce the awful curtain which cut us off from all sight of the enemy. Always the black pall smoking and burning appeared ahead—just ahead of us—hiding everything we wanted to see."

While the assault troops advanced, the so-called "trench-cleaners" entered the trench. Using grenades, they blasted the defenders hunkered down in an underground city. Hundreds of Germans, who had survived the bombardment, were slain and entombed.

As the regiment advanced further, the gaps between the legionnaires increased. "[E]ach man did not get out two yards from the next. Frequently, the other man was dead or wounded," recalled Legionaire John Bowe. "Nearer the front line, the worse the carnage. Dead were lying so thick, soldiers walked on upturned faces grazed by hob-nailed shoes."

Morlae recalled walking on a veritable carpet of dead Germans, torn apart by French shells as they tried to fall back to the next trench line. As the day ended, Morlae toted up his own losses—two-thirds of his section of 60 men were killed or wounded that day.

The initial advance was very rapid. The center force was abreast of Navarin Farm in less than an hour, while the attack on the right, toward the Butte of Souain, progressed more slowly. But much hard fighting still lay ahead. Sweeny's regiment had captured the Wagram earthworks, the Eckmuhl trench, a battery of German 77-millimeter guns and many machineguns.[46]

The next day, September 26, the Legion—both the Second and First Foreign Regiments—shifted eastward toward the Butte of Souain, which was still in German hands. The purpose was to draw enemy fire so reinforcements could be moved into position for an assault against the butte and Navarin Farm. The legionnaires came under intense shell fire and suffered heavy casualties.[47]

The third day of the offensive brought a pause in the attack but on the fourth day, September 28, the Legion joined in a renewed attack on Navarin Farm. The Legion attacked the Bois Sabot (Horseshoe Wood), an earthwork that guarded the farm's right flank. The German engineers considered it one of the strongest points in the entire line of defense. Rockwell called the Legion's attack "a blind sacrifice assault." That seems an apt phrase, considering the results. The Legion's attack enabled French army units to capture the Navarin Farm from the rear. But the Legion's casualties were horrific. Relatively few legionnaires made it into the earthwork, and all who did were lost. Entire companies were wiped out. Seeger and Genet were among the lucky ones. They survived the brutal, bloody attack on Navarin Farm. But it left an indelible mark. "None of the men who came out of the attack untouched ever knew how they escaped death or injury," said Paul Rockwell. "Facing the enemy fire was afterward likened to trying to go out in a heavy rainstorm without being hit by a single raindrop."[48]

While the overall offensive penetrated two miles into the German trenches and captured 1,800 prisoners and many machineguns, it ultimately failed to achieve a breakthrough. The depth of the German defense and the inability of the French to get reinforcements into the opening before the Germans could realign their forces doomed the offensive.

When the Second Foreign Regiment assembled after the battle, only 852 men were present out of 3,200 who began the attack.[49] In fact, the Legion's losses in the battles of 1915 were so great that by November of that year the four foreign regiments in France had to be combined to create a single regiment.

Many of the original American volunteers who were still in the Legion when the battle began were not there when the Second Foreign Regiment assembled afterwards. Sweeny was one of those absent. Sweeny had been shot in the chest by a machinegun bullet that penetrated one lung and his liver.[50]

The newly minted lieutenant was thought to be mortally wounded and he lay unattended on the battlefield for four hours before being carried to an aid station. The physician who examined Sweeny suggested he summon a priest, but Sweeny replied, "No dying for me." Yet his condition was critical. He had an American flag wrapped around his body when he was hit, and the bullet carried bits of cloth into the wound, causing it to become infected.[51]

There is no detailed, authoritative source of information on Sweeny's actions during the battle. *The Official Journal of the Republic of France* simply states that Second Lieutenant Sweeny, a "committed volunteer for the duration of the war" and "a very distinguished officer who sacrifices a comfortable position to become a brilliant servant of France, was seriously wounded while attacking the second line of enemy trenches."

However, his heroism seems undeniable given what happened next. While still in a hospital in the war zone in October, a French general presented him with the Legion of Honor, the highest award the French government can bestow on a soldier or civilian.[52] According to Paul Rockwell, Sweeny was the first American to receive this supreme honor.

American newspaper articles published during the war credit Sweeny with capturing a machinegun nest and six Germans. Some of the accounts say he did so "single-handed."[53] One article, written two years after the war, goes farther. It says Sweeny also saved the life of his superior officer.[54]

Left: **Lieutenant Charles Sweeny of the French Foreign Legion in 1916, wearing the Legion of Honor and Croix de Guerre awarded to him following the Champagne offensive (courtesy Mark Trapp).**

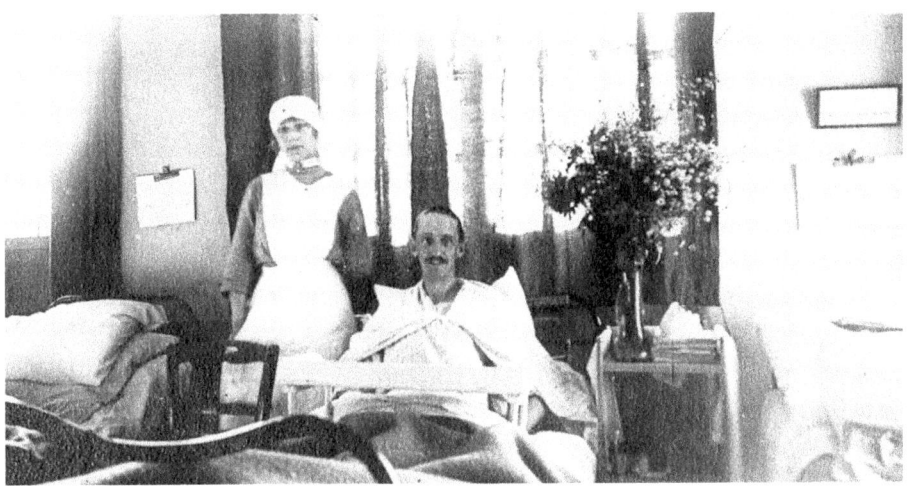

World War I photograph of a wounded and emaciated Charles Sweeny in a hospital recovering from gunshot wound to the chest (courtesy Georges Rolland).

In his 1972 biography of Sweeny, Donald McCormick adopted this last version. McCormick added that with all the other officers dead or wounded, Sweeny then took charge of the depleted company and led it into an attack on the German lines.

McCormick quoted from a dispatch by a war correspondent named C.F. Martelli. In Martelli's account, Sweeny was shot on September 26, the second day of the attack, as he "dashed boldly across a mile of shell-drenched ground." According to Martelli's account, Sweeny was wounded while leading a reconnaissance of "a salient on the German second line west of Tahure hill." Sweeny's service record seems to support Martelli's account as far as the date. It states that Sweeny received a "penetrating chest wound by gunshot" on September 26.[55]

When Sweeny later visited his hometown, a reporter for the *Spokane Review* mentioned to him that no account had yet appeared as to how Sweeny won the Legion of Honor. According to the *Spokane Daily Review*, Sweeny replied that no account was likely to appear because the decoration is not awarded for a single act but only after multiple acts. He also declined to discuss details of the war, saying that, as a soldier in wartime, he was duty-bound not to give out any information concerning the army.

According to Paul Rockwell, Sweeny "was given an excellent citation in Army orders" for his actions during the Champagne offensive, but he also did not provide any details.[56]

Sweeny's wound in the Champagne offensive required many months to heal. When he was finally well enough to travel, but not yet sufficiently recovered to return to combat, Sweeny sailed home to America for a visit in February 1916. While letting him go to America to recuperate, the French authorities also encouraged him to make speeches, give interviews and write articles that might rouse support for their cause among Americans who were reluctant, to say the least, to enter the war.

Sweeny visited his mother and siblings while in America. News reports also said he visited his seriously ill father. They may have reconciled their long estrangement during that meeting. Sweeny "always felt frustrated and misunderstood because his father had never given him full credit for making a success of his life as a soldier, more especially as his father had himself run away from home to enter the Civil War," said McCormick.[57]

Sweeny returned to France in late April. His father died in Portland on May 31.

An article in the *Ontario Argus* mentioned Sweeny's visit to his father in Portland, but focused primarily on his comments to friends about the war. The article quoted him as saying: "Winning a battle or being defeated in battle is not a matter of losing men, nor even of losing or winning a position. No matter how many men you've lost in a battle, you have won that battle if you have made the enemy believe he cannot stop you, that no matter what your losses or what he does you are coming right along. In other words, winning a battle is a question of getting the other man's goat. And you've lost when you have the feeling that no matter what efforts you make you cannot be successful."[58]

Ironically, Sweeny's near-fatal wound in the Champagne offensive may have saved his life—twice.

The first occurred in April 1916 when the French created what was initially called the Escadrille Americaine, a squadron of American pilots. After the Germans complained about the name, noting that America was still a neutral nation, the French changed the name in December 1916 to the Lafayette Escadrille, in honor of the French nobleman who fought in the American Revolution. The first seven members of the squadron—Victor Chapman, Eliot Cowden, Bert Hall, James McConnell, Norman Prince, Kiffin Rockwell and William Thaw—all had been members of the Foreign Legion. Of these, three—Hall, Rockwell and Thaw—had been in the first group of 43 volunteers who joined the Foreign Legion with Sweeny. The Lafayette Escadrille was credited with shooting down 41 German planes. After the United States entered the war, the Lafayette Escadrille was disbanded in February 1918 and 12 of its pilots became part of the U.S. 103rd Aero Squadron. Of the 38 Americans who served in the Lafayette Escadrille, 11 lost their lives, including five of the original 43 Legion volunteers—Chapman, Cowdin, McConnell, Prince and Rockwell.

Five more from the original group of 43 Americans in the Legion later

Lieutenant Charles Sweeny in front of his Foreign Legion troops (courtesy Georges Rolland).

left the trenches for the skies over France—James Bach, Edgar Bouligny, Robert Soubarin, Charles Trinkard and Frederick Zinn. Of these, one died. Trinkard was killed in a crash while doing stunts over an aerodrome at Toul for some of his legionnaire pals. Jack Casey was among those who witnessed the crash, said Rockwell.[59] There were a total of 265 American volunteers in all units of the French Air Corps during the war, according to the Lafayette Flying Corps Memorial Foundation. Of these, 225 received their wings as pilots, 180 flew in combat, 51 were killed in action, six died in training accidents and six more died of disease. They are credited with 199 aerial victories.[60]

Upon his return to France from America in April 1916, Sweeny wanted to join the newly formed Lafayette Escadrille, but his still festering chest wound rendered him unfit, according to McCormick.[61] Instead, he was assigned to drill new soldiers. Had Sweeny qualified to join the Lafayette Escadrille, he might have suffered the same fate as so many of his fellow legionnaires who became pilots.

The second occasion in which Sweeny's wound may have saved his life occurred in July 1916. Following France's humiliating defeat by Germany in 1870, the French army had built and reinforced a ring of forts around Verdun, making it both a strategic and iconic strongpoint in the nation's defense. In February 1916, the Germans determined to turn this commitment to the defense of Verdun to their advantage. They assembled 1,200 guns on an eight-mile front and two-and-a-half million shells. They then deluged the French fortress. "The French, forced to fight in a crucial but narrowly constricted corner of the Western Front, would be compelled to feed reinforcements into a battle of attrition where the material circumstances so favored the Germans that defeat was inevitable," wrote historian John Keegan in *The First World*

War. "If the French gave up the struggle, they would lose Verdun. If they persisted, they would lose their army."[62]

Within days, the German barrage forced the devastated French forces to abandon the outer ring of forts to German assault troops and retire to the inner defenses. In Keegan's analysis, the French would have been well-advised to have withdrawn from Verdun and taken up new defensive positions on the hills and ridges south of the city. In this dire situation, however, the French installed General Philippe Petain, a man whose reputation was based on stubborn resistance even in the face of heavy losses. He arrived with 20th Corps as reinforcements and ordered the French forces to "hold fast." He quickly made more effective use of the artillery and established a more efficient system of supply. A tidal wave of German troops washed up against the French lines, but the line refused to break. The war of attribution that the Germans had wanted now began in earnest.

Over the ensuing months, both sides fed more and more troops into the killing machine in a see-saw struggle where positions were repeatedly lost and retaken. One decimated village near Fort Vaux changed hands 13 times, said Keegan. By late June, 20 million shells had been fired into the battle zone and aerial photos show a moonscape of craters and forts reduced to mere outlines in the dirt. The human toll was even more terrible, with some 200,000 casualties on either side in less than four months. The Germans were forced to shift some of their forces westward in July to resist the British offensive in the Somme, but the struggle at Verdun continued.[63] In August and December, French attacks recovered some of the lost ground, including Fort Vaux and Fort Douaumont. The battle of Verdun lasted 303 days and the casualties were enormous, with estimates of French losses exceeding 370,000 and German losses topping 330,000. Some estimates put the total losses for both sides at more than one million.

To relieve pressure on Verdun, the Allies launched the Somme offensive on July 1. The Somme River meanders through Flanders before emptying into the English Channel. The area is marshlands and meadows topped by hills, including Vimy Ridge and Thiepval. There had been no major offensive here for two years and the Germans had used the time to build a "defensive system of enormous depth and strength."[64] The British massed 1,500 artillery pieces on an 18-mile front. The French added artillery support. Sizeable gains were made but with devastating losses. A breakthrough was nearly obtained near Deville Wood on July 14, but a German counterattack arrived before British reinforcements and the breach was closed. The offensive resumed after two months of smaller actions and gains were made with the aid of tanks before winter weather again halted the fighting. The French lost 195,000 men, the British 420,000 and the Germans 650,000. But there was no decisive breakthrough.

As part of this offensive, on July 4, despite inadequate artillery support, the Legion charged across 200 yards of open ground to attack the fortified village of Belloy-en-Santerre. German machineguns cut down the first wave. The second wave advanced on their bellies, crawling through a wheat field until they were close enough to rush the few remaining yards. "A final bound behind a hail of grenades and they were in the village, which they seized after two hours of house-to-house fighting." They then held the village against repeated German counterattacks through the night, the next day and the next night until finally relieved on July 6. They also took 750 prisoners, but at a terrible cost. The Legion's dead, wounded and missing totaled 25 officers and 844 soldiers out of 62 officers and 2,830 enlisted men engaged in the attack, or nearly one out of three.[65] Alan Seeger, the Harvard-educated poet, was among those killed in the first wave.

Sweeny's French military service record states that on September 1, 1916, he was assigned as a second lieutenant to the First Foreign Regiment. There is no indication in the record of his activities during this period. The next entry in the record says he was assigned to command the 30th Battery of the 81st Regiment of Heavy Artillery at the Trou de'Enfer (Fort Hell Hole) at Marly-le-Roi, a suburb west of Paris, from January 18 to February 5, 1917.[66] A certificate issued to Sweeny at the Center for Instruction at Marly-le-Roi indicates he was a student there from February 5 to April 11, 1917. The certificate does not indicate the nature of the instruction, but the fort is an artillery bastion so it may be the instruction was in the use of artillery.[67]

Sweeny's service record doesn't reflect it but news accounts of the period report that, once his wound healed, Sweeny engineered his transfer to an entirely new form of warfare—the tank. Rockwell, too, stated that after drilling recruits at La Valbonne and teaching at an officers' training school at Montelimar, "he trained for some months with the new 'tank' corps."[68]

Starting in 1916, the British and French armies employed a variety of these lumbering behemoths with the hope of finally breaking the stalemate of the trenches. Sweeny apparently threw himself into this new assignment with characteristic zeal, so much so that McCormick reports he upset a superior officer with his repeated requests to be given command of more tanks. There weren't enough tanks to go around.

Sweeny was ultimately given command of a squadron of 16 "iron babies, the caterpillar tanks which have wrought havoc on the western front," according to a wire service report.[69] Sweeny apparently saw enough action with the tanks to make a name for himself on both sides of the Atlantic. There is nothing in his service record about this involvement, but news accounts began referring to him as "Sweeny of the Tanks." Sweeny became so proficient at tank warfare that he wrote a pamphlet on the utilization of tanks with infantry in battle.[70]

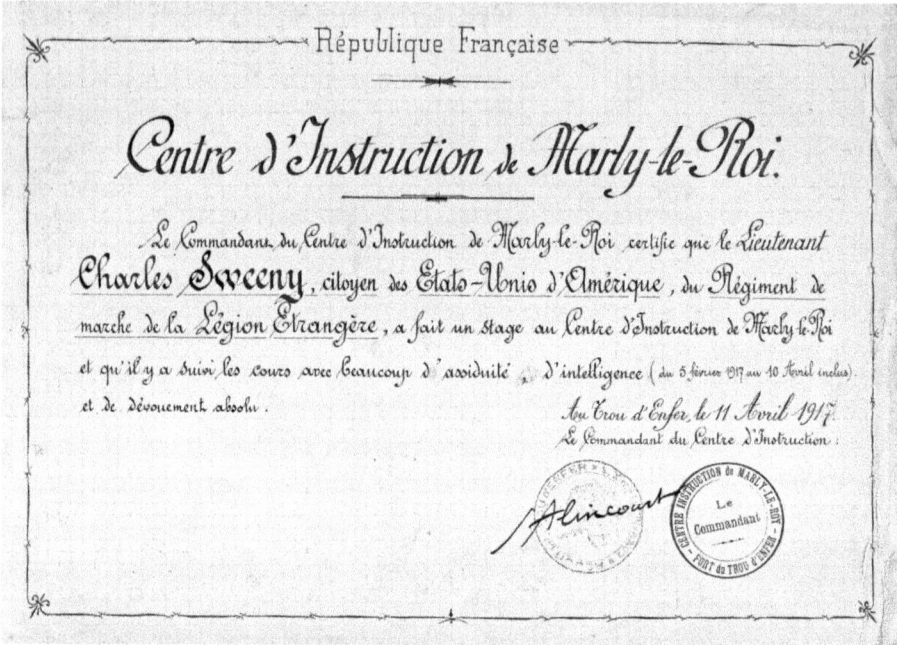

Lieutenant Charles Sweeny's certificate from the Marly-le-Roi instruction center for completing many intelligence courses between 5 February and 10 April 1917 (courtesy Georges Rolland).

It was not until April 16, 1917, that the French finally had enough tanks to launch a large-scale tank assault—the Nivelle Offensive in the Aisne section, west of Rheims. The offensive was a tactical success but a strategic failure. It pushed the German lines back but did not achieve the long-awaited breakthrough.

By then, however, Sweeny was headed to America with a promotion and a new assignment, although there is nothing in his service record about either. On April 6, 1917, a reluctant United States declared war on Germany. While his service record states that he was promoted to first lieutenant on April 8, five days later the *Sun* reported that Sweeny had been promoted to captain and granted an "unlimited leave of absence" so he could come to the United States to help train its forces for the fight ahead.[71] The *Washington* (D.C.) *Times* described his task as "instructing American officers in the 'rough stuff' of trench fighting."[72]

Sweeny arrived in New York on April 24; the same day that Marshal Joffre and his mission to the United States arrived for meetings with U.S. officials in Washington, D.C., Joffre's convoy was escorted into port with great fanfare. "American warships broke out French colors from their mastheads and American bands played the French national anthem for them," according to a wire service report.⁷³

Joffre's arrival briefly put Sweeny at the center of the action. The marshal had appointed Sweeny his aide-de-camp for the purposes of this mission to America. Following Joffre's meetings with U.S. officials, Sweeny resigned his French commission on May 23 so he could formally offer his expertise and services to the U.S. Army.

A little more than 13 years after leaving West Point in disgrace, Sweeny was returning to the U.S. Army as a decorated, celebrated war hero with combat experience and apparently a sizeable chip on his shoulder. The student was about to become the teacher, or so he thought. A head-on collision between the head-strong Sweeny and the hard-headed Army establishment was inevitable.

Chapter 9

"Over the Top" with the U.S. Army

Sweeny arrived back in America in April 1917, convinced he was destined for a senior leadership role in the U.S. war effort. After all, he had two-and-one-half years of experience with trench warfare and tanks while the American military had none; he had risen rapidly through the ranks from private to captain; been decorated for valor; and was, quite frankly, famous, thanks to copious media coverage of his exploits. If he had any doubts about his worthiness, two events before he left France should have banished such qualms. First, Sweeny—along with James Bach, Edgar Bouligny and George Camese—were honored in a public ceremony in the courtyard of the Hotel des Invalides, where they had been sworn into the Legion in August 1914. The event was a tribute to all of the foreign volunteers who enlisted at the outbreak of the war. Second, after the ceremony, Sweeny was accorded the rare privilege of a 45-minute private meeting with Marshal Joffre, during which Joffre made him his aide-de-camp for the impending mission to America.[1]

However, instead of being greeted with open arms by the U.S. Army as he expected, Sweeny's request to serve his homeland was met with what fellow legionnaire Paul Rockwell described as "red tape and jealousy."[2] Officers, who had spent decades slowly climbing the Army's seniority-based promotion ladder and genuflecting to the Army's timeworn traditions, were not inclined to make room in the upper echelons for someone who had broken the rules at West Point, bent the laws of neutrality and now expected to cut ahead of them in line for the prestigious ranks and assignments the war offered.

When the War Department's failure to act quickly on Sweeny's request became public, William Graves Sharp, the U.S. ambassador to France, wrote to Washington to point out that Sweeny was "the only American who has actual experience in command of a tank unit." He added that Sweeny's performance with one battery of tanks had so impressed the French that they had given him command of four batteries. "It would, in my opinion, be a tragedy if full advantage was not taken of his services, experience and technological knowledge."[3]

While he waited, Sweeny undertook a speaking tour to cities along the Eastern Seaboard to explain to U.S. audiences the nature of the war the country had just entered. The tour led to public criticism by some in the Army that Sweeny was engaged in shameless self-promotion and that his lauding of the French army was a slap at the U.S. Army. The ruckus quieted down once the War Department let it be known that the tour was being conducted at its behest. However, Sweeny didn't help himself with the War Department when he suggested, in response to an audience question, that he'd "like nothing better than to command an infantry regiment raised in Washington or Idaho."[4]

In the end, Sweeny was allowed to enlist on May 28, 1917, and given the rank of major. The fact that federal law at the time made that the highest rank to which any reserve officer could be appointed failed to diminish Sweeny's indignation. Subsequent events only stoked his anger.

Despite his field-grade commission and considerable experience, Sweeny's first assignment was as a student at the Reserve Officers Training Camp at Fort Myer, Virginia, across the Potomac River from the nation's capital. He soon discovered other battle-tested veterans, as well as politically connected novices, among the 2,300 student officers there. The veterans included John Crum, a former U.S. Army officer who had also fought in the Mexican civil war with outlaw-turned-revolutionary Pancho Villa and with the British Expeditionary Force in France; and Henry A.C. deRubio, a U.S. Army officer in the Spanish-American War and a soldier of fortune who had served under various flags in Mexico, Central America and the Philippines. Crum was made a captain; Rubio, a major.[5] The neophytes included Bennett Champ Clark, a 27-year-old parliamentarian for the U.S. House of Representatives and son of House Speaker Champ Clark. He was made a captain and put in charge of a 30-man training company, whose members included Major Sweeny.[6]

One can only imagine Sweeny's disgust and anger when Clark, who had no experience but because of his political connections, was assigned to be his training officer. Clark issued orders based on outdated Army combat manuals and the training bore no relation to the ferocious trench warfare taking place in Europe. Trench warfare required quick thinking and the ability to change tactics at a moment's notice.

In typical Sweeny fashion, he rebuked his superiors for failing to use him to better advantage, criticized what the students were being taught, and lectured the instructors on the French tactics that he believed they should be teaching. Not surprisingly, his protests had the opposite of their desired effect. Sweeny was drilled like a lowly recruit.

The matter came to a head when Sweeny submitted his resignation and word of it appeared in the press in July. The *Washington Herald* reported that "Sweeny stated no reason for submitting his resignation, but it is reported that he felt that in view of his experience with the Foreign Legion he should have been assigned to more important commands at the camp than has been the case."[7]

Sweeny's resignation was quickly disapproved, and the War Department publicly announced that student officers would not be allowed to resign. As the commander at Camp Myer explained, the students would not be the judge of their own qualifications, nor of the quality of their training.[8]

At the same time, however, the War Department quietly made changes to Sweeny's situation, placing him in charge of training those he had previously served alongside and even some of those from whom he had taken orders. He wasted no time in implementing the sort of practical training he had earlier proposed. In time, this included large-scale field exercises in trench warfare involving as many as three battalions of students. He employed French tactics, but with some innovations of his own. While the leading assault troops stormed the first two lines of trenches, Sweeny had the supporting troops advance single-file behind them to be shifted left or right to reinforce any advancing troops that needed support or to fill gaps that developed in the line.[9] This is similar to a tactic described by Sergeant Morlae in the attack on Navarin Farm.

On August 27, 1917, Sweeny reported to the 318th Infantry Regiment, 159th Brigade, 80th Division, which was being formed at Camp Lee, near Petersburg, Virginia.[10] Fittingly, given the nature of the fighting in France, the area around Petersburg had been the scene of a nine-month siege during the Civil War that involved the most extensive use of trench warfare ever employed on the North American continent.

While the officers of the 318th came from across the nation, the enlisted personnel in the regiment were drawn exclusively from the eastern counties of Virginia. Together with the 317th Infantry, which was drawn from Virginia's western counties, and a machinegun battalion, they formed the 159th Brigade. The 80th Division consisted of two brigades of infantry, one brigade of artillery, a regiment of engineers, a signal battalion and various logistical and headquarters units. The 80th Division drew its enlisted personnel from Virginia, West Virginia and the western counties of Pennsylvania, which gave rise to its name "The Blue Ridge Division." The first enlisted personnel began arriving at Camp Lee on September 4.

Sweeny was assigned to command the regiment's 2nd Battalion, comprised of Companies E, F, G and H. The regimental commander, his deputy and the leader of the 1st Battalion were Regular Army officers. All of the other officers were reserve officers, although some, like Sweeny, had prior military experience, including John Crum, who was assigned to command Company F.

In late November, Secretary of War Newton Baker came to Camp Lee to inspect the 80th Division. Sweeny's battalion was selected as the honor guard of the division, a coveted assignment because it implied that the chosen unit was the best.[11]

Through the winter and early spring of 1917-18, more recruits arrived to fill out the ranks of the 80th Division, construction of the camp was completed, non-commissioned officers were selected and training progressed. It consisted of close-order drill, bayonet practice, rifle marksmanship, long hikes, trench warfare tactics and gas-mask use.

Finally, in May 1918, the regiment took trains to Hoboken, New Jersey, where they boarded the former German luxury liner *Vaterland*, which had been seized by the U.S. government and renamed the *Leviathan*. The ship sailed for Europe on the afternoon of May 22. Private Rush S. Young, Company B, 1st Battalion, later recalled, "As we sailed down the river past the Statue of Liberty, we were allowed to come on deck to wave a hearty farewell. To many it would be farewell forever for they will rest 'with poppies now blowing overhead between the crosses row on row.'"[12]

Six days later, the ship was met by five destroyers and escorted the final two days to the French port of Brest. Within sight of the Brittany coast, German submarines tried to intercept the *Leviathan* but the destroyers drove them off with depth charges.[13]

In the 13 months between Sweeny's departure from France and his return with the American Expeditionary Force, much had changed. The Germans had withdrawn to better, stronger defensive positions in the Somme sector. The Bolshevik Revolution of 1917 had led to Russia's exit from the war in March 1918, allowing Germany to send more troops to France. The British naval blockade had reduced German industrial output. Allied gains in the Middle East against the Ottoman Turks had allowed British troops to be shifted from that front to France. But some things had only changed for the worse. French troops were on the verge of rebellion. Casualty lists had lengthened, with terrible losses at Arras, Ypres, the Aisne, Passchendaele and Cambrai. Tensions between the Allies had sharpened, with repeated clashes and changes in the high command. And the stalemate had deepened, despite some forward movement by the Allies.

The United States' entry into the war lifted the Allies hopes while making the Germans situation desperate. They had to achieve victory before the Yanks arrived in sufficient numbers to tip the scales against them. By the spring of 1918, time was running out. The Germans had time and resources enough for one last push in three phases. The first began in March in the Somme sector. The second began in April in Flanders. The third began in May in the Aisne sector. Each of the drives succeeded, at least at first. But dogged British resistance, made famous by General Douglas Haig's "backs to the wall" order demanding a fight to the last man, ultimately checked the first two drives. The third drive caught the Allies by surprise and quickly achieved a deeper penetration than the Germans themselves had expected. As a result, the Germans outran their ability to resupply their forces. At this point, the U.S. 2nd Division was rushed into action and stopped the German advance at Chateau Thierry. German attempts to mount fresh drives were broken up by preemptive Allied artillery bombardments, using information gleaned from captured German soldiers. The German offensive sputtered out. The Allies then mounted counterattacks in July and August to erase each of the German salients.[14]

It was now the Americans turn, but first the green U.S. troops needed some seasoning before they would be ready to "go over the top." Sweeny's unit disembarked at Brest on May 30. Three days later, they took trains across northwestern France to the city of Calais on the English Channel. They arrived on June 5 and were billeted in big tents on the wide beach. The military posts and munitions plants in the vicinity were a regular target of nightly German aerial bombing raids and the green American troops came under enemy fire for the first time, although there were no casualties.

At Calais, the Americans turned in their U.S. Model 1917 rifles and were issued British Enfield rifles and bayonets. The troops were then transported to the British front line on the Ancre River, near the battered city of Albert, in the area of the epic slaughter of 1916 dubbed the Battle of the Somme. The Americans spent ten days there training with the Welsh Fusiliers. After that, they were moved to Samer, closer to Calais, for training with the 16th Irish Division. From there, they hiked eight miles with full packs to Enquin, and two days later they marched five miles, again with full packs, to Cormont. While there, the regiment was reviewed, first on June 30 by the Duke of Connaught, who was the governor-general of Canada and uncle of Britain's King George V, and then on July 2 by General John J. Pershing, commander of the American Expeditionary Force.

It was at Cormont that the battalions of the 318th received their nicknames. The British called the members of the regiment "squirrels," apparently because the troops came from rural locales. The troops adopted the nickname for themselves and named the 1st Battalion the "red squirrels," the 2nd Battalion the "grey squirrels," and the 3rd Battalion the "flying squirrels." These became code names for each of the battalions.[15]

It also was in the Cormont area where the men of the 318th saw their first fighting, albeit with their fists instead of firearms and against British troops

Charles Sweeny in a World War I trench (courtesy Spokane Library).

instead of German. Private Rush Young later wrote that there were frequent brawls in the "wine joints" where British troops taunted the Americans for failing to arrive until, in their view, the war was nearly over. The men of the 318th got along better with the Canadians, Welsh and Irish troops. In fact, it was not uncommon for the Irish to join the Yanks against the British when a fight broke out.

Next, the troops spent 16 hours in boxcars being transported 60 miles south to Fieffes-Montrelet. The local crossroads town is 85 miles north of Paris and ten miles north of the heavily fought over regional rail hub of Amiens.[16]

Here the 318th trained under 17th and 66th British Divisions and the 38th Welsh Division in and near the front lines. And it was here, in late July, that the regiment suffered its first casualties. Sweeny's 2nd Battalion had four men killed and five wounded from random shell fire. The other two battalions had two killed and ten wounded.[17]

A reorganization of the regiment to conform more closely to British regiments resulted in Sweeny, now the senior major in the regiment, receiving a lateral move from command of the 2nd Battalion to regimental operations officer on July 27.[18]

In August, the regiment went into support in the second line of trenches in the Albert sector, east of Amiens. This was the first time the regiment had come under direct enemy artillery fire. The Germans showered them with six-inch shells. "The air became arched with black smoke from the bursting shells, and the fumes of acid tasted bitter in our mouths," recalled Young. "Our faces turned scarlet, the earth quivered, and we were trembling."[19]

On August 12, the troops moved into the front line trenches, relieving the 14th Welsh Fusiliers in Aveluy Wood. The regiment was assigned to hold a 2,200-yard front, across the Ancre River from heavily fortified Thiepval Ridge, 2,000 yards to their front.[20] Today, a massive brick monument, the size of a 10-story building, sits on the ridge. Carved on its walls are the names of 72,000 Commonwealth soldiers whose bodies were never found after the battles of the Somme.

Young recalled that the trenches were dry but shallow. The ground was chalk and gravel; it was simply to hard to dig deeper. The trees were reduced to shattered stumps. The sickening smell of death hung in the air. The British had only taken the area a few days before and rotting corpses littered No Man's Land.

The Ancre River posed a challenge to cross under fire so the regiment was not attacked here. By the same token, the 318th was unable to get patrols across the river. But German shellfire still took a toll. By the time the regiment finished its training on August 18, it had lost two officers and five enlisted men killed and one officer and 31 enlisted men wounded.

On August 20, the regiment marched 20 miles to the vicinity of Domleger, where it exchanged its British rifles and bayonets for U.S. weapons. Then they were off again, this time by train, to the American sector. They arrived at Recey sur Ource, a town about 175 miles southeast of Paris in the heart of the Burgundy region.

Here they were issued the French Chauchat automatic rifle to replace the British Lewis machinegun, which they had been required to turn in when they left the British sector. Young called the Chauchat "a damn poor excuse of a gun after using the Lewis gun on the Somme."[21] His opinion was widely held among U.S. troops.

The troops boarded trains again on September 2 and were moved about 60 miles north through mountains and along the Marne River to Longeville. That same day, Sweeny was shifted from regimental operations officer to command of the 1st Battalion, comprised of companies A, B, C and D.[22] He would continue in command, and under Young's observant eyes, through the end of the war.

Five days later, the regiment marched about five miles to Resson, near Bar-le-Duc. They were now in the reserve for the U.S. First Army's first real offensive: the attack on the St. Mihiel salient, 23 miles south of Verdun on the Meuse River. The ultimate goal was to capture the rail hub at Metz, which would cut the German supply line and force a large-scale withdrawal. The attack began September 12.[23] But the 318th was not needed. The Germans were in the process of evacuating the salient and the attack turned their retreat into a near rout until congested, muddy roads bogged down the artillery and supplies supporting the U.S. advance. The planned breakthrough fizzled out and with it the hope of capturing Metz.

On September 19, the regiment marched 14 miles in a hard rain to a wooded area near Fort-du-Regret. This was one of a ring of forts around Verdun, where the Germans had tried in 1916 to bleed the French dry and ended up hollowing out both armies.

Nearly two years later, in September 1918, when the U.S. 80th Division arrived in the vicinity of Verdun, it was the first time the entire division had come together in one place since leaving Camp Lee. While the division had missed the battles of Chateau Thierry, Belleau Wood and St. Mihiel, it was destined to play a prominent role in the final, climatic clash of the war: the Meuse-Argonne offensive. The battleground was essentially two parallel valleys running north between the Aire and Meuse Rivers, 135 miles east of Paris. The valleys were separated by a broken ridge line with high points at Montfaucon, Romagne, Cunel and Barricourt. Overlooking these valleys on the west was a wide, rugged series of steep hills topped by the Argonne Forest and on the east by a line of hills on the east side of the Meuse River. These hills, known as the Heights of the Meuse, enabled the German artillery to put plunging fire into the valleys.[24] The French army had learned this the hard way in 1914. After the initial German advance had been halted, the French had counterattacked here and suffered considerable pain for no gain. The French army had not tried any more major assaults here since 1914.

In the intervening four years, the Germans had constructed a defensive network in this sector 12 miles deep. Now, the Allies intended to throw the full weight of the 300,000 American First Army, plus the French Fourth Army, against this 25-mile-wide section of the German line. At the same time, British and French forces would attack in the Somme. The objective of both drives was to sever the main German supply line that ran between Lille in Flanders and Strasbourg on the Rhine River. The Meuse-Argonne offensive was aimed like a dagger at the rail hub at Sedan. Cutting that line would force either a general withdrawal or a complete collapse of the German center. It was a worthy goal, but there was little room for maneuver in the Meuse Argonne sector. The assault forces would have to attack straight ahead into the best natural and man-made defenses almost anywhere on the Western Front.

Nine American infantry divisions, divided into three corps of three divisions each, would make the initial assault, with six more American infantry divisions in reserve. Ten American and French artillery brigades, totaling 2,775 guns, would fire a preparatory barrage and then shift the shelling northward so the assault forces could advance behind a curtain of fire toward the enemy positions. There were 156 guns per mile of the front.[25]

The 80th Division was assigned to Lieutenant General Robert Lee Bullard's Third Corps, which was the right wing of the offensive. The 80th Division was in center of Third Corp's assault force, on the west side of the Meuse, with the 4th Division on its left and the 33rd Division on its right. (The First Corps was on the right wing, with the 77th, 28th and 35th Divisions making the initial assault through the Argonne Forest and the Aire River Valley. In the middle, between the First and Third Corps, was the Fifth Corps, comprised of 91st, 37th and 79th Divisions. Its route led through Montfaucon, the steep, 500-foot height that was the key strongpoint in the German's first line of defense.)

The terrain in front of the 318th was an irregular series of hills, woods, clearings and ravines. The ruins of a hamlet called Mallancourt was on the right and another called Bethincourt was on the left. The White Tower of Montfaucon was visible to the division's left front. From this tower, Germany's Crown Prince had directed the savage fighting around Verdun in 1916.

The Allies began the offensive at 11:30 p.m. on September 25 with a massive artillery barrage. "If they call the barrage at St. Mihiel the All American $1,000 000 barrage," said Private Young, "certainly they must call this one the All American $5,000,000 barrage."[26]

As the troops girded themselves for what lay ahead, Sweeny moved from company to company in his battalion reading a message from the division commander, Major General Adelbert Cronkhite, exhorting them to "make the enemy know that the 80th Division is on the map; make him know, when he faces you in the future, that resistance is useless."[27]

Young described the soldiers waiting to assault Germany's Western Wall as "blood thirsty, because that is what we were now, after all the hard hikes we had had since we left the English sector, and after being away from all the sympathizers, or ones who did not want to fight. We now had the fighting spirit, courage, and ambition that later carried the 80th on to the top. We had confidence in our officers and the officers in the men. With that, any organization can win."[28]

That invincible attitude expressed in his remark, that sense of inevitability of success that it projected, and hidden within that remark a naiveté about what they really faced, seems to be the key to what ultimately led the American forces to prevail in the Meuse-Argonne offensive. The vastly more experienced French and British troops, as well as their German opponents, had long since lost such attitudes. When they attacked now, they did so simply to avoid letting their comrades down. When the Americans went over the top, they advanced confident of victory because they had no idea that what they were about to do was seemingly impossible.

The preparatory bombardment consisted of thousands of high-explosive shells plus 800 mustard gas and phosgene shells into the German positions in the Meuse-Argonne. Historian Edward G. Lengel wrote in his excellent history of the Meuse-Argonne offensive, *To Conquer Hell*, that the Germans introduced gas warfare in April 1915 and the British and French countered with their own poison gas. The Germans started with chlorine gas, which caused retching and coughing. They then switched to phosgene gas, which could be inhaled without any telltale signs but brought death within 48 hours as the lungs dissolved. Mustard gas was first used by the Germans in September 1917. Like phosgene, it had no effect until a few hours later. Then painful blisters would develop on the skin, particularly under the arms and in the crotch; the eyes would burn and swell shut, sometimes causing permanent blindness; and, if inhaled, would lead to blistering of the lungs and a slow, agonizing death.

The American soldiers, Lengel said, had "a reasonably effective gas mask" but they were uncomfortable to wear for long and the eyepieces tended to mist up, "a serious problem in the Meuse-Argonne, where the troops often had to fight in foggy conditions." Soldiers who removed their masks to see where they were going suffered the effects of the gas while those who kept them on ran the risk of walking into an unseen machinegun.[29]

After six hours of bombardment, the ground assault began at 5:30 a.m. on September 26 with a mighty rush forward. The sky was cloudless and clear as the sun came up, with ground fog that obscured the advancing troops but also sometimes required a compass to keep moving due magnetic north. As the troops advanced, the American barrage moved ahead of them at the rate of 100 yards every four minutes. The troops made their way across Forges Creek, a swampy area over which engineers had hastily erected some footbridges.[30] As they advanced, the troops encountered land mines, barbed wire entanglements and a moonscape of shell holes.

German and Allied aircraft appeared overhead to gather intelligence and for a time the soldiers lifted their attention from the ground to the sky. Four Allied observation balloons were turned into flaming gasbags in quick succession and their observers took to their parachutes to escape the flames. The German planes also flew over the American lines, at a height of 200–300 feet, firing their machineguns at the advancing troops on the crowded road. Surprisingly, they inflicted few casualties. Young said this was the only time he witnessed the regimental commander, Colonel Ulysses Worrilow, engaged in actual combat. "He began to fire at them with his pistol for all he was worth. I often wondered what he thought he could hit with a pistol, shooting at an airplane in flight."[31]

By 4 p.m., the regiment had reached Bethincourt, but as the divisions on either side pinched in toward the center to use a bridge thrown up by the 80th Division engineers, congestion slowed the advance.

A German counterattack was easily beaten back by massed machinegun fire during the afternoon and the troops resumed their advance toward wooded areas ahead.

Sweeny's battalion fell behind at one point and he tried to make up time by trying to move his men across the main road being used by trucks hurrying to the front. But the truck drivers wouldn't let the battalion through. "The major knew when he was licked and told the men to fall out until the transports were all past," recalled Young. "You are never supposed to halt transports, but had he got by, he would have made up the time he was behind."[32]

As daylight faded that first day, the 80th Division approached the village of Dannevoux, four miles north of the line of departure. Owing to resistance early in the day, it had not kept pace with the divisions on either side. Nightfall brought darkness and rain, but the officers of the 318th kept the men advancing under new orders from division to assist the 4th Division by reaching Cuisy, four miles northwest of Bethincourt. Slippery mud and shell holes added to the soldiers' labors. About midnight, after advancing about 12 miles in 15 hours since the start of the offensive that morning, Sweeny's weary battalion arrived at Cuisy.

While Sweeny may have been slow in reaching Bethincourt, he apparently made up for it later. The history of the regiment, written by regimental officers in 1919, said that the leading element reached Cuisy a little after midnight, which is when Sweeny's battalion arrived. Succeeding units straggled in until 3 a.m.[33]

Despite some delays along the 25-mile front, all of the forward elements in the Meuse-Argonne offensive achieved their first-day objectives except the high ground around Montfaucon, which was taken on the second day.

The offensive had momentarily caught the Germans off balance. The covert movement of U.S. troops from the St. Mihiel area northwest to the Meuse-Argonne line of departure had gone undetected. The Germans were expecting the Americans to try to continue their advance around St. Mihiel. But the German defenders in the Meuse-Argonne quickly recovered. While only 5,000 shells fell on Bullard's Third Corps the first day, 65,000 shells landed in its area on the second day. Shells rained down on Cuisy while orders from higher headquarters to the regiment were received and then countermanded. The fog of war had briefly descended on the offensive and it took a day to sort things out.

Finally, on the afternoon of September 28, Sweeny received orders to attach his battalion to the 59th Infantry of the neighboring 4th Division at Septsarges, northeast of Cuisy. The following morning, this combined force renewed the attack, with Sweeny's 1st Battalion behind the other two battalions as they attacked side by side. Dense underbrush and fog reduced visibility to 30 feet, and machinegun fire from various directions soon created confusion and disorder.

According to the official regiment history, "Due to the failure of these two battalions [of the 59th Infantry] to make the progress anticipated [the sector of this attack was in a heavily wooded area known as the Bois Brieuelles], the 1st Battalion soon found themselves pushed to the front, forming the apex of a triangle. Their position was an extremely perilous one, from which the splendid judgment, great coolness and personal bravery of Major Sweeny, the battalion commander, finally successfully extricated them, after they had suffered very heavy casualties."[34]

Private Young offered a different view of Sweeny's conduct during this engagement. He recalled that Major Sweeny discovered a gap of about 300 hundred yards between the battalions on either side of him and ordered Lieutenant Robert C. Duval, commanding Company A, "to close the gap with one of his platoons." After reconnoitering the situation, Duval advised Sweeny that no such action was possible in daylight, owing to machinegun fire from woods nearby. Sweeny "flew into a rage," saying, "I'll not have my orders debated." He then asked the other officers who among them would carry out his order. Lieutenant James D. Bebout volunteered. He had just been reassigned to Company D after serving as transportation officer and had been the butt of jokes for his "soft" job. Rebout then led the first of two waves of troops out of the cover of the woods. Within 25 yards, machinegun fire cut the entire first wave down like an invisible scythe. The second wave halted, and no more attempts were made. "Lieutenant Duval was right; the job could not be done in daylight," recalled Young, clearly critical of Sweeny's actions.[35]

During this period, the remainder of the 318th also was heavily engaged. The 2nd Battalion was ordered to close a gap that had developed between the 4th Division on the left and the 79th Division on the right. "For five days," the regimental history said, "the 2nd Battalion held this position on Hill 295, exposed to frontal and enfilade fire from 77s [artillery pieces] and 5.9s [mortars], to say nothing of harassing fire from machineguns. Many casualties were suffered, among them Captain John Crum, who had commanded F Company since its organization."[36]

Sweeny's battalion spent two more days in the Bois de Septsarges, dodging shells and repulsing counterattacks. Young described having to spend hours at night standing with their heavy packs because heavy rain had turned the ground to mud. Finally, he gave in to exhaustion, took off his pack and laid down in the mud on his raincoat.

The battalion tried to advance but was repulsed. There seemed to be no way forward and the battalion was taking many casualties. "As we tried to advance, we ran into a barrage of machinegun fire," said Young. "We couldn't keep liaison between the platoons and companies, the woods were too thick. Confusion seemed to prevail among the troops. Owing to the density of the underbrush and fog we could not see thirty feet ahead. We were like drowned rats and were covered with mud from head to foot. They were getting hit on both sides from the machinegun fire. The rat-tat-tat was constant and although they did not see us, they were putting down a fine barrage."[37]

Young credited Sweeny with getting the battalion out of this difficult situation "through coolness and good judgment." The battalion withdrew 200 yards to the rear and dug in. The Germans continued shelling them with "whiz bangs" (Austrian 88s) and 155 mm guns.

Sweeny then sent a runner to have the local artillery commander report to him so he could arrange shelling of the strong points blocking the advance. When the commander reported to Sweeny, he turned out to be the major's own brother, Captain Sarsfield Sweeny of the 4th Division's 16th Field Artillery. Moments later, the 23-year-old Sarsfield was struck by shrapnel while standing at the major's side.[38] A news article said he died in his brother's arms. Sweeny apparently escaped physical harm but the incident left a psychological wound that never healed. In later years, Sweeny refused to talk about his kid brother's death.

Sarsfield had been a student at Yale University when the United States entered the war and he was said to be the youngest captain in the Army at the time he was commissioned in November 1917. He had married a childhood friend, 20-year-old Louise Daly of Baltimore, Maryland, in February 1918, and she was pregnant when he shipped out for France in May. He never saw his namesake son, who was born six weeks after he died.[39]

The following day, October 3, the battalion was ordered to advance again, back to the same position that Sweeny had just gotten them out of. Once again the shelling took its toll. It was the same story up and down the line. The 4th, 80th and 33rd Divisions were all stalled. It got so bad that Young expressed sympathy for the officers because everyone was looking to them to act and they were "catching hell coming and going."[40]

The shelling on Sweeny's battalion intensified and all his men could do was hug the side of whatever shell hole they had crawled into. "The woods were strewn with dead and wounded," recalled Young. "The ones who had been shell shocked were screaming like maniacs, and the wounded, groaning in pain. Further back in the woods could be heard the horses and mules that had been hit, nickering and groaning. If this had lasted much longer, we would all have been crazy. It was getting on my nerves."

Finally, on October 4, despite having been under almost constant, heavy shelling for four days, the 80th Division was ordered into a frontal assault on the Bois des Ogons the following day.[41] The 4th Division and 79th Division had each suffered heavy losses trying without success to get into these woods. Now the Blue Ridge boys would be thrust into this killing field.

On the night of October 4–5, Sweeny's battalion was restored to the 318th to join in the regiment's assault on the Bois des Ogons on October 5. Sweeny's battalion shifted position and Young recalled being able to see the village of Nantillois 250 yards to the left being attacked by 2nd Battalion. (On October 3–4, the 2nd Battalion under Major Jennings Wise had participated in the earlier attacks on Nantillois and the Bois des Ogons, and had lost all of its company commanders and 60 percent of its other officers as casualties.)[42]

Sweeny's battalion and the rest of the 159th Brigade (the 317th and 318th Infantry Regiments) was tasked with attacking the Bois de Fays from the neighboring 4th Division sector in hopes of flanking the Bois des Ogons from the east.[43] Once the Bois des Ogons was taken, the 80th Division would join the 4th Division's attack on the Heights of Cunel. That, at least, was the plan.

But the attack ran into trouble even before it began. One of the lead battalions of the 317th got lost on its way to the line of departure and a reserve battalion had to be brought up to fill the gap. The half-hour delay left the advancing troops without the support of a rolling barrage.[44]

Sweeny's troops went over the top and were heading down a slope in the direction of the Bois de Fays when mustard gas and shrapnel rained down on them. Then German long-range guns joined in the chorus of exploding shells. The tanks advanced up a low ridge but when one of them was blown to bits by a direct hit, the others retreated, leaving the infantry to go it alone. The German rain of shells turned into a cloudburst.

"We had no long-range guns to silence them," said Young. "We had to advance at all costs, or be driven back, and we were shouting that we would stay here until Hell froze over, yet the farther we advanced across the open slope the better targets we were." Looking around, Young said he saw thousands of troops advancing. "What a sight as I look back on the hill. Nothing seemed to stop them. It was indeed tragic."[45]

Scrambling from shell hole to shell hole, the troops moved forward. Reaching a ravine, they paused. Half of the battalion's machineguns had been put out of action by this time. Then came the order to advance in single files, 50 yards apart and at 25-yard intervals. The men raced over the hilltop as fast as they could and headed toward the Bois-de-Fays, not knowing what they would find there.

"All along the ridge," recalled Young, "I could see the boys being mowed down by machinegun fire, and the runners were being picked off by snipers. Another runner would try his luck, by running to the wounded or dead one, getting the message and trying to get it through. Down he would go and another would try."[46]

Young took shelter in a shell hole with Private Willie B. Mitchell. He could see men nearby "shivering and shaking in their shell holes, praying to God Almighty to help them, as we were waiting for orders to advance." Mitchell "had tears in his eyes and was shaking like a leaf." Young tried to calm the man, telling him it would be all right. But the man was convinced he would be killed if he tried to advance. Finally, Young told him, "We must go now, Mitchell. Lieutenant Hort has given the signal. I will go first and you follow. We'll see you in the woods." Young started up the hill. Mitchell didn't budge. That's where death found him a short time later, when a shell exploded in the hole.

German planes appeared overhead, spotting for the artillery. The men were now crouched in shell holes just below the crest of the final hill, about 150 yards from the woods. Soon the German artillery found them there and showered them with shells. They had to move. Young said it was certain death to stay where they were.

"As we reached the crest of the hill, it was one solid sea of shell craters, not one foot of land remained that had not been torn up by the big shells," said Young. "Machineguns were popping in every direction. Off we went for the woods as fast as we could go. Whiz-Bang, Whiz-Bang, Crash! Crash! And a big shell burst in front of me at the edge of the woods, scattering chunks of human flesh all over the ground. On a limb of a tree about ten feet high, hung a man's leg with the shoe and wrap leggings still on it. Poor soldier! Who could it be?" He found out later.[47]

To everyone's surprise, Sweeny's battalion entered the western part of the Bois de Fays without incident and discovered the German shells were now falling behind them. The German artillery was trying to cut off the unit from reinforcements reaching them. Moving on, they found the Germans had built a "town" within the wood. They found officers' houses with flowerbeds with beer bottles stuck in the ground as decoration and board walkways between the dwellings. They also found a teenage machine gunner chained to a tree with his gun. He immediately surrendered without firing a shot. He had a broad smile on his face as he was led to the rear, clearly happy to be a live prisoner.

As they continued to advance to the northwest part of the Bois de Fays, they found concrete bunkers dug into the earth and numerous machinegun nests, some of which the battalion was able to destroy. Then the shelling began again. They were bombarded by trench mortars, which could fire 30 rounds in a minute, and whiz-bangs. Machineguns were "popping" all around them. Sweeny's battalion had finally reached its objective, but now it was taking fire from three sides. The battalions on either side in the advance were slow in arriving. The troops were ordered to take cover in a ditch in the rear. The German fire increased. "Such a barrage I have never seen," said Young, "with all companies huddled in the ditch. Although this violated certain tactical principles of massing, it undoubtedly saved us."[48]

Throughout the day, elements of the 80th Division attacked the Bois des Ogons, seizing a piece of the wood for a time before being driven out with heavy losses. That evening, Major General Cronkhite ordered the entire 80th Division into a renewed attack on the Bois des Ogons. Instead of fierce resistance, the advancing troops found the woods empty. The Germans had pulled out, having bought time and inflicted many casualties.[49]

Early on October 7, the 318th was relieved and Sweeny's men crept quietly to the rear.[50]

During this part of the Meuse-Argonne offensive, between September 26 and October 7, the regiment lost 108 men killed, 832 wounded and two missing out of a total of about 3,750 men, a casualty rate of 25 percent. Sweeny's battalion, with a little more than 1,000 men, had 33 killed, 250 wounded and two missing, a loss of 28 percent. The casualty rates for the 2nd and 3rd Battalion were 35 and 19 percent, respectively.[51]

On October 23, the 80th Division was transferred from Bullard's Third Corps to the First Corps, commanded by Lieutenant General Hunter Liggett. This was in preparation for the division's return to the fighting. This time they would be on the left wing of the advance as part of First Corps.

A number of new officers arrived but even these replacements left the battalions with an average of less than two officers per company. Owing to the gaps in its ranks, the regiment was reorganized into three smaller platoons per company. The platoons also were reorganized to respond better to rapid changes as the troops advanced. Instead of four sections—two of automatic riflemen and riflemen, one of rifle grenadiers and one of hand grenadiers— the new 49-man platoons were divided into two identical sections of three squads each—a rifle squad, an automatic rifle squad and a grenadier squad. By putting the full range of light infantry weapons in each platoon, the units were more adaptable, more maneuverable and easier to control.[52]

During this period in the rear, the regiment was issued overcoats as well as Browning automatic rifles and machineguns. The American-made Browning automatic rifle was lighter, more durable and more accurate than the French Chauchat, which tended to jam and break. It was a welcome change. The regiment spent the time training the new arrivals and practicing with the new weapons.

The training included sham battles, with the battalions arrayed against each other. In one such practice engagement, one of the newly arrived lieutenants got separated from his platoon and couldn't find it. Private Young recalled Sweeny chewed out the rookie officer in front of the men. The lieutenant "must have felt rather cheap," said Young.[53]

There was even time for some fun. On October 27, a group of young

American women from the Y.M.C.A. put on a show with a banjo, singing, dancing and telling jokes.

Three days later, the regiment hiked 23 miles north and east through the Argonne Forest and took up a position on the east side of the forest between the villages of Chatel-Chehery and Cornay to relieve the 82nd Division.[54] As the 318th prepared to return to the front lines, more officers arrived, bringing the regiment up to near its full complement.[55]

By the end of October, the U.S. Army's objectives of the first part of the Meuse-Argonne offensive had been achieved. It had pushed the Germans back about ten miles to a line running roughly from Grandpre on the west, beyond the heights of Cunel and Romagne, to the River Meuse on the east. The Germans had been driven entirely out of their stronghold in the Argonne Forest and swept from the Heights of the Meuse as far as the southern portion of the Bois de la Grande Montagne. There was now more room for maneuver with a clear path ahead to the ultimate objective, the rail line running roughly west to east through Sedan.[56]

The First Corps prepared to attack with three divisions in line, from left to right, the 78th, the 77th and the 80th. The 80th was tasked with seizing the high ground north of Sivery lez Buzancy on the first day and protecting the flank of the Fifth Corps on its right.

On November 1, after a three-hour artillery barrage, the 80th Division launched an attack northward as part of a general advance. The 317th Infantry Regiment of the 80th was in the lead, with the 318th behind it, and captured the town of Buzancy. The 318th then passed through the 317th and took the lead. The objective was high ground studded with machinegun nests between Imecourt and Alliepont, with the goal of breaking the German's final line of resistance south of the Meuse. According to Young, the pace of advance was about 100 yards every six minutes. The advance was held up for a time by rugged terrain and later by machinegun fire from woods on Hill 214.

The advance resumed the next day and by the following day the entire brigade had reached the area of Imecourt. During the night of November 2–3, Sweeny's Battalion advanced 12 miles through Imecourt to Sivery, despite torn roads and slippery mud. "This was the hardest hike I have ever experienced," said Young. "We were sliding and slipping, falling into shell holes full of water and were getting completely exhausted."[57]

In the early hours of November 3, all of the officers of the 318th as well as of the 317thInfantry, the 313th Machinegun Battalion and the brigade were in a conference in a barn in Sivery when a German shell crashed through the roof and exploded above them. The 318th's casualties included three lieutenants killed and one captain and four lieutenants wounded. Sweeny apparently emerged unscathed, as there is no report of his being wounded.[58]

Despite these losses, the 80th Division advanced on a front about two miles wide between the 77th Division on its left and the 6th Marines on its right. The advance continued on November 4 with the capture of Sommauthe and Hill 314 by Sweeny's battalion. But the troops were soon halted at the Sommauthe-St. Pierremont ridge by fire from machinegun nests they couldn't see. The 318th had outrun the artillery's ability to move up and support them.

Private Young was wounded here by a bullet that broke the fibula bone below his left knee and was evacuated. After the war, he married in 1921, divorced in 1928, and became a chef in a restaurant in Washington, D.C. He died in San Diego, California, in 1969.[59]

Once the artillery was in place, it delivered a 2,500-round barrage and Sweeny's battalion resumed its advance toward La Polka Farm. It was delayed by the inability of the unit on its left to take high ground there that allowed German machineguns to cover the approach. When night fell, Sweeny's battalion captured the farm after a fierce fight. The 2nd Battalion then relieved Sweeny's 1st Battalion on November 5 and the advance continued for 24 hours until the 1st Battalion again took the lead. It was at this point on November 6, just 15 miles southeast of the final objective, Sedan, that the 80th Division was relieved by the 1st Division.[60] That was the end of combat for the 80th. The armistice silenced the guns five days later.

Why certain regiments were replaced on the front line in the final days of the war is a subject of some controversy. The regimental history states that the reason for relieving the 80th at that moment, considering the results obtained and the relatively low casualty rate at the time, "has never been made clear to us." "[I]t is believed that we were relieved simply to enable the 1st Division, which had been the first to come over, to be in the line at the signing of the armistice, which was expected momentarily at the hour of our relief. Certain it is that no division had advanced further or suffered fewer casualties from November 1st to 6th than had the 80th Division." The regimental history states that during the last three days in the line, it advanced ten miles while sustaining casualties of 25 killed, 93 wounded and one missing. "The regiment takes pride also in the fact that at the hour of its relief it was further north than any unit on the American front."[61]

In a message of praise delivered to the troops of the 80th Division by its commander, Major General Cronkhite noted that the division advanced more than 15 miles in the final five days of combat, "always led," "captured two Huns for every man wounded," "captured one machinegun for every man wounded," "captured one cannon for every man wounded" and accomplished all this with a lower rate of casualties than any other division.

The regimental history notes that Sweeny was twice singled out by the regimental commander for special mention and divisional citation. Only seven other officers in the 318th received this recognition, and Sweeny was the only officer cited more than once.[62]

The first citation states: "This officer displayed rare tactical ability in handling his battalion. He met with strong opposition at one point in his attack, and the fact that he gained ground with as few casualties as he had reflects great credit on his ability and judgment."

The second citation reads: "This officer gained his objective with dash and ability. He showed excellent tactical judgment and initiative in exploiting the success of his advance after reaching his objective, which action enabled the relieving corps of the 1st Division to make immediate progress without serious opposition."

The citations carry no dates, but it appears the first refers to the attack on the Bois-de-Fays on October 5, and the second involves capture of Sommauthe and La Polka Farm on November 4.

Four members of the 318th received the Distinguished Service Cross, the second highest U.S. Army decoration for valor after the Medal of Honor. Two of them were in Sweeny's battalion.

Private William F. Tignor of Company D, during the attack on Sommauthe on November 4–7, "repeatedly went forward and by calling and making noises, drew machinegun fire upon himself in order to locate machinegun nests, which were subsequently put out of action."

Sergeant William T. Johnson of Company A, on October 5 at the Bois-de-Pays, was leading a patrol when it came under heavy machinegun fire. He ordered his men to take cover and then advanced alone. Working his way closer to the gun, he destroyed the nest. Later in the same patrol, he "braved the perils of an extremely heavy barrage to bring to safety a comrade who was lying 300 yards in advance of the lines."

Sweeny also endorsed a recommendation of the commander of Company D that Lieutenant Daniel Clovis Moomaw be awarded the Distinguished Service Cross for his actions on October 5 at the Bois-de-Fays. Moomaw had been assigned to deliver his platoon to brigade headquarters to serve as liaison with the 4th Division. Informed that he personally was not needed, and knowing that his battalion had been ordered to attack the Bois-de-Fays, Moomaw undertook a lone reconnaissance of the wood. Sweeny said Moomaw "reported to me at the southern edge of the Bois de Fays shortly after my arrival there. The information which he had gathered proved afterward to be extremely accurate and of the greatest value." Minutes later, Moomaw entered the wood just moments before an enemy shell burst at that location. No body was found at the time and he was reported missing. Sweeny delayed sending in the medal recommendation while waiting to learn if Moomaw was living or dead. It was not until May 1919, when Moomaw's brother, aided by battalion officers, visited the spot and located remains that were then positively identified as Moomaw's by a wristwatch and teeth. (Moomaw turned out to be the man whose leg Young had seen blasted onto a limb of a tree at the edge of the Bois de Fays.) By then, Sweeny had been transferred. When he was contacted in 1938 and asked to support a belated award of the medal to Moomaw, Sweeny readily agreed and wrote to the War Department. No action was taken then and despite subsequent efforts, no award of the medal has been made.[63]

There is no mention in the regimental history of any other decorations being distributed to members of the regiment. A resume that Sweeny wrote many years later for his publisher lists his many decorations from other nations but doesn't mention any U.S. military medals.

In *One Man's Wars*, McCormick wrote that Sweeny received another bullet wound during the final days of the war, but he hid this fact and continued to lead his battalion until the 80th Division was sent into reserve four days before the Armistice. According to McCormick, Sweeny was in a Paris hospital when the war ended on November 11, 1918.[64]

There is no mention of Sweeny being wounded while serving in the 318th, either in the regimental history, which includes detailed casualty lists, or in any of Sweeny's personnel records now at the National Archives. Nor is there any mention that Sweeny was absent from the regiment in the final days before the armistice. A fire in 1973 destroyed most of the personnel files of First World War soldiers, including Sweeny's, but a partial reconstruction has been made by the archivists. This is not to say that Sweeny wasn't wounded during the Meuse-Argonne offensive. It simply cannot be established with the records available. Sweeny may have concealed his wound from the regiment, and the medical staff may have failed to report the nature of his ailment to the regiment, either by neglect or at Sweeny's request.[65]

Following the armistice, the regiment began a march of 160 miles in ten days that ended on November 29 at the 15th Training Area near Asnieres-en-Montagne in Burgundy, 145 miles southeast of Paris. Everyone wanted to go home immediately, but it took some time before the 318th's turn finally came.[66] In fact, it was not until May 17, 1919, that Sweeny's "red squirrels" of the 318th Infantry sailed out of Brest harbor aboard the U.S.S. Maui. It arrived in Newport News, Virginia, ten days later. To honor their service, the men of the 318th received a hero's parade through the state capital, Richmond.

Sweeny, however, wasn't among them. On Feb. 24, he was promoted to lieutenant colonel, and on March 11 he was transferred to A.E.F. headquarters in Paris, where his wife and children had spent the war. He was honorably discharged on July 11, 1919, at Camp Lewis, Washington,[67] a location that facilitated a visit with family members in Spokane. However, his mother had died January 3, 1919, in Spokane and was buried there next to her husband three days later, so it would have been impossible for Sweeny to be there for the funeral.

Sweeny had survived four years of war and earned fame and glory. But during those years he had had precious little time with his wife and children and had lost his father, mother and youngest brother. His world was forever changed.

Most soldiers of the "war to end all wars" had had their fill of war. Not Sweeny. He was just getting started.

Chapter 10

Polish-Soviet War

Despite the long separation during the war, Sweeny didn't spend much time afterward with his siblings in the Pacific Northwest, or even with his wife and children in Paris. After four years of living on the edge of eternity and serving a noble cause, he was uncomfortable in a humdrum civilian world where nothing momentous was at risk. He craved action and a cause larger than surviving everyday life. It wasn't long before he found it.

After his army discharge in July 1919, he set about organizing a contingent of 200 former U.S. Army officers with combat experience in France. On September 2, 1919, he obtained a new U.S. passport. On his application, he wrote that he intended to "rejoin my wife and children at my residence in France and continue my profession as publicist that I followed before 1914." Based on what happened four days later, those were clearly not his true intentions.

On September 6, while the ink was still drying on the Treaty of Versailles that formally ended "the war to end all wars," Sweeny sailed back to France with the first group of his volunteers to get into a new war. In an appropriate coincidence, the ship they traveled on was the French ocean liner *Rochambeau*, named for the French nobleman who had fought beside the American colonists in their war for independence.

Sweeny's new cause was another war for independence, the struggle of Polish and White Russian forces against Russian and Ukrainian Bolsheviks. "Col. Sweeny has his professional eye on the operations against the Bolsheviks," reported the *Sun*, which quoted Sweeny as saying, "There is considerable going on and plenty of opportunity for a military man."[1]

For more than a century, Poland had been split into three pieces by its monarchist neighbors: Germany's kaiser, Russia's czar and Austria-Hungary's emperor. With the end of the World War in 1918 and the toppling of these potentates, Polish nationalists saw a chance to realize their dream of reuniting the three pieces into a single independent Republic of Poland. The Allies had beaten Germany and Austria-Hungary, and Russia had forfeited its claim to victors' spoils at the Paris Peace Conference. Russia had made a separate peace in March 1918 and ceded all Polish territory to the Central Powers. In addition, the Bolsheviks now running Russia were anathema to the Allies.

In his 14 Points, which set forth his parameters for the peace negotiations, U.S. president Woodrow Wilson specifically addressed Poland in point number 13: "An independent Polish state should be erected which should include the territories inhabited by indisputably Polish populations, which should be assured a free and secure access to the sea, and whose political and economic independence and territorial integrity should be guaranteed by international covenant." Given all of these circumstances, Poles believed 1919 was their golden moment.

However, the Poles weren't the only country to see opportunity in the post-war turmoil. As German troops withdrew from Poland, as required by the armistice, Russia's Red Army began advancing westward. Its goal was to drive through Poland to invade Germany and take advantage of the chaos there to export the revolution throughout Western Europe. Bolshevik agents in the West were already fomenting disruptions aimed at facilitating regime changes.

By February 1919, the Red Army had pushed as far into Polish territory as the Bug River, about 125 miles east of Warsaw. The Poles, under General Jozef Pilsudski, the provisional chief of state of the Second Polish Republic, then counterattacked and drove the Bolsheviks back nearly 300 miles to the Berezina River, in what is now Belarus, and into Ukraine. The fighting continued, despite an attempt by the Allied Supreme Council to establish a temporary eastern border for Poland. The Poles wanted the border where it had been in 1772, which would have been within the current boundaries of Russia. The Russians wanted the border to be along the current battle lines, much farther west. The Poles joined forces with anti–Soviet Ukrainians and marched on Kiev, capturing the city in May 1920. However, a powerful Soviet counterattack drove the Poles and White Russians back nearly 500 miles to the outskirts of Warsaw. Here the Polish and White Russian forces routed the Red Army in a fierce 10-day Battle of Warsaw in August 1920.[2] Fighting continued with more Polish victories until the Soviets agreed to accept some of Poland's territorial claims in October 1920. The Treaty of Riga divided the disputed territory in Belorussia and Ukraine between Poland and the Soviet Union.

Despite declarations of support for Polish independence, most of the Allies did little to redeem their pledges. The United States credited the Poles with $56 million (equal to the cost of one day's Allied operations on the Western Front in the World War) to cover the release of U.S. Army surplus in France and then adopted a position of "interested observer."[3] Great Britain gave the Poles 50 airplanes, but mostly paid lip service to aiding Poland. France, alone among the Allies, made a serious effort to provide material assistance to the Poles against the Soviets. The French saw the Poles as natural allies in future confrontations with Germany or Russia.[4]

Both the Polish and Russia forces were in desperate need of equipment. Most of what they used was scrounged from leftover supplies from the World War. Tanks, aircraft and artillery were in short supply. As a result, wrote historian Norman Richard Davies in *White Eagle, Red Star: The Polish-Soviet War 1919-1920*, "Cavalry remained the principal offensive arm." The battles in this war more closely resembled those bloody horse, lance and saber clashes of pre–20th century conflicts.[5]

France shipped surplus rifles and ammunition to Poland, equipped a Polish army under General Jozef Haller and sent 400 officers there to help train the Polish officer corps in French military procedures and tactics. Gen. Paul Prosper Henrys, commander of French forces in the Balkans, led this French Military Mission to Poland in 1919. While the Poles regarded Henrys as a "featherbrained busybody," they had an entirely different view of the other officers. "In contrast to its chief," wrote Davies, "the French mission commanded considerable respect and influence through the activities of its 400 officer-instructors."[6] The French officers served as advisors to Polish units at various levels. Their most significant impact was on organization and logistics.

Among the French officers was Charles de Gaulle, a 28-year-old captain who had distinguished himself in combat in the World War and been captured while defending Fort Douaumont at Verdun in 1916. In May 1919, he traveled to Poland as an advisor with Haller's army. He later served as an instructor in tactics at the officers' school, and in the summer of 1920 he distinguished himself at the Zbrucz River, was awarded Poland's highest military award, the Virtuti Militari, and was promoted to major.

Exactly when Sweeny reached Poland and what he did there is unclear. As usual, Sweeny never bothered to clear up the confusion. This has led to various tales about his involvement. One story suggested that Sweeny played a role in recruiting American pilots for a Polish version of the Lafayette Escadrille.[7]

While there was a Polish version of the Lafayette Escadrille, the story of the 70th (Kosciuszko) Squadron[8] is well documented in Kenneth Malcolm Murray's *Wings Over Poland*, and there is no mention of Sweeny. Murray was a member of the squadron, which had 23 pilots, including 16 Americans. He provided a detailed account of how Merian C. Cooper, a captain in the U.S. Army Air Service in the World War, recruited American pilots for the squadron, starting with another Air Service veteran, Major Cedric E. Fauntleroy, in a Paris café.

Cooper left Paris by rail with the first contingent of seven recruits, all veteran American combat pilots, on September 11, 1919, while Sweeny was at sea heading to France with his own recruits. Cooper's contingent arrived in Warsaw on September 26, where two more Americans, who had served in the World War with the British Royal Flying Corps, joined them.

There was a hiatus in the fighting during the winter of 1919-20, in part because of the weather and in part because of international efforts to broker an end to the fighting. When the fighting resumed in the spring, the Kosciuszko Squadron was first used in the Kiev offensive in April 1920. The pilots became quite successful at low-level strafing of Bolshevik cavalry units, and earned the admiration of Polish ground commanders.

By war's end, the squadron had flown more than 400 combat sorties, three of its American members were dead and ten of them had been awarded the Virtuti Militari as well as other important Polish decorations.

Cooper was shot down in July 1920 and spent nine months in a Soviet prisoner-of-war camp before escaping before the end of hostilities and making his way back to Poland, where he had been given up for dead. He was among the squadron members awarded the Virtuti Militari. General Pilsudski presented him with the medal personally.[9]

It is likely Cooper and Sweeny met during the Polish-Soviet War. There is later correspondence between the two men that indicates they became good friends. However, there is nothing in the books about the Kosciuszko Squadron that mentions Sweeny.

Cooper was a larger-than-life character, like Sweeny. While serving with the U.S. Army Air Service in the World War, Cooper was shot down and held in a German P.O.W. camp until released at the end of the war. He decided to recruit fliers for Poland after seeing the aftermath of a Bolshevik atrocity while administering post-war relief aid there. After Poland, he was a founding board member of Pan American Airways. During the Second World War, he was a colonel in the U.S. Army Air Corps, serving as a logistics liaison to the Doolittle Raid on Japan, setting up the India-Burma-China Ferry Command, serving as chief of staff to the Fifth Air Force and attending the Japanese surrender on the battleship Missouri. He also became a Hollywood screenwriter, director and producer. He is best known for the 1933 film *King Kong*, which he co-wrote, co-directed and appeared in. After World War II, he collaborated with movie director John Ford on his trio of cavalry classics *Fort Apache*, *She Wore a Yellow Ribbon* and *Rio Grande* as well as *The Searchers* and *The Quiet Man*, all starring John Wayne.

One piece of the correspondence between Sweeny and Cooper serves to illustrate the easy banter typical of two old friends. In January 1956, Sweeny sent Cooper the following letter[10]:

> My dear Coop:
> I am sending you the manuscript of a play written as a thesis at the University [of

Utah] here. It is different. Jack Ford I feel could do wonders [with it]. My only interest is to bring it to your attention. Treat as you would any other manuscript.

I am walking as gently as my disposition will permit down the stairs from seventy to eighty. My mind is fertile of memories: the men and women I have known, those I have loved, even those I have despised, the things I have seen, the things I have done. Could old age be more fitingly [sic] lived? I once wrote a play on this plot. I did not then know "The Tales of Hoffman [sic]."[11] Fortunately the Professor of English at Notre Dame in 1898 said it was no good and there and then destroyed my theatrical ambitions.

My best regards to Shorty and his wife, to Jack Ford and to your good wife and yourself.

Bien a vous,
Charles Sweeny

There is no response from Cooper among Sweeny's personal papers.

Before leaving Paris for America to recruit his volunteers in mid–1919, Sweeny had consulted with famed pianist and composer Ignacy Jan Paderewski, who was then in Paris attending the peace conference as the Polish prime minister. Sweeny consulted Paderewski about recruiting American volunteers to fight for Poland.[12]

If Sweeny arrived in Poland with his volunteers in late 1919, it is likely he met with the same cool initial reception from General Pilsudski as Cooper had when he was introduced to the Polish leader upon his arrival in Warsaw. Pilsudski told Cooper that Poland could defend itself. Later, of course, Pilsudski changed his mind after witnessing the valuable contributions made by Cooper, and apparently Sweeny as well. On August 29, 1920, the *New York Tribune* glowingly reported that Sweeny had been made a brigadier general in the Polish army "in recognition of his splendid services." The article said, "Recent dispatches say that he has been marked out by his gallantry and leadership." The article was widely reprinted in newspapers across the United States.[13]

It is worth noting that Sweeny was appointed a brigadier general in the Polish military, which outstripped both Cooper's and Fauntleroy's eventual promotions to lieutenant colonel and colonel, respectively, suggesting that Sweeny's role was more significant.

While in Warsaw, Sweeny also renewed his friendship with Henry J. Reilly, a West Point classmate who would play a useful role in a more important chapter later in Sweeny's life. Reilly was the son of an up-from-the-ranks artillery captain who had been killed in action in the Boxer Rebellion in China in 1900. Reilly had graduated 80th out of 124 in the class of 1904. Since then, he had been a war correspondent in the Far East and a civilian instructor at West Point. Returning to the Army, he went to France as a colonel in command of the 49th Field Artillery Regiment and later the 83rd Brigade of the 42nd (Rainbow) Division, the youngest brigade commander in the A.E.F.[14]

After the war, he became a war correspondent again and covered armed conflicts in Poland, Spain, Albania and France. He also became the first president of the Reserve Officers Association and a brigadier general in 1920. He died in New York City in December 1963. While in Poland, Reilly made a name for himself as the only commentator or military advisor to correctly predict the Poles would win the Battle of Warsaw and how they would achieve this surprise victory.

Although Reilly's and Cooper's activities in Poland are clear, Sweeny's are murky.

The *New York Tribune* article about Sweeny being named a brigadier general contained a lengthy account of Sweeny's earlier career and his recruitment of former American officers to fight for Poland. But it offered no details of when he arrived in Poland or what he did there.

In his 1972 biography of Sweeny, McCormick quoted an ex–British officer named Edward Myers, who he said met Sweeny in Warsaw in 1920, as saying that Sweeny was made a brigadier general to enable him to organize guerrilla forces to fight the Bolsheviks. Myers said Sweeny got along well with the Poles but "quickly despaired of getting any effective cooperation with the White Russians."[15] Myers thought Sweeny was an "unofficial member" of General Weygand's mission to Poland.

The latter statement is consistent with a resume Sweeny wrote for his publisher in 1942. In the resume, Sweeny said he was a "member of [a] Mission sent to Poland by [the] French Government in 1920 under command of General Weygand [and that he] assisted at Battle of Warsaw."[16]

French General Maxime Weygand, the chief of staff to Marshal Ferdinand Foch, arrived in Warsaw on July 21, 1920, at the head of the Inter-allied Mission to Poland. Although the mission was a diplomatic rather than a military one, Weygand arrived thinking he was going to assume command of the Polish army. This did not occur, and a bad situation turned toxic when Pilsudski asked Weygand, "How many divisions did you bring?" and was informed that the answer was none. Weygand was made an advisor to the Polish chief of staff on July 27, but his tactical proposals were rejected. He departed after barely a month in Poland on the final day of the Battle of Warsaw, which began August 12 and ended August 25. While Weygand was hailed back in France as the architect of the Polish victory, historian Jean Lacouture wrote that Weygand's "part in the 'miracle on the Vistula' has never been made quite clear."[17] Similarly, historian Norman Richard Davies concluded that Weygand "was the first uncomprehending victim, as well as the chief beneficiary, of a legend already in circulation that he, Weygand, was the victor of Warsaw. This legend persisted for more than forty years even in academic circles."[18]

If Sweeny was part of Weygand's entourage, it is hard to see how he could have overcome the Poles' negative attitude toward Weygand's mission or how he had enough time to make a sufficient impression on his own to earn a high rank. We're left to conclude that he either (1) arrived long before Weygand's mission, perhaps with the 100–200 American volunteers he reportedly raised,[19] or (2) he arrived with Weygand and commanded a division of Polish guerrillas,[20] or (3) his commission as a brigadier general had more to do with public relations than military prowess. His resume for his publisher offers a clue. It makes no mention of him being made a brigadier general by the Poles, suggesting he took no pride in that honor.

There's also the question of what became of the 100 or more former American officers that Sweeny recruited, some of whom reportedly sailed with him to France on the *Rochambeau* back in September 1919. There is no mention of them in the subsequent news coverage of Sweeny, and no list of the officers accompanying him was published.

According to McCormick, who had the benefit of interviewing Sweeny's son as well as some of his contemporaries, Sweeny steadfastly refused to talk or write about his time in Poland. Likewise, Sweeny's French military record contains no clues as to his service there, and most of the official Polish records from this period apparently have been lost.[21]

Both sides finally agreed to a cease-fire, with the Soviet forces in hopeless disarray and the Poles too exhausted to continue the pursuit. The Treaty of Riga, which formally ended hostilities and established national boundaries, was signed March 18, 1921. By then Sweeny had returned to his family in Paris. However, it wasn't long before he was off again on another military adventure, this one with a bit more intrigue.

Chapter 11

Greco-Turkish War

In the immediate aftermath of the World War, the victorious Allies were intent on settling scores with the vanquished Central Powers as well as securing territorial gains for themselves. Complicating the peace process, Great Britain and France had made a number of promises during the war to other nations to induce them to join the fight against Germany, Austria-Hungary and the Ottoman Empire. As it turned out, they had promised more than they could deliver. This, in turn, created expectations that fueled post-war border conflicts, although none was quite as large as the Polish-Soviet War.

One of the prime targets was the once sprawling Ottoman Empire, which at its zenith in the 17th century had stretched from Budapest to Baghdad and from Algiers to the Arabian Peninsula. Russian expansionism, ethnic nationalism (often encouraged by European powers) and internecine political rivalries in the 18th and 19th centuries gradually weakened and shrank the empire until it was reduced to roughly modern-day Turkey and the Levant. By 1908, when a military coup overthrew the sultan, and hard-line nationalists and Islamists took power as the Young Turks, the empire was commonly referred to as "the sick man of Europe." It was ripe for dismemberment.

Following the empire's defeat in 1918, the Young Turks were ousted and a feeding frenzy of land grabbing by the empire's neighbors began. In 1920, the victorious Allies sought to impose the Treaty of Sevres, which would break up the Ottoman Empire into several small nations and zones of foreign influence. In the west, Greece would get Thrace as well as eight Turkish islands in the Aegean Sea while Italy would get the Dodecanese islands. In the east, there would be an independent Armenia, an autonomous Kurdistan, and much of the rest of Anatolia would be divided into French and Italian zones of influence. Turkey would lose all of its territories in Arab Asia and North Africa. In addition, the Allies would control Turkey's finances and reduce its military to a token force. Historian Patrick Kinross concluded, "All that was to remain of Turkey was a rump of an inland state, with most of its outlets to the sea under foreign control, and its sovereignty reduced to a shadow."[1]

Not surprisingly, the Turks rejected the treaty. There were too few British military forces in the area to turn the treaty into reality on the ground. So, the Allies, led by Great Britain's David Lloyd George, accepted an offer from Greece to mount a military campaign to enforce the terms. They did so over strong opposition from France's Marshal Foch as well as the British General Staff, who feared Greece would overreach.

The Greeks, eager to seize as much territory as possible, scooped up Thrace, captured several cities on the east side of the Bosphorus and the Dardanelles, and thrust deeper into western Anatolia. Faced with this invasion, the Turkish nationalists regained power and set up a provisional government in the city of Ankara, in central Anatolia.

The Greek offensive involved four separate advances, with little coordination. They appeared to easily overwhelm the opposition as Turkish forces fell back eastward. It was, however, a strategic retreat, not a rout. And when the French and Italians became alarmed at the scope of the Greek gains, they joined forces against Lloyd George and ordered the Greeks to halt where they were. This left the Greeks stalled in mountainous terrain, widely separated on a lengthy front and with no access to railways for resupply.[2]

The delay in the Greek advance allowed Turkey to reorganize its forces and also form a strategic alliance with the Soviet Union to secure Turkey's rear from the Armenians and Kurds. Meanwhile, a change in government in Greece led the Greeks to break with the Allies and ignore the order to halt. Their immediate goal was to reach the main railway and seize key points. The Greeks continued to advance deeper and deeper into the mountains until they were defeated in a three-week battle in September 1921 at the Sakarya River, only 50 miles west of Ankara. The Turkish "army of liberation" was led by Mustafa Kemal, who later took the name Ataturk ("Father of the Turks") and became the first president of a reborn Turkey. The Greeks were driven back 250 miles to the city of Smyrna (now known as Izmir) on the Aegean Sea, which the Turks besieged and captured in September 1922 with a heavy loss of life among both Greek soldiers and civilians. The Allies tried to force the Turks to give up Thrace but in the end the Treaty of Lausanne in July 1923 forced the Greeks to return Thrace and the Turkish islands, and exchange their Turkish population for the empire's Greek population.

In January 1921, Sweeny applied for a new U.S. passport. The application states that he had credentials as a correspondent from the managing editor of the *New York World*. Sweeny arrived in Turkey in early 1922 with his friend, Larry Rue, a U.S. Army pilot in the World War who arrived in France too late for combat and remained in Paris to become a foreign correspondent for the *Chicago Tribune*. It was Rue who got Sweeny the job with the *New York World*.[3]

While Sweeny's role in Poland "has to some extent been clouded in secrecy, there is no doubt that in Turkey he was first and foremost acting as an agent for French Intelligence," wrote biographer Donald McCormick. "His job as a war correspondent was simply a cover."[4]

There seems to be no way to independently verify this story. McCormick served in British naval intelligence during the Second World War. This, no doubt, enabled him to make many contacts in that secret fraternity. His reporting on this aspect of Sweeny's career appears to be based entirely on his covert sources.

McCormick wrote that British intelligence officers in Constantinople followed Sweeny around the city. They noted that he made frequent trips to the Tatavia quarter, an area of bars and brothels near the port to service sailors and others willing to risk its dangerous streets. They assumed he was simply seeking the usual services of these establishments until they saw him meeting with the French military attaché. Upon further inquiry in the quarter, the British officers reportedly learned that Sweeny was ferreting out information on an international arms merchant: a Greek, born in Turkey, living in Paris, who had been knighted by the British crown. Sweeny wrote a number of articles about the Greco–Turkish War that were seen as pro–Turkey/anti–Greece and that, in McCormick's words, he had "gone out of his way to discredit accounts of Turkish atrocities against the Armenians."[5] But Sweeny never wrote about the arms merchant, known in England as Sir Basil Zaharoff.[6, 7]

British intelligence would have had good reason for wanting to keep a close eye on Sweeny if his sleuthing was intended to expose Zaharoff's dealings. Zaharoff was a board member and international sales representative of Vickers Ltd., the giant British armaments company and one of the world's foremost munitions makers at the time.

American journalist John T. Flynn traced Zaharoff's career in his 1941 book *Men of Wealth*. He reported that over several decades and across several continents, Zaharoff became rich and influential by manipulating nations into arming themselves against real or phony threats from other nations, and then selling arms to both nations. In 1915, at the secret urging of the British and French governments, Zaharoff played a key behind-the-scenes role in engineering Greece's entry into the World War on the side of the Allies. This involved funding an underground public relations campaign, issuing pamphlets, subsidizing newspapers, bribing Greek officials, and ultimately aiding in the ouster of King Constantine, who was intent on keeping his nation out of the World War.[8] Constantine was forced to abdicate in 1917 by a revolt led by his pro-war former prime minister, aided by Allied troops landed at Athens. Constantine was replaced on the throne by his son, Alexander, who sided with the pro-war faction. Greece then joined the Allied cause, and Zaharoff added Greece to his customer list for arms.

According to McCormick, Sweeny met Zaharoff once briefly in Latin America and took "an instant dislike to him." Sweeny's dislike stemmed from Zaharoff fomenting revolutions in Latin America to boost arms sales. His dislike increased to loathing during the World War when Zaharoff persuaded the Allies not to bomb two enemy munitions plants.[9]

Flynn, the American journalist, explored the curious situation involving these two munitions factories. The factories were located on either side of the French-German border, just 15 miles apart near the city of Metz. One factory, at Briey, was owned by a French company; the other, at Thionville, by a German company. When the war began, the French forces fell back, leaving the French factory intact. As the war progressed, both factories turned out armaments for German soldiers to kill French and British soldiers. When French army officers asked to bomb the factories, they were denied permission. When a French general took it upon himself to order a bombardment, it was stopped immediately by higher ups. "Deputies clamored for its destruction. A committee of the Senate urged it. Even the Cabinet asked why Briey and Thionville were not stopped. But nothing was done," wrote Flynn. When the war was over, the Briey factory was handed back to its French owner "unscathed." Zaharoff's interests were protected at the cost of a great many Allied lives, a fact that incensed Sweeny.[10]

Following the Armistice in 1918, Zaharoff worked with the Greek prime minister, Eleftherios Venizelos, to promote Greece's territorial claims in Turkey and to finance Greece's invasion of Anatolia, with the blessing of the Allies' Supreme Council.

The political situation in Greece changed dramatically, however, when King Alexander died suddenly in October 1920 after being infected by the bite of a pet monkey. The following month, Prime Minister Venizelos, whose absence to attend the Paris peace conference had created an opening for his opponents, was defeated in an election. With his son dead and the prime minister defeated, Constantine regained the throne. This time Constantine did not balk at committing his country to war, and Greece renewed its advances into Turkey with, as we have seen, Greece's defeat in 1922 and subsequent humiliation in the Treaty of Lausanne.

Despite the setback in Greece, Zaharoff's influence and prosperity continued unabated until his death at age 87 in 1936, the same year the Spanish Civil War began.

Meanwhile, Sweeny, in his role as a foreign correspondent, obtained an interview with Ataturk. According to McCormick, "The two had much in common: both were soldiers and both had a fondness for playing poker. With the tacit approval of French Intelligence and a personal recommendation from General Weygand, Sweeny was appointed a military advisor to Ataturk."[11]

This new role didn't last long, however. The Turks soon vanquished the Greeks and Sweeny returned to Paris.

Sweeny's involvement in the Greco-Turkish War was of little consequence in all but one respect: He made a friend who would be a major figure in his life for the rest of his days. His name was Ernest Hemingway. He was still a neophyte reporter when he met Sweeny, who impressed him as a man of the world with a brilliant military mind. Sweeny became a mentor to the young Hemingway, helping him obtain information for his dispatches from Turkey, tending to Hemingway during his illness, and creating a bond that would endure through many more wars to the end of their lives.

Chapter 12

Morocco and the Rif War

The armed struggle of Moroccan tribesmen to expel Spanish colonial rule from northwest Africa in 1921–26 rarely rates more than a footnote in history today. However, noted military historian Douglas Porch believes the Rif War deserves greater attention. Rather than the Arab Revolt led by T.E. Lawrence in World War I, he considers the Rif War the true transitional event that signaled the shift from "failed prenationalistic resistance to European colonialism into successful post–World War II insurgencies, infused with nationalism and guided by Maoist revolutionary strategies."[1]

Whereas Lawrence of Arabia's Arab Revolt ultimately required the assistance of European armies to defeat the Ottoman Empire, the Moroccans succeeded on their own, at least for a time, to defeat European forces superior in both size and weaponry.

The Rif War also proved to be an important and controversial episode in Sweeny's saga. Once again he made international news; once again he was seen as a devil-may-care soldier of fortune; and once again he defied U.S. laws and upset U.S. officials. In the end, it tarnished his reputation for a time in America but polished it in France.

* * *

Morocco has had a turbulent history dating back to ancient times and the events that led to the Rif War can be traced back to 1492. That year Spain finally succeeded in pushing the Muslim invaders out of Europe and back across the Mediterranean Sea to Africa after seven centuries of occupation. The Spanish then began their own long period of conquest and colonization of foreign lands, not only in North Africa but in the newly discovered Western Hemisphere.

Morocco, located just across the narrow Strait of Gibraltar from Spain, was an obvious target, and the Spanish moved quickly to establish fortified enclaves along its Mediterranean shore during the reign of King Ferdinand and Queen Isabella, the monarchs who bankrolled the voyages of discovery of Christopher Columbus. These outposts withstood innumerable sieges by the Rifs, the Berber tribe indigenous to the northern part of the country, and Arabs, who migrated to the area with the spread of Islam in the 7th century. The danger posed by the Rifs as well as the arid mountain terrain discouraged Spanish colonial expansion deeper into Morocco for four centuries.

Finally, in the early 20th century, internecine strife weakened Morocco to such an extent that Spain, France, England and Germany began a scramble to gain dominance over it as one of the last areas in Africa left to colonize. In 1912, internal and external pressures forced the sultan of Morocco to agree to the partition of his country into two protectorates. The Treaty of Fez gave France control over the central plains and Atlas Mountains adjacent to its colony in Algeria. Spain received a narrow strip in the north dominated by the rugged Rif Mountains plus Western Sahara to the south. Germany was placated with colonies in French Equatorial Africa (now in the Republic of Congo and Cameroon). The city of Tangier became an international zone. The treaty also gave Spain mining concessions in the Rif Mountains and a railroad concession to connect the mines to the fortified enclave at Melilla on the Mediterranean coast.[2]

After a millennium of independence, Moroccan nationalists reacted violently to having their sovereign nation split into subservient colonies of France and Spain. The treaty caused a mutiny by indigenous troops under French command and riots in Fez, then the capital of Morocco. The uprising was put down, but it ultimately led to a full-fledged rebellion, the Rif War of 1921–26.

So how was this conflict different from previous revolts against colonial rulers and the first of our modern wars of liberation? In an article analyzing this aspect of the Rif War, William Dean, of the U.S. Air Force Air Command and Staff College, drew upon a paper published in 1925 by Captain Charles Willoughby, a U.S. Army intelligence officer who had traveled extensively in Spain and Morocco. Willoughby said the critical difference was what indigenous peoples learned during World War I, which ended just two years before the Rif War began. In World War I, European powers deployed native troops from their colonies to the battlefields stretching from France to the Middle East. There they learned the ways and weapons of modern warfare and something else as well. "[T]he colonial empires were based on a legend, the legend of the invincible white man," wrote Willoughby. "The subject races had discovered a strange truth: the white overlords, those unfathomable masters of their destinies, were opposed to each other. Demigods who had their secular pedestal had been reduced to fragments of clay."[3, 4]

Willoughby saw the Rif War as an opportunity to reverse the direction of this narrative and re-establish "the supremacy of the white man and the Western colonial empires" by brutally suppressing this revolt. "Only an aggressive war, led to the heart of their country by punitive expeditions, burning villages, destroying wheat reserves and dispersing herds, could accomplish the subordination of the rebel tribes," wrote Willoughby.

"To do so," wrote Dean, "Willoughby suggested the use of tanks, armored cars, flamethrowers and gas." The use of poison gas in war was outlawed by the European powers after the World War but Dean wrote that thousands of tons of mustard gas were used on Moroccan villages.[5] Willoughby also suggested Spain and France join forces to ensure victory against the rebels. This happened as well.

* * *

The rebels confronting the colonizers in Morocco were a clannish, fiercely independent people skilled in the hit-and-run tactics of guerrilla warfare. In the Rif War, they were led by Mohammed ben Abd el-Krim (1882–1963), a university-educated teacher, translator, journalist, and civil servant in the colonial bureaucracy. He also was a tribal chief and a Muslim judge. He was imprisoned in 1916 for alleged anti-colonial activities but escaped in 1918 and managed to regain his position as a judge in Melilla. In 1919, fearing he was about to be imprisoned again, Abd el-Krim fled to the mountains. In 1921, he launched the rebellion with the goal of uniting the fractious Berber tribes, casting out the colonizers and forming an independent republic. The effects of Spanish colonial exploitation drove many downtrodden tribesmen to his cause.

As thousands of Spanish colonists moved to Morocco, Spain set about exerting its control over northern Morocco. The Spanish built a system of blockhouses along 300 miles of roads and a railroad from Ceuta to Tetouan. In late 1920, the Tercio de Extranjeros (Regiment of Foreigners, also known as the Spanish Foreign Legion) was formed, with Major Francisco Franco as its second in command, for service in Morocco.

Abd el-Krim's strategy was to lure the Spanish out of their fortresses and into the mountains where their stretched out lines of troops and extended supply lines would leave them vulnerable to being destroyed piecemeal.[6]

In early 1921, Spanish troops occupied Chechaouen, a medieval fortress city in the Rif Mountains between Tetouan and Tangiers where Abd el-Krim had been imprisoned. In May 1921, Spanish General Manuel Silvestre set out from Melilla toward Alhucemas Bay with 25,000 troops to subjugate one tribe and provide an object lesson to other tribes. As his troops marched, they became strung out for miles along the mountain road. On July 17, at a place called Annual, Abd el-Krim ambushed Silvestre, inflicting heavy casualties. After five days under siege, Silvestre ordered a withdraw 70 miles back to

Melilla. However, it soon turned into a rout as the Spanish troops abandoned their blockhouses, dropped their weapons and fled in a panic for the safety of Melilla's walls, falling prey to more attacks along the way. Many of the troops never made it, including Silvestre. Abd el-Krim inflicted this loss with just 4,000 fighters.

According to Porch, "The Spanish officially put their losses at 13,192 killed, although many thought this a gross underestimate. Worse, 20,000 rifles, 400 machine guns, and 129 cannons had been swept up by the enemy. The Spanish had suffered the worst military disaster in the history of European colonialism, besting by several thousand deaths the Italian debacle at Adowa in Ethiopia in 1896."[7]

Abd el-Krim put the captured weapons to immediate use. Spanish outposts throughout the mountains came under attack. When relief columns were sent to rescue them, they were ambushed and slaughtered. When soldiers tried to escape, the rebels hacked them to death. When the soldiers tried to surrender, they suffered the same fate. By the end of August, more than 130 outposts had been overrun.

The humiliating defeat led to official investigations, revelations of corruption in the military that undermined its fighting ability, and recriminations on all sides. Spain then doubled down, increasing its troop strength in Morocco to 150,000 and attacking villages in an effort to deprive rebels of the wherewithal to continue the fight. Civilians suspected of siding with the rebels were summarily shot. However, the campaign seemed to have more impact on Spain's military and public opinion than on Morocco's tribes. Spanish military conscripts staged mutinies and civilians held anti-war protests.

In 1923, General Miguel Primo de Rivera y Orbaeja, a Spanish nobleman and captain general of Catalonia, stepped in, dissolving the national legislature, tossing out the constitution and setting up a military junta to run Spain as a dictatorship.

Meanwhile, the fighting in Morocco intensified. Casualties spiraled, Spanish troop morale plummeted and neither side could see a path to victory. Finally, in July 1924, Rivera decided to withdraw his forces from Chechaouen and concentrate on protecting Tetouan and the coastal enclaves. In November, the 40,000-man garrison began their march from Chechaouen to Tetouan 40 miles away. After four days of march, the troops were strung out on the road. That's when 7,000 rebels struck. The Spanish troops didn't panic this time, but the attacks splintered the column into smaller groups that were soon decimated. By the time Francisco Franco, commanding the rear guard, reached Tetouan after a month, up to 20,000 of the original 40,000 lay dead behind him.[8]

Abd el-Krim marketed himself to the world press as the leader of a proud people subjected to cruel abuse by colonial authorities and his rebellion as a war of liberation. His message resonated in many quarters where he was seen as a freedom fighter, not a terrorist. "Abd el-Krim fights for an ideal, to defend his native land," read a leaflet encouraging Spanish and French legionnaires to desert and join his cause.[9]

At this point, an over-confident Abd el-Krim made a fatal error. In April 1925, he attacked French military positions with 4,000 rebels in an effort to draw the southern tribes into an alliance against the colonial powers. However, Porch said, no tribal uprising in the south was likely because the French had a firm hand on the territory.

France had remained on the sidelines during the earlier rebellion against the Spanish. Now it entered the fray with a much better and stronger military than their Spanish allies. France had 64,000 troops, including the French Foreign Legion, in Morocco, supported by modern artillery and aircraft. According to Porch, the French believed that was sufficient to deal with rebels. Nevertheless, Abd el-Krim dealt some early blows to the defenses, overrunning two-thirds of France's 66 blockhouses by June 1925.[10]

Abd el-Krim then advanced to within 20 miles of Fez, the capital. Along the way, he scooped up French arms and ammunition to resupply his rebel army. The French discovered what the Spanish had already learned: isolated outposts could not hold out or be reinforced; artillery was ineffective against enemy fighters spread out in gullies and behind boulders, and aerial bombing added little unless coordinated with ground assaults. The commander of French forces called for reinforcements. The rebels appeared to be on the cusp of victory. But the French position was not as dire as it appeared. The advance on Fez turned out to be Abd el-Krim's high-water mark. He had won several major battlefield victories and gained widespread attention for his independence movement but he had not achieved any strategic benefit.

* * *

It was at this point in the Rif War that Sweeny swaggered onto the world stage once again. He proposed to the French prime minister, Paul Painleve, to raise a squadron of American pilots to support France's war effort in Morocco. Because of the demands created by its mandates over Syria and Lebanon and the occupation of the Rhineland following World War I, France's military was stretched thin. So Sweeny's offer was seen as a godsend. In addition, French officials saw in Sweeny's offer a public relations ploy to change public opinion in the United States about the war. As a result, Painleve "warmly welcomed Colonel Sweeny's request," according to records in the French Army Historical Center at Vincennes.[11]

Abd el-Krim's fight resonated with Americans, who, after all, had once been a colony and fought their own war for independence. His propaganda campaign had generated editorials in U.S. newspapers against the war and against Americans siding with Spain and France.[12] Stories of heroic Americans in action might change public opinion.

However, before the French could accept Sweeny's offer, there was a familiar obstacle to be overcome, namely U.S. neutrality laws and the opposition of the U.S. Department of State. As in the World War, the solution was quickly found and it was dealt with in much the same way as before. Sweeny and his pilots would not be members of the French military. Instead, they would be employed by the sultan (or cherif) of Morocco. This, of course, was a transparent ruse, as everyone knew the sultan was merely a puppet of the French colonial regime. Painleve asserted that the American volunteers would be fighting "to defend the cause of the peaceful Moroccan population."[13]

In June 1925, Sweeny sent a telegram to a number of American veterans of the World War. The telegram received by Paul Ayres Rockwell, who had served with Sweeny in the French Foreign Legion, read: "Propose reforming Lafayette Escadrille, service Morocco. Have half dozen old members already lined up, would like you to join."[14] Rockwell was quick to accept, as were many others approached by Sweeny.

By July, Sweeny had assembled 17 volunteers, including 12 pilots, and they made their way to Morocco. Eventually, 16 pilots served with the squadron. (There are several lists that name the pilots, but no two lists are identical.) They included the following from the Lafayette Escadrille and French Flying Corps: Major Paul F. Baer (nine aerial victories in the World War), Captain Thomas Buffum, Major Charles Craig (14 victories), Colonel Charles W. Kerwood (12 victories), Major Austin Gillette Parker, Major Granville A. Pollack and Captain William B. Rogers (eight victories). Other pilots in the squadron had flown with the U.S. Army Air Service.

In addition to Rockwell, the non-pilots included Sweeny and James V. Sparks, an Indiana-born dentist who had served as an ambulance driver in the World War and later set up a dental practice in Paris where Sweeny was one his patients. Sweeny recruited Sparks to serve as the squadron's medical officer. According to Sparks, both he and Sweeny learned to fly while serving with the squadron and they each flew as pilots on many sorties. Sweeny also participated in many missions as an observer.[15]

The U.S. Department of State issued instructions to its consul in Morocco to advise the Americans that they risked losing their U.S. citizenship and being imprisoned and fined if they continued to do battle against a people with whom the United States had no quarrel. The consul in Tangier, Maxwell Blake, passed this advice along to the volunteers.

The *New York Times* reported from Washington, D.C., on September 19, 1925, that the State Department was threatening to prosecute the American pilots if they didn't immediately end their involvement. The State Department cited section 5282 of the Revised Statutes of the United States as follows: "Any

American pilots at Paris' Le Bourget Airport about to leave for the Rif War in Morocco, 1925. From left, Granville Pollock, R.H. Weller, Austin Parker, W. Graham Bullen, Charles Sweeny, Charles Kerwood, and Lansing Holden (courtesy Bibliotheque nationale de France).

person subject to jurisdiction of the United States who enters into enlistment in service of any foreign prince, state, colony, district or people, as a soldier ... shall be deemed guilty of a high misdemeanor and shall be fined not more than $1,000 and imprisoned for not more than three years." In referring to its instructions to the U.S. consul in Morocco, the State Department cited section 4000 to the effect that this U.S. official may issue writs to prevent U.S. citizens from entering into military or naval service of other countries to make war upon any foreign power with which the United States is at peace, or against a portion of the same people of that foreign power. The *Times* said the State Department's action was prompted by embarrassment over the impression that the United States was supporting a colonial power against the people of that colony, which was having a negative impact on both domestic politics and international relations.[16]

An Associated Press dispatch from Morocco on September 22, 1925, reported that the State Department's ruling that they were violating U.S. neutrality laws did not worry the American volunteers. "The aviators declare that they feel fully justified in serving under the Sultan of Morocco," the AP reported. It quoted the pilots as saying that they had taken no oath of allegiance, signed no enlistment papers and can leave whenever they wish. The article added that the squadron had done it's "hardest day's work" that day, having dropped three-tons of bombs on "Moorish concentrations" in morning and afternoon flights.[17] In any event, according to Rockwell, Secretary of State Frank Kellogg was forced to retract the threat after consulting with Attorney General John Sargent, and no action was ever taken against the volunteers.

The *New York Times* reported on September 26, 1925, that the "State Department said it had gone as far as it could when it had called the situation to the attention of America's representative in Morocco." The department declined to say whether it would intercede on behalf of any of the volunteers if they were ever captured by the Riffians.[18]

Overall, the men were inspired to volunteer by a yearning for adventure and a desire to recreate their earlier camaraderie, not by any sense of racial superiority.[19] Sweeny was not a racist, but he did have a low opinion of Moroccans in general and Abd el-Krim in particular. He did not believe they were capable of self-government. "This man is no Ataturk, no genuine progressive," he told friends, according to biographer McCormick. "He is a reactionary, committed to putting the clock back a hundred years in Morocco."[20]

Sweeny offered a fuller explanation for siding with the colonizers in this fight in an article he wrote for the *New York World*, published shortly before leaving for Morocco. "We are going to Morocco believing we can sustain the civilizing work the French have done under the Protectorate." He added that the sultan has accepted the squadron "in the same spirit he has accepted the Protectorate, which has changed Morocco from a backward country, full of warring tribes, to a flourishing, sane, cultivated country." He concluded, "In our view, France, in fighting Abd el-Krim, is fighting the cause of the white man's civilization, and all who have formed this squadron know enough of the world to appreciate what the white man's civilization means."[21]

Sweeny's phrase "white man's civilization" tended to remind people of the phrase "white man's burden," the title of an 1899 Rudyard Kipling poem justifying imperialism. The phrase had acquired a bad odor during the Boer War in South Africa (1899–1902) and the Philippine Insurrection (1899–1902). Sweeny was criticized in some American newspapers. He refused to recant, saying other nations should be backing France in Morocco. Later, according to McCormick, Sweeny offered a more caustic comment in a Paris bar:

> "It's no use winning a major war and then turning your back on every little war just because it doesn't directly concern you. This is yellow-bellied isolationism spouted by crocodile-tear shredding, middle-aged senators who have grown fat and maudlin out of war profits and now want to turn their backs on the world and doze away the rest of their lives."[22]

Despite technically being mercenaries, the volunteers certainly were not motivated by money. The pay was the equivalent of about 40 American dollars a month and they had to pay for their own meals. There were no formal enlistments, no oaths of allegiance and, when it was all over, there was no formal discharge.

The initial name of the squadron, the Lafayette Escadrille, was dropped even before the volunteers left Paris for Morocco. The reason, according to Rockwell, was that none of the pilots in the new unit had flown with the famed World War squadron, despite stories then and now to the contrary.[23] The name Escadrille Americaine also was nixed to avoid further riling the U.S. government. In the end, the squadron was named the Escadrille Cherifienne, the 19th Squadron of the Moroccan Aviation Regiment. The French provided the ground crews.

There were calls from some Americans to block the squadron's departure for Morocco but nothing came of it and Sweeny and his volunteers were soon on their way.

While the military mission of the squadron was important, the "psychological effect and media impact" was of equal or greater importance to the French government, according to an article by historian El-Mostafa Azzou of Morocco's University of Oujda. A telegram from the French minister of war to the resident general in Morocco, Marshal Hubert Lyautey, underscored this point: "This American expression of solidarity seems particularly interesting at the moment and capable of bringing a share of American propaganda to our cause, strengthening American sentiment against the aggression of Abd el-Krim."

Thus, the journey of the squadron from Le Bourget Airport in Paris to Morocco became a carefully choreographed publicity campaign that would have done a Hollywood agent proud. The squadron was accompanied by journalists hand-picked to deliver positive stories. In a report to the French General Staff, Lyautey wrote that "this trip has especially designed propaganda," with "holidays organized at points," involving local personalities, at each of three planned stops as the squadron flew south through Spain. The stops were in Barcelona, Alicante and Malaga before arriving in North Africa at Rabat. Azzou wrote that "reporters, photographers and America cinematographers were as numerous as the French," when the squadron departed. The campaign generated support in France and Spain, as well as in the United States, with public opinion polls showing a marked rise in support for the cause among the American public.

The propaganda campaign was a rousing success, and Azzou credits Sweeny with not only coming up with the idea but of playing a major role in devising the strategy.[24]

The squadron's arrival in Morocco coincided with dramatic strategic changes. France and Spain agreed to joint operations against Abd el-Krim, and Paris dispatched Marshal Philippe Petain, the hero of Verdun, to Morocco to take charge. Petain was determined to mount an aggressive campaign to bring the war to a close. He intended aerial bombardment to be a key component in his planned advance.

The squadron was assigned ten French Breguet biplanes to conduct their observation and bombing missions, although some reports say there were only seven. They usually flew at low attitudes at relatively slow speeds. The Riffians had no aircraft or anti-aircraft artillery, but they did have rifles and they used them to considerable effect. In a letter to his sister, Gertrude Finucane, Sweeny wrote: "The Riffs are excellent infantrymen and first-class shots. You may judge when I tell you that they have already shot out of airplanes from 500 to 1,000 feet up and going from 80 to 100 miles per hour over 20 French aviators."[25] There were other hazards as well. The terrain was mountainous, their maps were often of little help and exhaustion soon became an issue as the pilots sometimes flew five sorties a day.

According to one official French report, the squadron flew 350 combat missions in a six-week period and dropped 40 tons of explosives. While the majority of the squadron's missions involved bombing rebel fighters in the open countryside, some attacks were carried out against villages and towns, with significant numbers of civilian casualties.[26]

In September, a flotilla of 63 ships landed a Spanish invasion force along on the Mediterranean coast and they stormed inland seizing rebel positions. Supported by artillery, aircraft and poison gas, the troops swiftly drove toward Abd el-Krim's capital. That same month, Petain launched his offensive in the south, aided by 100,000 fresh troops. The advance soon recovered all of the territory the French had lost to the rebels since April. A combined total of 360,000 French and Spanish troops were now closing the ring on the leader of the rebellion.

While public opinion about the squadron's role had been mixed, it turned increasingly negative after the bombing of Chefchaaouen, a city of 7,000. It had not been bombed before because it was the holy city of the Djebala tribe. On September 17, 1925, the city bombed for precisely that reason, to drive the Djebala out of the war, Rockwell later wrote. "The city looked lovely from the air, hugging its high mountain and surrounded with many gardens and green cultivations.... I looked down upon the numerous sanctuaries, the six mosques, the medieval dungeon, the big square with its fountain playing and fervently hoped none of them had been damaged. I regretted having to attack a town that always had maintained its independence except for a few years of Spanish occupation."[27]

In his article analyzing the Rif War, Dean wrote that American newspapers savaged the volunteers. *The Literary Digest*, an influential weekly magazine, headlined the news "U.S. bombs and Rif babies." The *Pittsburgh Post* said it would be chivalrous to fight beside these people seeking freedom, "but

General Henri Gouraud, military commander of Paris, commends six members of the flying squadron that Charles Sweeny commanded in Morocco's Rif War at a ceremony January 22, 1926, in the courtyard of the Hotel of the Invalides. Front row, left to right: Granville Pollock, James Sussan and Shuyler Cousins. Back row, left to right, Charles Sweeny, Charles Kerwood and Dr. James Sparks.

it is nothing gallant or chivalrous in the rain of bombs, dropped on defenseless villages." The *Christian Century*, the leading mainline Protestant magazine, roared: "These American soldiers of fortune have no other pretexts than the exaltation of the manhunt. This is a royal sport and the fact that these women and children who have had the misfortune to be born in the Rif villages as victims has no more meaning for them than the death of a rabbit during a hunt."[28]

As public opinion turned sharply against the air campaign, diplomatic pressure from the United States led the French government to disband the squadron in November 1925. Sweeny and his men had flown 470 missions and logged 653 hours in the air since their arrival.[29] There is no record of any loss of life among the squadron members.

While they were loathed by many Americans, they were lauded by the French military. In his order disbanding the squadron, Marshal Petain praised Sweeny for having "brilliantly commanded" the unit and all of volunteers for devoting themselves to the French cause. On Petain's recommendation,

Charles Sweeny at a French military ceremony with his son, Charles (courtesy Frank Goodbold).

Sweeny's Legion of Honor was raised to the rank of Grand Officer, the second highest.[30]

Winter gave Abd el-Krim a respite but the end was in sight. He still had 12,000 men but Spain and France now had half a million troops in the field. Meanwhile, a poor harvest and a typhus epidemic had weakened the rebels' ability to fight and they could not get fresh supplies of rifles through Tangier. Eight rebels now had to share each rifle.[31]

When spring arrived, the offensives against the rebels resumed. Facing likely execution if captured by the Spanish, Abd el-Krim bargained with the French and struck a deal. On May 27, 1926, he arrived at a French camp to surrender, along with his family, a line of mules loaded with possessions, and reportedly a quarter million dollars. The Spanish demanded he be turned over to them for a war crimes trial, but the French sent him into exile on the island of Reunion, off the southeast coast of Africa. In 1947, he slipped away from French custody and obtained asylum in Cairo, Egypt, where he died in 1963.

Sweeny returned to France. In February 1926, he was asked to present himself in his Escadrille Cherifienne uniform to receive, with appropriate military pomp, the wings he earned in Morocco. A news account of this event said Sweeny now had been decorated 19 times.[32] Among his decorations were two medals he had received from the sultan of Morocco: the Croix de Guerre of Morocco with two citations (meaning two awards) and the Commandeur d'Ouissam Allouite (Commander of the Order of Ouissam Allouite, an award similar to the Legion of Merit awarded by the U.S. military).

According to a story his son told McCormick, the sultan also gave Sweeny the title of pasha and he may have offered him a harem. Sweeny's son said he tried to learn the truth about that tale from his father, but Sweeny "just laughed and said nothing."[33] While this story of a harem sounds like a tall tale, it may actually be true. Dr. James Sparks, who flew with Sweeny in the Rif War squadron, told an interviewer in 1948 that, in addition to awarding him medals for his service, the sultan offered him 1,000 acres of land and 16 wives, "a deal that the young, handsome doctor tactfully refused."[34]

When a newspaper reporter covering the ceremony asked Sweeny what he planned to do next, he replied, "Well, one of the things that interest me most just now is north polar exploration. I have been across the equator on several occasions, but I have never been across the artic circle. It would be a new experience." He added that he was considering accepting an invitation to join a French "transpolar" mission, "which proposes to cross the Polar basin from Spitsbergen [Norway] to Alaska on motor sledges." The reporter included his own reply in the article: "It sounds risky."[35] There is no mention of Sweeny's reaction, but it is likely he cracked a smile at that response.

Sweeny's decision to support a colonial power in the Rif War was a departure from past behavior and would not be repeated. It was all the more strange a departure given that he was born in America, a nation founded on the principle of self-determination; he was born to the children of immigrants from Ireland, a country oppressed for centuries under foreign rule; and he was a true believer in the cause of liberty, justice and fair play.

Sweeny said on more than one occasion after the Rif War that he was motivated by a conviction that Britain and France represented the best of civilization and preserving their influence was in the long-term interest of mankind. He pointedly did not include Spain in that assessment. Alternatively, he may have simply sided with his adopted country, France, without regard to principle in this instance.

Chapter 13

Spanish Civil War

After the Rif War, Sweeny returned to Paris. While he spent some time with Eva and their three children, he also disappeared for long periods. He traveled extensively across North Africa and the Middle East. Some of his travel was on behalf of the French intelligence services and the French military but some was simply sightseeing.

A photo of Sweeny has an intriguing inscription on the back: "Charles Sweeny, Colonel, Air Force, Syria 1926." It is further inscribed: "To Helen, affectionately, Charles Sweeny, January 1949." The photo was among those in Sweeny's files when he died and retained by his grandson, Frank Goodbold. That suggests it was never sent. Helen may have been a friend of Sweeny's in Salt Lake City, where he was living in 1949.[1] The portrait shot is certainly one of the more attractive photos of Sweeny. France was heavily involved in Syria, but what was Sweeny doing there in 1926?

Following World War I and a brief period of independence, Syria was made a French protectorate by the League of Nations.[2] King Faisal[3] resisted French control of Syria but his forces were defeated in battle in 1920 and he was expelled. However, the French authorities antagonized the tribal leaders by creating their own governing institutions instead of working through the local elites. This led to a second revolt, in which rival religious and ethnic factions combined against French rule in Syria and Lebanon, in 1925. The French had fewer than 15,000 troops in Syria at the time and the rebels, led by Sultan Shaykh Hilal al-Atrash,[4] won several battles. These initial results led the French authorities to withdraw temporarily to regroup and build up their manpower. This move emboldened more indigenous factions and created a broader conflict. Following the winter of 1925-26, the French dispatched thousands of troops from Morocco and Senegal to Syria and recaptured the nation's cities. Eventually, the French had 50,000 troops in Syria, a number roughly equal to the entire Druze population. The revolt was finally put down in 1927 with an estimated 6,000 rebels dead and 100,000 Syrians homeless. French casualties were about 2,000.

The photo of Sweeny in pilot's gear suggests he was once again engaged in the air on behalf of the French. However, there is nothing in his French military record about Syria. It is unclear whether the rank of "colonel" refers to his former U.S. Army rank of lieutenant colonel or a newly minted French rank.

The French air force had a large and active operation in Syria during the rebellion there. Coming at the same time as the Rif War in Morocco, the French air force was stretched thin for personnel, so Sweeny's help would have been welcomed. Aerial resupply drops were crucial to sustaining the 700-man French garrison besieged by rebels at Suwayda for 65 days until a relief column arrived in September 1925. French aircraft also were used extensively for reconnaissance and communication. Planes dropped messages from the high command to ground forces to direct their movements. According to historian David E. Omissi, the French made heavy use of aircraft to bomb villages in rebel territory and an aerial bombardment broke up a rebel attack aimed at Damascus. Omissi said the bombing of villages in the Haraun area so intimidated the populace that it "thwarted the efforts of Druze activists to inspire a general uprising." The bombings were carried out without warning to the villagers with the intent of increasing the intimidation factor. These terror tactics provoked an international outcry, and some French officials privately expressed concerns about such measures.[5]

Charles Sweeny, Syria, 1926 (courtesy Frank Goodbold).

In 1928-29, Sweeny accompanied French General Paul-Francois-Maurice Armengaud on a mission for the French government. According to Alfred Wintle,[6] an eccentric British army officer who knew Sweeny well between the world wars, the mission was to assess how North Africa could be prepared as a base of operations in the event of another major European war. Wintle said Sweeny and Armengaud visited Morocco, Algeria and Tunisia, and made several proposals, including fortifying the Tunisia border with Libya to deter encroachment by Mussolini. However, no action was taken on this recommendation.[7]

Sweeny also spent time during the 1920s and 1930s working as a journalist, which accounts for some of his travels. This included a short stint managing the Paris office of the *New York World*, during which he provided some work for Hemingway.

The Spanish Civil War began in July 1936 when the Nationalists—generals, conservatives, monarchists and fascists—sought to oust the democratically elected leftist government of the Second Spanish Republic. The revolt had its roots in the Republicans' repression of the aristocracy, army and Catholic Church after centuries of their tyranny. The liberal Popular Front won the election in February and by mid-June extreme elements of the leftist alliance had created chaos, with 160 churches burned, 269 political murders, ten newspapers wrecked and 113 general strikes. Armed peasants had seized estates and divided up the land, and gun fights had erupted between two large trade unions.[8]

The Spanish Civil War became an international proxy war between fascism and communism, and a proving ground for advanced weaponry. Nazi Germany sent munitions, planes and military personnel to the Nationalists while the Republicans, also known as Loyalists, received some support from the Soviet Union. Britain, France and the United States adopted a non-interventionist position, although volunteers from all three countries joined the fight, mostly on the Republican side. The Nationalists, led by General Francisco Franco, finally prevailed in March 1939. The war became infamous for the atrocities committed by both sides. According to historian Antony Beevor, the Loyalists executed at least 38,000 alleged Nationalist sympathizers, including many members of the clergy, while the Nationalists executed up to 150,000 suspected Loyalist supporters, including many schoolteachers and trade unionists. About one-third of the Loyalists who died were killed after the war. Murder, rape and looting were also common. Aerial bombing of villages in earlier conflicts, such as the Rif War and Syria, escalated to the bombing of cities.[9]

The civil war not only deeply divided the Spanish people, but also people in nations around the globe. While communism and fascism each had its committed followers, both ideologies were abhorrent to many people. This made the choice of which side to support in the civil war—and what to think of those people who supported the other side—a highly emotional decision, sometimes with serious, long-term consequences.

Sweeny hated Bolshevism and had even fought against it in Poland. But he saw fascist Germany as a much more immediate threat to Western civilization and world peace, especially to the security of his adopted homeland, France. If the Nationalists prevailed in the civil war, France would be nearly surrounded by fascist regimes in Germany, Italy and Spain. Sweeny saw the Spanish Civil War as the best hope of heading off a new general European war. If the Nazis could be stopped in Spain, then France might be spared. As in the Rif War, Sweeny saw France and Britain as the promoters and protectors of the values he cherished. And so, despite having no affection for the leftist elected government of Spain, he found himself on the side of the Loyalists.

His decision to support the Republican cause not only led some to suggest that Sweeny had become a communist but also a traitor to his church. As we have seen, the Catholic Church in Spain was one of the prime targets of extreme elements of the democratically elected leftist regime, so supporting the Loyalists was seen as a mortal sin in some circles. Sweeny was raised in the Catholic faith, had attended Catholic schools and regularly attended Catholic services. Consequently, it was not an easy decision for him to make. As usual, however, Sweeny refused to be deterred by criticism from doing what he believed was right. As he told Hemingway, "God changes like the rest of us. The only thing about God is that he changes his mind long before we change ours. If Jesus Christ could see the German menace in our midst, he would lose no time in telling us that for once we could support the devils against the supposed angels. He would just clip the angels' wings and send them back to school again."[10]

Both Hemingway and Sweeny spent a good deal of time in Spain during the civil war. Hemingway was there as a journalist, but he also was collecting material for future novels. During the war, Hemingway helped raise money to supply ambulances and drivers for the Loyalists and helped organize committees to aid the cause. This led to the FBI keeping tabs on Hemingway for decades as a possible communist.[11]

One of the legends about Sweeny was an incident that involved his support for the Republican cause. In his biography of Sweeny, McCormick states that a party had been called in a cellar in the Montmartre district of Paris by young French students and Basque exiles. Everyone who arrived at the party was supposed to give a donation to the Republican cause. Sweeny had been drinking at the Crillon Bar on the Plaza de Concorde and was told by a journalist friend about the party. Sweeny challenged all of his drinking buddies at the bar to a game of poker dice and quickly won 500 francs, pocketed the money and headed directly to the party in the cellar. He not only donated the 500 francs but all the money in his pocket. He then offered his services as a chauffeur to drive volunteer Republican combatants to the Spanish border at 4:00 a.m. He spent the rest of the following week driving volunteers from Paris to the Spanish border, a distance of nearly 500 miles.[12]

Sweeny and Armengaud arrived in Spain in the guise of journalists, but they were actually there to assess the situation for members of the French government. According to biographer McCormick, Sweeny went to Spain in the spring of 1937 to evaluate the military situation, determine what sort of aid the Loyalists needed to defeat the Nationalists, and make a report to the French politicians who sent him.[13]

Hemingway and journalists covering the war made the Hotel Florida in central Madrid their base of operations. While its location on the Plaza de Callao meant Nationalist artillery shells landed nearby, its 200 rooms each had a bathroom and, most prized of all, hot running water. The journalists tended to congregate in the hotel.[14] While the rooms at the front of the hotel were more attractive, Hemingway used his fame and relative wealth among the correspondents to secure one of the lesser rooms at the rear of the hotel. The reason: the rear rooms were less likely to be hit by incoming artillery. According to Hemingway biographer Carlos Baker, the boulevard in front of the hotel was "so often strewn with glass" from the shelling "that Ernest came to think of it as one would think of a hailstorm that happened every day."[15]

Although supposedly in competition with each other for original reporting, the hordes of journalists living at the hotel "ate together at a communal table in the basement of a Gran Via restaurant, observed the same incidents together, repeated the same anecdotes together, kept track of the shelling together, checked over the rubble together, and they all studied one another like crows."[16] Sweeny was well known to many of the journalists as a soldier of fortune and a reporter, and counted some of them among his friends. He would have spent time in this milieu to make contacts, gather information and maintain his cover as a journalist. Some of the world's best-known journalists and authors were covering the war. In addition to Hemingway, they included John Dos Passos, Josephine Herbst, Martha Gellhorn (who was having an affair with Hemingway and would become his third wife), Herbert Matthews, Ladislas Farago, Floyd Gibbons, H.R. Knickerbocker, Robert Neville, and Alan Moorhead.

Sweeny later returned to Spain and served as a military advisor to the Loyalists. In a letter to Max Perkins in February 1940,[17] Hemingway described an incident he witnessed during the war when Sweeny weighed in as a military advisor. The incident involved the Battle of Teruel, a climatic struggle for a city in a river valley in the mountains of eastern Spain, 100 miles from the coast and about 125 miles east of Madrid. The city had no strategic value but once gains were announced by the Loyalists, both sides threw whatever they could into the fight so as not to lose face in the propaganda war.

The battle lasted from December 1937 to February 1938. Teruel was defended by only 6,000 Nationalist troops. Against this, the Loyalists mustered 100,000 men. The Loyalists began by attacking Muela de Teruel Hill, a heavily fortified position with concrete machine gun emplacements and tank traps. It was considered "impregnable," but four companies of Loyalists seized it in a mighty rush.[18] After encircling the city, the Loyalist forces captured the city on January 8 after a three-week siege.

General Francisco Franco, who had risen to prominence in the Rif War a decade before, was in overall command of Nationalist forces in the war. He tried to reinforce the Nationalist forces in the city but it fell before relief could arrive. This was due to the rugged, remote location and harsh winter conditions. The winter of 1937-38 was the coldest in Spain in 20 years. A blizzard dumped four feet of snow on the ground and sub-zero temperatures produced as many casualties on both sides from frostbite as from enemy action. Hemingway described the challenge of trying to hold binoculars steady with 50 mph winds battering him.

Over the objections of the German and Italian advisors plus his own staff, Franco then delayed a major offensive aimed at Madrid to focus on Teruel. It was necessary, he told them, to preserve the notion that the Nationalists could not be defeated even if they were not always victorious.[19] Nationalist forces, supported by German and Italian warplanes, launched their attack on January 17. A large-scale cavalry charge by the Nationalists on February 7 broke the Loyalists' position north of the city and the Nationalists gained final victory on February 22. The heavy losses in men and equipment drained the resources of the Loyalists, enabling the Nationalists to achieve major gains in eastern Spain in the succeeding months.[20]

In his February 1940 letter to Perkins, Hemingway said of Sweeny, "He made plans for the Teruel offensive. Rather he corrected them and showed everything that was wrong with the Russian staff work and every goddamned thing came out exactly as he said it would including how we lost the town and why because of not doing one thing, which should have been done when it was taken."[21]

In *One Man's Wars*, McCormick described another incident where Sweeny acted as a military advisor to the Loyalists. It involved a column of Nationalist troops having to cross a bridge in a narrow valley. Sweeny positioned the Loyalist artillery on ridges on either side of the valley with instructions to hold their fire until the enemy was across the bridge. The artillery was then to destroy the bridge, closing the trap before annihilating the enemy. However, the Russian gunners opened fire before the Nationalists crossed the bridge. Sweeny saw this fight as the Loyalists' last best hope of winning the war. Frustrated, he soon left for Paris, but he remained firmly committed to the defeat of fascism as the prime threat to democracy and the likely cause of another great war.[22]

This incident also may have been Teruel. In *Hell and Good Company*, historian Richard Rhodes described a two-day battle by the Nationalists at a bridge crossing of the Alfambra River, north of Teruel. Once the Nationalists succeeded in crossing the river, they were able to encircle Teruel and finally retake it. Rhodes said the Loyalists lost 15,000 dead and wounded and 7,000 prisoners were taken in this action alone.[23]

In a conversation with Col. Wintle, Sweeny blamed internal squabbling among the Loyalists for the defeat of their cause. He said, "the Spanish Government officials and the Russians spent far too much time quarreling and too little time tackling the enemy."[24]

Public opinion in England, France and the United States was sharply divided over which side in the Spanish Civil War represented the greater danger if they prevailed. Those who favored the Loyalist cause saw the conflict as the defense of a democratically elected government and the final opportunity to stop the rise of fascism, which they believed, correctly as it turned out, would lead to another general European war. Those who sided with the Nationalists saw the war as the defense of property, stability and traditional institutions against an onslaught by socialists, communists and anarchists, which would lead to the end of civilized society.

Sweeny's involvement with the Loyalist cause was sufficient to earn him the unyielding enmity of Franco and the Republicans. He was barred by the Franco regime from ever returning to Spain.[25] His involvement on the Loyalist side also led some in the governments of the United States, and even France, to refer to Sweeny as "the red colonel," implying he had become a convert to the communist ideology. However, nothing in Sweeny's conduct or correspondence supports such a conclusion. As Sweeny explained in a letter to an old friend in Paris, Rene Barsini:

> "Washington has its Pharisees who turn a blind eye to the suffering of Spain, but keep a keen eye on an old reprobate like myself who, they think, is the Devil's advocate in this Civil War, hand in glove with the Ruskies and breathing fire against Wall Street. It is so very far from the truth, yet I still wouldn't yield to anyone in my determination to see this Spanish thing to the right conclusion—never mind a damn who runs Spain, but, more to the point, to see that the Germans and Italians get kicked firmly out."[26]

In a February 1940 letter to Perkins, Hemingway offered a few additional thoughts about Sweeny's actions during the Spanish Civil War: "Charley got into the Spanish war late.... Then the minute he got into it he acted as though all the rest of us were simply criminal lunatics and the minute the war started was when he entered. And the war stopped when he left. He's wonderful. But I would rather listen to him on military things than anybody I have ever known."[27]

While Sweeny's involvement in the Spanish Civil War did nothing to diminish his friendship with Hemingway, it impacted his standing with U.S. officials who were already upset with him over his actions in the Rif War. That impact would be felt soon enough.

Chapter 14

Dodging the FBI to Recruit Pilots for France

By the time the Spanish Civil War ended in March 1939, Europe was sliding inexorably toward another general war, although many politicians and citizens of democracies on both sides of the Atlantic Ocean tried not to notice. One man who refused to ignore the threat was Sweeny. He earned a reputation around Paris as a Cassandra[1] for his belligerent predictions of imminent war.[2] This included many loud toasts in the Crillon Bar denouncing Hitler and any Nazi sympathizers in France. Some people soon tired of his harangues and even friends began to avoid him.[3]

As a keen observer of European politics[4] as well as a voracious reader of world history, Sweeny, like Winston Churchill, was very clear eyed about where fascism in general and Hitler's Germany in particular, were headed. He had closely followed the career of General Hans von Seeckt, the architect of Germany's resurgence as a military power between the world wars. It was Seeckt who "wheedled [British prime minister David] Lloyd George into … a 150 percent reinforcement of the Reichswehr [German army] in 1920," wrote Sweeny. It was Seeckt who, in the 1920s, saw Hitler as a man he believed could lead Germany back to greatness and still be controlled by the German General Staff. And it was Seeckt who mapped out the steps to conquest that Hitler would methodically follow in the 1930s.[5]

In many respects, the march toward a Second World War had begun with the harsh terms the Allies imposed on Germany at the end of the First World War. Hitler came to power in Germany in 1933 as part of a backlash against the hard economic times that stemmed from those terms. In 1935, Benito Mussolini, the fascist dictator of Italy, invaded Ethiopia to make a colony of the ancient kingdom. When the democracies failed to stop this aggression, Hitler saw an opening to put Seeckt's plan into action. In 1936, Germany violated the terms of the Versailles treaty by remilitarizing the Rhineland. Again the democracies failed to act. Germany then formed an alliance with Japan to oppose possible aggression by the Soviet Union. The following year, Japan began its invasion of China. In 1938, Germany annexed Austria and then struck a deal at Munich to seize Czechoslovakia while promising Britain and France an end to its territorial claims and "peace in our time." When Hitler then laid claim to the Polish city of Danzig in 1939, Britain and France belatedly tried to deter Germany by promising to come to the aid of Poland if it was attacked. In August 1939, having gotten away with all of his previous land grabs without a muscular response from the democracies, Hitler set the stage for what he thought would be the unchallenged conquest of Poland by signing a mutual nonaggression pact with the Soviet Union. The two dictatorships agreed to divide Poland between them. The following month, Germany invaded Poland. To Hitler's surprise, Britain and France reluctantly declared war. However, once Germany had devoured Poland, a period now known as the "Phoney War"[6] set in until the spring of 1940. Although technically at war, none of the warring European nations launched any major land offensives for the first eight months after declaring war.

While the world waited to see what would happen next, Sweeny did more than just talk. He began to act. His first move was to contact his West Point classmate, Henry J. Reilly, who was now a brigadier general in the Officers Reserve Corps and a journalist. Since covering the Polish-Soviet War of 1920 as a war correspondent, Reilly had served as editor of *The Army and Navy Journal* from 1921 to 1925, become the founding president of the Reserve Officers Association in 1922 and written a number of books about war. Sweeny proposed that, in the event of war, they raise and lead an infantry division of American volunteers to fight for France. Reilly, who had been watching developments in Europe with the same deepening sense of despair as Sweeny, readily agreed. On August 25, 1939, they announced their plans in Paris. Exactly one week later, September 1, 1939, hostilities began with Germany's blitzkrieg of Poland.

According to the *New York Times*, planning for the American volunteer venture began nearly a year earlier, at the time of the Czecho-Slovak crisis in September 1938. In the intervening months, Sweeny and Reilly worked quietly with members of the American Legion, Veterans of Foreign Wars and former members of the French Foreign Legion and Lafayette Escadrille to plan the organizing, recruiting and financing of their volunteer division. In addition, they anticipated creating an aviation brigade to be named for Norman Prince, who is credited with selling the concept for the original Lafayette Escadrille to the French and who died in a crash landing in 1916.[7]

Sweeny told the *Times*: "It has seemed to us that apart from what the United States Government may or may not do provision should be made so those young Americans who feel deeply that the cause of freedom is at stake will have an opportunity to enlist in its defense. We thought also that the response which we are certain of getting may make those in Germany, who by their pressure on Poland are endangering the peace of the world, reflect before they commit an irreparable act. What we did in 1914 has never been disapproved and we see no reason why we should not do it again."

While always an idealist, Sweeny was realistic about the likely impact of what he was doing. He saw the announcement as more of a morale boost to stiffen the spines of the French and British to oppose Hitler than a serious deterrent to German aggression.

In an effort to avoid a clash with the U.S. government over the neutrality laws as in the Rif War, Sweeny announced that they planned to only enlist Americans who came to Canada to join up. In addition, enlistments would not begin until war was declared. The plan envisioned the cooperation of the French consular service.

Judging by newspaper reports of the period, the reaction to the idea was swift. On September 6, 1939, an Associated Press story from Paris quoted the American Legion as saying that 300 Americans had already volunteered. The same article quoted Sweeny as saying, "2000 other men" had contacted him about serving, while "a prominent American congressman" had sent him a telegram offering to "furnish you 1000 American volunteers and [a] company [of] 250 men from Texas." Sweeny added that his division would become a unit in the French Foreign Legion.[8]

In his biography of Sweeny, McCormick recounted a story about how two FBI agents soon turned up in Paris asking questions, and Sweeny "frog-marched" one of them out of the Crillon Bar. When Sweeny returned to the bar, he commented that he had been "removing a dirty rotten little spy who is doing Hitler's work for him without realizing it."[9] If this story is true, and J. Edgar Hoover learned of it, it might explain why the FBI director gave Sweeny's later recruiting activities so much personal attention. Hoover was obsessive about protecting the FBI's carefully cultivated tough-guy image, and such an incident could have given that public face a black eye.

A number of newspaper articles during this period said that if the volunteer division was activated, Sweeny would be made a major general in command of the unit. However, French government support for the plan went from lukewarm to cold and Sweeny's appointment never materialized.

The *New York Times* reported from Paris on September 15, 1939, that "the question of raising an American division under the leadership of Colonel Charles Sweeny is held in abeyance as it does not seem feasible to form such a division now. Many applications have been received but the French would have to treat these enlistments as made in the regular Foreign Legion with no guarantee of keeping the Americans together."[10]

Sweeny sent a memo to French president Edouard Daladier outlining actions that needed to be taken to defend the nation and he followed up with a face-to-face meeting. In his memo, Sweeny asserted that France's plan to sit behind fortifications on its border with Germany to await attack was folly. "By sitting tight behind the Maginot defense France runs the psychological risk of making herself incapable of attack and therefore encouraging the enemy to take the initiative," he wrote. Instead, he said France should launch columns of tanks into Germany while deterring Mussolini from joining Hitler by threatening to invade Italy. He argued that North Africa was the key to ultimate victory. It would enable the Allies to open fronts in Greece, the Balkans and the Middle East, confronting more fronts than their enemies could defend against. Swelling the ranks of the Foreign Legion with volunteers from America and elsewhere would help France achieve these aims.[11]

Sweeny was discouraged by the lack of support from Daladier but determined to push on. At the urging of his old friend and mentor, General Armengaud, Sweeny decided to focus his efforts on raising the aviation brigade that was part of his plan. It was hoped that a new Lafayette Escadrille, comprised of Americans, would, in the words of Armengaud, "shake France out of her lethargy."[12] Sweeny also was motivated to raise an aviation brigade by his knowledge of Seeckt's plans to combine German armor and air power in a future war and by Armengaud's personal observation of the effects of German blitzkrieg in Poland, which he imparted to Sweeny.

In December 1939, Sweeny sailed to Canada to begin recruiting American pilots to fight for France. His goal was 150 recruits.[13] He quickly encountered some challenges. One, of course, was the U.S. neutrality laws. Upon the outbreak of war in Europe, President Roosevelt had issued a proclamation on September 5, 1939, stating that it would be illegal for Americans to join the military of a warring nation or to hire someone to do that. Another challenge was hostility from isolationist portions of the U.S. press. "For months I was hounded like a criminal," he said, comparing himself to Baby-Face Nelson, a notorious bank-robber who was killed in a shootout with FBI agents in 1934. A more serious obstacle was what he called "the complete apathy of the American people."

Sweeny's first task was to organize a network of people into an "underground railroad" of sorts to help him find potential recruits, provide them with instructions and money, and assist them in getting out of the United States, into Canada, and on to Europe. Both the U.S. Federal Bureau of Investigation and Canadian authorities were watching Sweeny, so his movements and communications required stealth and deception. It was a classic game of cat and mouse, but the cats in this case were no match for the mouse's decades of experience as a soldier, journalist and spy.

Although Sweeny had said he would not enlist any American volunteers on American soil, he apparently did not intend that pledge to mean he and his helpers wouldn't meet with American pilots on American soil and encourage them to travel to Canada to enlist there. By January 3, 1940, he had slipped away from the government agents watching him, crossed the U.S.-Canadian border and quietly taken a room at the Hotel Carmel in the west Los Angeles suburb of Santa Monica, California, to begin recruiting. It was probably no accident that Sweeny chose the Hotel Carmel. The owner was the father of Paul E. Penrose, a well-known local flight instructor who later became a test pilot for North American Aviation. Santa Monica also put him near Mines Field (now Los Angeles International Airport) and Clover Field (now Santa Monica Municipal Airport), the home of the Douglas Aircraft Co., maker of the DC-3 civilian airliner that became the workhorse of the U.S. military as the C-47 military cargo and paratroop carrier.

Among the first potential recruits that Sweeny met with were student pilots Clyde Hamilton Hodges, 19, of Los Angeles and Kendall Winton Everson, 18, of Inglewood. According to Everson's unpublished autobiography,[14] his friend Hodges saw Sweeny's August 1939 announcement and wrote to him in Paris. Sweeny wrote back in October to say he would be in contact soon. In January 1940, Sweeny invited Hodges and any of his pilot-friends who were interested to a meeting at mid-day in "a dark, back corner in the bar" at the hotel, located a block off the beach at 201 Broadway. Hodges and Everson brought along two other student pilots, William Scott Raney, 21, and Walter Edwin Palmer, Jr., 20, both of Los Angeles. The foursome's flying experience ranged from 30 hours for Everson to several hundred hours for Palmer.[15]

Everson recalled that Sweeny "was dressed in a dark civilian business suit and we were all impressed by his demeanor and especially impressed by the small civilian replica of the Croix de Guerre, France's highest decoration, which he wore on his left coat lapel."[16] Sweeny told the young men he was recruiting pilots to form a new Lafayette Escadrille. He inquired about each man's flying experience but only glanced at their logbooks. "I don't think Sweeny even read the stuff; he seemed more interested in the fact that here were four young fliers willing to join up with his squadron." Sweeny told them they would receive training at a French air base in Morocco and then be sent to Finland to fly with the Finnish air force against the Russians, who had invaded Finland. After some combat experience, they would return to France to fly against the German Luftwaffe. Everson said the men were excited at the offer of flight training that they wouldn't have to pay for, and by the thought of flying planes "larger, faster and more powerful than a Piper Cub." All four were eager to sign up.[17]

Sweeny told the men they would leave for Detroit by train from Los Angeles' Union Station. They would be met in Detroit by one of Sweeny's men, who would get them across the border into Canada. They would then proceed to the Wellington Hotel in Toronto, where they could enlist and then take a ship to Le Havre, France. "Sweeny spoke in low tones so as not to be overheard by anyone passing or sitting nearby," said Everson. "He swore us to secrecy, admonishing us to speak to no one about this meeting or our plans." They knew what they were planning to do was illegal. "Mr. Sweeny was well aware of this, lending a decided 'cloak and dagger' air to everything he did and said, and by extension to everything we did after becoming associated with him. All this seemed to add to the excitement and appeal of the whole adventure."[18]

A couple of weeks later, the four men met again with Sweeny at the hotel. This time they received train tickets to Detroit, $20 to cover expenses and detailed instructions. They were told other recruits would board the train as it traveled through Southern California but they should avoid any contact with them for fear of disclosing their purpose. They were to board the train at 9 p.m. on Friday, February 23, 1940.[19]

The young men had agreed among themselves to mail letters from the train station telling their parents where they had gone. However, the day before they were to leave, Everson decided a letter wouldn't do so he told his father his plans. Instead of telling his son he couldn't go, Everson's father offered him an alternative. If the son would forgo Sweeny's offer, the father would help him join the Army Air Corps. Everson accepted the offer.[20]

Everson informed the other young men of his decision and agreed to drive them to the train station. After seeing them off, he put their letters in a mailbox on his way home. However, what none of them had figured on, he said, was how long it would take the train to reach Detroit. The letters were delivered on Monday while the train was crossing Kansas. Hodges' parents immediately called the FBI. The next day, a *Los Angeles Examiner* story, "Allies Lure L.A. Boys Into War Air Service," was front-page news across the nation. Palmer's parents called relatives in Illinois and "five of Walt's uncles met the train in Chicago and dissuaded him from going any further," said Everson. FBI agents met the train in Detroit and prevented Hodges and Raney from crossing into Canada. Hodges and Raney had no money for train fare so they found an auto dealer who needed two new cars delivered to California and agreed to drive them there plus money for expenses. All three of the men returned to Los Angeles.[21]

Everson's father kept his word and supported his son's attempt to become a U.S. military pilot. However, the recruiter said that even a parent's permission could not waive the requirement that pilot applicants be at least 20 years old. Everson would have to wait. He was devastated. He thought he had missed his big chance. However, he soon found a Civilian Pilot Training program at Los Angeles City College, enrolled and earned his private pilot's license.[22]

After America entered the war, Everson became a U.S. Marine Corps aviator. He flew Grumman TBF Avenger torpedo bombers with the VMTB-232 "Red Devils" in the South Pacific and was awarded the Distinguished Flying Cross with two stars and the Air Medal with two stars. After the war, he was active in military and commercial aviation. He retired after 29 years with United Airlines as a captain, and he retired from the Marine Corps Reserve as a colonel. He died in 2002.

While Everson lived a long life and realized his ambition, the lives of the other three young men were cut tragically short. All three died within 18 months of boarding the train, before America even entered the war. Hodges died, apparently in an accident of some sort, in Alpine, California, in the Sierra Nevada Mountains south of Lake Tahoe on July 14, 1940. Raney and Palmer died together in a plane crash on August 10, 1941. They had rented a new Interstate Cadet monoplane from Young Air Academy at Metropolitan Airport in Van Nuys at 4 p.m. Palmer, who had married only five days before, was giving Raney a final flying lesson before he took his private pilot's test. After gaining altitude and making figure eights and steep turns, the plane "slipped into a spin, witnesses told police, and instead of leveling off dived to the ground." It landed in a bean field at Woodley Avenue and Oxnard Street in Van Nuys. Both men were killed instantly. Airport mechanics had to cut the wreckage apart with acetylene torches to remove the bodies.[23]

The newspaper stories about the young pilots on the train identified Sweeny as their recruiter. An Associated Press story on February 28, 1940, quoted Palmer as saying that "at least 20 youths" had been recruited on the West Coast for war air service.[24] The same day, the *Los Angeles Examiner* reported that while Sweeny was in Santa Monica, he sent telegrams to persons in several cities in the United States and Canada. The article concluded that Sweeny was "only one of several individuals involved in the asserted foreign recruiting operations." It said one telegram on February 19 went to Dudley Hill in New York City. It read: "Wire if you have confirmed deposit of money. If deposited, proceed as outlined. First shipment leaves here Friday. Desirable you should be on ground prepared to receive it. Shipment about the size of yours, which I suppose is already sent. Keep me informed. Ted delighted." Another telegram the same day went to Sweeny's nephew, Robert Sweeny, in Palm Beach, Florida.[25] It said: "Time for action has arrived. Highly important I be advised use necessary funds with minimum delay. Inform me if I can count on this." A third telegram, sent February 22 to Kenneth Archibald in Montreal, Canada, mentioned money being deposited in Sweeny's name.[26]

The same *Examiner* article also reported that Sweeny's phone records showed he called the French consulate in Los Angeles and "talked in French to someone there." It quoted the French consul in Los Angeles, J.J. Viala, as saying he had heard of Sweeny but had never met or spoken with him.

The proprietor of the Hotel Carmel, Leo Penrose (Paul's father), told the *Examiner* that Sweeny had been a guest January 3–6 and again February 12–23, and that on February 22 Sweeny had made a large number of phone calls to numbers in Los Angeles. He recalled that large numbers of young men "flocked to the hotel" that night and the next morning, waving train tickets but refusing to say why they were there. When Sweeny first registered at the hotel, he gave the Royal Bank of Canada in Toronto as his address. When he returned, he listed the Stewart Hotel in San Francisco as his address. Letters for Sweeny that arrived after he left came from the Toronto bank and were forwarded to San Antonio, Texas, his next stop.

Clearly, Sweeny and his helpers had managed to start several "shipments" on their "underground railroad" as part of their recruiting operation. Sweeny later credited two men in Southern California with coming forward at the outset and saving the plan. One was Joseph Everett Weddle of Los Angeles. The other was Edwin T. "Ted" Parsons of Hollywood, a member of the original Lafayette Escadrille. (Parsons was undoubtedly the "Ted" that Sweeny referred to in the telegram to Dudley Hill in New York.)

A February 26, 1940, memo from the FBI's Los Angeles Office reported that two individuals (names redacted) "formerly employed at the Douglas Aircraft Company, Santa Monica ... were enroute from Los Angeles, California to Toronto, Canada for the purpose of enlisting as cadets in the French Aviation Service, and that a Colonel Sweeny connected with the French Government purchased their railroad tickets." The memo was based on information from U.S. marshal A.A. Sanders in Cheyenne, Wyoming, who had spoken to the two individuals when their train stopped there briefly.[27]

None of the four young men previously mentioned worked for Douglas Aircraft. Thus, this memo appears to refer to other recruits en route to Canada at about the same time. Among a group of recruits who had worked at Douglas Aircraft and entrained for Canada about that time was 19-year-old Chesley Gordon Peterson. Born in Idaho, he had been raised in Santaquin, Utah, and graduated from Payson High School. He dropped out of Brigham Young University after his sophomore year to join the Army Air Corps but flunked out of pilot training at Randolph Field near San Antonio, Texas. From there he took a job with Douglas Aircraft in Santa Monica. He and some of his coworkers formed a club of washed-out fliers with R.A. Moore of Fort Worth as president and Peterson as vice president. Peterson later told historian Vern Haugland[28] that he learned that Sweeny was at a local hotel to recruit pilots to fight for France and he and his friends went to meet him. Sweeny outlined the scheme to get them to Europe and said one of his men, Weddle, would let them know when they were to leave. The call from Weddle came in February 1940. The group of recruits boarded the train and after several days arrived at the train station in Windsor, Ontario, Canada, across the river from

Detroit. "There they were met by two men," Peterson said. "They read out our names, and when we responded they told us to get on the train going back to where we had just tried to come from, or we would be thrown into jail. They were the FBI.... One of them said that if they ever caught up with Sweeny, he'd never get out of jail."

When the men returned to Los Angeles, Weddle told them that Sweeny had a new plan. This time they would travel as Red Cross workers for an ambulance unit in France. Once there, they would join the French Foreign Legion as fliers. In due course they were told to meet in a shed behind a house one night. There they met what Peterson described as "a man with a long beard, looking like Jeremiah straight out of the Bible." The man was Sedley Peck, a former newspaper reporter, World War I aviator and Paris Post commander of the American Legion. (On May 29, 1940, Peck arrived in Paris at the head of a detachment of Dr. Sparks' volunteer ambulance unit. He later served as an intelligence officer on General Dwight Eisenhower's staff.) However, the new plan fell apart in late April or May, said Peterson. So members of the group made their own plan. They took the train to Chicago and then split up, taking different trains and crossed into Canada. They reassembled in Ottawa. The plan changed again on May 10 when Germany invaded France. Now, instead of heading to France, seven Sweeny recruits sailed to England. In addition to Peterson and Moore, they were Paul Anderson, Edwin Orbison and Dean Satterlee, all from Sacramento; Byron Kennerly from Pasadena; and James McGinnis from Hollywood. Ironically, Anderson was the son of the head of the FBI's San Francisco office.[29]

Two more Sweeny recruits left Los Angeles by train bound for Canada on May 10. One was Eugene Quimby "Red" Tobin, 23, the son of a Los Angeles real estate broker. He had cut classes in high school to take flying lessons and in time he scraped together enough money to buy his own plane. That led to a job flying actors and studio executives around California for Metro-Goldwyn-Mayer movie studios. The other was Andrew Mamedoff, 27, a White Russian immigrant, who grew up in Thompson, Connecticut. He had flown in air shows and operated a small air charter service, first in Florida and then Southern California. Tobin and Mamedoff had been contacted by Weddle at Mines Field and received their instructions in the backyard shed. When their train reached the Canadian border, FBI agents questioned them but accepted their claim of going to visit a cousin to go fishing. When they detrained in Montreal, they went to the Queen's Hotel and asked for a letter that was supposed to be waiting for them with cash and train tickets to their next stop. It wasn't there. They asked if any other American guests had asked for a letter and were pointed to a man sitting in the lobby reading an aviation magazine. The man was Vernon Charles "Shorty" Keough, 26, a 4-foot-10 Brooklyn-born barnstormer and parachute jumper. While the three men were having a drink in the hotel bar, the letters arrived. They contained tickets to Halifax, Nova Scotia. They were met by a man who gave each of them a pink card that stated they were persons of "indeterminate nationality" and were to be given free passage to France because they were to join the French Air Service. They sailed the next day and arrived at St. Nazaire in Brittany on May 31. Tobin spent the next four days arguing with French port officials before he was allowed to proceed and join up with Mamedoff and Keough in Paris on June 4. There were now eight American volunteers at the hotel there.[30]

Sweeny had returned to France in the spring but his efforts to pave the way with the Air Ministry to get his pilots into the air had been met by what historian Alex Kershaw described as "infuriating lethargy, disorganization and crippling bureaucracy."[31] The first of his volunteers had reached Canada on April 13, 1940, and been promptly packed off to Europe. By May 10, a total of 32 men had begun this journey.[32]

Unfortunately, Sweeny's recruits arrived too late to fight for France. In April 1940, Germany invaded Denmark and Norway. Denmark surrendered within hours while Norway fought back for two months. On May 10, the day Tobin, Mamedoff and Keough departed for France, Germany invaded the neutral nations of Holland, Belgium and Luxembourg. The French army responded by moving into Belgium to meet the German advance and quickly found itself outflanked by a German attack through the Ardennes Forest on the French right. This is precisely the series of events that Sweeny had warned would happen in his memo to Daladier months before. It also was the same day that Winston Churchill was installed as Britain's prime minister, replacing the discredited Neville Chamberlain. The British and French forces that had advanced into the Low Countries to meet the German attack soon found themselves pinned into a rapidly shrinking area on the northwest coast of France. In an epic move, the British put to sea with every warship, freighter, fishing trawler and pleasure craft available and plucked 338,000 troops off the bombed, strafed and shelled beaches around Dunkirk between May 26 and June 4. France gave up two weeks later. The proud nation that had withstood the German onslaught of 1914 for four long years fell in 1940 in just six short weeks. The French were forced to sign an armistice on June 22.

Britain now stood alone and practically defenseless as it awaited a cross-channel German invasion. Sweeny was determined to be of whatever help he could to resist the scourge of fascism. Sweeny whole-heartedly agreed with Churchill when he said: "What General Weygand has called 'The Battle of France' is over. The Battle of Britain is about to begin. Upon this battle depends the survival of Christian civilisation."

In the chaos that ensued in the French collapse, Sweeny tried to get his recruits out of France but some never received his message about escape routes.

Of the 32 Sweeny recruits who reached France, four were killed and nine were captured by the Germans. The others made their way out of France just barely ahead of the invaders. Some returned to America. Six made their way to England.[33]

Tobin, Mamedoff and Keough were at an air base near Tours in central France, waiting for a chance to get into the air, when the base was bombed and strafed on June 12. They spent the next four nights sleeping in a ditch to avoid being killed in subsequent air raids. When German troops rolled into the base, they, and everyone else there, fled south. They boarded a train to Bordeaux on the Atlantic coast and then hitched a ride on a truck to the little port of St. Jean de Luz near the Spanish border. They arrived on June 22, the day France signed the armistice. The next day they sailed out of the harbor on the *Baron Naim*, the last ship to depart before German troops captured the port. They arrived in Plymouth, England, on June 25, took a train to London and went directly to the U.S. Embassy. There, Ambassador Joseph P. Kennedy ordered them to go home. Instead, they looked for a way to get into the fight they had come so far to join.[34]

Back in America, FBI agents were still trying to break-up Sweeny's recruiting network. In addition to FBI agents in Los Angeles, FBI offices across the country were drawn into the hunt, including San Francisco, Portland, Salt Lake City, Denver, San Antonio, Chicago, Detroit, Miami, Philadelphia and New York City.

While FBI agents chased Sweeny around the country, FBI Director J. Edgar Hoover pursued the State Department, seeking to enlist it in his efforts to reel in Sweeny. Hoover and Assistant Secretary of State Adolf A. Berle, Jr., exchanged no less than nine memos about Sweeny, delivered by special messenger, between February 5 and April 19, 1940.[35] On February 5, Hoover complained that American citizens were able to cross into Canada without passports. Berle replied that the State Department had been assured by Canada that no American would be allowed to travel on a belligerent ship to a combat area without a valid passport.[36] On February 26, Hoover pleaded with the State Department to take some sort of action. Berle replied that any violation of neutrality laws would be a criminal matter for the Justice Department, of which the FBI was a part. Hoover responded in a March 1 memo that Sweeny had recruited an individual (whose name was blacked out in the memo) and the FBI had referred the case to the Justice Department for action. Berle replied that he would be "pleased to learn of the decision of the Criminal Division" in the matter.

Given the tenor and tempo of Hoover's memos, it is somewhat surprising that the FBI director met with continued resistance. Hoover had a well-earned reputation as a skilled infighter, so it is fascinating to watch Berle parry each of Hoover's thrusts in this bureaucratic fencing match. One can imagine how the State Department's slow-walking approach to this issue infuriated the FBI director.

The back-and-forth continued on March 13 when Berle wrote to Hoover, "It is the understanding of this Department that the French in accepting for military service its own citizens are careful to see that those with allegiance also to the United States do not perform any act in violation of American law." The following day, Berle advised Hoover that a search of the State Department's files "has failed to disclose any record … relating to [name redacted, but given the hometown it is most likely Chesley Peterson] of Payson, Utah, who is said to have been recruited for service in a foreign army." On March 15, Hoover sent Berle a copy of an "anonymously received report" regarding "the enlistment of American citizens for French military duty, on the part of the French Consulate in New York City." Berle wrote back on March 20 to thank Hoover for the report and to say another report about Sweeny by an FBI agent (name redacted) had been transmitted to the assistant to the attorney general "for his information and consideration." On April 19, Berle thanked Hoover for sending him yet another report from an FBI agent about Sweeny.

Hoover's memos beseeched the State Department to use its influence to shut down Sweeny's operation. Berle's memos are exquisitely polite and yet unyielding to Hoover's entreaties. While many officials in the State Department despised Sweeny for meddling in foreign affairs, the White House likely took a different view, given Roosevelt's efforts to aid the Allies. Hoover fared somewhat better with the Justice Department. Several memos signed by the head of the Criminal Division between March 5, 1940, and October 28, 1941, urged Hoover to keep investigating Sweeny's recruiting, which he did.

As the pace of Sweeny's operation picked up speed, the FBI's pursuit intensified. An April 2, 1940, memo from the New York City FBI office to the Los Angeles office states that it had learned of a group of "about 30 fliers who were reported to have enlisted in New York, ten of whom left for Europe in January 1940." FBI headquarters and the head of the Criminal Division directed that any recruits found be interviewed about who sought to recruit them, and under what terms and inducements.

Sweeny was never prosecuted for his role in the recruitment effort. A memo dated December 21, 1944, from the FBI office in Los Angeles states that the investigation of Sweeny for "sedition" has been closed. A full page of text explaining this action is blacked out. The uncensored portion of the memo states, in part, "This file reflects that Sweeny was formerly an officer in the United States Army, that he is very much pro–British and pro–French and very much opposed to the Nazi form of government. There was nothing in the file to indicate that Colonel Sweeny was un–American or unpatriotic."

In 1962, Hoover responded to a written inquiry from an author (name redacted) seeking information about an incident in which "a group of American fliers were intercepted by Agents of the FBI at the Canadian border and returned to the United States." Hoover replied that the FBI had nothing in its records about such an incident, even though press accounts at the time reported on it. Attached to the letter in the FBI files was a note, which read in part: "In 1941, the U.S. Attorney at Los Angeles, California, declined prosecution of Sweeny and those associated with him for the reason that there was no direct evidence of a violation of federal law."

While the Justice Department declined to prosecute, Hoover certainly seems to have believed there was evidence aplenty. There is a memo in the FBI files signed by Hoover dated August 30, 1940, with a photo showing Sweeny in England with British forces being trained. Hoover wrote in the memo, "If Sweeny has gone to England and is an American citizen, he has violated the Neutrality Act by proceeding through a combat area."[37] It appears the evidence was there, but the Roosevelt Justice Department ultimately decided to ignore it. Sweeny remained free to fight another day.

Chapter 15

The Eagle Squadrons and the Battle of Britain

While in Paris in the spring and summer of 1940, Sweeny came to the realization that his recruiting efforts for France had become a lost cause. Germany now occupied two-thirds of France and the armistice between France and Germany would be signed June 22, 1940. The aging Marshal Philippe Petain was forming a new French Government at the spa town of Vichy that was forced to collaborate with the Nazis.[1] Under the terms of the armistice, the French military was to be disbanded and France was forced to pay Germany for the cost of the invasion.

The Nazis were well aware of Sweeny's bitter hatred of Hitler and National Socialism, and the Gestapo was determined to silence him.[2] One night during a Gestapo sweep of Paris, he was shot at while returning to his apartment. The bullet ricocheted off a nearby wall. Sweeny spent a restless night peering out of his apartment window where he saw two Gestapo types nearby watching his apartment. Even though he had notified a gendarme of the attempt on his life, nothing was done to give him protection. It was then he decided that it was time to get out of France and go to England where he could resume his recruiting activities. He borrowed some old clothes from the apartment manager and disguised himself as a crippled old woman with a body racked by arthritis. He was able to sneak by the German agents who he believed were plotting to assassinate him. He then went to the home of two friends, Marcel Labonne and Marcel de Maugenet, to hide.[3] They put him up for a day as he finished his plans to escape. Sweeny confided in his friends and told them of his scheme to go to England and invited them to join him later.

Sweeny resolved that his recruiting efforts should not be wasted because of the fall of France. He had set up an underground escape route so that he and his volunteers could escape to Britain. He also had set up three secret wireless stations, one in Lisbon, one in France, and one on a small fishing boat at Bordeaux, so his people could communicate freely. He was determined to send a coded message when he got to England to let them know that he was ready for them to come. "You'll never be able to get a message through," said de Maugenet. Sweeny replied, "If I do get to Britain I shall insist on making a [BBC] broadcast to France. I will send you a secret message in this broadcast. It's got to be a g__ d__ simple code that you can understand and the British security people don't get suspicious about it, otherwise they won't let me talk on the radio." He decided on the code word "Verdun." It was a word that referred to the great World War I battles that struck a sense of pride in both the French and the British. So Sweeny suggested that if he didn't mention Verdun in his broadcast, they should lay low because he couldn't help. If he mentioned Verdun once, they were to stay at home and lay low and await another message. If he mentioned it twice, then they were to get in touch with his underground contacts to arrange for their escape to England.[4] How Sweeny escaped from France is unverified but his friend, Professor Wormuth, thought he escaped in a fishing boat. While his plan to form a new Lafayette Escadrille in France was in tatters, Sweeny felt that if he could get his pilots to Britain he might yet win the day.

To understand how the Eagle Squadrons—a celebrated unit of American volunteers in Britain's Royal Air Force (R.A.F.)—came about, it must be understood that there were four Sweenys who played a role in their creation. They were Colonel Charles Sweeny, his brother Robert,[5] Robert's son Charles and his other son Robert.[6] (For clarity, we will refer to the elder Sweeny as the Colonel, to his brother as Robert Sr. and Robert's sons as Charles and Robert). Robert Sr. and his sons were Americans living in England, pursuing financial and business interests. Charles had been active in aiding the British war cause as early as 1939. Over the objections of U.S. ambassador Joseph P. Kennedy, he had organized and recruited several Americans living in England to form a Home Guard Unit known as the First Motorized Squadron.[7]

After forming the motorized home guard unit, he moved on to assisting his uncle, the Colonel, in forming the Eagle Squadron. He wrote to Sir Hugh Seeley of the British Air Ministry in June of 1940 requesting that an American Air Defense Corps be created. He backed up his request by claiming that his uncle still had a well-organized recruiting organization in place with a large number of potential American recruits. He also made the request to Lord Beaverbrook, minister of Aircraft Production, and Brendan Bracken, Winston Churchill's personal assistant. Through persistence, Charles was able to make a presentation to the British Air Council, which approved the proposal on July 2, 1940, provided that they had 25 pilots and 25 reserve pilots ready to go. Without Charles' efforts, the Eagle Squadrons never would have gotten off the ground.

There also was another American, Clayton Knight, who started recruiting pilots and staff from the United States with the support of the British and Canadian governments. Knight had been a combat pilot during World War I and had been shot down by the Germans, taken prisoner and held until war's end. He had no love for Germany. Nor did Canadian Vice Air Marshall William Bishop, who called Knight in September 1939 to request Knight recruit training pilots for the Royal Canadian Air Force (RCAF). Homer Smith, another World War I pilot and coincidentally a cousin of the Sweenys, became Knight's assistant and set up an office in New York City to begin operations. Knight then met with U.S. major general Henry H. "Hap" Arnold, chief of the Army Air Corps, and Rear Admiral John Towers. They supported Knight's efforts as long as he didn't draw from their recruits for the United States Army and Navy. Knight then met with U.S. Department of State officials and received the go ahead as long as he operated covertly without much fanfare. The Roosevelt administration was concerned about the political opposition and bad press that the isolationist movement in America could generate against Knight and the President. As the war in Europe evolved, the Knight Committee played a key role in acquiring pilots for the Eagle Squadron. With Knight's support, the Eagles were later able to expand into three separate squadrons.

A few days after escaping to England, on June 29, 1940, the Colonel had lunch with Constantine Brown, the foreign editor of the *Washington Star*. Brown agreed that the formation of an American squadron to fly for the R.A.F. would boost English morale, hopefully enough to keep Britain in the war long enough until America could get involved.[8] The Colonel then went back to the America for a short time to renew his recruiting contacts.

Early in July, the Colonel got a cable from London that some of his American recruits who had been in France—Newton Anderson, Vernon Charles Keough, Michael Luczkow,

Group Captain Charles Sweeny of the R.A.F. Eagle Squadron (courtesy Nicole Hess).

Andrew Mamedoff, Virgil Wilson Olson, and Eugene Quimby Tobin—had arrived safely in England through his underground network and were trying to enlist in the R.A.F. The British were reluctant to accept such a small number and were worried about accepting men from a neutral country.

The Colonel returned to England with his nephew Robert to convince the British to accept his recruits.[9] The Colonel pointed out to the British officials that he had several more recruits left in France and he could get even more from France, Canada, and the United States.[10]

He sought out high-level English officials, including Winston Churchill, for permission to broadcast an appeal to the French people to join the fight against the Germans. He was told that he couldn't recruit from the defeated. This angered the Colonel and he demanded, 'Then to who else do I appeal?' Do you want me to recruit from the Germans? By God, if I thought they'd listen, I would do just that!"[11]

Quentin Reynolds, a well-known war correspondent for *Colliers* magazine, and Tallulah Bankhead, the flamboyant American actress whose father had been speaker of the U.S. House of Representatives, made appeals to the British government on the Colonel's behalf to allow him to make his broadcast to France. He was finally given permission to make the broadcast over the British Broadcasting Corporation (BBC) network on October 24, 1940. In an emotion-filled speech, he made this plea:

> Frenchmen, my brothers, the truth of this war is that by words you have been led to defeat and to misery. Those of us who already are here are the Vanguard, as we were in 1914. We airmen of the Lafayette squadron, American volunteers, men of 1914, soldiers of the Foreign Legion, have rallied to the cause of England. We will fight with her, for her, for ourselves and for you. Millions will come after us as they did in 1918. Great Britain has become the Verdun of this war. She is the rock against which barbarism will be broken as it was broken in 1916 at the gates of Verdun. In this struggle you will be reunited with us and in victory you will win back your joy and pride in France.[12]

News of the broadcast was published in newspapers worldwide over the next few days.[13]

The BBC censors who were editing the Colonel's speech told him to use the word "Verdun" only once because it was redundant to mention it a second time. He nodded agreement but left it in the broadcast and pretended he had forgotten to cut the second one. As a result, the signal reached Labonne and de Maugenet, who escaped France along with others.[14]

Response to the Colonel's speech was immediate and negative in America. The American press accused the Colonel of irresponsible loose talk in his broadcast and then gave some incorrect details about his life. They stated that he had been an aviator with the Lafayette Escadrille during the First World War and was now a flyer with the Eagle Squadron. After making a few more remarks to defame the Colonel and his speech, they came to this conclusion:

> America has no intention of sending millions of her sons to fight in foreign lands. England does not need those millions. What she does need is munitions of war, guns, tanks, airplanes, medicines, surgical instruments, food and clothing and most people of the United States want England to have them.
>
> Britain is fighting for America, for democracy everywhere as well as for her own salvation. It is for America to support her with those necessities and make the British Isles the Verdun of the Second World War.[15]

Although the article had incorrect facts, it expressed the general American attitude toward the war at the time.

Many Americans in London turned their backs on the Colonel and American Embassy officials threatened to withdraw his passport and force him to return to the United States. The Colonel remained undaunted in the face of opposition. Recruiting and training pilots was extremely costly and threatened to end his crusade. He had spent most of his own money getting recruits to France and was running low on funds. His family and friends rallied around him to help pay for the endeavor. About $100,000 was raised. While the Colonel donated a small amount, Robert donated $40,000 and his father Robert Sr. donated an undisclosed sum. A good friend of Robert, Barbara Hutton, the Countess Reventlow, an heir to the Woolworth fortune, donated $15,000. This was enough capital to continue on and to treat the recruits like royalty during the recruiting process.[16]

Finally, the Colonel prevailed and the British Air Ministry on September 19, 1940, announced that 34 young American pilots had been chosen to form their own squadron of the Royal Air Force. The Eagle Squadron was finally born with 71 Squadron the first to be created. It was stationed at Church Fenton, near the city of York. On October 9, a press release went out worldwide with many newspapers picking it up. The headline read: "The 'Eagles' Are Ready: Ace U.S. Squadron for R.A.F. Led By Famous Fighter"—referring to the Colonel.[17] Two additional Squadrons, 121 and 133, would soon follow.[18] The Colonel was appointed as the honorary commanding officer with the rank of group captain but he had no flying duties. The Colonel's candidate for squadron commander was William E.G. Taylor, a former U.S. Navy and Marine Corps pilot who flew for the British Royal Navy as an aircraft carrier pilot. However, a decorated British fighter pilot, Walter M. Churchill (no relation to the prime minister), was chosen to be the squadron commander. He had eight confirmed kills of Nazi aircraft to his credit.

Robert Sweeny, Sr., was given the honor of naming the squadron. His son Charles designed a special patch to be worn on the shoulder of the uniforms to designate that the pilots and officers were members of the American Eagle Squadron. Charles based the design on the eagle on the cover of U.S.

passports. Robert Sr.'s son Robert was chosen by Air Marshal Sholto Douglas to be the adjutant of the squadron to keep the high-spirited pilots in line. Robert resigned a few months later to become a decorated bomber pilot.[19]

The first aircraft the R.A.F. equipped the Eagles with was the American-made Brewster Buffalo, an antiquated, cumbersome airplane that paled in performance to the British Hurricanes and Spitfires. The British had received the Buffalos through Roosevelt's Lend-Lease Program. Squadron Leader Churchill devised a plan to get rid of the unwanted Buffalos. He told the pilots not to lock the tail wheel when they came in for a landing knowing that an unlocked tail wheel would cause the airplane to go into a ground loop and cause considerable damage. The danger to the pilots was minimal. So the pilots followed instructions, the planes were damaged and were replaced by Hurricanes in November 1940.[20]

As honorary commanding of officer, the Colonel visited R.A.F. bases to observe and ensure the Eagle pilots were being properly trained. In October 1940, a newspaper article by reporter G.H.P Anderson described one of those training sessions while flying as a passenger in a two-seater Miles Master trainer. As they took off they climbed to 2,000 feet and dove on an imaginary target in the middle of the airfield while Sweeny and Squadron Leader William E.G. Taylor and several thousand spectators looked on. Then they practiced formation flying with eight other trainers. Anderson concluded the article by writing:

> Back in the Americans' mess later some of the pilots told of their adventures in reaching England. Richard A. Moore of Garland, Texas, and Chesley Gordon Peterson of Santaquin, Utah, for example, said they had set out from California last February after resigning their cadetships in the United States Army Air Corps. They told of traveling 3,000 miles and then being turned back, and of trying again in the concealment of a freight car and getting "G" men on their trail and then finally hurrying to Canada when the recruiting of flyers for an American Squadron began.[21]

The American pilots had never flown in military formations before and had to learn the techniques and terminology of aerial combat. The British fighter formations had to fly close together while on missions so the pilots wouldn't lose each other in the dense fog. They flew in a triangle formation with the two rear aircraft about six feet back just below and inside the trailing edge of the leader's wings. This was different than in America where the rear planes flew just above the leader. During an attack the leader and number two plane first engaged the enemy while number three flew cover in case the formation was ambushed by enemy fighters.[22] Number three would then join in after the other two had made their run or when they were engaged in a dogfight. The British used the term "Rhubarbs" when their fighter squadrons were on search and destroy missions looking for enemy aircraft to destroy. When the fighters were escorting bombing missions, those missions were called "Circuses."[23]

What the Americans had to learn seemed overwhelming. For example, they had to learn vectoring. The British had developed an early warning radar system to alert the nation and pilots of incoming German aircraft. Through vectoring, the radar operators would give the pilots a compass heading so they could intercept and engage the Luftwaffe before they reached their targets, which greatly reduced the damage their bombers inflicted. Vectoring also was used to direct the pilots to their rendezvous points to form up with British bombers to escort them on their bombing runs on German-held targets. They also had to learn how to pack, wear and land in parachutes in case they were shot down.[24] Flying night patrols and night fighting was especially dangerous and they received instruction and training on night fighting. They attended lectures from R.A.F. officers on gunnery, the use of oxygen at high altitudes, and how to keep from blacking out in tight turns and dives when centrifugal force forced the blood from their brains.

The Americans needed additional training because the British fighters, the Hurricane and the Spitfire, were powered by the famous high-performance Merlin Rolls Royce V-12 engine that outperformed anything in the American arsenal. Later, when the American P-51 Mustang fighters were fitted with the Merlin, they became one of the premier long-range fighters of World War II. When the Eagle Squadrons pilots transferred into the U.S. Army Air Corps, they were assigned P-51s and P-47 Thunderbolt's to fly. Their experience fighting the Germans in the high-performance British fighters gave them an advantage over the other American pilots.

In November 1940, several of the Eagles volunteered for night patrols. Although the Eagles were inexperienced at fighting at night they were accepted because the British pilots had been pushed to the point of exhaustion. On the 14th, Byron Kennerly and others were scrambled to intercept large squadrons of German bombers headed toward Coventry, England. Due to his lack of experience, Kennerly only got one burst of machine gun fire at a Heinkel bomber. On his return flight back to his base as he flew over Coventry, he could see that the city had taken a terrific pounding. The Germans had dropped tons of conventional bombs and incendiary bombs on Coventry and there were fires everywhere. The next morning, he, Phil Lechrone and Jim McGinnis had a day pass and planned to go to London for some relaxation. As Kennerly approached the other two to go to breakfast, they were talking to Andy Mamedoff. He was telling them that his mechanic had a sister in Coventry, who was part-owner of a tea shop, and he couldn't get through to her because of the bombing. Neither Mamedoff nor his mechanic could get away to check on her because they were on call in case of a German air attack. McGinnis then said, "Looks as if we take a trip to Coventry today." The three of them then drove an R.A.F. truck two-and-a-half-hours to Coventry and saw first-hand the destruction and carnage the German bombers inflicted on the city. Unfortunately the mechanics sister was killed in the raid.[25]

While eager to get into combat, it was apparent from a few missions they had flown, that the Eagles still weren't quite ready. In late November 1940, the Colonel accompanied several of his men and others on an ocean liner, sailing under the Belgium flag, to Canada for further instruction. The men included R.A.F. fledgling pilots, officer instructors, Canadian R.A.F. officers, American pilots, and sailors of the Royal Navy. The sailors were sent to man destroyers the British had acquired through Roosevelt's Lend-Lease Program that were anchored in Canadian waters. They were to take them to England to serve in the Royal Navy. The Colonel, dressed in a RAF uniform, when asked by a reporter about their mission, declined to comment, wary of the isolationists in America and the bad publicity they could generate.[26] The Ottawa *Evening Citizen* ran an article anyway that featured a picture of the Colonel and described him as an important individual and group captain in the R.A.F. It described the Eagles as a R.A.F. squadron manned entirely by American pilots with ground staff from England. It gave a short background on Squadron Leader William E.G. Taylor and ended with this statement about the Colonel:

> Group Captain Sweeny was a former newspaperman in Paris until the outbreak of the war, he was special correspondent for the Exchange Telegraph, official British news agency. He is an American, however, and hails from Spokane, Wash. When the Citizen reporter spoke to him he was perusing the Oxford Book of Greek Readings, with obvious relish as a pastime.
>
> During the last war he served in the Foreign Legion, commanded a U.S. Infantry regiment, and later served on the general staff.[27]

If the usually talkative Colonel seemed unusually uncommunicative, it might be because he had more on his mind than just his fliers. He had left his wife Eva and their children—Charles Jr., Emeline, and Patrick—in France, and he was increasingly worried about their well-being. Although he had neglected them in recent months because of his crusade against Hitler, he feared for their safety. The Gestapo was infamous for brutalizing the families of its enemies. In addition, Patrick's mental and physical infirmities made his safety a special cause for concern. The Nazis' despicable eugenics and genetics program, in an effort to create the "Master Race," called for the elimination of persons they deemed inferior, especially those with disabilities. The Colonel was aware of this and for a time considered having them rescued, but felt it was unlikely that his wife would leave because of her devotion to France and her family.

Sweeny received a false report that his son Charles had been taken prisoner by the Gestapo. He asked the U.S. State Department to have Admiral William Leahy, the U.S. ambassador to the Vichy Government of France, intervene for him. The Colonel was viewed by the State Department as a meddler who had no business recruiting pilots for foreign powers. The State Department bluntly told him that he should have looked after his family to ensure their safety before he started to meddle in a war that didn't directly involve the United States. Privately, the accusation must have stung. He probably acknowledged the truth. He had let his fear of Hitler and Germany blind him to his duty to his family.[28] One U.S. newspaper article reported that Eva spent time in a Nazi concentration camp during the war.[29] However, the Colonel's grandson, Frank Goodbold, believes that the Nazis kept a close eye on her but didn't imprison her and the children. Regardless, the family was left in a perilous situation.

The Colonel and his men returned from Canada in January 1941 and the squadron was moved to Kirkton-in-Lindsey in 12 Group where Taylor took command when Churchill became ill. Although he held no operational authority, the Colonel had become the public face and spokesperson for the Eagles. He sought publicity for this squadron at every opportunity and was extremely successful in this role as the squadron became internationally famous. He and the Eagles appeared in numerous newspaper and magazine articles and he appeared in Movietone newsreels promoting their cause.[30] Just a few months later, the Squadron got a two-page write up in *Life* magazine that explained the mission of the Eagles and offered photos of the pilots engaging in horse play.[31] This was the Eagles' way of relieving the stress and tension of being fighter pilots who faced death every day. The isolationists in America nearly went insane with rage because of the Eagles' popularity and created some negative press for the Colonel and the squadron. Many people in the United States didn't want to be drawn into another European war and failed to see the inevitability of war with Germany. They didn't understand that world domination was Hitler's ultimate goal with the German people as the Master Race and himself as Supreme Fuhrer. If he hadn't been stopped, the world would have sunk into the abyss, ruled by unspeakable terror, brutality, mass murder, and intimidation. There would have been a worldwide holocaust.

In the spring of 1941, U.S. major general "Hap" Arnold was touring England on a fact-finding mission. He met with Colonel Sweeny, who he called the "coordinator of the Eagle Squadron," and Air Chief Marshall Douglas. Arnold expressed his opinion to Douglas that the time had come for the squadron to stop training and be moved up to frontline combat duty.[32] Douglas was very negative about the Eagles and denigrated them as being "prima donnas." This prompted Chesley Peterson, one of the squadron's most successful pilots and later a squadron commander, to break military protocol and speak to Air Marshall Hugh Sanders, Douglas' superior. He requested the Eagles be transferred to 11 Group's sector of operations because most of the action throughout the war was in the 11 Group's area. That area included London and other cities that bore the brunt of the Luftwaffe attacks. The eastern most area of 11 included Dover, which was closest to France (Calais), and most attacks by the R.A.F. on German targets on French soil originated from 11. The Eagles were assigned to 12 Group, whose area included the cities of Liverpool, Coventry, and York in northwest England and only saw periodic action against the Germans. Most of 12's missions were convoy duties over the North Sea.[33] As a result of Peterson's request, in April 1941, 71 Squadron was transferred to Martlesham Heath as part of 11 Group of the British Fighter Command. Their Hurricane I fighters were replaced by the new Hurricane II model. The new model was fitted out with the recently re-engineered Rolls Royce Merlin XX engine that gave the airplane better performance. Unfortunately, the Hurricane II still couldn't hold its own against the German Messerschmitt Bf109 but the pilots welcomed the improvement just the same.

The pilots of 71 Squadron didn't have to wait for long for action. After being re-assigned, they flew frequent missions, including one south of Boulogne off the French coast, where they engaged German aircraft but didn't score any aerial victories. A month later, on May 15, two Eagles were involved in a dogfight with three Bf 109's over the English Channel where they damaged one Bf109 near Calais. Unfortunately, the Americans suffered an embarrassing loss when one of their Hurricanes was damaged by a volley of gunfire from another American airplane and had to crash land.[34] This case of friendly fire was probably due to their lack of combat inexperience.

In June 1941, the squadron was moved again to North Weald, just north of London. Squadron Leader Taylor was replaced at this time by Henry de Clifford Anthony "Paddy" Woodhouse, a British pilot who had flown during the Battle of Britain. Taylor had exceeded the allotted number of operational hours permitted and was 36, too old by R.A.F. standards to command a squadron. While being too old to command, he was still qualified to take control of a fighter training unit but turned down the offer to fly for the U.S. Navy.

The squadron scored its first aerial victories on July 2, 1941, while escorting 11 Bristol Blenheim bombers to Lille, France. The bombers' mission was to destroy an electric power plant and steel and engineering works there. Fighter Command hoped to draw German fighters into the battle, and 25 to 30 German fighters attacked. Not only did the bombers hit their targets, but the R.A.F. claimed 11 German planes downed with the Eagles scoring three of those kills, plus one probable kill, and one damaged. But 71 Squadron lost one airplane, and the pilot, William Isaac Hall, was taken prisoner for the duration of the war. The squadron remained busy for the rest of July, flying 568 operational missions.[35]

In August 1941, the Eagles got some exciting news. Their Hurricane fighters were being replaced by the Super Marine Spitfire Mark IIA's. The

Spitfire had as many machine guns as the Hurricane, eight .303 Brownings, but it had a higher top speed of 370 mph, 30 mph more than the Hurricane, and could climb higher and faster. They finally had an airplane that would put them on equal terms with the Bf109's. Later that month they received the Spitfire VB that had studier longerons and could support an even more powerful Merlin Engine. The VB also had better armament. Now the pilots could choose to fire four .303 machine guns or two 20 mm Hispano cannons. Better yet, they could fire all of them at the same time to give them devastating firepower. Because of the increased performance of the VB, the R.A.F. changed their fighter formation from the triangle with a lead aircraft and two trailing close behind to protect the lead, to a two-airplane formation with a lead and a wingman. This freed up more aircraft for combat but still gave adequate cover for the lead pilot.[36]

On August 3, 1941, Eagle pilot Gregory Augustus "Gus" Daymond, 20, shot down a German Dornier 17 bomber while on convoy escort duty. Daymond was flying with another Eagle Squadron plane when he spotted the Dornier. Leaving his companion to keep a lookout over the convoy, he went in pursuit of the bomber. He later described to a reporter what happened. "The German dived to within 50 feet of the water at full throttle. I opened fire at 200 yards range dead astern. That Dornier was going all out and we were traveling nearly 300 miles an hour. I could see my bullets hitting the water so I put up my nose and raised my aim. Suddenly smoke began to pour from the Dornier and it touched the water. It bounced 50 feet into the air and then went in nose first. Only a small patch of oil was left on the sea."[37]

While the Colonel was overseeing the building and training of 71 Squadron, two additional squadrons were formed. On May 14, 1941, 121 Squadron was activated, operating out of Kirton-in-Lindsey, and given the Hurricane I's to fly. By this time, the Knight Committee in America was a well-oiled operation and was able to supply pilots and personnel for all overseas postings. Knight made sure that the personnel sent to 121 Squadron received intensive training before they got to England, to cut down on the time they took to become combat ready. The R.A.F. assigned Squadron Leader Peter Powell, a British pilot, as commander of 121. The squadron reached full strength by mid-June and in July it received Hurricane II's to fly combat in. On August 8, 1941, the unit claimed a probable kill of a German Ju 88 twin engine bomber.[38]

The third and final Eagle unit, 133 Squadron, became active on August 1, 1941, at Coltishall, near Norwich, in Norfolk. Fighter Command chose George A. Brown, a pilot from 71, to be the commander. Andy Mamedoff, one of the first pilots to join 71 Squadron, and one of the Colonels first recruits from France, transferred with Brown to become a flight leader. To give his pilots a dose of reality, Brown told his pilots, "have a look around the mess hall [today] as in a year from now most of you will be dead." His startling prophecy turned out to be true.[39]

It took 133 Squadron some time to achieve combat readiness, attaining day operational status September 26, 1941, when the pilots completed Operational Training Unit that instructed the pilots on coastal patrol duties. 133 Squadron relocated a few times over the next few weeks while flying patrols over the North Sea. In October, it transferred to Eglinton, Northern Ireland, to carry out convoy patrol duties protecting allied shipping from the German surface ships and U-boats. During the transfer on October 8, 15 airplanes took off for Eglinton. Their flight plan called for them to land at the Isle of Man for refueling. The weather was bad with poor visibility as they approached the runway at Man. Four of the flight misjudged their altitude and crashed into the side of a mountain. All were killed. Sadly, they had missed clearing the top of the mountain by only a few feet. Of particular note, Andy Mamedoff, who had recently married an English girl, was one of the men killed.[40]

August was a significant month for 71 Squadron too. Paddy Woodhouse was replaced as squadron leader by E.R. Bitmead. Regrettably, Bitmead couldn't handle the assignment. He had flown during the Battle of Britain and developed battle fatigue and hadn't fully recovered. He was in no mental condition to lead the squadron and was replaced after a few weeks by Stanley T. Meares. Meares also had seen action in the Battle of Britain and at Dunkirk. Under Meares' command, 71 made great progress and recorded the destruction of nine enemy aircraft during August, the highest of all R.A.F. squadrons.

Toward the end of August, Colonel Sweeny and Luke Allen, one of the pilots of 71 Squadron, were on an inspection tour of R.A.F. training bases in Great Britain. The Colonel was proud of the job the Eagles and R.A.F. had done in overcoming great odds in repelling the Luftwaffe. He commented to a newspaper reporter: "Britain has regained control of the [English Channel]. Enemy planes seldom venture more than a few miles beyond the British border, and German planes now must base themselves 25 miles or more inland from the French coast." He also was impressed with the engineers in Great Britain who were constantly making design changes to their airplanes to increase performance, to give their pilots and aircrews an advantage in the air war. He was aware of the importance of their work and said, "control of the air is based on horsepower, and horsepower will settle the war in Europe. At the start of the war the German Messerschmitt 109 had 600 horsepower. Now it has 1350. Our own planes are developing 2,000 horsepower and over." Then Luke Allen got in a plug for the Eagle Squadrons: "There are three Eagle Fighter Squadrons of about 25 men each, with a bomber squadron now in formation. There are 163 American pilots in England now, most of them in British squadrons, and 412 more men in training."[41]

In September 71 Squadron suffered a tragic loss when Squadron Leader Meares and pilot Ross Scarborough were killed in a mid-air collision during a training flight. Pilot Chesley "Pete" Peterson, a 21-year-old from Santaquin Utah, became the squadron leader. Despite the loss of Meares and Scarborough, 71 Squadron again led the R.A.F. that month in enemy aircraft destroyed. Sadly though, Eugene "Red" Tobin, another one of the Colonel's recruits who escaped from France to join the Eagles, was killed during a rhubarb mission over Boulogue on the coast of France.

England's King George VI, to recognize the achievement of 71 during Meares' command, awarded squadron members Chesley Peterson, Carroll McColpin, and Gregory Drummond the Distinguished Flying Cross. By now the squadron also had three aces—pilots with five or more kills—William Dunn, Gus Daymond, and Carroll McColpin. On October 2, 71 recorded five enemy aircraft destroyed in an intense battle with Bf 109s from the famous German fighter unit Jagdgeschwader (JG) 2 over Abbeville, near the coast of France.[42] The Eagles had come into their own as one of the best fighter units in the R.A.F.

On December 7, 1941, the Japanese attacked the American naval base at Pearl Harbor, Hawaii. The next day, President Roosevelt, in his famous "Day of Infamy" speech, asked Congress to declare war on Japan and Congress approved it. The pilots of 71 Squadron and 121 went to American Ambassador John Winant in London to request a transfer to the Pacific Theater so they could fight against Japanese forces. Winant told them that they would eventually be transferred into the U.S. Army Air Corps but to be patient.

In December 1941, the Eagles learned that they were going to be transferred from 11 Group to 12 Group. The R.A.F. had a standing policy that, due to the length of time they had been in 11 Group, the most dangerous area, they had to be rotated to a base in 12 Group, further away from frontline action. The transfer to 12 was supposed to give 71 Squadron a reprieve and some rest and relaxation from the constant threat of being shot down or killed in action. Chesley Peterson, infuriated at this policy, protested to 11 Group's commander, Air Vice Marshall Trafford Leigh-Mallory, who curtly told him and the squadron to do as they were ordered. Instead, the bullheaded Peterson went over Leigh-Mallory's head to the leader of Fighter Command, Air Chief Marshall Douglas, to register his complaint. Douglas reversed Leigh-Mallory's order and 71 was moved to Martlesham Heath in Suffolk, which was still in 11 Group's zone of operation. 121 Squadron was transferred to North Weald in Essex and 133 Squadron to Kirton-in-Lindsey in North Lincolnshire.[43]

As 1942 began, the Eagles and the R.A.F. faced a new and terrifying challenge from the Luftwaffe einheiten (units) of Western Europe. The Germans introduced a new fighter, the Focke-Wulf Fw 190, which was faster than the

Spitfire Mark V, carried strong weaponry, and had superior maneuverability. Although the Germans had a superior fighter, the Eagles, during the first six months of 1942, bravely pressed on by flying rhubarbs, circuses, and convoy escort duties while continuing to score victories that added to their impressive total of German aircraft destroyed. The R.A.F. wouldn't have a comparable airplane to the Fw 190 until July when the first Spitfire Mark IXs were put into service. With the Mark IX's increased performance, it somewhat leveled the Fw 190's advantage.

121 Squadron flew missions in February 1942 to find the German battle cruisers Scharnhorst and Gneisenau and the heavy cruiser Prinz Eugen. These ships had been harassing and sinking vessels of English convoys in the Indian Ocean and were returning to Germany for repairs and refitting. They were now anchored off Brest, France, while the German navy tried to figure out how to get them through the English Channel without being destroyed by the British navy and Royal Air Force. Winston Churchill wanted them sunk before they could return and inflict more damage on British convoys. Bad weather allowed the German ships to initially escape without being detected. When they were soon discovered, British air and naval attacks were repelled with the help of German escort ships and air cover. As the Scharnhorst and Gneisenau neared home, they struck mines that were laid by the British and suffered severe damage. But the ships survived, which infuriated Churchill.[44] After the battle it was recorded in 121's record book: "Eight of our pilots took part in large scale operations today [12 February].... Our job during these operations was to get and maintain air superiority while bombing was carried out by Hurricane bombers. Stirlings, and Beauforts. The targets were the German battleships Gneisenau and Scharnhorst and the cruiser Prinz Eugen. It is believed no great damage, if any, was done to these three ships [by the RAF]."[45]

In the spring of 1942, the squadrons participated in several circus bombing missions. 121 Squadron on March 24, 1942, along with six other fighter units, flew in a bomber mission to escort 12 Boston bombers to Comines, France, to bomb a power station there. As they approached Comines about 50 Fw 190s attacked the British formation and got through the escort's outer ring, almost getting to the bombers. But the Eagles and their comrades were able to turn them back without losing any bombers. On the return flight to England, the Fw 190s continued to harass the British over French territory, but the Eagles again successfully turned them back. 121 claimed one enemy aircraft probably destroyed but lost one Spitfire when it ran out of fuel and had to crash land. The R.A.F. pilots continued a widespread night and day offensive. During the night they would attack enemy airfields and during the day fighters and bombers would fly circus missions against targets in Belgium and France. British and Eagle pilots flew more than 22,000 fighter sorties, averaging more than 180 per day.

During this period, the R.A.F. lost more than 300 fighters. British light bombers during the same period flew 700 sorties across the English Channel, losing 11 airplanes. The combined British losses totaled 314 airplanes while they claimed 205 German aircraft destroyed. German records after the war showed that the real count of German losses was only 90 airplanes, but the R.A.F. still scored an important victory: the Luftwaffe had to keep two of its best fighter wings in Western Europe to protect German assets there, which took pressure off the Soviet Union fighting Germany on the Eastern Front.[46]

In July 1942, the full-length motion picture *Eagle Squadron* premiered in London. The movie starred Robert Stack, Diana Barrymore, John Hall, Eddie Albert and Nigel Bruce. 71 Squadron thought the film would be a documentary because movie crews had filmed the unit at North Weald before it started production. Pilot Art Roscoe remembered: "They [the movie crew] were taking shots around us getting in and out of airplanes. I guess it was background footage. William Geiger and I were to be in one scene together and every time they would go to take it the two of us would start giggling and they would have to cut. This went on several times, then they switched to something else and never did get back to us so we weren't in the film at all. I never did see the film until after the war." The Eagles who attended the premiere were extremely disappointed and walked out when they realized it was another run-of-the-mill, fictionalized Hollywood movie.[47]

By the summer and fall of 1942, Soviet leader Joseph Stalin was pressing for a second front to be established in Western Europe to draw more German forces away from the Eastern Front where his forces were fighting. Roosevelt and Churchill were keenly aware of the Stalin's urgent request. However, the Americans and the British weren't ready to attack Western Europe. They lacked the ships, troops and supplies to open a Western Front. Nevertheless, the Allies had to prepare for a second front. To test German defenses, they decided to attack the Germans at Dieppe, France.. The raid was codenamed Operation Jubilee. It included 6,100 troops, of which 5,000 were Canadian troops, and air cover from the R.A.F. The objective was to destroy German fortifications at Dieppe, capture prisoners, destroy airfields, and seize ocean-going vessels including landing craft. Air Vice-Marshall Leigh-Mallory was assigned to direct the air umbrella for the operation, which included all three Eagle Squadrons. This was the only time all three would fight in the same battle.

On August 19, 1942, Operation Jubilee got underway with the ground forces coming under intense fire from the Germans. The Canadians suffered 3,367 casualties. As the ground battle raged below, a deadly air battle took place overhead. 121 Squadron flew three missions on the 19th while 71 and 133 each flew four. At the end of Jubilee, 121 claimed one German aircraft destroyed, two probably damaged, and one damaged, with two of its own aircraft missing or lost in battle. 71 claimed one destroyed, one probably damaged, three damaged and two of its planes destroyed. 133 faired even better with seven destroyed, one probably damaged, and en damaged with no loss of their own airplanes. The Eagles were credited with a good number of the R.A.F.'s claim of 48 German aircraft destroyed and 24 damaged. Although the ground attack was a costly failure, the R.A.F. succeeded in fending off the Luftwaffe, thanks to the help of the Eagle Squadrons. Newspapers across the United States featured an article titled "Allied Raid On Dieppe Sets Pattern For Real Invasion," stating that many lessons were learned that would be valuable when the real invasion took place.[48]

Over the next few months the Eagles became celebrities as they were the subject of many articles in the *New York Times*, the *Washington Post*, and *Time* magazine.

When the United States entered the war in December 1941 it was grossly unprepared and needed time to ramp up wartime production and recruit personnel for each branch of the armed forces. The Eagles knew that the Army Air Corps wanted them because it would give the Air Corps experienced fighter pilots, but by September 1942 they were wondering why it was taking so long. They didn't realize the time required to build and either ferry or ship aircraft to Britain. In addition, pilots and flight crews had to be trained to man those aircraft. The Eighth Air Force, which was to be the backbone of the air war in Europe, was formed on January 28, 1942, at Savannah, Georgia, and a few days later the Eighth Bomber Command and the Eighth Interceptor Command were organized, eventually being transferred to South Carolina. U.S. major general Carl Spaatz was assigned as commander of the Army Air Force in Britain (AAFIB). His command spent the next several months readying for the move to England. On July 2, 1942, the first American airplanes of the Eighth Air Force started to arrive in the United Kingdom after the long air crossing from Nova Scotia to Iceland and on to England. Others were shipped in crates by the Merchant Marine, which was constantly harassed by German U-boats. The first American fighter groups of the AAFIB were equipped with English Spitfires and the extremely fast and versatile twin-engine P-38 Lightning fighter-bombers, so the American pilots could fight the German Fw 190s and Bf 109s on equal terms.

As more American men and equipment started to arrive in England, on August 8, 1942, Major General Spaatz opened a dialogue with the Air Chief Marshall Wilfred Freeman, vice-chief of the Air Staff of the British Fighter Command, on transferring the Eagles to the U.S. Army Air Corps. There were several issues that needed to be addressed before the transfer could happen. The Eagle pilots who held rank in the R.A.F. wanted the same rank in the American Air Corps. To solve this issue, all the Eagle pilots who were to be transferred were interviewed and assigned a rank based on their qualifications and experience. Chesley Peterson, after his interview, was given the rank of lieutenant colonel. Another issue was that the Eagles didn't want to be split up and sent to different units, and they were given assurances that that would not happen.[49]

The transfer was scheduled to happen on September 29, 1942. Just before the transfer, 133 Squadron flew one more circus mission that ended in disaster. They were to escort 24 B-17s on a bombing mission to Morlaix, France. In their mandatory briefing before the flight, they were told to expect 35 m.p.h. winds. When they took off, they faced 100 mph winds and poor visibility and couldn't find the bombers they had been ordered to escort. As they continued to search for the B-17s, they didn't realize that the bombers had reached the rendezvous point early and gone on to Morlaix. The Eagles then lost radio contact with ground control but continued to fly south looking for the bombers. They eventually met up with some bombers returning to England and formed up with them. The fighters were critically low on fuel so Flight Lieutenant Edward Brettell, who was acting as flight leader, descended through the clouds to figure out where they were. To their great distress, instead of being over England, they had been blown off course and were over Brest, France. Being low on fuel, they panicked and tried to land on an enemy airfield but were attacked by Fw 190s and fired upon by German anti-aircraft guns. 133 Squadron lost all 12 planes on this mission. Six of the pilots became prisoners of war and four others were killed when they ran out of fuel or were shot down. One pilot bailed out and made his way back to England with the help of the French underground. Another pilot managed to fly back to England but crash landed and was seriously injured.[50] Brettell became a prisoner of war after being shot down. He was later executed by the Germans for taking part in "The Great Escape," which became the basis for a movie of that name starring Sir Richard Attenborough and Steve McQueen.[51]

On September 29, 1942, at Debden, 17 miles northwest of London, a ceremony transferring the three Eagle Squadrons from the R.A.F. to the U.S. Army Air Corps finally took place. Air Chief Marshall Douglas addressed the crowd saying:

> We of Fighter Command deeply regret this parting for in the course of the past 18 months, we have seen the stuff of which you are made and we could not ask for better companions with whom to see this fight through to a finish.
>
> It is with deep personal regret that I today say "Goodbye" to you whom it has been my privilege to command. You joined us readily and of your own free will when our need was the greatest.
>
> There are those of your number who are not here today—those sons of the United States who were first to give their lives for their country. We of the R.A.F. no less that yourselves will always remember them with pride.[52]

At the time of the ceremony, the Eagle Squadrons had accounted for 73.5 enemy aircraft destroyed with 71 Squadron credited with 41 of those.[53] With the lowering of the British flag and the raising of the American flag, 71 Squadron became the 334th Fighter Squadron, 121 became the 335th and 133 became the 336th. They all became part of the 4th Fighter Group.

One of the positive things that came about by the transfer was increased pay. Eagle pilot and ace William Dunn explained the pay the Eagles received as R.A.F. pilots: "My monthly pay as a pilot officer was about 18 Pounds a month [roughly $85 U.S.], and out of that I had to pay 4 pounds 5 shillings income tax, which left me with 13 pounds 15 shillings [about 65 U.S.] to pay my mess bills, batman, laundry etc." When people asked him why he joined the R.A.F., he sardonically replied, "For the high pay, what else."[54] As U.S. pilots, their pay was increased to $240 a month and they got a free $10,000 life insurance policy. As one pilot put it, "we went from buses to taxis and from beer to scotch. Living got considerably better."[55]

The squadrons flew Spitfire Vs until more American aircraft arrived in England. They would later be assigned P 47s and P 51s to fly. They went on to become one of the most successful fighter units in the U.S. Air Force, accounting for 1,016 enemy aircraft destroyed. Donald Blakeslee and Chesley Peterson went on to storied careers, giving credit to the leadership and combat skills they learned with the Eagles. Blakeslee became commander of the 4th Fighter Group and Peterson became one of the youngest colonels in the Air Force. An obituary for Blakeslee in Britain's *Guardian* newspaper described him as the most decorated American fighter pilot of World War II. Peterson retired as a major general after also serving in the Korean and Vietnam wars.

Of the 244 Americans who flew for the R.A.F. Eagle Squadrons, 140 were either killed in action, killed on active service (such as in training flights), or were shot down and became prisoners of war.[56] Their sacrifice for the cause of freedom should never be forgotten.

Chapter 16

"Wild Bill" Donovan and the Office of Strategic Services

By the end of 1941, Sweeny's involvement with the Eagle Squadrons had drawn to a close. He had returned to New York City and was searching for a new crusade on which to embark. He had become discouraged that he wasn't taking an active part in the war against his bitter enemy, the Germans. He wasn't deterred, however, and he spent his days studying war maps and troop movements so he could devise plans to "stir it up inside enemy territory." He formed different scenarios to explore the possibilities of causing revolts against the Nazis among the people in Eastern Europe. He discussed them with his friends and fellow recruiters. One of them was his friend from the Morocco Rif campaign against Abd el-Krim, Dr. James Sparks. Sweeny went to Washington and told Sparks about a plan he had for organizing a coup in Yugoslavia.

Germany had invaded Yugoslavia on April 6, 1941, and within two weeks had forced its surrender. The Nazis then established puppet state governments in each ethnic region. But guerrilla units were organized to resist the German occupation. Those who wanted to restore the monarch formed the Chetniks under Draza Mihajlovic. Those who wanted a communist regime joined the Partisans under Josef Broz Tito. Sweeny felt of all the enemy-held territories Yugoslavia was ideal for resistance because of its bleak mountainous landscape, which provided cover where guerrilla forces could hide their bases. They could strike at the Axis forces and then disappear back into the mountains before the enemy could react.

Sparks was happy to see the excitement building in Sweeny; he was his old self again. "Charlie was immensely enthusiastic about this project he had cooked up to recruit American flyers for Yugoslavia," said Sparks. "He intended where possible to use immigrants who were Slavs as well as American-born subjects. Together we obtained an interview with Franklin Roosevelt, the President, who said it was 'wonderful idea.'"[1]

Roosevelt admired Sweeny for organizing the Eagle Squadrons and listened intently as he explained the Yugoslavia plan. Sweeny compared Yugoslavia to Morocco and explained the terrain was similar to what he had experienced in the Rif War. He believed that a few operatives and planes could supply and direct guerrilla activities in Yugoslavia as well as attack enemy convoys from the air. This could force the Germans to commit large numbers of troops there instead of in North Africa or Russia. The president was tremendously impressed and told them to go ahead with their recruiting. He cautioned that he could not give them his official blessing since America wasn't officially in the war yet.[2] Roosevelt still had to appease the isolationists in America. He told them he would inform them when they could start sending the pilots overseas.

Sweeny, true to form, had no difficulty in finding and signing up pilots for Yugoslavia. "He paid several visits to the White House to ask for permission to go ahead with his plan, but each time officials kept putting him off, telling him to wait a few more days," said Sparks. "The delays and evasions continued and when Tito gained the upper hand over the Mikhajlovic forces in November 1941, the project was abandoned."[3]

Sweeny, already distrustful of politicians, was developing a resentment of Roosevelt and his administration. His next experience with Roosevelt pushed his resentment over the edge into a bitter and deep hatred of the president and his policies.

After the Yugoslavia plan fizzled out, Sweeny was still anxious to get back into the war. He met with William J. Donovan, Roosevelt's appointee to coordinate the government's intelligence-gathering efforts. They came up with a plan to use Sweeny's experience and contacts in Morocco to form a guerrilla force to battle the Germans in North Africa.

As the Second World War raged in Europe before U.S. entry, fears of fascism and communism prompted Roosevelt to propose creation of an office to coordinate the intelligence arms of America. Up to that time, intelligence gathering was conducted by several federal departments and agencies with competing notions of how best to serve the nation. These agencies included the Office of Naval Intelligence (ONI), the intelligence branch of the Army (known as G2), the Federal Bureau of Investigation, the State Department and Secret Service. It was Roosevelt's desire that through a spirit of cooperation the intelligence services could take a more strategic approach in protecting America. He was fed up with having to referee the agencies' bureaucratic rivalries and petty disagreements about the best solutions for intelligence gathering.

On July 11, 1941, Roosevelt appointed Donovan, a New York City lawyer, to head the office of Coordinator of Information (COI), which later evolved into the Office of Strategic Services (OSS) and was the forerunner of the Central Intelligence Agency (CIA). It was the Presidents' wish that Donovan stop the infighting and bickering between the agencies to improve the quality of the intelligence that the White House was receiving.[4]

Since America had yet to enter the war, Roosevelt wanted to know if England and Churchill could withstand the German onslaught until the United States could get involved. According to the official history of the CIA:

> The office of the Coordinator of Information constituted the nation's first peacetime, non-departmental intelligence organization to collect and analyze all information and data, which may bear upon national security: to correlate such information and data, and to make such information and data available to the President and to such departments and officials of the Government as the President may determine; and to carry out, when requested by the President, such supplementary activities as may facilitate the securing of information important for national security not now available to the Government.[5]

Donovan was not an intelligence professional, but he had prior federal government experience and a reputation as someone who could get things done. The son of Irish Catholic immigrants, he became a successful Wall Street lawyer. In 1912, he joined the New York National Guard and was commissioned a captain. In 1916, his guard unit, the famous 69th "Fighting Irish" New York Regiment,[6] helped pursue Pancho Villa in Mexico. With America's entry into World War I, his guard unit became part of the U.S. Army's 42nd "Rainbow" Division. Promoted to major, he led a battalion to France, was wounded three times, rose to the rank of colonel and received the Medal of Honor, Distinguished Service Cross and Purple Heart. Later, he and Theodore Roosevelt, Jr., the son of the former president, became co-founders of the American Legion.

In 1922, he was appointed U.S. attorney for the Western District of New York by President Warren G. Harding, and then served President Calvin Coolidge as an assistant attorney general specializing in anti-trust litigation. For a brief time he supervised a young J. Edgar Hoover and his newly formed FBI. He then went on to practice antitrust law in New York City and entered politics, running unsuccessfully as the Republican candidate for lieutenant governor of New York in 1922 and governor in 1932.

In 1940 and 1941, Roosevelt secretly sent Donovan on a mission to England to gather intelligence and report on Britain's resolve and ability to continue the fight against Hitler. During this time, Roosevelt was fighting the Isolationists in America who wanted to stay out of the war at all cost. The president needed accurate intelligence so he could develop covert operations to supply England with enough aid to keep fighting. British prime minister Winston Churchill understood Donovan's mission and, hoping to win America's further support for England's desperate war effort against Germany, gave him complete access to defense and intelligence secrets. Donovan completed his mission by touring the Balkans and British installations in the Mediterranean in early 1941. Roosevelt was so impressed with Donovan's report and his conclusions on how to help England that he appointed him to head the COI.

The Army and Navy didn't like the idea of an outsider like Donovan having access to their intelligence data. Another huge obstacle to Donovan was FBI Director Hoover, who made it perfectly clear he would not share his FBI files with anyone. Shortly after Pearl Harbor, the Joint Chiefs of Staff (JCS) was formed to coordinate the efforts of all U.S. armed forces. To pacify and gain the support of the JCS, Donovan sold them on the idea that the COI would become the Office of War Information and would be placed under the Joint Chiefs. The JCS readily agreed to Donovan's proposal, believing that it would put him totally under their control. However, Donovan had outsmarted the JCS because on June 13, 1942, President Roosevelt issued an executive order creating the Office of Strategic Services (OSS), whose mission was intelligence gathering and sabotage, with Donovan as director. Roosevelt gave the OSS access to the president's unlimited, "unvouchered funds" provided by Congress to be spent as the president wished and not subject to public scrutiny. Donovan now had a secret war chest to draw from to fund his projects. It only took a short time for the JCS and Hoover to become jealous of Donovan's power, suggesting to the president that he should be reined in or even fired. Their requests fell on deaf ears; Donovan had told the president what he intended to do and Roosevelt liked it. Hoover, the consummate grudge holder, responded by creating one of his now-notorious files and spending considerable FBI recourses trying to dig up dirt to blackmail and control Donovan. Hoover met with little success.[7]

As the threat of Hitler loomed, Donovan recruited several Americans to join in the struggle against the Axis powers. They tended to be well-educated, well-traveled individuals who had studied world affairs and shown an interest in joining the struggle against fascism.[8] Charles Sweeny was one of them. In Sweeny, Donovan saw a man who was cut out of the same mold as himself. Sweeny was a bitter enemy of Hitler and had risked everything, including his life, citizenship and own money to oppose him.[9]

On December 7, 1941, the Japanese attacked Pearl Harbor and the following day the United States declared war on Japan. Hitler, as Japan's ally, then declared war on the United States. The United States and England adopted a "Hitler First" policy, making the defeat of Germany their first priority. During the month after the attack on Pearl Harbor, Donovan and Sweeny devised a plan to send Sweeny to North Africa to recruit the indigenous tribes there to join the allies in the fight against Hitler. Donovan first proposed the plan to Roosevelt's army chief of staff, General George C. Marshall, and his chief of naval operations, Admiral Harold R. Stark, for their approval. They whole-heartedly agreed, so Donovan put together a memo and proposed the plan to President Roosevelt on January 9, 1942. Here is the text of the memo:

> 1. It is proposed to send Colonel Charles Sweeny to Morocco to investigate and eventually organize an uprising of native tribes against German Occupation. Colonel Sweeny was one of the organizers of the American Volunteer Corps in the French Army in 1914. He served in the Foreign Legion from 1914 to 1917, reaching the grade of Captain. He was attached to the Viviani-Joffre Mission to the United States in 1917. Transferred to the American Army, he served in France until after the Armistice.
>
> In 1925 he served in Morocco in the Air Force and was Honorary Commander of the Sultan's Guard. During the operations against Abd-el-Krim that summer and autumn, he commanded the Air Force in support of the columns engaged in the Ouergha Valley and Riff Mountains. The most active of these columns was commanded by Colonel Nogues. In execution of his mission, Sweeny attached himself to this column and, for three weeks, lived in the same tent with the Column Commander. This is the same Nogues who, today a full General, is Resident-General of Morocco. General Juin, Commander in Chief of the French Forces in North Africa, then a Captain, was Nogues' Chief of Staff. The three have remained firm friends.
>
> 2. While in Marrakech, Colonel Sweeny knew intimately the three great Caids of the South: El Glaoui, El Gundelfi, and El M'Tigue. The latter two are now dead and El Glaoui remains Supreme Lord of the Atlas Mountains under the French.
>
> El Glaoui, the Chief of the Glaoua tribe, was chosen by Lyautey, Conqueror and First Resident General of Morocco, to pacify and organize the territories of the Sus and the Atlas Mountains of Southern and South Eastern Morocco. It was Lyautey's policy to count on the great land and religious chiefs more than on the force of arms. Even with this policy, it required 25 years to subdue the Atlas Definitely.
>
> El Glaoui, by this association with the French, has become a wealthy man. French and English bankers estimate his wealth in the neighborhood of twenty-five million dollars. He is convinced that a German occupation of his country would entail the certain loss of his position and fortune. To attach him to our cause, arms, and eventually money, would have to be supplied.
>
> 3. The tribesmen of the Atlas and of the Anti-Atlas Mountains towards the Sus and the Sahara Desert are very warlike. It would be possible to arm at least 100,000 of them, and possibly 250,000. The road system from Morocco to the South toward Dakar, passing through mountains and desert, is very open to attack by bands of guerrillas. The French, in spite of their long experience in colonial warfare, found this their greatest difficulty in the Conquest of Morocco. For example, Marshal Petain required ten months and a force of 150,000 men and 30 batteries of 65 mm mountain guns to put down the Abd-el-Krim insurrection of 1925-26. Native African troops and the Foreign Legion, men hardened to the desert heat and the mountain cold, made up 90% of this force. Even then the operation was finally successful only because of the support of certain local tribes. The Germans, who know nothing of the art of colonial warfare would, at first, find the problem almost impossible of solution and would always be in difficulties. Colonel Sweeny does not feel that it would be possible to prevent the Germans from reaching Dakar once they had occupied Northern Africa, but

16. "Wild Bill" Donovan and the Office of Strategic Services

he does feel that communications could be made extremely difficult and at times impossible.

4. As soon as it was certain that the Germans intended to occupy Northern Africa, rifles and machine guns would have to be landed on the Moroccan Coast in the region of Agadir, or further to the south.

Colonel Sweeny proposes to go to Morocco to contact El Glaoui and other friends in the tribes and among French Colonials. He will report with the least delay possible. Any effective plan will inevitably call for the landing on the Coast of requisite arms and munitions, an estimate of this would be furnished with report of Colonel Sweeny.[10]

Roosevelt approved the plan with the notation on Donovan's memo: "OK. go ahead. FDR." The money to fund the operation would be available from Donovan's secret war chest.

When news of the plan to send Sweeny to North Africa got to Secretary of State Cordell Hull, departmental jealousy and infighting reignited, and Hull stopped the plan by refusing to give Sweeny a passport. Besides, Hull had a score to settle with Sweeny. In 1933, Sweeny was hired by the *Chicago Daily News* to be a correspondent to an international monetary conference in London attended by the United States and most of the major powers of the world. The Depression was in full swing and the countries of the world were exploring, through revalorization, the possibility of using silver to bolster their economies and raise the value of their currencies. Sweeny wrote of Hull's participation in the conference, "Cordell Hull proved himself a charming southern gentleman, liked by everybody, although nobody considered he spoke with any authority." Sweeny went on to say, "How do the European countries feel towards the United States? They're sick and tired of our evangelism. They don't want us to tell them what to do and how to do it. Every American goes there with the attitude that he is right and they are wrong. As a matter of fact, we've been wrong most of the time."[11] The disrespect Sweeny showed to Hull and the United States had to anger Hull.

Hull called Donovan into his office and lectured him saying, "You are trying to interfere with the conduct of my relations with a friendly country."[12] He reasoned that even though Sweeny's mission was secret and not connected to the United States, he might offend the Vichy French and their generals.[13] When journalist Drew Pearson's nationally syndicated *Washington Merry-Go-Round* newspaper column detailed Hull's reaction, articles lambasting Hull appeared nationwide. They accused Hull of being severely depressed by the war and lacking the sound judgment for which he had become famous. The newspapers also compared Sweeny to Lawrence of Arabia, speculating that if his plan was implemented, he would be able to inflict severe damage on the Germans.

Hull's objection to Sweeny's mission was without merit. Who better was in a position to acquire the allegiance of the Vichy French forces than Charles

Sweeny? He had risked his life and was severely wounded for the French cause during World War I, had fought for the French cause in the Rif War, and recruited pilots for the French air force before Germany overran France in World War II. France had bestowed on him some of the country's highest military honors and he was highly regarded in French military circles. He also was the perfect man for the mission because of his friendship with the tribal leaders and his knowledge of the terrain and military tactics. One can only guess as to the problems Sweeny could have caused Erwin Rommel and his Afrika Korps if he had been allowed to complete his mission.[14] If a hostile force of Berber and Arab tribesmen had been in control of Morocco and Algeria, instead of the Vichy French regime, Rommel would have faced a different strategic situation there. If he had tried to defeat or pacify the tribes, the Afrika Korps might have gotten bogged down as Spain and France did in the 1920s. If the Germans attacked east out of Libya with the tribesmen behind them, they would have had to put some sort of force on the border with Algeria or Tunisia to guard against an attack on their rear and their base of supply.

After this blunder, Hull took a long vacation.

Sweeny developed an intense hatred for the State Department, calling it "the most devious, two faced, freewheeling political institutions in the United States ... so hell bent on appeasement that it would appease its own rectum if it had one." His opinion of the FBI was just as critical, describing it as "small-time dicks chasing their own shadows and seeing a spy in every independent-minded American citizen."[15] Sweeny had a general contempt for all politicians too and he decided to use his writing skills to become a vocal critic of Roosevelt and his administration.

Chapter 17

Moment of Truth, or How Sweeny Would Have Won World War II

In 1942, after failing to secure an active role in the war for himself in either Morocco or Yugoslavia, Sweeny cast about for a way to participate, even if only as an armchair combatant. Sweeny had strong opinions about how the war was being fought and how it should be fought, and he decided he could be most effective by publicizing his views in a book. If the elected and appointed officials running America's war effort didn't want to listen to him, he would go over their heads to their bosses, the voters, to influence events. The result was a well-researched book that reached some startling conclusions.

Correspondence between Sweeny and Max Perkins, his editor at Charles Scribner's Sons, offers unique insights into both Sweeny's thinking and behavior during this period.

Sweeny's two-page outline sets forth his goals for the book, which he titled at this point *Our Chance to Win*. He planned to offer a steely-eyed analysis of the challenges and solutions to winning the war.[1]

Perkins commented favorably on the outline and asked Sweeny to send some autobiographical material for use in marketing the book. Sweeny responded on August 1, 1942, with a two-page resume that is as noteworthy for what it includes as it is for what it fails to mention. Here is the text from that document[2]:

Colonel Charles Sweeny
Born San Francisco, California, January 2[6], 1882
Two years West Point
Mexican Revolution, 1910-11
French Army, Foreign Legion, 1914–17, all grades from private to captain. As captain

in 1816 [sic] was a member of a board appointed to study a new tactic for the infantry and to draw up a regulation based on this study and on a study of the liaison between infantry and other areas during the attack.

One of the first officers to study liaison between infantry and Air Force. Wrote a pamphlet on this subject which was issued to all arms.

Designated to study utilization of tanks with infantry in battle. Wrote pamphlet on this subject.

Attached to French Mission to United States in 1917 as Aide-de-Camp to Marshal Joffre.

Transferred to American Army, May 1917 as Major. Commanded Battalion of infantry in France. Assistant G3 [Operations] of First Corps, Acting G3 of Fourth Corps. Demobilized in 1919.

Member of Mission to Poland by French Government in 1920 under command of General Weyand, assisted at Battle of Warsaw.

Organized and Commanded American Flying Squadron which served with French Forces in Morocco in Abd-el-Krim War, 1925.

Assistant Chief of Mission which, under command of General Armengaud, studied the organization of Northern Africa as a base of operations in case of a General European War, 1928-29.

Occasional lecturer at Ecole De Guerre, Paris from 1928 to 1939 on Strategical and Tactical Subjects.

Designated Commander of the First Foreign Division to be formed with Regiments of the Foreign Legion, 1940.

Organized and commanded the First Eagle Squadron, England, 1940

Commander de la Légion d'Honneur (Military Grade)

Croix de Guerre 7 citations

Croix de Guerre (Morocco) 2 citations

Commander d'Ouissam Allouite (Morocco)

Commander Nichan Iftikhar (Tunis)

Commander Order de Leopold (Belgium)

Croix de Guerre (Belgium)

Military Cross (Great Britain)

What stands out among the missing items is any mention of his role as a commander of a French tank unit, as a brigadier general in the Polish army, as a military advisor to Ataturk, or as a military advisor to the Loyalists in the Spanish Civil War. All of these items had been cited in numerous articles about Sweeny. So why did he omit them? These omissions are made all the more intriguing by his inclusion of the Mexican Revolution of 1910-11, when he was actually in Paris, and his role as commander of the Eagle Squadron, when that was a purely honorary title. Were his omissions an attempt to correct the record in some way? And what are we to make of his two questionable inclusions? Were they cherished parts of the legend he couldn't bear to lose? Unfortunately, there is no explanation for why he included some items and not others.

On August 19, 1942, Sweeny wrote to Perkins to say that after writing 20,000 words on the book, he had become dissatisfied with it and had gone "back to the beginning and started over from another base." Since then, he had written 10,000 words. "The difficulty," he added, "is to say these things without getting into trouble." This last comment was prophetic, not only for this book but also his future writing endeavors.[3]

Perkins wrote to Sweeny on August 20, to say that they would have to find a different title for the book. He said the salesmen at Scribner's had "all rebelled against the title [*Our Chance to Win*] as being too discouraging in implication, too uninviting. Perhaps *Winning the War* would do."[4]

After reading the first nine chapters of the book, Perkins wrote on September 14 to say he was "very greatly impressed," and that "they seem to be extremely interesting, cogent and vigorously expressed." On October 16, however, Perkins wrote to express concern about "certain passages" that would offend America's British allies.[5]

Sweeny sent the final chapters of his book to Perkins on October 15. He enclosed a letter and a galley proof of Hemingway's introduction for the book. "The first part is very brilliant," Sweeny wrote of the introduction. "The rest did not impress me. I disagree with his judgment both military and political." Apparently, Sweeny disliked it enough to leave it out because the book was ultimately published without Hemingway's introduction.[6]

Sweeny apparently took Perkins' advice to heart and set about revising the chapters. But, even as he did so, world events were casting doubts on some of his assessments. Instead of losing control of the Suez Canal, the British were driving the German forces westward out of Egypt. Meanwhile American and British forces had landed in North Africa and begun a drive eastward to catch the Germans in a giant pincers. Suddenly, the wheels had come off the German juggernaut, and Sweeny had to reconsider some of his judgments and projections.

Sweeny wrote on November 9 to say that he agreed battlefield events would require some rewriting. However, he felt that his basic assessment was still sound, that Allied victory was hardly assured and that an invasion of Western Europe was certain to fail.[7]

Given Allied gains in North Africa and the Pacific,[8] however, Perkins wrote on November 20 that perhaps Sweeny's basic assessment was overly pessimistic.[9]

The book was sent to the printer the first week of January 1943, although revisions to the galley proofs continued and so did the give and take between Sweeny and Perkins over some of the author's harsher views of Roosevelt, Churchill, and the British Empire.

On January 31, Sweeny wrote to reassert what he considered the four key points of the book: (1) the American people must be shown the seriousness and enormity of the task; (2) England and America could not win the war by themselves as they lacked sufficient population to defeat the Axis powers; (3) Roosevelt and Churchill must hand over direction of the war to military professionals; and (4) the war could only be won with the aid of Russia's and China's large populations. He then gave Perkins carte blanche to edit the book so long as his four key points were preserved.[10]

The book was published in May 1943 with the title *Moment of Truth*. The title came from that climatic moment in the bullring when the matador, armed with a sword, faces the bull, a mighty beast with two lethal horns. One of them is about to die. But which one? He said the Allies and the Axis now faced that moment of truth.

Moment of Truth received a good deal of attention in the press. It went through multiple printings and many book stores sold out of copies. Sweeny was aided in the marketing by endorsements by several of his famous friends. Among them:

Broadcaster and writer Lowell Thomas, who made Lawrence of Arabia a household name, encouraged people to read the book "if you want the tough, realistic, picture of the war."

War correspondent and writer Frazier Hunt, who covered both world wars and the Russian Revolution, said of Sweeny's book, "Here is a strong and biting antidote to the millions of words of mouthwash that have been written and spoken about the war."

Washington political columnist Drew Pearson said, "Professional, armchair and hunch strategists ought to read carefully Col. Charles Sweeny's book. He does not pull his punches ... and while fully confident that we shall get the better of the Nazis, he warns us against over-optimism which can play only into the hands of the enemy."

Foreign correspondent, editor and columnist Constantine Brown wrote that "Sweeny is a soldier who has seen probably more actual fighting than any other living soldier. As a fighting man he is a realist and has written a realistic book which should be a 'must' for all thinking Americans.... It is to my mind, the best and most readable geo-political book that has been written yet."

Sweeny made several other pronouncements that provoked controversy. For example, Sweeny asserted that the most common cause of war has been the need by nations to find living space, food and economic opportunity for their growing populations to prevent internal revolt.[11] He suggested that European leaders could have solved the Balkans problem by moving large portions of its population to more sparsely populated Anatolia (Turkey), Syria and Mesopotamia (Iraq).[12] This is a disturbing idea for someone who professed respect for the civilized norms of France and England. It presents Sweeny as playing with civilian populations like pawns on a chessboard.

While Sweeny's grasp of geography is stunning in its breadth and depth, and his ability to marshal facts is impressive, his strategic conclusions don't fare very well when compared to how the war actually ended up being fought.

Sweeny asserted that it would be impossible to land a million men on the European coast from England. "No sound military man considers it practicable," he wrote. There simply was not enough transport to deliver and resupply an army that size, and the capacity did not exist to build such a fleet. The problem is "beyond resolution."[13]

History proved him wrong, of course. On June 6, 1944, the Allies put 160,000 troops ashore on D-Day. They sustained 10,000 casualties, but the Germans failed to halt the invasion. By July 4, less than a month after D-Day, fully one million men were ashore in a beachhead 70 miles wide and 25 miles deep. Ten months later, Germany surrendered.

Sweeny also wrote that a stalemate between Germany and Russia seemed probable.[14] The Soviets had finally won the climatic five-month battle of Stalingrad in February 1943. The pivotal tank battle near Kursk, after which the initiative passed to the Russians, still lay ahead. So, Sweeny's assessment at the time is reasonable. In the event of a stalemate, Sweeny said Germany and Russia might come to an "arrangement" rather than continuing their death match while England and the United States waited to finish off the exhausted winner and claim the world's riches. "Our hope for salvation rests in her [Russia's] hands," he wrote.[15]

As to where the Allies could best launch their offensive against Germany, Sweeny considered the options of invasions through France or Italy, or through Iran and the Caspian Sea and the Caucasus.[16] One by one, Sweeny rejected each locale as impractical.

So, having rejected all of the likely scenarios, where did Sweeny imagine the Allies could find this battlefield? His answer: Siberia. Sweeny's idea was to transport all of the necessary troops and supplies through the Bering Straits off Alaska into the Arctic Ocean. They would then sail down three large rivers—the Lena, Yenisei and Ob—to central Siberia between Omsk and Irkutsk. There, the Allies would assemble a force of three million men who would be transported westward to join the Soviet offensive. The Siberian front met all of Sweeny's conditions, which he said were laid down by the great military strategists, Karl von Clausewitz and Alfred von Schlieffen.[17]

Given all of Sweeny's stated concern about logistics to mount and sustain an offensive elsewhere, it is hard to understand why he thought the solution was Siberia. To ship, rail and truck the men and material needed for Sweeny's Siberian offensive would be far more challenging than a cross-channel attack. Add in the harsh Arctic climate and the task becomes overwhelming. The distance from Alaska to Berlin via Siberia is some 7,000 miles. By contrast, the distance from Plymouth, England to Normandy is 120 miles, and from Normandy to Berlin is 840 miles. Sweeny described his plan as "logical" and "feasible." However, the best that can be said for his plan is that it is creative.

Chapter 18

A Thorn in the Side of Roosevelt

Upon completion of *Moment of Truth*, Sweeny was ready to start a campaign, a war of words, against President Roosevelt and politicians in general. It was the fall of 1943, with an election year coming up. It was his plan to write a book that would be an exposé on Roosevelt. He contacted his publisher, Charles Scribner's Sons, who agreed to publish his book once it was written. They agreed to advance him $100 a week during the writing period. When he returned the signed contract to Max Perkins, his editor at Scribner's, he stated in the November 15, 1943, letter: "The book is going to be a fighting one—a book for a Presidential year. It will be as brutally realistic about the political situation as 'Moment' was about the military situation…. The title is full of fight as I hope the book will be. *Ring in Our Nose* means just as it says. We are the bull and will suffer his fate as soon as our usefulness has passed."[1]

Sweeny had some harsh criticisms and radical ideas about Roosevelt and world politics in general that he felt the American people should know. Many of his ideas were well reasoned but others were inflammatory and seemed to be based on his personal opinion, not fact. As time went by, it will be seen, Scribner's chose not to print the book. Unfortunately, almost all of the manuscript was either lost or destroyed so we don't have much of it to ponder. But through letters between Sweeny and others, pamphlets and books, and the small part of the manuscript that survived, we can piece together many of the ideas that were in the book. During this time, he also was traveling throughout America on a lecture tour and did some campaigning for the Republican Party. He definitely proved to be an aggravation to Franklin Delano Roosevelt, the Democratic candidate, during the election year of 1944.

One of the things Sweeny was particularly critical of was the "Hitler First" policy that Churchill and Roosevelt adopted after the attack on Pearl Harbor. He wrote, "We shall be given long hours to reflect bitterly on our lack of foresight in concentrating all of our efforts on the defeat of Germany. As long as the American and English Navies and Armies are locked in a death struggle with the Japanese, Russia will be the undisputed master of Political and Geographical Europe. This is under the supposition that Germany has been destroyed and that France has not been restored and strengthened." This was written in late 1943, approximately six months before D-Day, the invasion of Normandy on June 6, 1944. Sweeny could see that the defeat of Germany was a strong possibility. He went on the say, "The conclusion of this analysis is now clear and indisputable: it is to the advantage of Russia that the war between the Western Powers, the United States and England, [against Japan] continues as long and as indecisively as possible."[2] Sweeny felt like General George S. Patton, that war between the western powers and Russia was inevitable.[3] He was fearful that, once Germany was defeated, the surviving German government would form an alliance with the Russians to conquer and dominate Europe. Max Perkins, Sweeny's editor, in a letter to his friend Elizabeth Lemmon, wrote of Sweeny, "He has been a soldier all of his life and fought in every war, and he ought to know something about the matter. He is pessimistic. He says there is a great danger that if the Germans beat the Russians, or the Russians the Germans, the two will join forces."[4]

Sweeny's fears were well founded. Before the war, in the mid- to late 1930s, Hitler made his territorial claims by taking control of the Rhineland, annexing Austria, and invading and occupying Czechoslovakia. Each of those moves was in direct violation of the Treaty of Versailles, and yet England and France did nothing to stop Hitler; they were wary of another long and protracted world war. Stalin became suspicious and paranoid about the British and French motives. Each of Hitler's territorial gains after the Rhineland were eastward towards Russia. Stalin felt that the British and French were appeasing Hitler and with each territorial gain they were forcing a showdown between Germany and Russia. So, on August 23, 1939, Russia signed a non-aggression pact with Germany that guaranteed Germany's eastern border in case of war. Russia agreed it would not invade Germany or give aid to any country that did. In return, Germany agreed not to invade Russia. The pact gave Hitler the assurance that, if hostilities broke out in Western Europe, he wouldn't have to fight a two-front war. A few days later, on September 1, 1939, Germany invaded Poland, breaking Hitler's promise to Chamberlain, and World War II began. Stalin, by making this self-serving alliance with Germany, unleashed Hitler's blitzkrieg on France and Western Europe.

However, by signing the non-aggression pact, did Stalin really expect Hitler would not attack him? Years earlier, Hitler, while in prison for organizing the Beer Hall Putsch in Munich, wrote his book *Mein Kampf*. In it, he outlined his vision for Germany. He stated that the German people needed more Lebensraum (living space) to obtain food and resources for the people of the Fatherland. That could only be achieved by conquering Russian territory and eliminating the Russian people who lived on it. In Hitler's mind, it was the destiny of the German "Master Race" to conquer and claim Russia as its own.

On June 22, 1941, after Germany had conquered France and most of Western Europe, Hitler double-crossed Stalin by unleashing Operation Barbarossa, his genocidal blitzkrieg on Russia, slaughtering tens of thousands of Russian peasants and captured Russian soldiers as the German army marched towards Stalingrad and Moscow. He was only stopped and turned back by a fierce Russian winter and the sheer determination of the Russian military, knowing they were fighting for their very survival. Surrender was not an option for the Russians, it was a fight to the death. Stalin had to know about *Mein Kampf* and Hitler's vision, but he made the mistake of trusting the half-mad, half-genius homicidal dictator of Germany. While Stalin initially thought he had pulled off a strategic move by signing the pact with Germany, it almost ended in disaster for him and the Russian people.

Given that history, Sweeny's mistrust of Stalin was logical. In many ways Stalin was as bloodthirsty a dictator as Hitler, and knowing his penchant for making self-serving deals with the devil, Sweeny wouldn't put it past Stalin, after conquering the Germans, to convince the German army to join forces with the Russians to dominate Europe. Stalin, by giving the Germans a promise of help to rebuild and restore Germany to power after the war, would have an unconquerable army.

Sweeny also had great misgivings about Great Britain. He had heard of the Morgenthau Plan, presented by U.S. secretary of the treasury Henry Morgenthau, Jr., and also of the Keynes Plan, developed by British economist John Maynard Keynes. These bold proposals being considered by the Roosevelt administration called for the pacification of Germany after the war, to ensure that the Germans would never be able to wage war again. They called for the destruction of some of Germany's industrial might with strict controls over what was left, leaving agriculture as Germany's main source of income. Both plans called for the establishment of a European Union of all the countries of Europe, with an international bank issuing a common currency called the Unitas (similar to today's Euro), for all member countries to use. Sweeny was suspicious that if either one these plans, or a combination of both, were implemented, the British would use it to control and dominate the economies of Europe.

In late 1943, Sweeny contacted Harry D. White, director of Monetary Research for the Treasury Department. White had carried out negotiations with Keynes and claimed authorship of the Morgenthau Plan, and Sweeny requested details of the plan from him. White wasn't forthcoming with information, which angered Sweeny. In a letter to Perkins on December 25, 1943, he wrote some scathing criticism of Roosevelt for even considering the plan.[5] When Nazi propaganda minister Joseph Goebbels received intelligence from his spies detailing the Morgenthau Plan, he set about creating hysteria among the German army by making them believe they were fighting for their very survival. This stiffened the resolve of the German troops, who became more fanatical and increased casualties among the Allies.

Another one of the Colonel's fears was that Great Britain would use an Allied victory to expand its worldwide empire to ensure that the sun would never set on the British Empire. Through this expanded empire, Britain would form the New World Wide British System to take over most industries. It would manufacture everything needed to assure its inhabitants a high standard of living. From the industrial plants of England, France, Belgium, Luxembourg and Germany, rebuilt and modernized with Marshall Plan dollars,[6] would pour a flood of merchandise to inundate the markets of the world. The coal of the Ruhr and of France, Belgium, and Wales would combine with the iron ore of France, Sweden, Spain and North Africa to produce a tidal wave of iron and steel products against which the mills of America would find it impossible to compete. In all the fields of commercial endeavor the story would be the same. The bauxite of France and Africa and India; the copper, lead and zinc of Spain, Tunisia, Morocco, Belgium, Congo and Rhodesia; the tin of Malaya; the rubber of the East Indies; the textiles of England, Ireland, France, Belgium, Germany, Spain and Italy, the silks of France, Italy and England and so forth and so on through the long list of industrial and commercial products the United States would have to compete with against a rival that would have the inestimable advantage of a customs-protected internal market of one billion consumers. It is only reasonable to conclude that America would soon find its export market of more than $18 billion a year shrinking and shrinking until nothing but remnants would be left.[7]

Although this British Super State failed to materialize, the United States, through international trade agreements, has seen many of its major industries decimated by letting them move to other countries. The promise of cheaper labor and material costs, lower tax rates, and higher profit margins has enticed American companies to move offshore. This has destroyed many major U.S. industries, such as auto and steel, putting millions out of work. In a way then, Sweeny's fears did come true.

In January 1944, Sweeny obtained a long talk with Admiral William D. Leahy. He was one of the most powerful men in Washington and Roosevelt's chief of staff. He also served as the chairman of the Joint Chiefs of Staff and was the spokesperson for General "Hap" Arnold of the Air Force, Admiral Ernest King of the Navy, and General George C. Marshall of the Army. All war plans went through him to the President. Leahy also was the liaison for the commander-in-chief and the military with the Allied Powers. He traveled with Roosevelt to all of the high-level conferences with other Allied leaders. Because Leahy performed well in his duties, Congress promoted him to five-star fleet admiral, the first man to hold that rank since Dewey in 1899 when he was promoted to admiral of the Navy. He was an advocate of a strong, two-ocean Navy and of greater effort in the war with Japan.[8]

Sweeny apparently got the interview with Leahy through his good friend Constantine Brown, the former Paris correspondent for the *Chicago Daily News* who was then foreign editor of the *Washington Star*. Sweeny described Brown as "Leahy's Man Friday" (his press contact). Sweeny wrote of Leahy, "I gathered from his very discreet remarks that the orientation of our foreign policy has already undergone a change or is about to do so. It appears that Roosevelt was greatly impressed by Stalin and seems inclined to abandon the British side and go over, lock, stock and barrel, to the Muscovite. Hull, Hopkins, Rosenman and Frankfurter[9] are trying to prevent this but the President showed evident signs of taking the bit in his teeth. Since I have arrived here I have had several letters from Constantine Brown to the effect that the situation is developing rapidly in that direction."[10] One has to wonder if Leahy was trying to manipulate Sweeny into writing something negative about the "Hitler First" policy, which would aid Leahy's advocacy of increased emphasis on the Pacific Theater.

Another of Sweeny's concerns was that the war was approaching a decisive period and Britain was preparing for two different outcomes. On one hand, the Allies were running the risk of a stinging defeat with a cross-channel invasion. In that case, it was his opinion that Great Britain would probably become a turncoat, leaving America and Russia alone to weather the Nazi storm. On the other hand, from all signs he could see, Roosevelt was arranging with England the conditions under which the post-war world would be compelled to exist if the Allies won. Sweeny feared the Allies would make the same mistakes they did in 1918 with the Treaty of Versailles, making the probability of yet another war in the near future a possibility. He was of the opinion that England, in her long history, had never honored her promises to anyone unless compelled.

"Today the world organization and Anglo-American cooperation are being put over by the same methods and by the same people who put over the prohibition in 1918," Sweeny stated in a May 22, 1944, letter to Perkins. "The whole proposition is just another one of those sanctimonious crusades under which manoeuvre [maneuvering] self seeking pressure groups, international finance, international Jewry, international labor, international communism and international buncombe in general are all friendly. By its friends you may know it." Sweeny felt the American people should be made aware of this so they could cast informed votes at election time.[11] "This book is, and such is its intention, an anti-Roosevelt book for election time," wrote Sweeny to Perkins on May 6, 1944.[12]

As Sweeny was writing *Ring in Our Nose*, his friend Frazier "Spike" Hunt was in the Pacific writing a book for Scribner's about General Douglas MacArthur. Hunt was given unprecedented access to MacArthur while writing the book. Sweeny reached out to MacArthur for information for *Ring in Our Nose*. Sweeny and MacArthur had attended West Point at the same time, although not in the same class, so Sweeny may have used that connection, as well as Hunt's access, to enlist the general's help. In any event, MacArthur offered to give him information to help him write his book. MacArthur harbored political ambitions and was talked about as a possible Republican nominee for president in 1944, so he might have seen a book critical of Roosevelt as furthering those ambitions. On May 6, 1944, Sweeny got a letter from Hunt with an added note from MacArthur stating, "Dear Chas: Could give you plenty of dope for 'Ring In Our Nose' Doug."[13] Like Sweeny, MacArthur had a low opinion of politicians running a war as evidenced by his later confrontation with President Harry S Truman that led to Truman relieving him from his command during the Korean Conflict.

Sweeny wanted to see America establish itself as the dominate world leader. In a May 22, 1944, letter to Perkins, he wrote: "We are Americans. God gave us a paradise in which to live and proper. We shall be held accountable for our stewardship. America's mission is not to be another cog on the European wheel. Our energy and enthusiasm should not be employed to perpetuate old tyrannies and old injustices. We are destined, if we are true to ourselves, to realize, as Rome did, that noblest of ideals, a world-wide empire of peace and justice. And we must use Rome's methods."[14]

This must have sounded imperialistic to Perkins and his patience was running thin with Sweeny. Perkins had written several letters to Sweeny trying to get him to tone down his rhetoric as he was writing the book.

On June 2, 1944, Perkins wrote to Sweeny pressuring him to finish the book. There were still two chapters outstanding and Perkins wanted them as soon as possible. "I hope it won't be long before we have all of the manuscript in our hands so that we can study the problem over carefully. I am prepared to personally agree with you as to the Rooseveltian tactics. Just the same, it would please Hitler, I suppose, to see a book come out which fomented suspicions among the Allies, and especially between us and Great Britain, just at this moment. I think you have a right to show how England has never regarded anything but her own interests, but I do not believe she is any worse in that respect than other peoples."[15] Sweeny was adamant that his book be published before the election while Scribner's insisted on waiting until after the election and after the negotiations between the Allies. They were at an impasse.

In the middle of July 1944, Max Perkins became ill and had to take a few weeks of sick leave away from the office. The last chapter of Sweeny's book was still outstanding along with a toned-down rewrite of some of his harshest rhetoric. While Perkins was absent from the office, Charles Scribner and his senior editor, John Hall Wheelock, along with others, got hold of Sweeny's manuscript and started reading it. They thought they were reading the completed book that included the missing chapter and the rewrite. They were shocked and appalled by Sweeny's harsh denunciations against Roosevelt and the Allies and immediately decided to cancel Sweeny's contract with Scribner's. In a carefully worded two-page letter dated July 13, 1944, they made it clear that it was "a publisher's privilege to make available to readers any honest book written from whatever point of view, regardless of the personal opinions he himself may hold, on the principle that the public is entitled to the best of what is being thought and said about matters that are of vital moment to all of us, and that the interests of all are best served by such free expression of opinion." While praising Sweeny as a "distinguished and loyal American," the letter said that with cooperation among the Allies so crucial to achieving victory, it would not be appropriate to publish a book that might "stir up latent animosities" between the Allies. Sweeny's book, they said, didn't offer any constructive suggestions to remedy his harshest criticism, and many of its points were unsubstantiated and seemed more controversial than factual. Scribner's felt that it could not publish the book and released Sweeny from his contract. They pointed out that they were within their rights to demand the return of the money they had advanced him, but Charles Scribner had decided to release Sweeny from that obligation.[16]

This, of course, enraged Sweeny. When Max Perkins returned after his illness, and saw what Scribner's had done in his absence, he immediately wrote a July 20, 1944, letter of apology to Sweeny. He pointed out that when Scribner and his associates had read the book they had all assumed that the last chapter had arrived. Perkins felt there was a chance to continue with the project and had sent a copy of the manuscript to Sweeny's friend, Frazier Hunt, in hopes that Hunt could suggest revisions that would make it publishable. However, Perkins went on to say that it would be impossible to publish the book before the election of 1944.[17]

On July 24, 1944, Sweeny sent a caustic reply to Perkins. He said he hadn't heard from Hunt but explained he had given Hunt carte blanche to revise the manuscript. He acknowledged the reasons why Scribner's canceled his contract, but defended his conclusions and opinions in the book. He claimed *Ring In Our Nose* was written to warn the American people they were going to be swindled again like in 1918-19.[18]

To understand Sweeny's concerns, it is necessary to look at the negotiations that took place leading up to the Treaty of Versailles after World War

I. President Woodrow Wilson wanted a "Just Peace" after the war. He believed there were underlying flaws in international relations that bred unfounded fears and mistrust that led to the outbreak of the war. Wilson offered 14 Points that he felt would make the world a better and safer place. Wilson recommended the end of secret diplomacy and alliances between countries, the reduction of armaments, freedom of the seas, easing of trade restrictions, a fair realignment of colonies, and respect between countries honoring their right to self-determination. He felt this would eliminate the nationalist sentiments and economic conditions that led to war. He also presented a bold proposal to organize an international organization, the League of Nations, so that nations could meet and work out their differences before hostilities could break out. Unfortunately, the Allies didn't share Wilson's views when the negotiations started. During the Paris Peace Conference of 1919, the major decisions were made by the "Big Four" David Lloyd George of Great Britain, Georges Clemenceau of France, Vittorio Orlando of Italy, and President Wilson. The Europeans weren't interested in a Just Peace. They only wanted to retaliate against the Germans. They ignored all of Wilson's 14 Points and demanded that Germany admit guilt for the war and they assessed excessive retributions to compensate the Allies for the war. The amount the Germans was assessed would cripple their economy for decades and caused the political unrest that allowed a madman like Adolf Hitler to rise to power. The treaty also restricted Germany to an army of 100,000 and restricted the size of their navy and other armed forces. The only thing Wilson came away with from the conference was approval for the League of Nations. It was his hope that it would prevent future wars. He returned home and presented the Treaty of Versailles to the U.S. Senate, which promptly refused to ratify it because it favored the European allies unjustly, and required League member-nations to send troops to repel aggression whenever directed to do so by the League. Senators Henry Cabot Lodge and William Borah asserted that only Congress could send the nation to war. In addition, Lodge detested Wilson personally and wanted to give the Republicans an issue to campaign on in the 1920 presidential election.

In his July 24, 1944, letter to Perkins, Sweeny went on to explain what he saw as the difference between 1919 and 1944. The first "swindling" was done behind Wilson's back while the second was being done with Roosevelt's full approval. Sweeny put the blame for Roosevelt's action on his "overweening ambition."

Sweeny asserted that his purpose in writing the book was "to prevent errors which would lead to another war." While Sweeny didn't claim to be a soothsayer, he did claim that by studying the men and countries involved, he could draw some deductions. "The history of Great Britain and of Churchill is so black that one has but to let the record speak for itself," he said.

Continuing, he argued that America was Great Britain's latest victim and "closing our eyes and keeping silent won't improve the situation." As an example of what he considered British machinations, he claimed that by trying to have the United States replace France as Syria's manager-protector after the war, Great Britain was creating a U.S.-Russia conflict while at the same time tearing down France. "If so, why have I lived?" he wrote. "Why have I fought? Why have I suffered?"[19]

Sweeny went on to make his case for publishing the book before the election. He felt that "we" could say whatever we liked about Great Britain and Churchill while that nation's fate depended on the United States. "The time to nail her to the cross is now when she is in our power. Afterwards it would be too late." He argued that Great Britain could not be trusted to live up to its promises when it no longer needs U.S. help. The American people had a right to know now while there was still time to act, he said. In his opinion, if Roosevelt was re-elected, there would be no stopping what he was predicting in the book.

Sweeny then drew a figurative line in the sand. "I leave Scribner's with some regrets because of the association with you. You have been a wise, an understanding and sympathetic mentor. I shall always be your debtor."[20] Sweeny was letting Perkins know that if Scribner's didn't publish the book before the election, he would go to another publisher. Sweeny felt he had powerful friends and contacts such as Hunt, Brown, MacArthur, and Hemingway who would give his book credibility to another publisher. In a letter to Perkins dated August 22, 1944, he stated that Double-Doran had expressed interest in publishing the book.[21]

However, in a letter to Perkins dated November 16, 1944, Sweeny began to realize his book was too controversial to print. "I have practically given up on the book. It must be a bad book as no one seems to consider publishing it. Yet when I read it over it seems to me to be better than *Moment*. But of course I am prejudiced." He went on to comment on the election that had occurred nine days before in which Roosevelt won by a landslide. "I did some campaigning for the Republican Ticket. What a licking we took. This fellow has a big bluff on the American people as Mohammed had on the Arabs or Napoleon on the French. I have come to the conclusion that it is silly to attempt to open their [the American people's] eyes to the gravity and the consequences of the situation. The American people just do not want to be saved. They are like an old whore—they like the job they are in."[22]

On November 20, 1944, Perkins wrote him back offering some encouragement. He said he had told Hunt to try further to place the book, but he felt other publishers would have the same fears about it as Scribner's did. Then Perkins suggested to Sweeny that he write an autobiography about his life.

While many adventurous people can write good enough narrative, few if any, can write as you do, particularly in respect to characterizing those you have seen, and in the vigor and cogency with which you state your convictions, and how you reach them. **All this should not be lost.**

What I am suggesting is that you write a book, at leisure, that would not be primarily "what happened to me," but "what I learned from what happened to me." You have very marked views on all military questions, including the one soon to be before us of universal military training. And you have your views also on the forms of political societies and on international relationships. The book might be primarily written to set forth these views, but it would be largely narrative, and the events recorded would illuminate your views. The book would not be so much what you did, but what you learned, and would not be strictly narrative, or at any rate, not a chronological narrative.[23]

On December 9, 1944, Sweeny replied to Perkins, "I have examined the project outlined therein. I have tried to receive it sympathetically but it is just no go. Writing about myself, my experiences and my deductions from them just does not interest me. I cannot work up the least enthusiasm." He went on to say, "One thing only is certain, the world is going to be the same old world with the same greed, the same hypocrisy, the same cruelty, the same injustice and the same barbarity. The same men are going to take up collection in Church on Sunday and lie and cheat the rest of the week." He then told Perkins he had soured on writing and it had done him no good to reread the manuscript to *Ring in Our Nose* and see that everything he had prophesied about England and Russia and especially Churchill and Roosevelt was coming true. It appears he was becoming discouraged or even depressed about the world situation. He did tell Perkins he was still going revamp and finish *Ring in Our Nose* for his own satisfaction. He then finished his letter by restating it was a no go to write his autobiography.[24]

It is astounding that he refused the book. Scribner's was a world-famous publishing house and was asking him to write the book. One has to think that maybe he was holding a grudge against them for canceling his contract for *Ring in Our Nose*. Or maybe Sweeny was hoping that they might yet give in and publish it.

On April 13, 1945, Sweeny wrote a letter to Perkins about the death of Roosevelt that occurred six days earlier. "I had about finished a complete and I hoped a final revision of 'Ring' when the old S.O.B. turned over and died on me. I had about fifty pages to do. Now I shall have to go back and do over another hundred pages. There is one consolation, he now belongs to history and one may say anything he pleases."[25]

Chapter 19

2600 Walker Lane

About this time a strange but interesting chapter opened in Sweeny's life. The Sweeny family had been friends with the Bamberger family of Salt Lake City, Utah, for decades. The two families probably met when Sweeny's father was negotiating with Jacob Bamberger for the sale of the Silver King and Daly-West Mines in Park City, Utah, in the early 1900s. When Sweeny went to Paris with his mother in 1910, the Bambergers were staying in the same hotel as the Sweenys. The Bambergers had a daughter, Dorothy, who was 12 years younger than Sweeny. She was attracted to him, and they later developed a close relationship.

Dorothy Bamberger Allen, friend and companion of Charles Sweeny (courtesy Maria Noble).

Sweeny's grandson, Frank Goodbold, had heard rumors from friends of both families that Sweeny and Dorothy had traveled extensively through Europe in the 1920s and 30s, sharing a room together. Although Dorothy married Lieutenant Colonel Charles J. Allen, a career Army officer and diplomat, in September 1925, she still had feelings for Sweeny. According to Dorothy's cousin, Betsy Bamberger Lesser, in late 1944 Dorothy had become severely depressed because she had lost her mother and her husband within five years of each other. She had always had someone living with her to protect her throughout her life as a result of an incident three decades earlier. When Dorothy was age 22, she was the target of an extortion plot that made national news. The extortionist, William L. Cummings, threatened to kill her by using a remote control bomb if the Bambergers didn't pay him $1,000 in cash.[1] Even though Cummings was caught and prosecuted, the experience left Dorothy with feelings of insecurity and vulnerability. When her mother Bertha died in May 1939 and her husband in August 1944, she felt alone and defenseless.[2] Lesser went on to say that Dorothy's brother, Clarence, invited Sweeny to go to Salt Lake City to live with her to bring her out of her depression. Sweeny accepted the invitation and moved in with Dorothy and stayed with her for the rest of his life.

Older Dorothy Bamberger Allen (courtesy Maria Noble).

Dorothy lived on a sprawling estate in a mansion built by the Bamberger family at 2600 Walker Lane, in a prestigious area of Salt Lake City. She had a full-time butler/bartender, chauffer, gardener, two full-time maids, and a cook. The estate had a large swimming pool, a guesthouse, a seven-car garage, and an animal run in which she kept dozens of stray cats. Even though she was small in stature she had a large heart especially for animals, and a veterinarian would visit her estate on a regular basis to administer medication and make sure the cats were in good health. Visitors to her home would find cans of open tuna fish around the house placed there for the cats to eat. Dorothy was a curious looking woman; she was barely five feet tall and weighed less than 100 lbs. with red hair and intense blue eyes. She was a chain smoker and always seemed to have a smoldering cigarette between her fingers or between her lips, which were heavily covered with lipstick. She never developed a lung disease from smoking and lived well into her 90s, but the cigarettes took a toll on her skin and complexion, and she appeared much older than she really was. She used copious amounts of makeup in an effort to mask her appearance. She eventually became almost totally deaf but vanity prevented her from wearing a hearing aid. To watch television, she had a special speaker

Older Charles Sweeny at Dorothy Bamberger Allen's home (courtesy Nicole Hess).

built that resembled a lamp with a flexible gooseneck with a speaker on the end instead of a light. Communication was a problem because she yelled at anyone she talked to and it was necessary to shout back at her to respond.

Dorothy and Sweeny had a peculiar companionship. The Bambergers always maintained that it was totally platonic, while friends and acquaintances insisted that it was a full-blown affair.[3] The Bambergers dismissed those rumors as based on conjecture and gossip from uninformed people. Regardless, there were accusations and strained feelings between Sweeny's estranged wife, Eva, living in France, and Sweeny and Dorothy.[4] Sweeny was unconventional in his relationships with women; he was a womanizer throughout his life, and even Hemingway admired his way with women. According to Sweeny's grandson, Dorothy could become impatient with Sweeny and verbally abusive to him. In some ways, she could hold her own with him.

Dorothy was a socialite and many important people came to her mansion as guests. She frequently had soirees that were well attended by the movers and shakers of society. In addition to Ernest Hemingway, she and Sweeny entertained the likes of Jack Dempsey, the heavy-weight boxing champ; Randolph Churchill, the son of the British prime minister; actors Gary Cooper (and his wife Veronica, "Rocky"), Amanda Blake (Miss Kitty on TV's *Gunsmoke*), Hugh O'Brien (TV's Wyatt Earp), Gene Tierney and other celebrities.[5]

Chapter 20

Defending Petain

By October of 1945, Sweeny's writing career had gone in a different direction. Instead of writing for a major publisher, he decided to write and publish his own works. In an October 25 letter to Max Perkins he wrote, "I can see that the world is going to hell fast in the midst of a general indifference on the part of the public. I do not believe that I would have anymore chance of getting a book published and read pointing out the real dangers of the present situation and present policy than I had previously. Enclosed you'll find a pamphlet I have published at my own expense. I do not expect it to have any success but [I] was so outraged by the trial and conviction of Petain that I have to do something to get it off my chest."[1] Henry Philippe Petain was the man chosen by the French Parliament to head a new French government after the Germans had overrun France in June 1940 when Prime Minister Paul Reynaud resigned. Petain was a lifelong army officer and the hero of Verdun whom Sweeny had first met in 1914 during World War I.

In the years between the world wars, Sweeny had several encounters with Petain. In August of 1920, after Sweeny had returned to France from Poland after the battle of Warsaw, Petain invited him to his office to discuss Sweeny's participation in the battle. He saw Petain again in 1923 after Sweeny returned to France from the Near East where he had accompanied French politician Henry Franklin-Bouillon to observe the unrest in Syria and the war between Turkey and Greece. According to Sweeny, Petain's questions were pointed and probing and he said the British were playing a dangerous game by supporting the Arabs, who could turn on them. In 1925, Sweeny served under Petain in the Rif War against Abd el-Krim. Sweeny was able to develop a social as well as a professional relationship with Petain during this time. One of Sweeny's most memorable experiences was a luncheon at the Trans-Atlantic Hotel at Meknes, Morocco in November. There had been a large parade preceding an awards ceremony bestowing military decorations on several people. Of the luncheon, Sweeny recalled, "I soon perceived that this man, whom I had always considered austere and distant, had a keen but kindly sense of humor doubled by a great joy of living. After the luncheon he entertained us for more than an hour with stories of men and events during his long career. Never once did I notice the least bit of malice or envy. Even when speaking of Foch, with whom he was then on very strained terms, he spoke with understanding and admiration."[2] Sweeny's high regard for Petain had evolved into love and respect. Petain was so impressed by Sweeny's service in Morocco that he raised Sweeny to the rank of Grand Officer of the Legion of Honour.[3]

Sweeny met him again in 1934 during the Popular Front movement demanding the reformation of the French Socialist government in power at the time. Operation of the government had been taken over by the cabinet, presided over by Gaston Doumergue, former president of the Republic, with Petain as minister of war. Sweeny felt this cabinet was nothing more than a stop gap to allow the storm to blow over until the crooked politicians could return to power and resume their former dishonest habits and schemes.

After Sweeny returned to France from the Spanish Civil War in 1937, he was taken by General Armengaud, the former air chief of France, to see Petain. Sweeny was impressed by "the lucidity of his mind and the great sadness of his spirit." Petain told Sweeny that the Ethiopian War and the Spanish Civil War were the opening shots of another world war. He said he had pushed for the completion of the armaments of the Maginot Line but the politicians wouldn't listen. His last words to Sweeny were that he "feared a disaster but hoped for the best." Over the next two years, before the outbreak of the war in 1939, Petain was very vocal in warning the French people of the oncoming disaster by giving speeches and publishing articles in magazines.

At the beginning of World War II, Petain was ambassador to Spain. Franco, the dictator in Spain, had been a student of his at the Ecole de Guerre some 30 years earlier. The French government felt that Petain was the man who could convince Franco to stay neutral during the war. He was successful.

The German invasion of France began on May 10, 1940. As the Nazi forces raced through France, the government of Prime Minister Paul Reynaud nearly collapsed before reorganizing in early June. At that time, Petain was appointed to the honorary position of vice-premier. Although the post carried no administrative or military authority, it was hoped that naming Petain would bolster the faltering French morale by putting the hero of Verdun into the government.

On June 16, the military position seemed hopeless for the French forces, so the cabinet voted 13 to 6 in favor of an armistice with Germany. The Reynaud Cabinet resigned after deciding to surrender and several prominent members fled the country. The president of the Republic, Albert Lebrun, called upon Petain to demobilize the military, saving as much as possible from the disaster. It was under these conditions the armistice was signed on June 22, 1940. By that time, Germany occupied three-fifths of French territory, the Italians had crossed the southern border and the French military no longer had the ability to resist the invaders.

On July 9, the French Parliament empowered Petain to form a new government as he saw fit. The vote on the proposal was 395 to 3 in the Chamber of Deputies and 225 to 1 in the Senate. On July 10, the members of the Senate and the Chamber of Deputies met in a National Assembly, as provided in the Constitution of 1875. By a vote of 569 to 80 with 17 absentees, they passed a constitutional law giving Petain the power to write a new constitution. At that point President Lebrun retired from office. He did not resign. If he had done so, it would have given the appearance that the old Republic of France still existed. By retiring, Lebrun admitted that the Republic had ceased to exist, explained Sweeny.

Sweeny declared that the government of the old Republic was a pack of scoundrels whose only god was money. He wrote that they had destroyed the influence of the church, and with it public morality and French culture, by turning religion into a political issue and accusing the clergy of every conceivable crime. Once the church was powerless, they seized its worldly goods and divided these spoils among themselves and their friends.[4]

In Sweeny's view, Petain had a chance to renew France when he took over the government in 1940. The French people were open to wholesale change But Petain blew his chance. While he named some honest military and naval officers to his cabinet, he shocked the French people by also naming several dishonest members of the old government. In the end, no matter how Petain tried to restore public confidence, this action and the subsequent intrigues of some of those disreputable politicians doomed his efforts.

Petain had an impossible task in dealing with the Germans. Under the terms of the surrender, Germany would occupy northern France. Southern France would remain supposedly independent with Petain as head of state with the government located in the spa town of Vichy. In southeastern France, the area around Nice would be under the control of Germany's Axis ally, Italy.

It's ironic that in the beginning the French people supported Petain and his new government. The French considered the British withdrawal from Dunkirk as a betrayal and many considered Charles de Gaulle a traitor because he abandoned his country and fled to England. De Gaulle was tried in absentia and sentenced to death by the Vichy government. Petain always maintained that he was not a puppet of Hitler. However, if he didn't do as Hitler wanted, the Germans would have completely taken over and made things even worse for the French people.

It was Sweeny's belief that Petain was trying to save as much of France and its surviving military as possible until a time when the Allies could rescue them. Unfortunately, in appeasing Hitler the Vichy government participated in the "Final Solution" and deported tens of thousands of Jews to the death camps. Vichy also conducted an aggressive campaign against the French resistance. Thousands of French citizens were jailed or killed. When the Americans launched Operation Torch, the invasion of North Africa, the French forces there fought against the Americans for a short time.[5] It was under these circumstances that Petain governed the French for four years When the war ended, Petain was indicted for war crimes in July and August of 1945. The charges were brought by none other than General Charles de Gaulle.

Before the war, Sweeny had heard de Gaulle lecture on tank warfare and strategy at the French war college and was immensely impressed by him.[6] But when de Gaulle abandoned France in 1940 and fled in the face of the enemy to England, Sweeny looked on him as a coward and became one of his harshest critics. In *Petain*, Sweeny wrote of de Gaulle, "He is a curious figure. He is the sort of man who could rise to an exalted position only in time of disorder and anarchy and then only as the tool of the stronger and more wily than himself. He is of mediocre intelligence but, like many stupid men, is determined and stubborn. His outstanding characteristic is an overwhelming vanity. He is one of those handsome, upstanding men who do not understand that beauty is only skin deep." Then as a comment on his escape to England, Sweeny wrote, "He pictured himself as the Joan of Arc of the twentieth century but he has not the moral courage to risk the execution pyre."[7] This criticism of de Gaulle would later come back to bite Sweeny when de Gaulle became president of France. He made it difficult for Sweeny to return to France for several years, a bitter pill to swallow considering Sweeny's love of France. Not being able to return probably added to his estrangement and separation from his wife Eva and son Patrick who were living in Nice.

In prosecuting Petain, the first big issue de Gaulle had to deal with was the question of Petain's authority. Petain had been named head of state in July 1940 by the National Assembly, which, under the Constitution of 1875, had all the power of a Constitutional Convention. Since Petain had been legally appointed at the Convention of 1940, he was lawfully the head of state under French Constitutional Law. To avoid the problem that this could cause at trial, one of the first acts of the de Gaulle government was to abolish the French State that Petain established and declare that the Republic had never ceased to exist. Thus, Petain could be tried for crimes against the Republic.[8]

Although the charges against Petain were many and varied, Sweeny concluded that they could be categorized into three general groups.

1. Conspiracy to overthrow the Third Republic.
2. Treason.
3. Intelligence with the enemy.

If Petain was guilty of conspiracy to overthrow the Republic so was President Lebrun, who had named him prime minister and then approved him as chief of the French State. Following this line of reasoning, the members of the Senate and Chamber of Deputies were equally culpable because the National Assembly voted Petain into power. The prosecution's solution to this thorny political and legal problem was to drop the conspiracy charge.[9]

The next charge was treason. Under the Code Penal of France, it is a capital offense for a French citizen:

1. To bear arms against the safety of France.
2. To plot with a foreign power or its agents, to commit hostilities or undertake war against France, whether war follows or not.
3. To plot with the enemies of the State to facilitate their entry into French Territory.
4. To deliver to them French ships or fortresses.
5. To supply them with munitions of war.
6. To aid the progress of their arms in French possessions or against French forces by sea or land.

It soon became obvious during Petain's trial that the prosecution had no evidence to support a conviction for treason under the first four charges or the sixth charge listed above. The fifth clause is liberally defined in French law to include furnishing any supplies, including moral aid and information, to the enemy. The specific crimes charged against Petain were (1) to have written a letter to Hitler congratulating him on the repulse of the commando raid on Dieppe, which was construed as giving moral aid to the enemy and (2) to have recruited labor for the munitions and other factories in Germany and to have delivered the workers to the German government, which was seen as giving material aid to the enemy. On these two charges Petain was convicted.[10]

Of the first charge, the congratulatory letter to Hitler, a copy of the letter was never introduced as evidence. The existence of the letter was established by hearsay testimony alone. At the time of the trial, the archives of the Petain government and the German government were in the hands of the Allies and yet no such letter was produced. In most courts of law, hearsay evidence would never be admitted into the trial. In Sweeny's opinion, it would be safe to assume that the charge of the congratulatory letter was "trumped up."

As to the second charge, furnishing material aid to the enemy, this was far more serious and, in Sweeny's view, better founded. However, Sweeny noted,

Petain did not act of his own free will. He acted under coercion. It appears that Petain received a non-negotiable demand from the Germans to furnish without delay a large number of workers to be sent to the war plants in Germany. Petain stalled as long as he could but if the Germans decided to push the issue he had no way to resist them. To fulfill the request, Petain made a deal with the devil.

According to Sweeny,

> It just happened that the workmen requisitioned were those whose cause would appeal the least to Petain. From the outbreak of the war in 1939 until the final catastrophe in June 1940, the workmen of the industrial regions of Paris and the north, but especially those of the center and the south had distinguished themselves by a series of strikes, sabotage and other disorders in the War Plants of the country. On the other hand, while these workmen were receiving very high wages and doing little to earn them, the men of the bourgeois and peasant classes were at the front. When the German demand was presented to Petain two million of them were prisoners. In this crisis Petain made the best bargain he could make under the circumstances. He exchanged those who had not suffered against those who had. Large numbers of farmers and small tradesmen—loyal Frenchmen who had given proof of their love of country on the battlefield—returned to their homes. Their places were filled by others whose loyalty and love of country were open to grave doubt. Who will blame Petain?[11]

As the trial progressed, Petain also was being tried and found guilty by the press. Sweeny commented on the effect of public opinion on the trial. "Issued a few days before the trial it [the press] informed the public that, among other crimes, Petain had ruined the French Army before the war, led it to defeat during the war and, finally, surrendered to the tender mercies of the Germans, both Nation and Army." As previously pointed out, none of that was true. In Sweeny's view, the French media considered Petain "a fascist who deserved not the slightest consideration from nations fighting in the defense of the democratic ideal. Anything which could happen to him would be less than he deserved."[12]

Many important people were called to testify at the trial. According to Sweeny, men like Daladier, Blum and Chevalier offered very little evidence but did a great deal to assassinate Petain's character by offering questionable hearsay testimony.

On August 15, 1945, Petain was found guilty of "intelligence with the enemy" and sentenced to death. He was immediately transported 500 miles from Paris to be imprisoned at the Fortress of Portalet. De Gaulle commuted Petain's death sentence to life in prison. On November 16, Petain was transferred to Fort de Pierre-Levee on Ile d'Yeu, a small island on the Atlantic coast where he died on July 23, 1951. Petain had requested that upon his death he be interred with his comrades at Verdun. But the government wouldn't allow it and buried him there on the island. Sweeny proposed an epitaph for his tombstone:

> **Here Lies**
> **Henri Philippe Petain**
> **Soldier Patriot Martyr**[13]

However, the government decreed a simpler epitaph: Phillipe Petain, Marshal of France.

On November 8, 1945, Sweeny wrote a letter to Max Perkins telling him of the success of *Petain*.

> The pamphlet is having a much better success than I ever hoped. Up to the present time five thousand copies have been printed and distributed in English, a French edition of ten thousand copies has been printed in Canada and distributed in French Canada and France proper, a Spanish edition of ten thousand copies has been printed at Mexico City and distributed in Spain and throughout South America. Of course none of this is going to do any good as far as getting the case retried or freeing Petain from prison. I feel that the Marshal is too old to permit us to free him. On the other hand I feel certain that, sooner or later, we shall succeed in forcing a revision of the trial and a rehabilitation of Petain.[14]

Chapter 21

Blaming FDR for Pearl Harbor

Sweeny's next project was an exposé about the mistakes the United States made leading up to the attack on Pearl Harbor. In a letter to Max Perkins dated February 3, 1946, he wrote,[1] "Am working on a pamphlet about Pearl Harbor. I am having some trouble in getting a copy of the official record. It appears that the transcript of the evidence before the Senate-House Committee will not be published for some months if then. It is risky to trust newspaper accounts." Then he added, "I am convinced that Roosevelt, by the end of 1941, had violated so frequently and so brazenly the Constitution and the laws of the land that only a war could save him from impeachment. One must be on solid ground before putting any such consolation on paper."

When it came to criticizing Franklin Roosevelt, Sweeny was like an old dog chewing on his favorite bone. He just wouldn't give up. The theme of his pamphlet on Pearl Harbor was that in order to be re-elected President, Roosevelt was somehow complicit with incompetence demonstrated by the government and the military that led to the disaster of December 7, 1941. Much of what he wrote in his Pearl Harbor pamphlet was a rehash of many of his points in *Ring in Our Nose*.

To say that America was not warned about an air attack on Pearl Harbor was absurd in Sweeny's view as well as some other critics. As early as 1925, General Billy Mitchell had foreseen the Japanese plans for expansionism in the Pacific. He predicted that in the near future the Japanese would attack Pearl Harbor from the air and inflict heavy damage on American warships and other assets there.

On August 30, 1945, the *New York Times* published portions of the official investigative proceedings and the conclusions about the Pearl Harbor attack. The *Times* singled out Army Chief of Staff General George C. Marshall, Secretary of State Cordell Hull, Chief of Naval Operations Admiral Harold R. Stark, Army War Plans Division Chief Lieutenant General Leonard Gerow, and the commanders in Hawaii—Lieutenant General Walter Short, Rear Admiral Husband E. Kimmel and Major General Frederick Martin—as most responsible for the American forces being caught totally off guard by the Japanese.[2]

However, Sweeny saw it differently. This was partly personal. He was resentful of Roosevelt and his administration for putting a stop to the plan to send him to North Africa to recruit the Arabs to fight against Hitler. His anger was fueled further when he wasn't permitted to recruit pilots to fight in Yugoslavia. He took the position that Roosevelt manipulated the circumstances so that adequate warning and preparation was not given to the American forces at Pearl Harbor. Japan's attack drew America into the war and that permitted Roosevelt to declare the unwanted war he wanted to wage on Japan and the Axis Powers. The war guaranteed his re-election, Sweeny surmised. These conclusions seem mind boggling because Sweeny had a front row seat to all of the events in Europe that led up to the beginning of World War II and he took a pro-active role in opposing Hitler and the Axis.

Despite the inherent contradiction, Sweeny reached the following conclusions. First, he criticized Roosevelt for the way he dealt with General Short, General Martin, and Admiral Kimmel, the military commanders on the ground at Pearl Harbor when the Japanese attacked. Sweeny concluded that Roosevelt didn't want a court-martial of these officers because it would show the president's complicity in the disaster. Since they were not on trial, they were denied legal counsel who could call and cross-exam witnesses. Roosevelt feared that the "facts" of his complicity would come out under cross-examination and expose him as a fraud. When the president took action and dismissed these officers, he abused his power as commander-in-chief because he found them guilty of malfeasance without a chance for the accused to defend themselves. Roosevelt constituted himself judge, jury, prosecutor while being one of the principle parties in the case.[3]

Next, since the commander-in-chief is ultimately responsible for all military matters, Sweeny concluded that the lack of preparation at Pearl Harbor fell upon the president's shoulders. Sweeny quoted the Roberts Report[4] stating that there was no adequately installed and staffed airplane-spotting system in Hawaii. Of course, this was inaccurate because there was a newly installed radar station at Opana Point on the island of Oahu that detected the large Japanese formation approaching Pearl Harbor from 130 miles out. The two privates manning the radar station called the information center on the island and reported it to the officer in charge, who erroneously concluded that they had spotted a flight of B-17 bombers scheduled to arrive from the mainland that morning. The officer told them the now infamous statement, "Don't worry about it."[5]

The Roberts Report also exposed the fact that the anti-aircraft command had received only 20 of the 500 37mm guns called for in the plan of defense for the island. The report noted that those guns had received ammunition for training or firing purposes on September 1941 of only 1,000 rounds (50 rounds per gun). The rate of fire of those guns under battle conditions was no less than 60 rounds per minute, so when the Japanese attacked, the gun crews had just 50 seconds of fire. Another 8,000 rounds for those guns were delivered December 6, 1941, and were issued to the batteries (only 400 rounds per gun). The next day when the attack started, the untrained crews of the anti-aircraft guns had only six minutes and 40 seconds of ammo in reserve to repel the two-hour attack.[6] Sweeny concluded, "Now we know that the Fleet in Pearl Harbor could not have been defended no matter what precautions had been taken, what diligence shown. The necessary weapons and material had not been furnished the Unit Commanders. The procedure of the Washington authorities in this matter is like sending a child to the corner to buy a loaf of bread and refusing to give him the necessary money."[7]

Sweeny's next conclusion was that the Roosevelt administration didn't keep the commanding officers in Hawaii adequately informed of the deteriorating relations between the Japanese and American governments. The two governments had been at odds for years over Japan's brutal expansionism that had begun with the Japanese invasion of Manchuria in 1931. Over the next few years, Japan expanded farther into China, which led to the second Sino-Japanese War of 1937. Japan then invaded French Indo-China so it could block all imports to China, including U.S. military supplies. The United States responded by placing an oil embargo on Japan. The Japanese navy estimated that it had only about a two-year supply of oil on hand. That was totally unacceptable to them. The conquest of the U.S.-held Philippine Islands was also a target of Japan. So, Japan put into action its plans for the Pearl Harbor attack, the invasion of the Philippines, Guam and other U.S. assets in the Pacific. Negotiations between America and Japan had reached an impasse.

On November 27, 1941, General Marshall sent this message to General Short in Hawaii:

> Negotiations with the Japanese appear to be terminated to all practicable purposes with only the barest possibilities that the Japanese Government might come back and offer to continue. Japanese future action unpredictable but hostile action possible at any moment. If hostilities cannot, repeat cannot, be avoided, the U.S. desires that Japan commit the first overt act. This policy should not, repeat not, be construed as restricting you to a course of action that might jeopardize your defense. Prior to hostile Japanese action, you are directed to undertake such reconnaissance and other measures as you deem necessary but these measures should be carried out as not, repeat not, to alarm the civilian population or disclose intent. Report measures taken.[8]

On the same day General Short replied: "Report Department alerted to prevent sabotage. Liaison with the Navy." It was received by the War Department, as it was rubber stamped and initialed by General Gerow. To prevent sabotage, the aircraft at Ford Island in Pearl Harbor and at other airbases on Oahu were lined up in the middle of the airfields and put under armed guard. While this strategy prevented sabotage from enemy agents on the ground, it exposed the aircraft to almost certain destruction if attacked from the air. They were lined up like ducks in a shooting gallery. Sweeny surmised that General Marshall didn't initial the report. He accused Marshall of some involved and artful dodging when asked about this report during the Army Pearl Harbor Board investigation. "After reading his [Marshall's] testimony and his embarrassed replies to the questions of the Board one obtains the impression that he would have liked to deny having seen it, but did not dare."[9]

Sweeny noted that since Marshall's November 27 memo to the field commanders ("If hostilities cannot, repeat cannot, be avoided the U.S. desires that Japan commit the first overt act") was sent the day after a U.S. ultimatum to Japan left no hope for peace, Marshall was convinced there would be a Japanese attack. Why then the call to avoid hostilities? And what was "the intent" that Marshall wanted them to avoid revealing?[10] Wouldn't active surveillance to seek out the enemy be the order of the day? In Sweeny's view, "the intent" of the actions Marshall outlined was "to entice the Japanese into committing an 'overt act.'"

Sweeny then offered his indictment of Marshall: "Therefore he is at least as fully responsible as Short for the success of the Japanese attack. In fact, his responsibility is far greater, for he is better informed than Short of the tenseness of the political situation. He also has at his command, which Short does not, the reports of the Army Intelligence Service as to probable Japanese intentions and the estimate of the War Plans Division of probable Japanese action. This latter bureau was convinced that a Japanese attack on Pearl Harbor was highly possible, if not certain."[11]

To better understand the tragic comedy of errors made preceding the attack, we need to briefly review the events that led up to the ultimatum given to the Japanese. On November 25, 1941, at 9:30 a.m. Secretary of War Henry Stimson and Secretary of the Navy Frank Knox were informed by Secretary of State Hull that he was going to hand an ultimatum to the Japanese the next day. Hull denied that the note was an ultimatum but Stimson's diary states that after informing him of the delivery, Hull stated: "Now it is up to the Army and Navy to take care of the matter. I have washed my hands of the Japanese."[12] There is some evidence that General Marshall contemplated notifying Short but instead the above message was sent after the president spoke with the Japanese representatives on the 27th. On November 28, the following message was sent by the War Department to General Short: "Critical situation demands that all precautions be taken immediately against subversive activities within field of investigative responsibility of War Department. Stop. Protective measures should be confined to those essential to security avoiding unnecessary publicity and alarm." It seems that the War Department feared sabotage on the ground more than an air attack.

Admiral Isoroku Yamamoto, the man who planned the Pearl Harbor attack, insisted that the United States be given at least a 30-minute warning before the attack that the peace negotiations were at an end. However, the Japanese army and Japanese prime minister Hideki Togo did not want any early warning that might interfere with the attack and took steps to subvert Yamamoto's demand.[13]

On December 6, 1941, the Japanese ambassador to Washington, D.C., received the first 13 parts of a 14-part message from Tokyo that clearly pointed out that war between the two countries was going to break out. The final part, stating that Japan was breaking off negotiations, did not arrive at the Japanese embassy until about 7:30 a.m. Washington time. At about 10 a.m. Washington time, the embassy received instructions to deliver the entire message to the State Department at 1 p.m. that day, which was 8 a.m. at Pearl Harbor, the time set for the attack to begin. The Japanese personnel took too long to decode and type the 5,000-word message and it wasn't delivered to the Secretary of State Hull until 2:20 p.m. (9:20 a.m. Hawaii time). By then the attack was well under way. American intelligence however, had intercepted Tokyo's communication to its ambassador on December 6 and by 9:30 a.m. Washington time (4:30 a.m. Hawaii time) on December 7 had decoded the message and delivered it to Admiral Stark. He immediately tried to contact Marshall, but the general was out riding his horse, and couldn't be contacted until 11:25 a.m. (6:25 a.m. Hawaii time). Marshall then ordered that Hawaii and other American bases in the Pacific be notified immediately. Due to poor atmospheric conditions over the Pacific Ocean, a radio message couldn't be sent. So the War Department sent it by the undersea cable service operated by the Radio Corporation of America (RCA). Although the cable wasn't secure, and the message could be intercepted, at least it would get there. Inexplicably, the message was not marked "URGENT" so it sat on the desk at the RCA Cable Office in Honolulu and wasn't delivered until after the attack had begun.

When President Roosevelt first read the Japanese communication, according to later testimony by a White House naval aide, he exclaimed, "This means war!" "Unfortunately," said Sweeny, "we are not informed in what spirit he made this statement: sad, firm, grave or—jubilant."[14] (However, Sweeny was clearly hinting at what he believed was FDR's complicity in orchestrating the events that led to the attack). After making that remark, the White House naval aide stated that Roosevelt tried to contact Admiral Stark, but he and

General Marshall were nowhere to be found. Stark it appears had gone to the theater that evening to enjoy a comic opera. In Washington at the time there was only one theater where a comic opera that would interest the admiral would be presented. It was the National Theater on Pennsylvania Avenue, between 13th and 14th Streets. It seemed incredible to Sweeny that the president didn't send one of his aides about 300 yards from the White House to deliver a warning to Stark about Japan's message.[15]

It is clear that General Marshall, Admiral Stark, President Roosevelt, and Secretaries Hull, Stimson, and Knox had ample warning of Japanese intentions for several weeks prior to the attack, although not necessarily the location. The Philippines, Formosa and Indo-China were also considered potential targets. Sweeny concluded that to prove Roosevelt and Company innocent of malfeasance, Kimmel and Short must be proven guilty. To see how this was accomplished, Sweeny looked at the first Pearl Harbor Report submitted by Frank Knox. Two of the many questions that came out of that report were: a) Was there any error in judgment that contributed to the surprise, and b) Was there any dereliction of duty prior to the attack? On the first count, Sweeny concluded that Short and Kimmel couldn't be convicted. Instead of Washington sending clear and detailed warnings of the imminent Japanese attack, they sent ambiguous, veiled messages with no detailed orders to prepare the fleet to repel the attack or be ready to seek out and destroy the enemy.[16] In fact, Kimmel and Short didn't learn of the November 27 ultimatum until December 1943 when the State Department released its findings. The only silver lining in the attack (if it can be called so) is that Admiral William F. Halsey had had the foresight to take his aircraft carriers out on the open sea for maneuvers and they weren't in the harbor on December 7. Halsey's carriers kept the Japanese at bay at the Battle of the Coral Sea and destroyed four Japanese aircraft carriers at the Battle of Midway, giving America time to recover from the Pearl Harbor disaster.

Given the problems with a finding of guilt on the first count, the only alternative the Roberts Commission had was to find Kimmel and Short guilty of the second count, dereliction of duty. Otherwise, the president wouldn't be justified in relieving them of their commands and blame would fall on the White House. The first thing the commission pointed out was that Kimmel and Short, along with several of their officers, were attending social functions the night of December 6. That point was hypocritical since Stark was at a play that night and Marshall was out riding his horse the next morning.

On the second count, the allegation was made that the Navy, Army, and Army Air Force commanders failed to cooperate and share intelligence. That led to lapses in communication that led to the disaster and resulted in dereliction of duty. They were given specific orders to have the aircraft warning system properly staffed and operating; the Navy should have been sending out reconnaissance aircraft to spot the enemy, and the anti-aircraft artillery located on the warships should have been manned and supplied and in a high state of readiness to repel the attack.[17] None of those steps were taken and blame was affixed to the commanders on the ground. To further bolster its case, the commission implied that the officers' use of alcoholic beverages the evening before the attack might have hampered their efficiency. The Army and Pearl Harbor Boards and the Joint Congressional Investigating Committee investigated and found that Kimmel, Short, and Martin and their junior officers were absolutely sober. The accusations of drunkenness were baseless.[18]

Sweeny concluded that the commanders on the ground were refused the basic rights granted to even the most evil of criminals. They were refused the right to hear the specific charges against them. They were refused the right to adequate counsel. They were refused the right to cross-examine witnesses. They were refused the right to present evidence in their defense. It was under these prejudicial conditions they were found guilty of "Dereliction of Duty." Despite such obvious unfairness, history has villainized them as incompetent traitors.[19]

After demolishing the credibility of the administration's case against the military men, Sweeny went on for the rest of his Pearl Harbor exposé ranting and raving and rehashing all of his old pet peeves against FDR. He stated that Roosevelt was elected for his first term in 1932 on a program of economic reform. It was picturesquely called the New Deal.[20] In 1937, Sweeny believed that the New Deal Bubble had burst and Roosevelt's domestic policy was in shambles. FDR realized that if judged by his record up to that time the election would be lost. The attention of the American people had to be drawn to other issues. With the world in turmoil with war raging in China and Spain, Italy having just conquered Ethiopia, and Germany and Russia plagued by civil unrest, Roosevelt focused on foreign policy. Sweeny wrote, "War, war alone, could save Roosevelt from political annihilation. Would Roosevelt, faced with disaster resort to … inciting war? No one knows. Would he profit by such a situation if it should occur? Without the slightest doubt. In the situation in which he found himself, he would naturally grasp any means of salvation." Sweeny admitted the weakness of his claim in the absence of direct proof, which he believed would eventually be found hidden in government files. But he argued that his conclusions were reasonable, given the evidence available.[21]

Sweeny's focus then shifted to criticize Roosevelt for the Republican (Loyalist) defeat in the Spanish Civil War. In early 1937, a British-sponsored initiative caused 27 nations to agree to ban all shipment of arms to all combatants in the civil war. Great Britain, which favored the legally-elected Republican cause, changed sides after Franco's forces seized the iron mines and manufacturing regions of the Asturias and the lead, copper, zinc and pyrite mines of Andalusia, the principle source of minerals for English industry. Since Germany and Italy were not parties to the agreement, they continued to furnish Franco with arms and supplies. Russia, the other source for Republican supplies, withdrew her support during the summer of 1937. To make matters worse, Leon Blum, the French prime minister, closed the French-Spanish border, halting the delivery of arms that were already in transit to the Republicans. The result of this British-inspired agreement was that the Republicans had no way to resupply. It was only a matter of time for Franco's forces to achieve victory. Roosevelt's contribution to the annihilation of the Republic was a joint resolution of the Senate and the House introduced January 8, 1937, at the request of FDR. The resolution deemed it unlawful to export arms, ammunition, or implements of war from the United States or its possessions to Spain or any other country shipping arms to either side of the opposing forces in Spain. By 1938, the Republican cause was in critical shape and Senator Key Pittman, chairman of the Foreign Relations Committee, proposed to repeal the ban for shipping arms to Spain. Secretary Hull, at the direction of Roosevelt, used the strong arm of the administration to stop the overturn of the ban. Sweeny then offered this indictment, "This combined action of the French and American Governments, in accord with the British Government, sealed the fate of the Spanish Republic. It should be noted here, and underscored, that in this affair Great Britain, France and the United States were the associates, we almost said accomplices of Germany and Italy in the assassination of a nascent Democracy."[22]

Towards the end of Sweeny's pamphlet on Pearl Harbor, he made the following list of precedents set by FDR that, under other and more ruthless Presidents, are capable of leading us into bloody and costly adventures:

1. He waged undercover war that favored Great Britain against the wishes of the American people.
2. He armed belligerent nations [Britain and her allies] without the consent of Congress.
3. He negotiated agreements in favor of Great Britain and her allies. And he took hostile actions against Germany and her allies, without consulting Congress.
4. He occupied British territory by agreement with Great Britain but without consulting Congress.
5. He planned to occupy foreign territory (probably French,) without the consent of its government, with which the United States was not at war.
6. He planned to make a "sneak attack" (D-Day) on a country without consulting Congress or the American people.

7. He placed elements of the Army and Navy under the command of one of the belligerents (Great Britain).
8. He acted in furtherance of his own wishes without regard to the Constitution and the laws of the land.[23]

At the end of his Pearl Harbor pamphlet, Sweeny made the following comment, "We must so modify our system of Government to the end that it cease to be a Government OF the People by the President and become a Government FOR the people by Congress."[24]

To accomplish this, he proposed a few specific changes. Starting with the judicial branch, he suggested that all federal courts be "completely independent" of the executive branch. This would entail depriving the president of the power to appoint federal judges. In addition, he proposed that the Supreme Court be given "untrammeled" authority to "scrutinize any initiative and/or action of the Executive and/or Congress." To handle this added workload, he proposed that the Supreme Court be divided into sections, with each having specific functions. He further proposed that one of these sections "should have the powers and initiative of a Council of State," adding that "it might be wise" to make former presidents and Supreme Court justices ex officio members of this Council of State. As to the duties and powers of the office of President, he proposed that the office be deprived of functioning as the commander-in-chief, leaving the President's role in foreign affairs to that akin to a minister of foreign affairs. The office of commander-in-chief would be filled by a person, nominated by the president but responsible to and removable by Congress "without concurrence of the President."

This is a brief summary of just a few of Sweeny's complaints against Roosevelt. It seems that regardless of what Roosevelt did, good or bad, Sweeny objected to it. There was no compromise in his mind.

Chapter 22

World Disorder and Revolution

During and after World War II, Sweeny traveled around the United States on a series of speaking tours. These speeches made full use of Sweeny's wide-ranging knowledge of war, politics, geography, economics, philosophy and culture.

One speech was a commencement address he delivered at Southwest Missouri State Teachers College in June 1944, just days before two milestones on the road to Allied victory—the D-Day invasion and the capture of Rome. While he began his remarks with rejoicing at the impending successful end to the war, he soon launched into a dire warning of what he imagined would be a failed peace. "Europe will still be overcrowded. Millions of her people will never … have enough to eat [and] more than half the total population on Earth will be still worse off than the starving Europeans. Meanwhile, the favored peoples and nations of the earth will strengthen their monopoly over the riches of the earth." He noted that Great Britain, with just 6 percent of the world's land and 6 percent of its population, controlled 30 percent of the world's wealth, reaped 36 percent of its income and will "do everything in its power to increase these percentages." Rather than see their families starve, he said, the hungry would fight to survive. "This means war."

"As we look forward into the vista of the years we see war succeeding war until the world will again conquer that equilibrium, that harmony, without which all is confusion and disorder." As future teachers, Sweeny told the audience, their task is to prepare their students to meet the stresses and trials inherent in that world.[1]

* * *

Sweeny made some of the same points in a speech to a group of bankers, also in the spring of 1944, about the long-promised Allied assault on Hitler's Atlantic Wall. He said there had been no great battles yet in this war like those of 1918. He dismissed as mere "large size skirmishes" the fighting that had taken place in North Africa, Sicily, Salerno and Anzio by mid-1944. "Up to the present time our men do not know what war is," he said. "They are going to learn."

Turning to his main topic, Sweeny described the geographic issues facing an invasion of Europe and concluded—as the D-Day planners had—that the most promising avenue was through either France's Picardy-Normandy coast or the coast of Brittany. He predicted two to five million casualties before the German surrender, and after that the final reckoning with Japan. He contrasted the amount of shelling during the final assault of the Meuse-Argonne offensive in 1918 and the recent battle at Cassino. "[S]hells were falling on the 150 kilometer front at the rate of approximately 200,000 a minute that is to say more than 1,000 a minute to every kilometer of front," he said. By comparison, the latest wire service report from Cassino said shells there were falling at the rate of two a minute. "That gives you some idea of the difference between what we are doing now and what we shall have to do once the attack on the Continent has commenced."[2]

* * *

The decades after the World War II were marked by turmoil. Wars of liberation erupted in Europe's colonies and Cold War tensions heated up between the capitalist West and the communist East. During this period, Sweeny put considerable effort into writing books that built on some of the themes in his speeches—world disorder and revolution—that he had honed as a guest lecturer to the Professor Wormuth's political science classes at the University of Utah.

Among Sweeny's personal papers obtained by his grandson, Frank Goodbold, were several drafts of chapters four and five of a book tentatively titled "World Disorder," which was never published.[3]

Sweeny asserted that a balance of power among the major powers could keep the peace in Europe. He envisioned two ways of doing this. The first was the creation of one power so much stronger than any of the other nations that none would attack it. The other way to keep the peace was to have two equally powerful rival nations kept in check by a third nation, which shifted its support to enforce the balance. Sweeny said the first way had not existed since the time of Charlemagne, the first Holy Roman emperor who united most of Western Europe in the Middle Ages. The second way existed between the 10th and 19th centuries and created an "uneasy equilibrium" among the powers in Europe. "If properly recreated," wrote Sweeny, a balance of power "could possibly write finis to the projects of world domination of Franklin

Delano Roosevelt, Harry Truman and Josef Stalin." Sweeny saw the two great rivals as the United States and the Soviet Union with either China or India serving as the third power to maintain the balance.

The multiple drafts of these two chapters suggest Sweeny struggled to find an approach that he could carry out. It is likely he abandoned the project when he couldn't find an approach that suited him. The bulk of the content involves lengthy recitations of historical events to illustrate and buttress the points that Sweeny sought to make. However, the content is repetitious at times, the arguments a bit muddled and the points a bit obscure. Sweeny was an excellent storyteller and a forceful advocate, but, as he himself admitted during one of his lectures, he tended to wander off topic at times.

A series of letters that Sweeny wrote to longtime friends suggests reasons why the book was never published.[4]

On February 25, 1952, he wrote to war correspondent and radio commentator Frazier Hunt: "I am still working on this damn book. It has been the scourge of my days and the incubus of my dreams. The only reason I undertook this plague was to prove to myself that I am not completely senile." In the final months of 1952, Sweeny's letters to old friends included comments about his frustrations with the book and with his health problems at age 70.

On December 29, Sweeny wrote to Hunt:

> I am sending you a copy of the first four chapters of the world stirring book. I am far from satisfied with any of it but especially the fourth chapter, like so many women I have frequented in the past, just refused to fall into its allotted place. I have written and rewritten it I forget how many times but it just will not flow.
>
> I am having the same difficulty with the fifth chapter which I have written and rewritten. I am now engaged on wooing the sixth chapter with the hope that that bitch will prove less recalcitrant than the others. I may yet have my pleasure with her.

Sweeny wrote to Hunt again on September 29, 1953, after some major health issues, including a cerebral hemorrhage in 1951, chronic lower back pain and the flu[5]:

> As to the book, I have done little about since last fall. I had tried to swallow too much and paid the penalty. I found myself firmly bogged down with 90,000 worthless words to weep over.
>
> I put the manuscript aside and began again. I had a new first chapter finished when Malcolm Cowley came to see me towards the end of May. He squirmed through the 90,000 words, shook his mane, scowled and asked me what I was shoot[ing] at. I had not thought from that angle. In fact, I have not yet digested the idea.
>
> He told me the public no longer reads books of 90,000 words except novels. Even their success depends on the greater or less degree of pornography which they offer to satisfy the vicarious appetites of their readers. Their objective is to incite to fornication and/or masturbation.

* * *

In the mid–1950s, Sweeny shifted his focus from writing "World Disorder" to writing a book about the causes of revolutions, which were much in the news. Unfortunately, relatively little of this intended book was found in Sweeny's files after his death. It is likely that Sweeny abandoned the project as his health gradually declined. In any event, it was never published.

In Sweeny's opinion, American intervention, sometimes to restore stability but more often to promote and protect American business interests, particularly in the Western Hemisphere, was a major factor in revolutions around the world. As he wrote in one brief draft of a section for the book, "Behind all the talk of world leadership, of solidarity of Free World Peoples, of realignment to contain and repulse a conjectural Russian aggression, one sees emerging from the fog of international politics, finance and economics the monstrous shadow of an American Universal Empire. This Empire, as one sees it building with an astonishing rapidity if not with an equal and correlative solidity is different in its fundamental construction from any empire of recent or ancient times although it will probably arrive at a like result in the end."[6]

Chapter 23

Sweeny's Last War

While fighting to sustain his health and finances, Sweeny also spent his final decade fighting for a cause unlike any other in his life. After putting his personal crusades ahead of his family for decades, Sweeny fought his last war for his children and grandchildren.

When the German invasion of France in mid–1940 became an unstoppable juggernaut, Sweeny had abandoned his family to engineer the escape of the American pilots he had brought to France. His wife, Eva, and their three children took up residence in Nice, a city on the south coast of France where her family had a home.

Sweeny's son, Charles, had served in the ambulance corps in France prior to the French defeat. In early 1941, the 29-year-old slipped out of Vichy France and made his way through fascist Spain to neutral Portugal. He sailed from Lisbon aboard the American cargo-passenger ship *Excambion* on a U.S. passport and arrived in New York City on March 18, 1941. He took a room at the Hotel Gotham in Manhattan.[1]

The following year, Sweeny's 28-year-old daughter, Emeline, followed a similar escape route. She left Lisbon on the Swedish-American liner *Drottningholm* on a U.S. passport and arrived in New York City on June 30, 1942.[2] She moved into an apartment at 3305 Cleveland Avenue NW, Washington, D.C.

Eva remained in Nice with invalid son Patrick.

Charles Jr. soon moved to Southern California and spent the war years there working as a cinematographer in the motion picture industry. In 1946, he listed his employer as the famed Metro-Goldwyn-Mayer movie studio[3] and his residence as 806 North Bedford Drive, Beverly Hills.[4] Charles Jr. used his father's fame to open doors and "blew his inheritance" trying to live the Hollywood lifestyle.[5]

He reportedly married several times. There are two confirmed marriages.

One was to Ginette Diamant-Berger, the 25-year-old daughter of French screenwriter, producer and director Henri Diamant-Berger. Her family lived in America during the war. On her 1941 citizenship application, Ginette listed her occupation as "script girl." The couple was married on July 28, 1942, by a Baptist minister at a commercial wedding chapel in a seedy part of west Los Angeles. The official witness was another minister at the chapel. Apparently no family or friends attended the wedding. The couple divorced a few years later. After the war, Ginette worked in film in Europe as a production assistant, screenwriter and assistant director.

Charles Jr.'s other confirmed marriage was to 28-year-old Utah native Patricia Anne Clarke on September 15, 1950, in Salt Lake City.[6] The couple had a daughter in 1952 and lived in Salt Lake City until at least 1957. Charles Jr. worked as a self-employed photographer and a videographer for KSL-TV.[7] During this period, his work included making a series of short films for Kennecott Copper Corporation about its mining operations. The films later appeared on television as the Kennecott Copper Theater.[8] The couple later divorced. Patricia and her daughter moved to Santa Barbara, California, where Patricia died in 1977. Charles Jr. later returned to France, reportedly to avoid creditors in Salt Lake City who claimed he owed them $300,000.[9]

Meanwhile, Emeline took a job as an interpreter for the federal government in Washington, D.C. In addition to her native French, she was fluent in English, Spanish and German, and possessed a photographic memory. In October 1945, she visited her father in Salt Lake City. A newspaper article said she stayed at the home of Dorothy Bamberger Allen, and was "extensively entertained." The article also said that "Col. Sweeny is now acting as vice chairman of the French relief effort for the state of Utah."[10]

On January 28, 1946, Emeline gave birth in Los Angeles to a son, whom she named Charles Sweeny O'Hare. Two months later, on March 25, 1946, she married Victor Edwin O'Hare in a civil ceremony in Nogales, Mexico, just over the U.S. border from Arizona.[11] Accounts differ as to where and how Emeline, 32, met O'Hare, 38. By one account, they met in Washington, D.C. By another, they met in Los Angeles while she was visiting her brother.

However it came about, the marriage was not a happy one and when Emeline tried to end it in 1947, O'Hare kidnapped her, took her to Mexico and demanded payment from her father for her return. Sweeny responded by hunting down O'Hare and freeing Emeline. The courts in Utah tended to reject divorce petitions from women, especially those with children, so Sweeny lodged Emeline in a hotel in Preston, Idaho, just over the state line from Utah. While obtaining a divorce there, she gave birth to a second son, Ernest Hemingway O'Hare, on November 3, 1947.[12]

A little more than a year later, on January 12, 1949, Emeline, 34, married Verden Lynn Talbot, 28, an Army Air Corps veteran and farmer who was liv-

Family photograph. Front row, from left: granddaughters Nicole, Elizabeth and Michele Talbot. Second row: grandsons Charles and Ernest O'Hare (Frank Goodbold). Third row: Colonel Charles Sweeny; his son, Charles; his daughter, Emeline Sweeny Talbot (courtesy Nicole Hess).

ing with his mother and sister, Thyra, in Lewiston, Utah, not far from Preston. The couple purchased a small farm with a two-room house in nearby Cove. Four daughters, Elizabeth, a set of twins, Nicole and Michele, and the youngest, Emeline, were born to this union between 1951 and 1955. Needing a larger house, the family purchased a larger farm, several new pieces of farm machinery and a herd of cows in nearby Richmond in late 1951. The farm and equipment were obtained with help from Emeline's parents and a loan from the federal Farmers Home Administration.

Despite the growing family, the marriage was in trouble. Emeline found it difficult to fit into the small-town culture. According to her younger son, her European lifestyle and outlook on life were incompatible with the views and values of many of the local citizenry. "She was divorced with children. She smoked and drank coffee. She even went to bars and drank," he said. These traits, and her independent thinking, led to her inability to be accepted by many of the people, particularly the women, of Richmond.[13]

The family situation worsened when one of Talbot's legs was smashed in a hay baler and had to be amputated in 1952. The next several years were difficult ones for Emeline and Verden. The loss of his leg affected his ability to work. The couple grew apart and the marriage gradually unraveled. Despite the marital discord, Emeline became pregnant again in 1957 but suffered a miscarriage. In August of that year, after the loss of the baby, she filed for divorce. The Utah courts made no move to block her petition.[14]

The divorce was granted in the spring of 1958 with sole custody awarded to Emeline. To manage her own affairs, Emeline purchased a 1951 four-door Plymouth sedan from one of her husband's relatives. She also began making plans to move herself and her children to France to join her mother. According to Emeline's younger son, the move to France was pushed by her parents. Eva purchased a home for them in Paris. The farm in Richmond was in the final phase of foreclosure, so she had little choice but to leave for France if she wanted a place to live.[15]

On August 14, 1958, ten days before the divorce was to become final and they were to leave for France, Emeline left her daughters with their aunt in Lewiston and drove with her two sons the 100 miles to Salt Lake City to purchase clothes and suitcases and make final preparations. It was late afternoon as they headed home. About two-thirds of the way home, she stopped at the Midway Inn between Brigham City and Wellsville for a beer. After they got back on the road, it began to rain heavily. There were no windshield wipers on the car, making it hard to see in the dark and rain. Emeline was forced to pull off to the side of U.S. Highway 91, a two-lane road between Wellsville and Logan, 16 miles from home. She parked to wait for the rainstorm to pass. She was seated in the driver's seat; 12-year-old Charles was in the backseat, and. 10-year-old Ernest was in the front passenger seat.

As they waited, a five-ton, ten-wheel truck approached their location. The truck, owned by the Utah By-Products Company, collected scrap fat, meat and bones from butcher shops and restaurants on a daily route but was empty at the time. The driver, Gene Ray Chidester, 32, of Logan, was driving on a suspended license. It had been suspended two months earlier for habitual reckless driving. Chidester changed lanes to pass a car and as he pulled back into the lane he swerved onto the shoulder and slammed into the left rear of Emeline's car parked on the shoulder. "The force of the crash threw both vehicles from the road, crossing a borrow pit.[16] They sheared off a utility pole, and came to rest in a field about 30 feet from the highway," the Provo *Daily Herald* reported the next day. The truck came to rest atop the car, with its front wheels resting on the hood of the car.[17] "The body of the car was knocked almost free of the frame," the *Deseret News* said. "The truck literally tore the sedan to shreds." A front-page photo shows a mangled hulk that is only recognizable as a car by the presence of a twisted steering wheel and a crumpled door.

Passport photograph of Emeline Sweeny Talbot and her children, 1958. Front row, from left: Michele, Nicole, Emeline and Elizabeth. Second row: Emeline. Third row: Ernest and Charles (courtesy Nicole Hess).

The truck driver was not seriously injured. The occupants of the car were not so lucky. Emeline was pinned against the dashboard by one of the truck's wheels. She was dead. So was Charles in the backseat. The rescuers had to cut the car apart to remove the bodies. They found Ernest jammed under the dash. Miraculously, he was alive, but with serious injuries to his head, chest and spine.[18]

It was a month after the accident before the boy was told that his mother and brother were dead. "I figured it out but I didn't tell them," he said in an interview in 2015. "Finally my grandfather [Sweeny] came to my hospital room to tell me. When he had trouble getting the words out, I said, 'They're dead.' He said, 'Yes.' I could see how badly he felt about lying to me since the accident. He left the room without another word."[19]

In addition to the surgeries and painful rehabilitation, there was at least one other never-to-be forgotten moment while he was hospitalized. "I'm in the hospital," he vividly recalled decades later. "I'm paralyzed from the chest down. The kid next to me is in a cast from his neck to his knees. His name was Dennis. He had septic arthritis. This guy walks in, sees Dennis and says to him, 'Hello son, I'm your father.' That was the first time I met my father," he recalled.

It had been ten years since the divorce, and the boy and his father, Victor O'Hare, had never had any contact. But when O'Hare learned his ex-wife had died and his son was alive, he made a beeline to the boy's hospital bed. His son was an heir to the fabled Sweeny fortune, and as the boy's sole surviving parent, O'Hare might be in for a big payday at last. In the son's opinion, his father was a "ne'er-do-well gold digger."

O'Hare spent the next two months hanging around Salt Lake City, visiting the boy in the hospital. When the boy was discharged from the hospital, Sweeny arranged for him to live with Raymonde Goodbold and her husband, Captain Thomas Goodbold, who was stationed at nearby Fort Douglas.[20] O'Hare tried to get the boy to leave with him. He cozied up to the boy's nurse, Hildegarde Land, hoping she could sway the boy.[21] When persuasion failed, O'Hare tried to kidnap his son. During a visit at the Goodbold home, O'Hare suddenly lifted the boy out of his wheelchair and started to carry him to his car. Only the timely intervention of Captain Goodbold stopped him. Goodbold grabbed hold of the boy and a tug-of-war ensued with the injured boy as the rope. Finally, O'Hare let go, got in his car and drove off. He soon returned with a police officer to try to enforce his parental rights. Goodbold warned O'Hare and the cop they were on a military reservation and he could have them both arrested by military police if they didn't leave. They left.[22]

Sweeny filed a lawsuit on behalf of Emeline's children against the truck driver and his employer. The company settled the suit for $60,000, with $15,000 going to the lawyers and $16,000 to the hospital for the boy's medical treatment. Each of the girls was to receive $3,000. The remainder was to be set aside for the boy's future medical bills.[23]

Sweeny also went to court to have himself appointed as the legal guardian of all five of Emeline's surviving children, seeking to deprive both O'Hare and Talbot of custody of their offspring. Sweeny alleged both men were unfit fathers. Both fathers fought Sweeny's petition in court. In addition, O'Hare made a personal appeal to Sweeny in a November 1958 letter, written in French. O'Hare said Sweeny's wealth could offer the boy many things, but he appealed to Sweeny to recognize that there are things beyond money that a father can give his son. When Sweeny didn't reply, O'Hare wrote to the Goodbolds, in English, to complain that Sweeny hadn't replied and to feel out their support for either his gaining custody or leaving the boy with them. There is no indication that the Goodbolds wrote back to O'Hare.[24]

The district court agreed to appoint a local bank to manage the children's estates, to oversee any inheritance while they were minors. The court also made the surviving son a ward of the court. But it declined to do the same for the four daughters. Instead, it let them remain with their father, who had taken custody of them immediately after the accident. Sweeny appealed the ruling as to the four girls, but the Supreme Court of Utah unanimously upheld the lower court's ruling. The court said state law required proof of actual neglect or harm to the children during the present period of custody, referring to the time since the accident. No such proof had been introduced, so the Supreme Court upheld the lower court's ruling allowing Talbot to retain custody.[25]

Talbot eventually left the farm in Richmond and he and his daughters moved into the family home with his sister, Thyra Griffeth. His health failed and on March 7, 1965, he died of a heart attack. Griffeth then took the responsibility of raising his girls.[26]

At Sweeny's urging, the district court sent the boy to live with Ray Goodbold and her husband. "In the beginning, I was taken in by her charm and glamour, the same as many others," he recalled. Unfortunately, it proved to be an uncomfortable fit. "Captain Goodbold was a very cold and distant disciplinarian," he said. "Being constantly reprimanded for not understanding the dos and don'ts of an army life, added to the control Ray Goodbold wanted over every minute of my life, led me to feel trapped."[27]

Years later, he learned from Sweeny's friends that she only agreed to take him in as a means of working her way into Dorothy Bamberger Allen's upscale social circle, and to receive a $200 a month stipend out of his trust fund.[28]

Raymonde "Ray" Glarner Goodbold was the daughter of André Glarner, a prominent French journalist and friend of Sweeny's in Paris in the 1920s and 1930s. Born and raised in France, Ray Glarner later claimed to have been France's figure-skating champion in 1931. However, official records do not support that claim. She also said she had served in the French Forces of the Interior (the French resistance) during the Second World War. She married a French architect and had a son in the 1930s. The couple later divorced and in 1948 she moved with her son to the United States and married Thomas Goodbold.[29] The Goodbolds offered to adopt Ernest after the accident but he declined.[30]

He still thinks about the what-ifs: "If we had not stopped for a beer; if we had arrived home before the rain; or if we had been sold a car with wipers, we would have made it." His life, and that of his mother, brother and sisters, would have been forever changed.

For many years, he believed Sweeny was in charge of his life. It was only much later he said that he learned he was actually a ward of the court. He spent a good deal of time with Sweeny at Dorothy Bamberger Allen's house between 1958 and 1960. "That's where I got to know him," he recalled.

In 1960, when the Goodbolds took a vacation without him, he spent the time with his half-sisters, who were living with their father. Lewiston, Utah, was a world he knew and understood. He asked to stay and the judge granted his request.

"When I decided to return to Lewiston, it was the final defeat for the Colonel," he said. "He seemed to have given up making a contribution to our lives. He was pleasant but distant. I only saw his disappointment at how things had turned out for his grandchildren."

Over the next three years, however, his relations with Verden and Thyra "deteriorated badly," he said. In 1963, now 15, he was offered a chance to rejoin the Goodbolds. "Given the conditions in Lewiston, the Goodbolds seemed the better of two lousy choices," he said. So he returned to the Goodbolds and agreed to be adopted. He also changed his name at that time from Ernest Hemingway O'Hare to Francis Ernest Goodbold. "It's funny," he said. "My mother always wanted to name me Francis, but my grandfather [Sweeny] insisted on naming me after Hemingway."[31] A few months later, Frank and the Goodbolds moved to Daly City, California, as Thomas Goodbold, now retired from the Army, could not find work in Salt Lake. Frank said he remained with the Goodbolds until age 21 because they refused to let him move out at 18.

He said he rarely saw Sweeny between 1960 and 1963, when Sweeny died. "We [he and his sisters] only learned of his death when someone pointed out his obituary in the paper. Uncle Charles didn't tell us. He took all the money he could for himself."[32]

However, there wasn't much money to be taken when Sweeny died. He had never been careful about money, and in 1952 he had invested in a company that was developing a piston engine that lost $420,000 in a single year.[33] Sweeny had also cashed out his trust fund holdings in the Sweeny Investment Co., selling it back to the Finucane branch of the family, which controlled the company. He netted about $12,000. At the end he was essentially broke and dependent on Dorothy Bamberger Allen.

While Sweeny's finances were depleted, Eva was continuing to manage on her own thanks to the foresight of her mother-in-law. When Sweeny more or less abandoned his family to go off to war, his mother gave Eva 225 shares of stock in the Sweeny Investment Company. Decades later, this generous act provided Eva with a steady income.[34]

Letters between Sweeny and Eva in the 1950s reflect no passion between them but an abundance of respect and an occasional flash of affection. The letters, written in French, begin "Mon chere Charles" and "Mon cher Eva," which translates to "my dear." One of Sweeny's letters to Eva begins "Ma cherie," which can mean "my darling," "my beloved" or "my dearest." One of Eva's letters signed off with "kisses." Curiously, Sweeny signed all of his letters to Eva with his full name, "Charles Sweeny." He also signed his full name to letters to old and dear friends, such as Hemingway.[35]

The letters were written while Sweeny lived in Utah with Dorothy Bamberger Allen, and Eva lived in Nice and Paris with their invalid son, Patrick. Most of the letters concern family money matters. The couple still shared some complex financial ties stemming from Sweeny's inheritance from his parents, so tax matters were a frequent topic.

The letters reveal that when their son, Charles Jr., turned 21, Sweeny gave him shares of stock in the privately held Sweeny Investment Company. This provided a monthly dividend sufficient to live on, if not a lavish lifestyle. The letters also indicate that Sweeny and Eva helped support their daughter, Emeline, especially after her husband was disabled in the farm accident and could no longer support her and the six children—two from her first marriage and four with Verden. They paid the medical bills for Emeline's pregnancies and Verden's leg amputation, and also gave her shares of stock in the Sweeny Investment Company.

Older Charles Sweeny at Dorothy Bamberger Allen's home (courtesy Nicole Hess).

In March 1956, Sweeny arranged with Eva to share some of her income with him. She agreed to give him part of her monthly income from the Sweeny investment stock. However, in July 1956, Eva lamented, "Why is it I have to live in misery before dying to benefit the children and grandchildren?"

The letters also mention some milestone family events and offer revealing comments by the parents about their offspring, as well as themselves.

On December 5, 1955, after discussing their children's personal and financial problems, Eva wrote, "I'm getting very sad thinking that our children have so stupidly organized their lives. I would like to protect them, even after my death. I could not have imagined my end with such sadness. Life is so ugly and so this life was not for my dear little Patrick. I would be thrilled to go."[36]

Eva also revealed her unhappiness with Charles Jr.'s spendthrift ways in a June 26, 1956, letter. "Charlie always wants to be the big lord, but he leaves the care of his children to the rich families," an apparent reference to his parents and his in-laws. With that criticism in mind, she advised Sweeny in the same letter, "We must especially think of Patrick. It is useless to believe that Charlie and Emeline will use their power to protect him. The boy cannot rely on anyone and he is unable to defend himself."[37]

On October 25, 1952, Sweeny wrote to Eva that Emeline was "holding up well" despite the hardships associated with her husband's accident as she prepared to give birth to twins, her fourth and fifth children, the following month. He also wrote as an adoring grandfather about Emeline's existing children. He wrote that Emeline's daughter, born the previous year, "is beautiful with blond golden hair, blue eyes and a firm chin with a pretty figure. In short, she is adorable. The two boys are growing up. Butch [Charles] is restless and bright. The little one [Ernest] is tougher and more manly."[38]

In the same letter, Sweeny wrote: "I hope to still have a few years to live in France. I'm not saying in peace because if offered the guarantee of a few years of peace I believe I would refuse. I'm not a type to live in peace. It is only the struggle that excites me. I am starting to believe there is a bit of Cyrano [de Bergerac] in me." He closed the letter: "I love you my good girl. Kisses to Alice [Eva's spinster sister and housemate] and Patrick."

On December 19, 1952, Sweeny wrote that Charles Jr.'s wife, Pat, had given birth that morning to a girl. "She's an eight-month child, very small but beautiful and well formed." He added that "Charlie is fatigued because of so much work. I'm all right. I'm still a jerk." After offering Eva best wishes for Christmas, he added, "We love you even if you do not think so."[39]

* * *

In later years, Frank Goodbold learned more about Sweeny from his friends, including Dorothy Bamberger Allen and her brother, Clarence. "My opinion of him changed for the better as a result of those stories," he said. "I still believe he was a bully, opinionated and probably a white supremacist; not Ku Klux Klan but one who believes that Europeans are superior to other races."[40] However, he now thinks that Sweeny spent his final years trying to make amends for not having been there for his wife and children. "Everyone wanted him to leave it [the children's custody issue] alone, but he wanted to save us," he said. "Fighting for my sisters and me was the Colonel's last war."

Sweeny visited Hemingway at his home in Ketchum, Idaho, in 1959. Upon his return, he called Hemingway to say he had suffered another stroke. The call left Hemingway depressed over his shrinking number of friends. Sensing his own mortality, Sweeny made one last trip to France and to see Eva and Patrick. Upon his return, he remarked on what had become of France:

"To have fought a world war only to lose a whole empire is an unparalleled folly."[41]

Sadly, Sweeny experienced one final loss when Patrick, age 44, died January 12, 1962, from injuries as a passenger in an auto accident on a mountain road above Nice.[42]

Sweeny's health continued to decline. He was hospitalized in Salt Lake City in early 1963 and died at age 81 on February 27, 1963. He was buried in Salt Lake City's Mount Olivet Cemetery, a non-denominational final resting place for many of Utah's political, social and military elite. Newspapers across the country carried obituaries marking his passing. They reverently recounted his many wars—often summarized as "7 wars under 5 flags"—as well as some of the myths that had piled up around him, which he had never brushed away.

Portrait of Charles Sweeny (courtesy Nicole Hess).

Eva, his wife of half a century although they spent more years apart than together, lived on until 1975. She is buried with Patrick in the Cimentiere Mairie de Saint Andre de la Roche in Nice.

Dorothy Bamberger Allen, who shared Sweeny's final years, died December 29, 1985, and is interred next to her husband and other family members in the Bamberger family vault in Mount Olivet Cemetery, not far from Sweeny's grave.

Sweeny's nephew Robert, the British amateur golf champion in 1937 and a decorated combat pilot in the RAF during the war, was a wealthy financier and playboy-sportsman. His engagements to Woolworth heiress Barbara Hutton and Lady Sylvia Ashley filled the celebrity columns, while his marriage to Manhattan's debutante queen of 1948, Joanne Connelley, ended in tabloid headlines. Robert divorced Joanne in 1953, citing her affair with international playboy Porfiro Rubirosa.[43] Robert died in London on October 21, 1983.

Robert's brother, Charles, the founder of the Eagle Squadron, was a socially prominent, wealthy financier. He first wife, Margaret Whigham, was the most famous beauty of her day and the "Mrs. Sweeny" immortalized in the Cole Porter song "You're the Top." The couple divorced in 1947.[44] He remarried and died in Miami on March 11, 1993.

Sweeny's son, Charles, was the last of the principal actors to leave the stage. He died in Nice on January 9, 2001, still trying to live off his father's fame.

Frank Goodbold, Sweeny's grandson, overcame his injuries received in the auto accident to become a successful businessman. He is married and lives in the Pacific Northwest.

His four sisters continue to live in Utah.

Despite having seen more wars than most old soldiers, Sweeny, the second oldest child in his family, outlived all of his siblings. He also outlived two of his three children and many of his famous contemporaries. In particular, it struck him as ironic that he had survived the passing of his long-time friend, Hemingway, who was nearly two decades his junior. One of the last things he said to a friend as he lay dying in his hospital bed was "Whoever thought I should outlive Ernest Hemingway."[45] Adding to the irony, Hemingway died violently, by his own hand, while Sweeny died peacefully in bed.

Chapter Notes

Introduction

1. Archibald MacLeish, the American poet and writer who was part of the same group of expatriates in Paris in the 1920s, said Hemingway "could exhaust the oxygen in the room just by coming into it." Jeffrey Meyers, *Hemingway* (New York: Harper & Row, 1985), 71.
2. George Seldes, *Witness to History* (New York: Bantam Books, 1987), 314.
3. *Ibid.*, 255.
4. Meyers, *Hemingway*, 212.
5. Michael Reynolds, *Hemingway: The Paris Years* (New York: W.W. Norton, 1989), 76.
6. *Ibid.*, p. 77.
7. Kenneth S. Lynn, *Hemingway* (New York: Simon & Schuster, 1989), 182.
8. Carlos Baker, *Ernest Hemingway: A Life Story* (New York: Charles Scribner's Sons, 1969), 98.
9. Donald McCormick, *One Man's Wars: The Story of Charles Sweeny, Soldier of Fortune* (London: Arthur Baker Ltd., 1972), 121.
10. Michael Reynolds, *Hemingway: The Final Year* (New York: W.W. Norton, 1999), 33.
11. Carlos Baker, *Ernest Hemingway, Selected Letters* (New York: Charles Scribner's Sons (1981), 553.
12. Waldo Pierce (1887–1970) was a prominent artist once called "the Ernest Hemingway of American painters." A long-time friend of Hemingway, he painted the novelist's portrait for a cover of *Time* magazine in 1937. He was married four times and had five children. In a 1930 letter, Hemingway offered this description of a visit to his Key West home: "Waldo is here with his kids like untrained hyenas and him as a domesticated cow." Like Hemingway, Pierce served as an ambulance driver during World War I, although he served in France while Hemingway was in Italy. France awarded Pierce the Croix de Guerre for bravery at Verdun.
13. Evan Biddle Shipman (1904–1957) was an American reporter and poet in Paris during the 1920s and 1930s. He met Hemingway in Paris in 1924 and lived in the Hemingways' home there. According to an article in the *Daily Racing Form*, Hemingway tutored Shipman in the local culture, boxing and drinking, and Shipman tutored the couple's son, Jack, in English. Hemingway dedicated his second collection of short stories, *Men Without Women*, to him. Shipman fought in the Spanish Civil War, where he was wounded, and served in a tank unit of the U.S. Army in World War II. He later became one of the premier horseracing writers in America.
14. Baker, *Ernest Hemingway, Selected Letters*, 553.
15. Rose Marie Burwell, *Hemingway: The Postwar Years and the Posthumous Novels* (Cambridge: Cambridge University Press, 1996). The other two influential men in Hemingway's life were General Charles "Buck" Lanham and Max Perkins.
16. Baker, *Ernest Hemingway, Selected Letters*, 501–502.
17. Baker, *Ernest Hemingway: A Life Story*, 154.
18. Reynolds, *Hemingway: The Paris Years*, 325.
19. Baker, *Ernest Hemingway: A Life Story*, 205.
20. Joe Fay, "From the Heritage Bookshelf: Hemingway, For Whom the Bell Tolls, and an Old Spanish Civil War Buddy," *Historic News*, September 10, 2010.
21. Baker, *Ernest Hemingway: A Life Story*, 275.

22. The Hurtgen Forest was the longest single battle ever fought by the U.S. Army and a totally unnecessary slaughter. Located on the Belgium-German border, it had no strategic or tactical value. However, Allied military planners in the rear ordered frontline commanders to push straight ahead through the forest rather than bypass it. The dense, dark forest became known as "the green hell." It took three months to capture, devoured units from no less than ten U.S. infantry divisions, inflicted 33,000 U.S. casualties and slowed the Allied advance into Germany. In many respects, the battle was a throwback to the infamous meat-grinder combat of World War I.
23. Reynolds, *Hemingway: The Final Year*, 204.
24. Meyers, *Hemingway*, 412.
25. Baker, *Ernest Hemingway: A Life Story*, 475.
26. Reynolds, *Hemingway: The Final Year*, 55.
27. Meyers, *Hemingway*, 429.
28. Baker, *Ernest Hemingway: A Life Story*, 457.
29. Reynolds, *Hemingway: The Final Year*, 149–150.
30. Baker, *Ernest Hemingway, Selected Letters*, 612.
31. Frank Goodbold Collection.
32. Frank Goodbold Collection.
33. "Viejo" is Spanish for "old-timer."
34. Frank Goodbold Collection.
35. "Melpomene" is the Greek muse of tragedy, and a "Baladron" is Spanish for a person who boasts that he is brave when he is not.
36. The Dromios are two foolish characters in Shakespeare's *The Comedy of Errors*, a slapstick farce.
37. Frank Goodbold Collection.
38. *Ibid.*
39. The Mau-Mau Uprising was a revolt between 1952 and 1960 against British colonial rule in Kenya.
40. Interview with Frank Goodbold, May 21, 2015.
41. Mary Welsh (1908–1986) was Hemingway's fourth wife. Biographer Jeffrey Meyers noted that while Hemingway had been the first husband of his first three wives, Mary had been married twice before. Her first marriage was to a fellow Northwestern University student in 1929 and lasted two years. Her second marriage to a fellow journalist in 1938 ended in divorce in 1945, after she began an affair with Hemingway. Mary met Hemingway in 1944 in London, where she was a correspondent for *Time*. According to Meyers (*Hemingway*, p. 394), "During the heightened sexual atmosphere of wartime London, where women reporters were rare, Mary openly used her attractions to obtain information from high-ranking officers." Hemingway later accused her of having sex with generals to get a story, wrote Meyers. Mary's other wartime lovers included Hemingway's brother, Leicester, and journalist/author Irwin Shaw. Biographer Kenneth Lynn (*Hemingway*, p. 508) wrote that "Mary's life, in the words of [her London colleague] Bill Walton, was 'full of lovers.'" The marriage of Ernest and Mary was, by all accounts, a turbulent one, so it is quite possible that she sought comfort in the arms of other men, including Sweeny.
42. Frank Goodbold Collection.
43. "Quod erat demonstradam" is a Latin phrase variously translated as "What was to be demonstrated," "Which is what had to be proven" and "Which had to be done."
44. "Cicerone" is an old term for a museum guide.
45. Frank Goodbold Collection.
46. Baker, *Ernest Hemingway, Selected Letters*, 544.
47. Frank Goodbold Collection.
48. "Services Slated for Hemingway," *New York Times*, July 5, 1961.
49. Sally Belfrage, "The Haunted House of Ernest Hemingway," *Esquire*, February 1963, 67.

Chapter 1

1. John Fahey, *The Ballyhoo Bonanza* (Seattle: University of Washington Press, 1971), 3.
2. *Ibid.*, 5.
3. *Ibid.*
4. Michael J. McAfee, 3rd New Jersey Volunteer Cavalry, 1864–65, http://3rdnjcavalry.com/A_Horse_to_Ride.html; Clyde A. Risley and Frederick P. Todd, "3rd New Jersey Cavalry Regiment, 1864–1865," http://3rdnjcavalry.com/ArticleVuksicBarbasic.html; Karen Denmark, "Tribute in Honor of the Third New Jersey," http://3rdnjcavalry.com/.
5. Civil War pension records of Charles Sweeny/James Nulty, National Archives.
6. 1870 Federal Census, San Francisco, California.
7. Affidavit from Charles Sweeny's Civil War Pension Application records.
8. Affidavit by Mrs. Lillian Edwards from Charles Sweeny's Civil War Pension records.
9. Fahey, *The Ballyhoo Bonanza*, 7.
10. "From Grocer's Clerk to Millionaire," *Spokesman Review*, July 23, 1916.
11. Fahey, *The Ballyhoo Bonanza*, 10.
12. "Fire in the Belcher Mine," *Daily Alta California*, October 31, 1874.
13. Fahey, *The Ballyhoo Bonanza*, 10.
14. "From Grocer's Clerk to Millionaire Mining Man," *Spokesman Review*, July 23, 1916.

15. "Charles Sweeny Tells Story of His First Trip in Placer Mining Fields," *Spokane Daily Report*, July 10, 1914.
16. *Ibid.*
17. "Charles Sweeny Tells of His First Trip in Placer Mining Fields," *Spokane Daily Chronicle*, July 10, 1914.
18. *Ibid.*
19. *Ibid.*
20. Fahey, *The Ballyhoo Bonanza*, 77.
21. *Ibid.*, 146.
22. *Ibid.*, 144.
23. "From Grocer's Clerk to Millionaire Mining Man," *Spokesman-Review*, July 23, 1916.
24. "Guggenheims Reported as Buying Big Buffalo," *Salt Lake Herald*, October 27, 1907.
25. Fahey, *The Ballyhoo Bonanza*, 191–192.
26. *Ibid.*, 126.
27. "From Grocer's Clerk to Millionaire Mining Man," *Spokesman Review*, July 23, 1916.
28. Under the U.S. Constitution until 1913, each state's senators were elected by the state legislature. As part of the Progressive Movement, direction of senators by the people came about in 1913 with the ratification of the 17th Amendment to the Constitution.
29. Fahey, *The Ballyhoo Bonanza*, 131.
30. *Ibid.*
31. *Ibid.*, 132.
32. "Gift of Twenty Thousand From Charles Sweeny," *Spokane Daily Chronicle*, January 6, 1906.
33. The Knickerbocker Trust was one of the largest banks in the United States. In 1907, its president used the trust's funds as part of a stock market manipulation aimed at cornering the market on copper, with the prospect of a huge profit. When the scheme failed to corner the copper market, the Knickerbocker Trust and some other banks collapsed, causing the Dow Jones Exchange to drop 50 percent and plunging the nation into a recession. Congress created the Federal Reserve System in 1913 to try to avoid future panics. Sweeny was not part of the scheme.
34. Fahey, *The Ballyhoo Bonanza*, 208.
35. *Ibid.*, 210.
36. "Charles Sweeny Dies in Portland," *Spokane Daily Chronicle*, May 30, 1916.
37. "Charles Sweeny Is Laid to Rest," *The Spokesman Review*, July 3, 1916.
38. Fahey, *The Ballyhoo Bonanza*, 214.
39. "Gift of Twenty Thousand from Charles Sweeny," *Spokane Daily Chronicle*, January 6, 1906.

Chapter 2

1. His date and place of birth are recorded on his United States Military Academy application. It also appears on his later various passport applications.
2. 1891 Gonzaga College Catalogue listing Sweeny as a student.
3. Gonzaga University website history page.
4. McCormick, *One Man's Wars*, 18.
5. *Ibid.*
6. *Ibid.*, 18.
7. *Ibid.*
8. *Ibid.*, 19.
9. *Ibid.*, 19–21.
10. 1897 and 1898 catalogues of Gonzaga College.
11. McCormick, *One Man's Wars*, 22.
12. 1900 Gonzaga Catalogue.
13. 1903 Gonzaga College Catalogue.
14. Appeal filed in the U.S. Court of Appeals for the Ninth Circuit, dated September 27, 1900.
15. "Bank Failures Were Big Outrages," *Spokane Press*, September 15, 1903.
16. Email from Angela Kindig, Archivist at Notre Dame University, dated May 6, 2005.
17. *Description and School History of Candidates, June 1900* (Archives, USMA), 67.

Chapter 3

1. "Charles Sweeny Jr of Spokane Selected as Cadet to West Point," *Seattle Post-Intelligencer*, May 24, 1899.
2. Jones served in the U.S. House of Representatives until he was elected to the U.S. Senate in 1908. He served in the Senate until his death in November 1932, two weeks after his defeat for reelection. He was a prohibition supporter and this helped cost him his reelection bid. Prohibition was repealed in 1933. He authored the Jones Act, which said that only U.S. flagged vessels could carry cargo between U.S. ports. This was a major boon to Seattle's port economy as a major shipper of goods to Alaska.
3. Letter to the George S. Shouhs from Col. A.L. Mill, West Point Superintendent, April 4, 1900 (USMA Archives).
4. Sweeny's classmates included two future four-star generals in World War II—Lesley J. McNair, killed by Allied bombs in the breakout of Normandy at St. Lo in 1944, and Joseph W. Stillwell, commander of U.S. forces in China.
5. *Book of Cadet Delinquencies, 1900* (USMA Archives).
6. "Hazing Their Fathers Sons," *The Sunday Call*, December 7, 1907.
7. McCormick, *One Man's Wars*, 29.
8. Stephen E. Ambrose, *Duty, Honor, Country: A History of West Point* (Baltimore: Johns Hopkins University Press, 1999).

9. McCormick, *One Man's Wars*, 31.
10. *Classification of Delinquencies, 1889-1911*, Department of Tactics (USMA Archives).
11. *Book of Cadet Delinquencies, 1900-1901* (USMA Archives).
12. Punishment tours required a cadet to march with a rifle at shoulder arms, back and forth across an area for a prescribed period of time, often an hour for each demerit. The cadet was not allowed to speak to anyone or stop.
13. Mills (1854-1916) was an 1879 graduate of the academy. He had won the Medal of Honor at San Juan Hill in the Spanish-American War in 1898. He had been shot in the face, losing an eye in the battle. Despite being temporarily blinded, he refused to leave the fight and continued to lead his men until the battle ended. When President William McKinley named him superintendent at West Point, the position resulted in his promotion from first lieutenant to colonel, skipping the ranks of captain, major and lieutenant colonel. He served as superintendent until 1906.
14. Letter in USMA Archives. Of the 169 candidates who became cadets in the class of 1900, 32 left before graduating. Thirty were discharged for academic deficiencies, one for physical disability and one—Sweeny—for conduct. Discharge for conduct is relatively rare, according to academy records. Two cadets were discharged for conduct from the class of 1898, none from the classes of 1899 and 1901, and one each from the classes of 1902 and 1903.
15. McCormick, *One Man's Wars*, 30.
16. Ibid., 33. The letters and thesis could not be located by the authors in a search of the academy archives in 2015.
17. Maghee (1882-1957) was the son of a surgeon in Wyoming. He went on to graduate in the class of 1905, serve on the general staff of the Allied Expeditionary Force (A.E.F.) and as operations officer (G-3) of the 91st Division in World War I, and retire as a colonel, according to the *Register of Graduates and Former Cadets* (1965).
18. The class of 1905 included Calvin Pearl Titus, who received the Medal of Honor from President Theodore Roosevelt as part of the academy's centennial celebration in 1902. Titus won the medal for volunteering to scale the wall of Peking's Forbidden City, under fire, to enable the 14th Infantry Regiment to relieve the 55-day siege of the foreign legations during the Boxer Rebellion of 1900. Sweeny was between appointments to West Point when Roosevelt visited the academy and so he did not witness this event.
19. The West Point course in Philosophy was not what we commonly think of as philosophy. It was the study of the mechanics of systems and how they worked.
20. The Drawing class at West Point involved geometry, topography, reconnaissance and map-making.
21. *Cadets Admitted, 1846-1912* (USMA Archives). In June 1903, the *Official Register of Officers and Cadets* listed Sweeny without a class standing because he was deficient in Drawing at that time. His other individual rankings were 97th in mathematics, 33rd in French, 16th in Spanish, 22nd in practical military engineering, and 55th in conduct, with 91 demerits.
22. McCormick, *One Man's Wars*, 34.
23. "Hazing Their Fathers' Sons," *The Sunday Call*, December 7, 1907.
24. "Army Inquiry Board Probing Into Hazing of Cadet Booz," *San Francisco Call*, December 18, 1900.
25. Albert Sidney Johnson entry, *The Cyclopedic Review of Current History, Volume 11*, 38.
26. As many as 200 cadets, or roughly half the entire student body, may have been involved in the demonstration according to transcripts of testimony by cadets at the 1901 board of inquiry in the USMA Archives.
27. Special Order 71, April 17, 1901 (USMA Archives).
28. "Dismissed Cadets Talk," *New York Times*, June 1, 1901; "Cadets Expelled from West Point Fight for Reinstatement," *Butte Inter Mountain*, June 15, 1901.
29. "Five Cadets Dismissed," *Evening Times*, Washington, D.C., May 22, 1901.
30. "Having Secured Positions," *Bismarck Daily Review*, May 24, 1901.
31. While the 1901 incident was judged a "mutinous demonstration," so-called "spirit pranks" have been and continue to be a tradition at West Point. Douglas MacArthur, who was the commander of the cadet battalion and graduated first in his class of 1903, led a group of cadets who moved the Reveille Gun to the top of the clock tower in what was then the Academic Building. They did it in a single night. It took the post engineers two weeks to get it back down. After that, the gun was bolted down. The difference between the two incidents seems to be the intent.
32. Mahaffey went to work for the Quayquil & Quito Railroad in 1901, became a second lieutenant in the cavalry in 1907, resigned from the Army as a captain in the Ordinance Corps in 1914 and died in 1958. Linton died in Brazil in 1922. Bowlby served as a lieutenant colonel in the Corps of Engineers in World War I and died in 1948. Cleveland worked as a civil engineer in Ecuador from 1901 to 1926 and died in

Florida in 1946. Keller became a major in the National Army during World War I, rising to the rank of colonel of cavalry by the war's end, and continued to serve in the Regular Army, retiring in 1938 as a colonel.

Chapter 4

1. Sweeny's comments are from notes for a lecture at the University of Utah titled "Some Aspects of Revolution, Especially in Latin America." The notes are from Sweeny's personal papers, held by his grandson, Frank Goodbold.
2. "New Era Being Opened," *The Oasis*, Nogales, Arizona, June 14, 1911.
3. *The Storm That Swept Mexico*, a 2011 PBS documentary on the 1910 Mexican Revolution.
4. Biography of Porfirio Diaz, About Education website.
5. One of the myths about Sweeny is that he met Francisco Madero while at Notre Dame. However, Madero never attended Notre Dame, nor as far as can be determined ever visited the school while Sweeny was there. The first opportunity for Sweeny to Madero would have been in Mexico in the years leading up to the 1910 revolution.
6. Spiritism is a philosophical doctrine or belief that human beings are immortal souls and that through successive lives they can learn from past mistakes and improve toward moral and intellectual perfection.
7. A medium is a living person who can contact someone in the spirit world.
8. Theosophy is a philosophy that seeks to understand the mysteries of the bonds between the universe, humanity and the divine to achieve individual enlightenment and salvation.
9. Annie Besant (1847–1933) was a British socialist, theosophist, women's rights activist and advocate of home rule for Ireland and India.
10. Enrique Krauze, *Mexico: Biography of Power* (New York: Harper Perennial, 1996), 248.
11. McCormick, *One Man's Wars*, 43.
12. Philip Russell, *The History of Mexico from Pre-Conquest to Present* (New York: Routledge, 2010), 236.
13. McCormick, *One Man's Wars*, 47.
14. *Ibid.*, 44.
15. *Ibid.*, 46.
16. *Ibid.*, 45.
17. "1906 Strike Signaled Changed at Cananea Mines," *Arizona Daily Star* (Tucson.com), June 3, 2013.
18. Russell *The History of Mexico from Pre-Conquest to Present*, 237.
19. McCormick, *One Man's Wars*, 44.
20. Ethan A. Nadelman, *A Cop Across the Borders: The Internationalization of U.S. Law Enforcement* (University Park: Pennsylvania State University, 2006), 78.
21. McCormick, *One Man's Wars*, 46.
22. "Arrest Being Made," *Ogden Standard Examiner*, December 26, 1906.
23. McCormick, *One Man's Wars*, 49.
24. "Francisco Madero and Jose Pino Suarez Killed While Being Transported to Penitentiary," *Daily Missoulian* (Missoula Montana), February 24, 1913.

Chapter 5

1. "Clash Is Expected Over Asphalt Mines," *St. Louis Republic*, July 4, 1901.
2. McCormick, *One Man's Wars*, 50.
3. "Story of Castro, a Midget Napoleon," *Spokane Press*, November 29, 1906.
4. "Castro's Curious Career," *The New Enterprise*, Madison, Florida, February 18, 1909.
5. *Harper's Weekly*, Volume 43, Part 2, 1196.
6. "Amazons Aiding Castro," *Evening News*, Washington, D.C., October 2, 1899.
7. "Castro's Curious Career."
8. "Castro Would Be Napoleon," *The Minneapolis Journal*, February 12, 1904.
9. "Castro's Curious Career."
10. "In a Steel House, Venezuela's Despot President Has a Bullet Proof Room," *Evening Star*, Washington, D.C., September 21, 1901.
11. Carlos A. Romero and Janet Kelly, *United States and Venezuela: Rethinking a Relationship* (New York: Routledge, 2002).
12. "Puerto Cabello Is Bombarded By British Cruiser Charybdis," *San Francisco Call*, December 15, 1902.
13. U.S. Department of State Website.
14. Kevin Singh, "Big Power Pressure During the Presidency of Cipriano Castro," *Revista/Review Interamericana*, Vol. 29 (1999), 1–4.
15. James C. Humes, *My Fellow Americans: Presidential Addresses That Shaped History* (Westport, CT: Praeger), 103.
16. Orray E. Thurber, *Castro and the Asphalt Trust* (New York, 1907), 4.
17. "Yankee versus Yankee," *Deseret Evening News*, Salt Lake City, Utah, January 26, 1901.
18. "Millions at Stake," *Arizona Republican*, March 17, 1906.
19. "Yankee versus Yankee."
20. *Ibid.*
21. Thurber, *Castro and the Asphalt Trust*.
22. *Ibid.*
23. "An Offer to Castro," *New York Daily Tribune*, July 2, 1908.

24. Based on research into the New York and Bermudez Company, the U.S. government may have been secretly involved in the company's opposition of Castro. Many company officials were friends of President Theodore Roosevelt and it appears great care was taken not to mention most of their names in McCormick's book.
25. "Put the Incivility Back Into Politics," *Wall Street Journal*, October 20, 1998.
26. Ibid.
27. "Venezuela Revolt Crushed," *Sun*, New York, February 20, 1907.
28. "Gen. Paredes Returns," *New York Tribune*, December 23, 1906.
29. McCormick, *One Man's Wars*, 50.
30. Ibid., 51.
31. "Castro Moving to Stop Revolt," *Cairo Bulletin*, Cairo, Illinois, February 15, 1907.
32. "Paredes in Venezuela," *New York Tribune*, February 9, 1907.
33. Eleanor Atkinson, Francis B. Atkinson, and Lewis A. Convis, *The World's Chronicle* (Little Chronicle Publishing Company, 1907).
34. McCormick, *One Man's Wars*, 52.
35. "Paredes Killed by Order," *Sun*, New York, March 3, 1907.
36. Ibid.
37. McCormick, *One Man's Wars*, 53.
38. "Asphalt Trust Trying to Force War with Venezuela," *Spokane Press*, April 1, 1908.
39. McCormick, *One Man's Wars*, 54.
40. Frank Moore Colby, George Sanderman and Thomas Nelson, *Nelson's Encyclopedia: Everybody's Reference*, 1907.
41. Ibid.
42. Ibid.
43. "Castro Is Taken to Ellis Island," *El Paso Herald*, December 12, 1912.

Chapter 6

1. McCormick, *One Man's Wars*, 54.
2. Ibid., 54–55.
3. Ibid., 54.
4. "Zelaya, the Man Without a Conscience," *Tacoma Times*, December 3, 1909.
5. Holly Sklar, *Washington's War on Nicaragua* (Boston: South End Press, 1988), 2.
6. Silvio Selva, *The United States and Central America* (self-published, 1913), 17.
7. Ibid., 18.
8. "Poverty Stricken Country Sucked of Its Life Blood," *San Francisco Call*, March 2, 1909.
9. "Zelaya's Stormy Regime as Dictator of Nicaragua," *Sun*, New York, May 25, 1919.
10. Lynn V. Foster, *A Brief History of Central America*, 2d ed. (New York: Facts on File, 2007), 165.
11. "Avalon Project, Convention for the Construction of a Ship Canal," November 1903, avalon.law.yale.edu.
12. Foster, *A Brief History of Central America*, 197.
13. "His Ambition Causes War," *Virginia Enterprise*, Minnesota, March 29, 1907.
14. "Recognition in International Law," CUP Archive, 129.
15. Foster, *A Brief History of Central America*, 197.
16. Lawrence Lenz, *Power and Policy: America's First Steps to Superpower, 1899–1922* (New York: Algora Publishing, 2008), 167.
17. Ibid.
18. "Zelaya Breaks Faith," *Evening Star*, November 23, 1909.
19. One of the warships was the USS *Tacoma* as mentioned in the newspaper article "Anxious Over Nicaragua," *Fergus County Democrat*, December 14, 1909.
20. McCormick, *One Man's Wars*, 56.
21. "Americans Are Refused Landing by Zelaya," *Daily Capital Journal*, Salem, Oregon, December 13, 1909.
22. McCormick, *One Man's Wars*, 56–57.
23. "Zelaya Is Defeated," *Topeka State Journal*, December 8, 1909.
24. McCormick, *One Man's Wars*, 57.
25. "Zelaya's Army Starving," *Evening Star*, Washington, D.C., December 24, 1909.
26. McCormick, *One Man's Wars*, 58.
27. Ibid.
28. Ibid., 59.
29. After fleeing Nicaragua, Zelaya moved to Spain and then to New York City, where he died in 1919.
30. "J. Madriz Patriot," *Evening Star*, January 6, 1910.
31. McCormick, *One Man's Wars*, 59.
32. "Insurgent Chief Made President," *Los Angeles Herald*, August 24, 1910.
33. "Nicaraguans Get Religious Freedom," *Norfolk Weekly News-Journal*, January 11, 1911.
34. In 1937, Somoza used his position to oust the elected president, his wife's uncle, and make himself president. The Somoza family ran the country until they were driven from power by the Sandinista insurrection in 1979.
35. Darol B. Rasmussen, *Roots for Revolt* (Personal Finance, 1996), 272, 273.
36. Smedley Darlington Butler, *War Is a Racket* (New York: Skyhorse Publishing, 2013, originally published by Roundtable Press, 1935).

Chapter 7

1. McCormick, *One Man's Wars*, 60.
2. "Successful Men of Utah," *Goodwin's Weekly*, May 13, 1916.

3. "After Silver King and Daly-West," *Salt Lake Mining Review*, December 30, 1903.
4. McCormick, *One Man's Wars*, 60.
5. James R. Lehning, *To Be a Citizen: The Political Culture of the Early French Third Republic* (Ithaca: Cornell University Press, 2001), 132.
6. McCormick, *One Man's Wars*, 63.
7. *Ibid.*, 61.
8. The dates of the marriage and birth come from Eva's U.S. passport application dated January 25, 1921.
9. McCormick, *One Man's Wars*, 62.
10. *Ibid.*
11. Eva Vons Sweeny's U.S. passport application provides birth dates and locations for the children as well as the date and location of her marriage to Charles Sweeney.
12. McCormick, *One Man's Wars*, 63.
13. A kepi is a French military cap with a flat, circular top and a horizontal visor.
14. McCormick, *One Man's Wars*, 64.
15. *Ibid.*, 65.
16. *Ibid.*

Chapter 8

1. The phrase was originated by author H.G. Wells when he published the book *The War to End War*. As the war progressed, it was referred to cynically.
2. McCormick, *One Man's Wars*, 65.
3. Casmeze's Certificate of Registration of American Citizen, #37538, February 4, 1913.
4. McCormick, *One Man's Wars*, 66.
5. In the first seven months of the war, more than 32,000 non-Frenchmen volunteered to fight for France, including more than 100 Americans. Martin Gilbert, *The First World War* (New York: Henry Holt, 1994), 62.
6. Douglas Porch, *The French Foreign Legion: A Complete History of This Legendary Fighting Force* (New York: HarperCollins, 1991), 1–6.
7. T. Bentley Mott, *Myron Herrick, Friend of France* (Garden City, NY: Doubleday, Doran & Co., 1929), chapter 20.
8. *Ibid.*
9. Gary Ward, "Engaged in Glory Alone, Yanks in the Foreign Legion Were First to Fight," *VFW, Veterans of Foreign Wars Magazine*, September 1, 2014, 34.
10. "American at Front to Become Lieutenant," *Sun*, New York, June 6, 1915.
11. Paul Ayers Rockwell, *American Volunteers in the Foreign Legion, 1914–1918* (Boston: Houghton Mifflin, 1930), 2.
12. Bert Hall, *In the Air: Three Years On and Above Three Fronts* (New York: The New Library, 1918), 5.
13. McCormick, *One Man's Wars*, 66.
14. John Bowe, *Soldiers of the Legion* (Chicago: Press of the Peterson Linotyping Co., 1918), 52.
15. *Ibid.*
16. Rockwell, *American Volunteers in the Foreign Legion, 1914–1918*, 8.
17. Charles Sweeny, "Tells of the Beginning of the Foreign Legion," *Evening Star*, Washington, D.C., June 29, 1917.
18. Rockwell, *American Volunteers in the Foreign Legion, 1914–1918*, 13.
19. Scott Kraska, "Legionaire! Americans in the French Foreign Legion, 1914–1918," *Military Trader News*, October 15, 2013.
20. Gary Ward, "Engaged in Glory Alone."
21. Charles Sweeny, "Tells of the Beginning of the Foreign Legion."
22. "American Legion Standard Enshrined with Napoleon's," *Sun*, New York, May 27, 1917.
23. Charles Sweeny, "Tells How It Feels to Face Battle Foe," *Evening Star*, Washington, D.C., July 1, 1917.
24. Sweeny's French military service record from the Veterans Office of the Foreign Legion in Aubagne, France.
25. "Sweeny Sails Away to More War," *Sun*, New York, September 7, 1919.
26. This conclusion is consistent with a news report in the *Richmond Times-Dispatch*, November 18, 1917, that Sweeny had received the "Croix de Guerre with four citations for bravery on the field of battle."
27. Sweeny's French military service record says he was promoted on December 3.
28. Rockwell, *American Volunteers in the Foreign Legion, 1914–1918*, 24.
29. "Sweeny Sails Away to More War."
30. Charles Sweeny, "Story of Sublime Courage in Face of Withering Fire," *Evening Star*, Washington, D.C., July 20, 1917.
31. Sweeny's French military service record says he was promoted on February 18.
32. "American at Front to Become Lieutenant."
33. Vincent J. Esposito, *The West Point Atlas of American Wars* (New York: Frederick A. Praeger, 1959), 32.
34. Gilbert, *The First World War*, 159.
35. Porch, *The French Foreign Legion*, 356.
36. "American at Front to Become Lieutenant."
37. Sweeny's French military service record says the promotion was by ministerial decree No. 5142, dated July 17 but effective July 11.
38. Rockwell, *American Volunteers in the Foreign Legion, 1914–1918*, p. 101.
39. "French Honor American," *Sun*, New York, July 23, 1915.
40. "Special Training for Men Who Charge Enemy Lines," *Evening Star*, Washington, D.C., July 22, 1917.

41. "Preparation of Foreign Legion for Attack on West Front," *Evening Star*, Washington, D.C., July 23, 1917.
42. "Charge in Modern Warfare Is Not a Romantic Dash," *Evening Star*, Washington, D.C., July 28, 1917.
43. Raymond Rouly (Captain, French Army staff), "The French Offensive in Champagne, September-October 1915," *Scribner's Magazine*, May 1916.
44. Edward Morlae, *A Soldier of the Legio* (New York: Houghton Mifflin, 1916), chapter 1.
45. *Ibid.*, chapters 3 and 4.
46. Rockwell, *American Volunteers in the Foreign Legion, 1914-1918*, p. 112.
47. *Ibid.*, p. 114.
48. *Ibid.*
49. Morlae, *A Soldier of the Legio*, chapter 8.
50. News accounts differ as to which lung the bullet struck. The *Sun* reported that the bullet penetrated the right lung and exited below the shoulder blade. McCormick quotes two other articles: one, by Martelli, said it was the right lung; the other, by novelist and war writer Gertrude Atherton, said it struck his left lung and liver.
51. McCormick, *One Man's Wars*, 86-88. An article in the *Spokane Daily Review*, May 18, 1917, said the infection was caused by "a piece of waistcoat in his lung where it had been imbedded with a German saber thrust." The wound healed once the cloth was surgically removed.
52. A December 14, 2015, letter to the authors from the Grande Chancellory of the Legion of Honor states that Sweeny was made a knight of the Legion of Honor by decree of October 7, 1915, published in the *Official Journal of the Republic of France* on October 25, 1915, and effective October 7, 1915, at the direction of the minister of war. He also received the Croix de Guerre with palm as part of this honor. Sweeny received the Legion of Honor with the rank of Chevalier (knight), the lowest of the award's five ranks on October 7, according to his French service record. Sweeny's Legion of Honor was later elevated two ranks to that of Commander in recognition of his subsequent service to France. On December 10, 1925, the *Spokane Daily Review* reported that Sweeny's Legion of Honor had been elevated one rank to Officer, based on the recommendation of Marshal Petain for Sweeny's service in Morocco's "Sherifian air force." In 1942, Sweeny listed the rank as one additional rank higher, Commander, in a resume for his publisher. Charles Sweeny, 1942-43, Archives of Charles Scribner's Sons, Manuscripts Division, Department of Rare Books and Special Collections, Princeton University Library.
53. Wire service story published in The *Evening Current*, Carlsbad, New Mexico, May 15, 1917; *The Bemidji Daily Pioneer*, Minnesota, May 25, 1917.
54. The article in the *Evening Sun* (New York) on September 8, 1920, was written by newspaper columnist Marguerite Mooers Marshall.
55. "Lieut. Sweeny Badly Wounded in France," *Sun*, New York, October 7, 1915; "Sweeny Refuses to Die," *Sun*, New York, October 13, 1915.
56. Rockwell, *American Volunteers in the Foreign Legion, 1914-1918*, 113.
57. *Ibid.*, 91.
58. "Winning Battles Is Only a State of Mind," *Ontario Argus*, Oregon, July 13, 1916.
59. Rockwell, *American Volunteers in the Foreign Legion, 1914-1918*, 285.
60. http://escadrilleamericane.wikifoundry.com/page/Pilot+Bio's.
61. McCormick, *One Man's Wars*, 96.
62. John Keegan, *The First World War* (New York: Random House, 1998), 279.
63. *Ibid.*, 282-286.
64. Esposito, *The West Point Atlas of American Wars*, 34.
65. Porch, *The French Foreign Legion*, 368.
66. Sweeny's French military service record.
67. Certificate d'Instruction de Marly-le-Roi, dated April 11, 1917.
68. Rockwell, *American Volunteers in the Foreign Legion, 1914-1918*, 260.
69. "First American Loaned to Country," *South Bend* (Indiana) *News-Times*, April 24, 1917.
70. Charles Scribner's Sons Collection.
71. "France Releases American: Capt. Sweeny Permitted to Return for Home Service," *Sun*, New York, April 14, 1917.
72. "Captain Sweeny Coming," *Washington Times*, April 25, 1917.
73. "Tank Like Big Hog," *Bermidji Daily Pioneer*, Minnesota, May 25, 1917.

Chapter 9

1. McCormick, *One Man's Wars*, 98.
2. Rockwell, *American Volunteers in the Foreign Legion, 1914-1918*, 60.
3. McCormick, *One Man's Wars*, 100.
4. *Ibid.*, p. 102.
5. "Seasoned Fighters at Ft. Myer Camp," *Washington* (D.C.) *Herald*, July 7, 1917.
6. "Military Units to Edsal Range," *Evening Star*, Washington, D.C., July 11, 1917.
7. "Regimental Review at Ft. Myer Camp," *Washington* (D.C.) *Herald*, July 11, 1917.
8. "Student Officers Forbidden to Resign Places," *Washington* (D.C.) *Times*, July 10, 1917.
9. McCormick, *One Man's Wars*, 105.

10. *History of the 318th Infantry Regiment of the 80th Division 1917-1919* (privately printed, 1919), 111.
11. *Ibid.*, 18.
12. Rush S. Young, *Over the Top with the 80th* (privately printed, 1933), 14.
13. *Ibid.*, 15.
14. Esposito, *The West Point Atlas of American Wars*, 62–65.
15. Young, *Over the Top with the 80th*, 24.
16. Amiens boasts the largest cathedral in France, built in the 13th century to house the head of John the Baptist. The head had been brought back from the Holy Land during the Fourth Crusade in 1206.
17. *History of the 318th*, 43.
18. *Ibid.*, 42.
19. Young, *Over the Top with the 80th*, 36.
20. *History of the 318th*, 47.
21. Young, *Over the Top with the 80th*, 45.
22. *History of the 318th*, 52.
23. *Ibid.*, 54.
24. Esposito, *The West Point Atlas of American Wars*, 70.
25. Edward G. Lengel, *To Conquer Hell: The Meuse-Argonne, 1918* (New York: Henry Holt, 2008), 62.
26. Young, *Over the Top with the 80th*, 59.
27. *History of the 318th*, 58.
28. Young, *Over the Top with the 80th*, 57.
29. Lengel, *To Conquer Hell*, 76–77.
30. *314 Machine Gun Battalion History, Blue Ridge (80th) Division* (Officers and Men of the Battalion, 1919), 28.
31. Young, *Over the Top with the 80th*, 64.
32. *Ibid.*, 66.
33. *History of the 318th*, 60.
34. *Ibid.*, 64.
35. Young, *Over the Top with the 80th*, 78.
36. *History of the 318th*, 64.
37. Young, *Over the Top with the 80th*, 75.
38. *Ibid.*, 80.
39. Public records on Ancestry.com.
40. Young, *Over the Top with the 80th*, 85.
41. Lengel, *To Conquer Hell*, 202.
42. *History of the 318th*, 66.
43. *Ibid.*, 68.
44. Lengel, *To Conquer Hell*, 203.
45. Young, *Over the Top with the 80th*, 89.
46. *Ibid.*, 92.
47. *Ibid.*, 95–96.
48. *Ibid.*, 98.
49. Lengel, *To Conquer Hell*, 239.
50. *History of the 318th*, 68.
51. *Ibid.*, 70.
52. *Ibid.*, 72, 74.
53. Young, *Over the Top with the 80th*, 109.
54. Hill 223, directly above Chatel-Chehery, was where Corporal (later Sergeant) Alvin York won the Medal of Honor for capturing several machineguns and 132 prisoners on October 3, after his squad of the 82nd Division found themselves behind enemy lines.
55. *History of the 318th*, 76.
56. *The 80th Division Summary of Operations in the World War* (Washington, D.C.: American Battle Monuments Commission, 1944), 36.
57. Young, *Over the Top with the 80th*, 115.
58. *The History of the 318th*, 79.
59. Public records on Ancestry.com.
60. *The History of the 318th*, 80.
61. *Ibid.*, 81.
62. *Ibid.*, 180.
63. Sweeny's affidavit on behalf of Moomaw's medal is in his personal papers in Frank Goodbold's collection.
64. McCormick, *One Man's Wars*, 109–110.
65. An article, "Sweeny of the Foreign Legion Lauds French," in the July 17, 1919, *Seattle Star* states that Sweeny's uniform following his July 11, 1919, discharge had four wound stripes—three French and one American. It states that he was wounded in August 1914 while fighting in the French retreat from Belgium. However, this is hard to believe given that he only enlisted August 21 and didn't complete training until October 2. Next, the article states that after the Battle of Verdun, which ended in December 1916, Sweeny was placed in command of 16 tanks and participated in the Chermin des Dames battle, in which tanks broke through the German pill-box line. However, that battle occurred shortly after Sweeny left France with Joffre's mission to America in April 1917. Finally, the article states that Sweeny was twice recommended for the Distinguished Service Cross. The article erroneously states that Sweeny lived in France for ten years before the war, that he graduated from West Point, and that he was attained the rank of colonel in the U.S. Army. As usual, the facts about Sweeny are mixed with fiction.
66. The troops were not idle during the months they spent at the 15th Training Camp. They spent the majority of their days engaged in every sort of battlefield maneuver, in the off chance that hostilities would resume. Sports competitions, stage shows and drill took up much of the rest of the time, according to the regiment's history, p. 93.
67. Sweeny's partially reconstructed military file in the National Archives.

Chapter 10

1. "Sweeny Sails Away to Find More War," *Sun*, New York, September 7, 1919.
2. George Kohn, *Dictionary of Wars* (New York: Facts on File, 1986), 397.

3. Robert Karolevitz and Ross S. Fenn, *Flight of Eagles: The Story of the American Kosciuszko Squadron in the Polish-Soviet War 1919-1920* (Sioux Falls: Brevet Press, 1974), 190.
4. Norman Richard Davies, *White Eagle, Red Star: The Polish-Soviet War 1919-1920* (New York: Random House, 1972), 85.
5. *Ibid.*, 46.
6. *Ibid.*, 94.
7. McCormick, *One Man's Wars*, 116.
8. The squadron took its name from Tadeusz Kosciuszko, a Polish military engineer who fought with the colonists in the American Revolution.
9. Kenneth Malcolm Murray, *Wings Over Poland: The Story of the 7th (Kosciuszko) Squadron of the Polish Air Service, 1919, 1920, 1921* (New York: D. Appleton, 1932).
10. Frank Goodbold Collection.
11. "The Tales of Hoffmann" is a French opera fantastique, written by Jacques Offenbach, based on three short stories by E.T.A. Hoffmann in the early 1800s, and first performed in 1881. A new production was mounted at the Opera-Comique in 1911, while Sweeny was living in Paris.
12. "Brave American in Polish Army," *Evening Herald*, Klamath Falls, Oregon, November 11, 1920.
13. "American Soldier of Fortune Wins Honors with Poles," *New York Tribune*, August 29, 1920.
14. "Henry Reilly, 82, Military Writer, General, Youngest Brigade Commander in AEF, Dies," *New York Times*, December 14, 1963; *Register of Graduate of the U.S. Military Academy*, 1965, Official Register of Officers and Cadets.
15. McCormick, *One Man's Wars*, 119.
16. Charles Scribner's Sons Collection, letter dated August 1, 1942.
17. Jean Lacouture, *De Gaulle: The Rebel 1890-1944* (New York: W.W. Norton, 1984), 50.
18. Davies, *White Eagle, Red Star*, 222.
19. Philip D. Caine, *Eagles of the RAF* (Washington, D.C.: National Defense University Press, 1991), 24.
20. In an article on the eve of the Second World War, the *New York Times* on August 25, 1939, included in Sweeny's career record that he had commanded a division in the Polish-Soviet War as a major general, not a brigadier.
21. McCormick, *One Man's Wars*, 119.

Chapter 11

1. Patrick Kindross, *Ataturk: The Rebirth of a Nation* (London: Orion Publishing Group, 1993), 231.
2. *Ibid.*, 239.
3. McCormick, *One Man's Wars*, 120.
4. *Ibid.*, 121.
5. Despite Sweeny's dismissive reports and Turkey's continuing denials of genocide, history's judgment is that the Ottoman government caused the deaths of 800,000 to 1.5 million Armenians in an act of ethnic cleansing in 1915.
6. McCormick, *One Man's Wars*, 122.
7. McCormick wrote more than 20 books, mostly about espionage matters, including *Peddler of Death: The Life and Times of Sir Basil Zaharoff* (New York: Holt, Rinehart and Winston, 1965).
8. John T. Flynn, *Men of Wealth: The Story of Twelve Significant Fortunes from the Renaissance to the Present Day* (New York: Simon & Schuster, 1941), 360-361.
9. McCormick, *One Man's Wars*, 123.
10. Flynn, *Men of Wealth*, 343-344.
11. McCormick, *One Man's Wars*, 124.

Chapter 12

1. Douglas Porch, "Spain's African Nightmare," *Military History Quarterly*, Winter 2006.
2. Dorothy Stannard, *Morocco* (Boston: Houghton Mifflin, 1993), 50.
3. William Dean, "Americans in the Rif Rebellion," *Revue Historique Armees*, 2007, 46-55.
4. Charles Willoughby (1892-1972) went on to become a major general and serve as General Douglas MacArthur's chief of intelligence during World War II. According to Dean, Willoughby was an admirer of Franco and Benito Mussolini and could be considered a fascist in terms of his political views.
5. Published reports in Spain state that Spain used chemical agents, including mustard gas, against the Rifs. The agents were purchased from Germany after all such agents supposedly had been destroyed and their manufacture and use had been banned by the Versailles Treaty of 1919. Sources: "Mustard Gas on the Rif" by Javier Espinosa in *El Mundo* (2001); "The Last of El Hoceima," by Javier Rada in *20 Minutos* (2006); and "ERC Requires Spain to Apologize for Use of Chemical Weapons in the Rif War" by Miguel Noguer in *El Pais* (2005).
6. Porch, *The French Foreign Legion*, 397.
7. Porch, "Spain's African Nightmare."
8. *Ibid.*
9. Porch, *The French Foreign Legion*, 396.
10. Porch, "Spain's African Nightmare."
11. El-Mostafa Azzou, "The Lafayette Escadrille: American Aviators in the Rif War (1921-1926)," *World Wars and Contemporary Conflicts*, 2003, 57-63.

12. Dean, "Americans in the Rif Rebellion."
13. Azzou, "The Lafayette Escadrille," 57–63.
14. Paul Ayers Rockwell, "Moroccan Bomber: American Fighters in the Rif War, 1925." *Aviation Quarterly*, 2nd Quarter, 1979.
15. McCormick, *One Man's Wars*, 132.
16. "Washington Moves to Halt Americans Fighting Riffians," *New York Times*, September 20, 1925.
17. "Fliers Say They Will Stay," Associated Press printed in *New York Times*, September 22, 1925.
18. "No Action Against U.S. Fliers," *New York Times*, September 27, 1925.
19. Dean, "Americans in the Rif Rebellion."
20. McCormick, *One Man's Wars*, 130.
21. Ibid., 133.
22. Ibid., 134.
23. Rockwell, "Moroccan Bomber."
24. Azzou, "The Lafayette Escadrille," 57–63.
25. "Riffs Bring Down 20 French Airmen," *Ogden Standard Examiner*, September 18, 1925.
26. Dean, "Americans in the Rif Rebellion."
27. Rockwell, "Moroccan Bomber."
28. Dean, "Americans in the Rif Rebellion."
29. David Woolman, *Rebels in the Rif: Abd el-Krim and the Rif Rebellion* (Stanford: Stanford University Press, 1968), 202.
30. McCormick, *One Man's Wars*, 146.
31. Dean, "Americans in the Rif Rebellion."
32. "U.S. Riff Flier Gets His Nineteenth Pair of Wings," *Oakland Tribune*, February 12, 1926.
33. McCormick, *One Man's Wars*, 145.
34. Joseph George Strack, "Px for Relaxation: Dentist James V. Sparks, Soldier of Fortune," *TLC*, September 1948. For a dentist by trade, Sparks (1893–1973) led an unusually eventful life. He served as an ambulance driver in World War I and with Sweeny in the Rif War. He then organized a flying squadron for another of his Paris patients, the King of Siam. Other patients included the King of Greece, Marshal Petain and General Pershing. Later, he was elected commander in France for the American Legion, received the French Legion of Honor and Croix de Guerre; met Hitler, Mussolini and other heads of state; accepted a colonel's commission in the French army to organize an American Volunteer Ambulance corps at the start of World War II; and talked his way out of a Spanish prison and fled Europe before the Nazis could catch him. Despite all that, his closest brush with death came in 1934 in Marseilles as one of three judges of the world bantam-weight title fight between Al Brown and Kid Francis, the French-Italian challenger. Sparks declared Brown the winner, as did one of the other two judges, setting off a riot. The *New York Times* said soldiers with fixed bayonets had to rescue Sparks from the "howling mob."
35. "Decorated, Wantes to Hop Over Pole," *Oakland* (California) *Tribune*, February 12, 1926.

Chapter 13

1. Sweeny was acquainted with several women named Helen in Salt Lake City. One of them, Helen Lowe Bamberger, was the widow of John E. Bamberger of the Bamberger mining family. She lived next door to Sweeny when he resided at Dorothy Bamberger Allen's home. John's father was Dorothy's brother.
2. The British had promised Faisal, leader of the Hashemites, that he would rule a united Arab state based in Syria after World War I. However, the French refused to honor that commitment when they took over control of Syria under a secret pact (the Sykes-Picot Agreement of 1916) that divided the post-war Levant into zones of influence between the two European powers.
3. Faisal (1885–1933) was the third son of the grand sharif of Mecca and the leader of the Arab Revolt during World War I. He is perhaps best known to Western audiences through director David Lean's 1962 film epic *Lawrence of Arabia* starring Peter O'Toole in the title role. Faisal was played by actor Alec Guinness. After his expulsion from Syria, Faisal was made king of Iraq by the British in 1921. He served as king until his death in 1933.
4. Al-Atrash (1891–1982) was an Arab Druze and an ardent nationalist who fought against the Ottoman Empire and then the French. After the 1925–27 revolt failed, he escaped to Transjordan, was later pardoned and in 1937 returned to Syria. He participated in an uprising in 1945 that led to Syria's independence in 1948.
5. David E. Omissi, *Air Power and Colonial Control: The Royal Air Force 1919–1939* (Manchester: Manchester University Press, 1990), 190–192.
6. Wintle (1897–1966) was the son of a British diplomat. In 1915, the 17-year-old Wintle became an officer in the cavalry and saw action at Ypres, the Somme and other battles. In 1917, a shell burst cost him an eye, a kneecap and several fingers. After that, he always wore a monocle in that eye. Despite his wounds, he returned to combat and won the Military Cross in November 1918 for advancing ahead of the infantry to gather information and personally taking 35 prisoners. When the German Army overran France in 1940, Wintle demanded an R.A.F. plane so he could rally the French Air

Force to fly their planes to Britain. When his demand was refused, he pointed a gun at an officer and was imprisoned in the Tower of London. He was soon released and sent into occupied France to gather intelligence. He was captured, escaped, recaptured and escaped again, this time making it back to Britain through Spain. After the war, he retired as a lieutenant colonel, and ran for a seat in Parliament but lost.

7. McCormick, *One Man's Wars*, 157.
8. Lynn, *Men of Wealth*, 442.
9. Antony Beevor, *The Battle for Spain: The Spanish Civil War* (London: Penguin, 2006).
10. McCormick, *One Man's Wars*, 160.
11. FBI files, http://webharvest.gov/peth04/20041015195614/http://foia.fbi.gov/foiaindex/ernesthemingway.htm.
12. McCormick, *One Man's Wars*, 161.
13. *Ibid.*, 162.
14. Richard Rhodes, *Hell and Good Company* (New York: Simon & Schuster, 2015), 107.
15. Baker, *Ernest Hemingway: A Life Story*, 311.
16. Elinor Langer, *Josephine Herbst: The Story She Could Never Tell* (Boston: Little, Brown, 1983), 213.
17. Baker, *Ernest Hemingway, Selected Letters*, 500.
18. Rhodes, *Hell and Good Company*, 211.
19. Brian Crozier, *Franco* (Boston: Little, Brown, 1967).
20. Beevor, *The Battle for Spain*.
21. Baker, *Ernest Hemingway, Selected Letters*, 501–502.
22. McCormick, *One Man's Wars*, 163–164.
23. Rhodes, *Hell and Good Company*, 514.
24. McCormick, *One Man's Wars*, 164.
25. *Ibid.*, 164.
26. *Ibid.*
27. Baker, *Ernest Selected Letters*, 502.

Chapter 14

1. Cassandra is a figure in Greek mythology who was cursed with the power of prophecy that no one would believe.
2. A January 22, 1944, *New York Times* review of journalist A.J. Liebling's new book, *The Road Back to Paris*, said: "In 1939 the only man in Paris within Liebling's hearing who predicted the disaster was Charles Sweeny, an American who had been a colonel in the Foreign Legion, a reporter for *The New York World* and a promoter of ice hockey at the Palais de Glace."
3. McCormick, *One Man's Wars*, 166.
4. Until the outbreak of the war, Sweeny was a special correspondent to the Exchange Telegraph, the official British news agency, according to "Eagle Squadron Organizer Is Here with Other Aces," *Evening Citizen* (Ottawa, Canada), November 16, 1940.
5. Charles Sweeny, *Moment of Truth* (New York: Charles Scribner's Sons, 1943).
6. "The Phoney War" is the English spelling rather than the American "phony." It is the generally accepted term.
7. "U.S. Volunteers Sought in France," *New York Times*, August 26, 1939.
8. "300 Americans Offer Services to France; Ambulances Donated," *Oakland Tribune*, September 6, 1939. The article said American citizens had donated 19 ambulances to France to be manned by American volunteers under the direction of Dr. James V. Sparks, the Paris dentist who had served in Sweeny's squadron in the Rif War.
9. McCormick, *One Man's Wars*, 169.
10. "U.S. Aviator in Action," *New York Times*, September 15, 1939.
11. *Ibid.*, 171.
12. Byron Kennerly, *The Eagles Roar!* (New York: Harper & Brothers, 1942), Introduction by Charles Sweeny, viii.
13. Vern Haugland, *The Eagle Squadrons, Yanks in the RAF, 1940-42* (New York: TAB Books, 1992), 9.
14. Kendall Everson, *The Lafayette Escadrille Escapade*, chapter 4 in his unpublished memoir, provided to the authors by Everson's son, Scott, in 2015.
15. *Ibid.*, 58.
16. Sweeny was known to wear the rosette of the Legion of Honor in his lapel, France's highest honor.
17. Everson, *The Lafayette Escadrille Escapade*, 58–59.
18. *Ibid.*, 59.
19. *Ibid.*
20. *Ibid.*, 60.
21. *Ibid.*
22. *Ibid.*, 61.
23. "Two Killed When Plane Falls into Bean Field," *Daily Mirror* (Los Angeles), August 11, 1941.
24. "Foreign Recruiting on Coast Related." Associated Press, February 28, 1940.
25. News stories and FBI memos played up Robert Sweeny's engagement to Woolworth heiress Barbara Hutton.
26. "New Evidence in Allied Recruiting," *Los Angeles Examiner*, February 28, 1940.
27. FBI memo, dated February 26, 1940, obtained through Freedom of Information Act.
28. Haugland, *The Eagle Squadrons*, 15.
29. *Ibid.*, 16.
30. Alex Kershaw, *The Few: The American*

Knights of the Air Who Risked Everything to Fight in the Battle of Britain (Cambridge: De Capo Press, 2006), 6–12.
31. Ibid., 37.
32. Ibid., viii–ix.
33. Kennerly, *The Eagles Roar!*, ix.
34. Kershaw, *The Few*, 38, 52 and 54.
35. These memos, along with a thick stack of other documents, were obtained using the U.S. Freedom of Information Act from the FBI, Justice Department and State Department concerning Sweeny. Many of the FBI documents were heavily redacted to remove any names other than Sweeny's as well as many large blocks of text containing other, unspecified information still deemed exempt from disclosure more than a half century later.
36. A March 2, 1940, story by Guy Richards appeared in the *Washington Times Herald*. It said Americans going to Finland to fight were able to go without a passport because none was needed to leave as long as the next stop on their route did not require one from a U.S. citizen. Many of the Americans were listed on ship manifests as "crew."
37. Ibid.

Chapter 15

1. To humiliate the French people Hitler demanded that the armistice be signed in the same railcar where Germany had been force to sign the armistice ending the First World War in 1918.
2. The Gestapo was the Nazi secret police whose mission was to identify the enemies of Germany and eliminate them through imprisonment or assassination.
3. Labonne and de Margenet were well known by the Colonel to shelter people being sought by the Germans. Labonne later joined the Free French Forces and de Margenet the Special Operations Executive (SOE), whose role was espionage and sabotage against the Germans. He was eventually caught and executed by the Nazis.
4. McCormick, *One Man's Wars*, 176–177.
5. Robert Sr. was a graduate of the University of Notre Dame and the Harvard Law School. He went into business in England, where the Sweenys had business interests, and became a member of London society.
6. Robert was a brilliant golfer, and both he and his brother Charles were well-known in London's social circles. Robert Jr. won the British Amateur Golf Championship in 1937. Later, in 1954, he finished second to Arnold Palmer on the last hole of the U.S. Amateur Golf Championship.
7. Caine, *Eagles of the RAF*, 29.
8. Kennerly, *The Eagles Roar!*, ix.
9. Caine, *Eagles of the RAF*, 26.
10. Of the 32 American pilots the Colonel recruited to France four were killed, six escaped to England, 11 were taken prisoner by the Germans, and the rest presumably escaped through Spain and returned to the United States.
11. McCormick, *One Man's Wars*, 181.
12. Ibid., 182.
13. "American Flier in Britain Tells French Millions of Yankees Coming Again," *Helena Independent*, October 26, 1940.
14. McCormick, *One Man's Wars*, 181–182.
15. "Promising Too Much," *Sunday Spartanburg Herald Journal*, October 27, 1940.
16. Caine, *Eagles of the RAF*, 33.
17. "The 'Eagles' Are Ready; Ace U.S. Squadron For R.A.F, Led By Famous Fighter," *Glasgow Herald*, October 9, 1940.
18. Kenneth Kan, "First in the Air: The Eagle Squadrons of World War II," Air Force History and Museum Program, 2007, 6.
19. On September 8, 1943, the *Milwaukee Journal* ran an Associated Press article titled "Golfer Robert Sweeny Cited for U-Boat Attack." It said that Royal Air Force Flying Officer Robert Sweeny, who won the 1937 British amateur golf championship and helped organize the American Eagle Squadron, had recently helped destroy two U-boats in the Bay of Biscay. As the pilot, Sweeny had pressed home his attack despite anti-aircraft damage to his Liberator bomber, and been awarded the Distinguished Flying Cross. After the attack, Sweeny nursed his damaged aircraft 400 miles back to England on three engines, flying at low attitude to avoid enemy fighters as all of the plane's guns had been jettisoned to lighten the load. The article noted that his uncle, Colonel Charles Sweeny, and brother, also named Charles Sweeny, had formed the Eagle Squadron. The article erroneously stated that Col. Sweeny also had formed the Lafayette Escadrille in the First World War.
20. Kan, "First in the Air: The Eagle Squadrons of World War II," 8.
21. "American Airmen Serving British Get First Test," *Helena Daily Independent*, October 14, 1940.
22. Kennerly, *The Eagles Roar!*, 65–66.
23. Kan, "First in the Air: The Eagle Squadrons of World War II," 9.
24. Vernon "Shorty" Keough was an experienced parachute jumper with more than 400 jumps to his credit before he became an Eagle. He often gave lectures to the other pilots on the proper use of parachutes. He had a great sense of humor. He said he was so short because sometimes the chute didn't open on his many jumps and his body had compacted.

25. Kennerly, *The Eagles Roar!*, 185.
26. "American Pilots in Canada: Reticent on Forming Yank Force," *Helena Daily Independent*, November 25, 1940.
27. "Eagle Squadron Organizer Is Here with Other Aces," *Evening Citizen*, Ottawa, Ontario, November 25, 1940.
28. McCormick, *One Man's War*, 190.
29. "Miss Sweeny Visits in Salt Lake," *Salt Lake Telegram*, October 16, 1945.
30. YouTube links to Sweeny Movietone Newsreels: https://www.youtube.com/watch?v=5_8G26mnZ9w; https://www.youtube.com/watch?v=_z2fVNnI6ms.
31. "Americans Fly For Britain In R.A.F. Eagle Squadron," *Life Magazine*, April 21, 1941, 51–52.
32. Kan, "First in the Air: The Eagle Squadrons of World War II," 10.
33. Caine, *Eagles of the RAF*, 131.
34. Kan, "First in the Air: The Eagle Squadrons of World War II," 11.
35. Ibid., 12; "American Eagle Squadron Joins British Bombers To Down 11 German Planes," *St. Petersburg Times*, July 7, 1941.
36. Kan, "First in the Air: The Eagle Squadrons of World War II," 13.
37. "Eagle Squadron Pilot Bags Dornier Bomber," *Montreal Gazette*, August 4, 1941.
38. Kan, "First in the Air: The Eagle Squadrons of World War II," 14.
39. "The First Americans to Fight the Nazis Revealed," *Daily Mail*, November 28, 2015.
40. Caine, *Eagles of the RAF*, 191–192.
41. "RAF Again Bosses Channel, Pushes Nazi's Inland, Says Eagle Squadron Commander," *Salt Lake Telegram*, August 29, 1941.
42. Kan, "First in the Air: The Eagle Squadrons of World War II," 15.
43. Ibid., 16.
44. Ibid., 18.
45. Caine, *Eagles of the RAF*, 205.
46. Kan, "First in the Air: The Eagle Squadrons of World War II," 18.
47. Caine, *Eagles of the RAF*, 249–251.
48. "Allied Raid on Dieppe Set Pattern for Real Invasion," *Eugene Register-Guard*, August 19, 1942.
49. Kan, "First in the Air: The Eagle Squadrons of World War II," 22–23.
50. Ibid., 24–25.
51. Caine, *Eagles of the RAF*, 269.
52. Kan, "First in the Air: The Eagle Squadrons of World War II," 25.
53. Caine, *Eagles of the RAF*, 278.
54. William Dunn, *Fighter Pilot: The First American Ace of World War II* (Lexington: University Press of Kentucky, 1982).
55. Ibid., 283–284.
56. Caine, *Eagles of the RAF*, 336–349.

Chapter 16

1. McCormick, *One Man's Wars*, 196.
2. Given the date of the German invasion of Yugoslavia and later events, the meeting with Roosevelt probably occurred in the summer of 1941, well before the December 7 attack on Pearl Harbor drew America into the war.
3. McCormick, *One Man's Wars*, 196–197.
4. When it comes to bureaucracies, some things never change. Following the September 11, 2001, terrorist attacks on New York City and the Pentagon, official inquiries determined that a failure to share information among the intelligence services had undermined the nation's security. Then-president George W. Bush established an intelligence czar to achieve greater cooperation among the agencies, just as FDR did 60 years before.
5. CIA website.
6. The regiment earned the official designation "The Fighting Sixty-Ninth" during the American Civil War as part of the famed Irish Brigade of the Army of the Potomac.
7. https://www.cia.gov/library/publications/intelligence-history/oss/art02.htm.
8. Ibid.
9. Sweeny had made many friends in the intelligence services of France, England and the United States. Marine Corps Lieutenant Colonel John Thomason, was well placed to aid Sweeny in his efforts to join Donovan's organization. In 1941–42, he was a section chief in the Office of Naval Intelligence. Thomason (1893–1944) won the Navy Cross at Belleau Wood in World War I, and an author and illustrator of several books and magazine articles.
10. Memo to President Franklin D. Roosevelt by William J. Donovan (COI) dated January 9, 1942, Archives, FDR Presidential Library. http://www.fdrlibrary.marist.edu/_resources/images/psf/psf000511.pdf.
11. "London Parley Helped Silver," *Spokesman Review*, August 1, 1933.
12. "The Washington Merry-Go-Round" column, *United Feature Press Release*, March 15, 1942.
13. "The Washington Merry-Go-Round" column, *Long Beach Independent*, February 22, 1942. When Germany overran France in World War II, the French government fled the country. When an Armistice was signed between Germany and France on June 22, 1940, General Philippe Petain became the acting president of France. The French State then moved to the spa town of Vichy in central France and collaborated with the Nazis. The Allies were leery that the remaining French military might fight on the side of Germany.

14. Field Marshal Erwin Rommel, known as the Desert Fox, led Germany's forces in the North Africa campaign. He met with early successes but the Allies eventually drove the Germans off the continent. Later, Rommel was forced to commit suicide by Adolf Hitler because of his involvement in the July 1944 plot to assassinate Hitler with a bomb. Hitler gave Rommel the choice between suicide or the death of his family. The Nazi propaganda machine staged an elaborate funeral for Rommel, claiming he had bravely lost his life in a battle defending the Third Reich.
15. *Ibid.*

Chapter 17

1. Charles Scribner's Sons Collection.
2. *Ibid.*
3. *Ibid.*
4. *Ibid.*
5. *Ibid.*
6. *Ibid.*
7. *Ibid.*
8. The United States had won a decisive naval victory at Midway in June 1942, had landed in the Solomon Islands in August 1942, and was pushing the Japanese back in New Guinea.
9. Charles Scribner's Sons Collection.
10. *Ibid.*
11. Charles Sweeny, *Moment of Truth* (New York: Charles Scribner's Sons, 1943), 92.
12. *Ibid.*, 93.
13. *Ibid.*, 206.
14. *Ibid.*, 245.
15. *Ibid.*, 252.
16. *Ibid.*, 256–258.
17. *Ibid.*, 277–287.

Chapter 18

1. Charles Scribner's Sons Collection.
2. Charles Sweeny, *Ring in Our Nose* (unpublished manuscript, 1943).
3. Charles Sweeny, *Britain Bids for World Power* (privately printed, Arrow Press, 1948) 1.
4. Maxwell Perkins and Elizabeth Lemmon, *As Ever Yours: The Letters of Max Perkins and Elizabeth Lemmon* (University Park: Pennsylvania State University Press, 2003), 194.
5. Charles Scribner's Sons Collection, Sweeny letter to Perkins, November 15, 1943.
6. The Marshall Plan, officially known as the European Recovery Plan, was a program developed by Secretary of State George C. Marshall. Through it, the United States gave $13 billion in aid to help rebuild western European economies after World War II.
7. Charles Sweeny, *Britain Bids for World Power*, 11.

8. John C. Fredriksen, *American Military Leader, Volume 1 A–L* (Santa Barbara: ABC-CLIO, 2009), 416.
9. Sweeny was referring to Cordell Hull, Secretary of State; Harry Hopkins, chief foreign policy advisor to FDR; Sam Rosenman, While House counsel, and Felix Frankfurter, a Supreme Court justice and an informal advisor to FDR.
10. Charles Scribner's Sons Collection, Sweeny letter to Perkins, February 2, 1944.
11. Charles Scribner's Sons Collection, Sweeny letter to Perkins, May 22, 1944.
12. Charles Scribner's Sons Collection, Sweeny letter to Perkins, May 6, 1944.
13. Charles Scribner's Sons Collection, Frazier Hunt letter to Sweeny, May 6, 1944.
14. Charles Scribner's Sons Collection, Sweeny letter to Perkins, May 22, 1944.
15. Charles Scribner's Sons Collection, Perkins letter to Sweeny, June 2, 1944.
16. Charles Scribner's Sons Collection, Charles Scribner letter to Sweeny, July 13, 1944.
17. Charles Scribner's Sons Collection, Perkins letter to Sweeny, July 20, 1944.
18. Charles Scribner's Sons Collection, Sweeny letter to Perkins, July 24, 1944.
19. *Ibid.*
20. *Ibid.*
21. Charles Scribner's Sons Collection, Sweeny letter to Perkins, August 22, 1944.
22. Charles Scribner's Sons Collection, Sweeny letter to Perkins, November 16, 1944.
23. Charles Scribner's Sons Collection, Perkins letter to Sweeny, November 20, 1944.
24. Charles Scribner's Sons Collection, Sweeny letter to Perkins, December 9, 1944.
25. Charles Scribner's Sons Collection, Sweeny letter to Perkins, April 13, 19445.

Chapter 19

1. "Wireless Infernal Machine Newest Weapon of Underworld," *Ft. Wayne Sentinel*, September 27, 1913.
2. Dates obtained from the website of Mt. Olivet Cemetery, Salt Lake City, Utah.
3. Interview with Frank Goodbold, May 21, 2015.
4. Interview with Betsy Bamberger Lesser by Leslie G. Kelen on the J. Willard Marriot website of the University of Utah. Lesser (1922–2004) was the granddaughter of Utah Governor Simon Bamberger.
5. *Ibid.*; McCormick, 210.

Chapter 20

1. Charles Scribner's Sons Collection.
2. McCormick, *One Man's Wars*, 18–19.

3. *Ibid.*, 146.
4. *Ibid.*, 21–22.
5. Sweeny took a curious stance on Operation Torch. He hinted that America should never have invaded North Africa since the U.S. was not at war with France. Much of North Africa was under French control at the time.
6. McCormick, *One Man's Wars*, 157–158.
7. Sweeny, *Petain*, 27.
8. *Ibid.*, 23.
9. *Ibid.*, 29.
10. *Ibid.*, 30.
11. *Ibid.*, 31.
12. *Ibid.*, 22–23.
13. *Ibid.*, 34.
14. Charles Scribner's Sons Collection.

Chapter 21

1. Charles Scribner's Sons Collection.
2. "The Army Makes Public the Findings of Its Inquiry into the Disaster on Dec. 7, 1941," *New York Times*, August 30, 1945.
3. Charles Sweeny, *Pearl Harbor* (self-published, 1946), 9–10.
4. The Roberts Report refers to the commission appointed by the President Roosevelt in December 1942 and chaired by Supreme Court Justice Owen Roberts to investigate the Pearl Harbor disaster.
5. "Radar, Built Here, Detected Pearl Harbor Attack but Futile Early Warning," *Baltimore Sun*, November 29, 1991.
6. Sweeny, *Pearl Harbor*, 12.
7. *Ibid.*, 13.
8. *Ibid.*, 14.
9. *Ibid.*
10. *Ibid.*, 15.
11. *Ibid.*
12. *Ibid.*
13. Robert B. Edgerton, *Warriors of the Rising Sun: A History of the Japanese Military* (New York: W. W. Norton, 1997), 257; "Pearl Harbor Truly a Sneak Attack, Papers Show," *New York Times*, December 9, 1999; "Historian Seeks to Clear Embassy of Pearl Harbor Sneak Attack," *Japan Times*, December 14, 2014.
14. Sweeny, *Pearl Harbor*, 16.
15. *Ibid.*, 20.
16. *Ibid.*, 20–21.
17. *Ibid.*, 21.
18. *Ibid.*, 22.
19. *Ibid.*, 22–23.
20. The New Deal included several economic and social programs such as the Civilian Conservation Corps, Works Progress Administration, Tennessee Valley Authority, and Social Security, all intended to put Americans back to work and offer long-term security.
21. Sweeny, *Pearl Harbor*, 37–38.
22. *Ibid.*, 39.
23. *Ibid.*, 69–70.
24. *Ibid.*, 74.

Chapter 22

1. Frank Goodbold Collection.
2. *Ibid.*
3. *Ibid.*
4. *Ibid.*
5. Frank Goodbold Collection.
6. *Ibid.*

Chapter 23

1. Passenger manifest for the *Excambion*, March 18, 1941.
2. Passenger manifest for the *Drottningham*, June 30, 1942.
3. Passenger manifest for the *Stevens Victory*, which departed Le Harve, France, for New York on May 5, 1946.
4. The home, built in 1924, has four bedrooms and five bathrooms in just under 4,000 square feet. In 2016, it was valued at more than $5 million.
5. Interview with Frank Goodbold, May 30, 2015.
6. Patricia was a graduate of Mills College, a private women's college in Oakland, California. Her father was a Canadian-born mining engineer working in Utah. In 1950, he was general manager of the Independent Coal and Coke Co. executive The family lived in a large, upscale home near Dorothy Bamberger Allen's estate.
7. Marriage record and city directories for Salt Lake City.
8. Interview with Frank Goodbold, May 30, 2015.
9. *Ibid.*
10. "Miss Sweeny Visits Salt Lake," *Salt Lake Tribune*, October 15, 1945.
11. O'Hare was born in Oklahoma. He began working on ocean liners at age 16. At 18, he married 26-year-old Katherine Dixon Riggs, a New York City magazine editor, published poet and writer for *Time*, *Look* and the *Reader's Digest*. It is likely he met Riggs on a two-week cruise with her parents to Jamaica and back. O'Hare and Riggs were married in New York City on April 28, 1927, two weeks after that cruise. He continued to work on ocean liners until the late 1930s. The 1940 census lists him as a typesetter in New York City. The marriage ended during the war and O'Hare moved to Los Angeles.
12. Interview with Frank Goodbold, May 30, 2015.
13. Interview with Frank Goodbold, April 30, 2016.

14. *Ibid.*
15. *Ibid.*
16. A borrow pit is where soil, sand or gravel is dug for use in construction at another location.
17. "Second Son in Poor Condition; Utah Mother, Son Killed in Crash," *Daily Herald*, Provo, Utah, August 15, 1958.
18. *Deseret News*, August 15, 1958.
19. Interview with Frank Goodbold, May 30, 2015.
20. According to Frank Goodbold, Sweeny couldn't prevail on Dorothy Bamberger Allen to let the boy live with them, so he "shopped" the boy around to families he knew until the Goodbolds agreed to take him in.
21. O'Hare wed nurse Land in 1960. They lived in Los Angeles until O'Hare's death in 1987. Land died in 2008.
22. Interview with Frank Goodbold, May 30, 2015.
23. *Ibid.*
24. Frank Goodbold Collection.
25. *In re O'Hare's Guardianship*, 9 Utah 2d 181 (1959).
26. Although Verden Talbot testified in court that he intended to raise the girls and would not need any financial help, the girls were actually in the care of one of his sisters and that "she wants the full amount of the income from the [girls'] trust funds," according to a December 18, 1958, letter to Sweeny from his lawyers. The trust funds included shares of stock in the Sweeny Investment Co. According to Frank Goodbold, the sister used the money from the girls' trusts to pay off the mortgage on her family's farm. Frank Goodbold Collection.
27. Interview with Frank Goodbold, May 30, 2015.
28. *Ibid.*
29. Thomas died in 1990 and Raymonde in 2014. In 1982, French president Francois Mitterrand awarded her the Medaille de Chevalier de L'Ordre National du Merite for her many years of service to France and the French expatiate community in San Francisco.
30. Interview with Frank Goodbold, May 21, 2015.
31. *Ibid.*
32. *Ibid.*
33. McCormick, *One Man's Wars*, 210.
34. Interview with Frank Goodbold, May 30, 2015.
35. Frank Goodbold Collection.
36. *Ibid.*
37. *Ibid.*
38. *Ibid.*
39. *Ibid.*
40. Interview with Frank Goodbold, May 21, 2015.
41. McCormick, *One Man's Wars*, 211.
42. Report of death of Patrick by U.S. consulate in Nice, France.
43. http://theesotericcuriosa.blogspot.com/2010/09/tarnished-life-of-1948-season-girl_07.html.
44. In 1943, Margaret fell 40 feet down an open elevator shaft, after which she became sexually voracious. In 1951, she married the Duke of Argyll. Their 1963 divorce case became an international sensation, in which the duke alleged his wife had had sex with as many as other 88 men during their marriage. A Polaroid photo was introduced into evidence showing the duchess, nude, performing a sex act on a naked man whose head was not visible. Analysis of handwriting on the photo focused on five candidates for the man in the photo. They included Minister of Defense Duncan Sandys, who was Winston Churchill's son-in-law, and movie star Douglas Fairbanks, Jr. The identity was never proven in court. Margaret died a pauper in July 1993. In one final bizarre twist, she was buried next to her ex-husband, Charles Sweeny. Their daughter, Frances, married the 10th Duke of Rutland in 1958.
45. McCormick, *One Man's Wars*, 211.

Bibliography

Books

Ambrose, Stephen E. *Duty, Honor, Country: A History of West Point*. Baltimore: Johns Hopkins University Press, 1999.

American Battle Monuments Commission. *80th Division Summary of Operations in the World War*. Washington, D.C.: Government Printing Office, 1944.

Baker, Carlos. *Ernest Hemingway: A Life Story*. New York: Charles Scribner's Sons, 1969.

Baker, Carlos. *Ernest Hemingway, Selected Letters, 1917–1961*. New York: Charles Scribner's Sons, 1981.

Bowe, John, and Charles L. MacGregor. *Soldiers of the Legion*. Chicago: Press of Peterson Linotyping Co., 1918.

Bruce, Robert B. *A Fraternity of Arms, American & France in the Great War*. Lawrence: University of Kansas Press, 2003.

Caine, Philip D. *Eagles of the RAF*. Washington, D.C.: National Defense University Press, 1991.

Cisek, Janusz. *Kosciuszko, We Are Here: American Pilots in the Kosciuszko Squadron, 1919–1920*. Jefferson, NC: McFarland, 2002.

Company F History, 319th Infantry. Flemington, NJ: Ryman Herr, 1920.

Davies, Norman Richard. *White Eagle, Red Star: The Polish-Soviet War 1919–1920*. New York: Random House, 1972.

Donovan, James. *A Terrible Glory: Custer and the Little Bighorn*. New York: Little, Brown, 2008.

Dunn, William. *Fighter Pilot: The First American Ace of World War II*. Lexington: University Press of Kentucky, 1996.

Eisenhower, John S.D. *Yanks: The Epic Story of the American Army in World War I*. New York: Simon & Schuster, 2001.

Esposito, Vincent J. *The West Point Atlas of American Wars*. New York: Frederick A. Praeger, 1959.

Fahey, John. *The Ballyhoo Bonanza: Charles Sweeny and the Idaho Mines*. Seattle: University of Washington Press, 1971.

Flynn, John T. *Men of Wealth: The Story of Twelve Significant Fortunes from the Renaissance to the Present Day*. New York: Simon & Schuster, 1941.

Furr, Herman. *314 Machine Gun Battalion History, Blue Ridge (80th) Division*. Officers and Men of the Battalion, 1919.

Gilbert, Martin. *The First World War*. New York: Henry Holt, 1994.

Glasscock, C.B. *The War of the Copper Kings: Builders of Butte and Wolves of Wall Street*. New York: Grosset and Dunlap, 1935.

Hall, W.B. (Bert). *In the Air: Three Years On and Above Three Fronts*. New York: The New Library, 1918.

Harrison, Gordon A. *Cross Channel Attack*. Saypoint, CT: Konecky & Konecky. 1950.

Haugland, Vern. *The Eagle Squadrons: Yanks in the RAF, 1940–42*. Boston: McGraw-Hill, 1992.

History of the 318th Infantry Regiment of the 80th Division, 1917–1919. Richmond: Byrd, 1919.

Karolevitz, Robert, and Ross S. Fenn. *Flight of Eagles: The Story of the American Kosciuszko Squadron in the Polish-Soviet War 1919–1920*. Sioux Falls: Brevet Press, 1974.

Keegan, John. *The First World War*. New York: Random House, 1998.

Kennerly, Byron. *The Eagles Roar!* New York: Harper & Brothers, 1941.

Kershaw, Alex. *The Few: The American Knights of the Air Who Risked Everything to Fight in the Battle of Britain*. Cambridge: Da Capo Press, 2006.

Kinross, Patrick. *Ataturk: The Rebirth of a Nation*. London: Orion Publishing Group, 1993.

Kohn, George C. *Dictionary of Wars*. New York: Facts on File, 1968.

Korda, Michael. *Ike: An American Hero*. New York: HarperCollins, 2007.

Krauze, Enrique. *Mexico: Biography of Power*. New York: Harper Perennial, 1996.

Lehning James R. *To Be a Citizen: The Political Culture of the Early French Third Republic*. Ithaca: Cornell University Press, 2001.

Lengel, Edward G. *To Conquer Hell, The Meuse-Argonne, 1918*. New York: Henry Holt, 2008.

Lenz, Lawrence. *Power and Policy: America's First Steps to Superpower, 1899–1922*. New York: Algora Publishing, 2008.

McCormick, Donald. *One Man's Wars: The Life of Charles Sweeny, Soldier of Fortune*. London: Arthur Baker, Limited, 1972.

Meyers, Jeffrey. *Hemingway: A Biography*. New York: Harper & Row, 1985.

Morlae, Edward. *A Soldier of the Legion*. Boston: Houghton Mifflin, 1916.

Mott, T. Bentley. *Myron Herrick, Friend of France*. Garden City, NY: Doubleday, Doran & Co., 1929.

Murray, Kenneth Murray. *Wings Over Poland: The Story of the 7th (Kosciuszko) Squadron of the Polish Air Service, 1919, 1920, 1921*. New York: D. Appleton, 1932.

Nadelman, Ethan A. *Cop Across the Borders: The Internationalization of U.S. Law Enforcement*, University Park: Pennsylvania State University, 2006.

Nelson, James Carl. *The Remains of Company D: A Story of the Great War*. New York: St. Martin's Griffin, 2009.

Omissi, David E. *Air Power and Colonial Control: The Royal Air Force 1919–1939*. Manchester: Manchester University Press, 1990.

Peck, Josiah C. *The 319th Infantry in the A.E.F.* Paris: Herbert Clark, Printer, 1919.

Perkins, Maxwell Everts, and Lemmon Elizabeth. *As Ever Yours: The Letters of Max Perkins and Elizabeth Lemmon*. University Park: Pennsylvania State University Press, 2003.

Porch, Douglas. *The French Foreign Legion, A Complete History of the Legendary Fighting Force*. New York: HarperCollins, 1991.

Rasmussen, Darol B. *Roots For Revolt: Why the Rich Get Richer and All Others Pay*. New York: Vantage Press, 1996.

Reynolds, Michael. *Hemingway, The Final Years*. New York: W.W. Norton, 1999.

Reynolds, Michael. *Hemingway, The Homecoming*. New York: W.W. Norton, 1992.

Reynolds, Michael. *Hemingway, The Paris Years*. New York: W.W. Norton, 1989.

Rockwell, Paul Ayers. *American Fighters in the Foreign Legion*. Boston: Houghton Mifflin, 1930.

Rhodes, Richard. *Hell and Good Company*. New York: Simon & Schuster, 2015.

Rue, Larry. *I Fly for News*. New York: Albert and Charles Boni, Inc., 1930.

Russell, Philip. *The History of Mexico from Pre-conquest to Present*. New York: Routledge, 2010.

Salmon, John L. *The Official Virginia Civil War Battlefield Guide*. Mechanicsburg, PA: Stackpole Books, 2001.

Silvio, Selva. *The United States and Central America*. Nabu Press, 2012.

Sklar, Holly. *Washington's War on Nicaragua*. Boston: South End Press, 1988.

Stannard, Dorothy. *Morocco*. Boston: Houghton Mifflin, 1993.

Sweeny, Charles (nephew of Col. Sweeny), and James A. Goodson. *The Autobiography of Charles Sweeny*. Canterbury, Kent: Harrop Press, 1990.

Sweeny, Charles. *Britain Bids for World Power*. Privately printed [Arrow Press], 1948.

Sweeny, Charles. *Moment of Truth, A Realistic Examination of Our War Situation*. New York: Charles Scribner's Sons, 1943.

Sweeny, Charles. *Pearl Harbor*. Privately printed [Arrow Press], 1944.

Sweeny, Charles. *Petain*. Privately printed [Arrow Press], 1943.

Sweeny, Charles. *Ring in Our Nose*. Unpublished manuscript, 1943.

von Feilitzsch, Heribert. *In Plain Sight: Felix A. Sommerfeld; Spymaster in Mexico, 1908 to 1914*. Henselstone Verlag, 2012.

Watson, Samuel N. *Those Paris Years*. New York: Fleming H. Revell, 1936.

Werstein, Irving. *Sound No Trumpet: The Life and Death of Alan Seeger*. New York: Thomas Y. Crowell, 1967.

Williams, Ashby. *Experiences in the Great War: Artois, St. Mihiel, Meuse Argonne*. Roanoke: Stone Printing and Manufacturing, 1919.

Woolman, David. *Rebels in the Rif Abd el-Krim and the Rif Rebellion*. Stanford: Stanford University Press, 1968.

Womack, John Jr. *The Mexican Revolution 1910-1920: Mexico Since Independence*. Cambridge: Cambridge University Press, 1991.

Young, Rush S. *Over the Top with the 80th*. Privately printed, 1933.

Articles

Azzou, El-Mostafa. "The Lafayette Escadrille: American aviators in the Rif War (1921–1926)." *World Wars and Contemporary Conflicts*, 2003.

Belfrage, Sally. "The Haunted House of Ernest Hemingway." *Esquire*, February 1963.

Civil War Trust. "The Battle of Third Winchester." Accessed 2015. http://www.civilwar.org/battlefields/third-winchester.html.

Dean, William. "Americans in the Rif Rebellion." *Revue Historique des Armees*, 2007.

Denmark, Karen. "Tribute Honoring Third New Jersey Cavalry." Third New Jersey Cavalry. Accessed 2015. http://3rdnjcavalry.com/.

Everson, Kendall. "The Lafayette Escadrille Escapade." Privately printed. From the collection of Scott Everson.

Gopnic, Adam. "Revisiting the Dreyfuss Affair." *New Yorker*, September 28, 2009.

Kan, Kenneth C. "First in the Air, the Eagle Squadrons of World War II." Air Force History and Museum Program, 2007.

Kraska, Scott. "Legionnaire! Americans in the French Foreign Legion, 1914–1918." *Military Trader Magazine*, October 15, 12013.

Porch, Douglas. "Spain's African Nightmare." *Military History Quarterly*, Winter 2006.

Recouly, Raymond (Captain, French Army staff). "The French Offensive in Champagne, September—October 1915." *Scribner's Magazine*, May 1916.

Reilly, Henry J. "Blitzkrieg." *Foreign Affairs*, January 1940.

Rockwell, Colonel Paul Ayers. "Moroccan Bomber: American Fighters in the Rif War, 1925." *Aviation Quarterly*, 2nd Quarter, 1979.

Strack, Joseph George. "Px for Relaxation: Dentist James V. Sparks, Soldier of Fortune." *TLC*, September 1948.

Time-Life Staff. "Americans Fly for Britain in R.A.F. Eagle Squadron." *Life Magazine*, April 21, 1941

Ward, Gary. "Engaged in Glory Alone: Yanks in French Foreign Legion Were First to Fight." *Veterans of Foreign Wars Magazine*, September 2014.

Correspondence

Sweeny, Charles. 1942–43, Archives of Charles Scribner's Sons, Manuscripts Division, Department of Rare Books and Special Collections, Princeton University Library.

Sweeny, Charles. Personal papers, correspondence and unpublished manuscripts from the files of Sweeny's grandson, Frank Goodbold.

Historical Records

Affidavit from Charles Sweeny's Civil War Pension Application records.

Affidavit by Mrs. Lillian Edwards from Charles Sweeny's Civil War Pension records.

1870 Federal Census, San Francisco, California.

Files and correspondence pertaining to Charles Sweeny from the Federal Bureau of Investigation, U.S. Department of Justice, U.S. Department of State, Department of the Army, Veterans' Administration, and National Archives and Records Administration.

Franklin D. Roosevelt Presidential Library Archives.

Gonzaga College/University Archives.

Notre Dame records, Hesburgh Library, University of Notre Dame.
Public records available on Ancestry.com.
Sweeny's French military service record, Veterans Office of the Foreign Legion, dated June 11, 1920.
Union Army Service Record of James McNulty aka Charles Sweeny (Sr.), National Archives and Records Administration.
U.S. Military Academy Archives.

Newspapers and Periodicals

Arizona Daily Star (Tucson)
Baltimore (Maryland) *Sun*
The Bisbee (Arizona) *Daily Review*
Bismarck (North Dakota) *Daily Review*
Breckenridge News (Cloverport, Kentucky)
Bryan (Texas) *Daily Eagle and Pilot*
Butte (Montana) *Inter Mountain*
Daily Alta California (San Francisco)
The Daily Capital Journal (Salem, Oregon)
Daily Herald (Provo, Utah)
Daily Mirror (Los Angeles)
Daily Missoulian (Missoula, Mont.)
Deseret News (Salt Lake City)
Esquire
Eugene Register-Guard (Oregon)
The Evening Citizen (Ottawa, Ontario)
The Evening Herald (Klamath Falls, Oregon)
Evening Star (Washington, D.C.)
The Evening World (New York)
Ft. Wayne (Indiana) *Sentinel*
The Glasgow (Scotland) *Herald*
Goodwin's Weekly
Grand Rapids (Michigan) *Daily Herald*
Helena (Montana) *Independent*
Long Beach (California) *Independent*
Los Angeles (California) *Examiner*
The Los Angeles (California) *Herald*
Milwaukee (Wisconsin) *Journal*
Montreal Gazette
The New York Times
New York (New York) *Tribune*
The Norfolk (Virginia) *Weekly News-Journal*
Oakland (California) *Tribune*
The Oasis (Nogales, Arizona)
The Ogden (Utah) *Standard*
Ogden (Utah) *Standard Examiner*
Ontario (Oregon) *Argus*
St. Petersburg (Florida) *Times*
Salt Lake (Utah) *Herald*
Salt Lake (Utah) *Mining Review*
Salt Lake (Utah) *Telegram*
Salt Lake (Utah) *Tribune*
The San Francisco (California) *Call*
Seattle (Washington) *Post-Intelligencer*
South Bend (Indiana) *News-Times*
Spokane (Washington) *Daily Chronicle*
Spokane (Washington) *Daily Report*
The Spokesman Review (Spokane, Washington)
The State Journal (Frankfort, Kentucky)
The Sun (New York)
Sunday Spartanburg (South Carolina) *Herald Journal*
The Tacoma (Washington) *Times*
Time Magazine
The Topeka (Kansas) *State Journal*
Valentine (Nebraska) *Democrat*
The Virginia (Minnesota) *Enterprise*
Washington (D.C.) *Herald*
The Washington (D.C.) *Times*

Index

Numbers in ***bold italics*** indicate pages with illustrations

Abd el-Krim 147–149, 152–154, 156, 196, 200, 221
Across the River and Into the Trees (by Hemingway) 11, 12
Aguilar, Porfirio 55
al-Atrash, Sultan Shaykh Hilal 158, 263*n*4
Albert, Eddie 192
Alexander, King of Greece 142, 143
Allen, Charles J. 218
Allen, Dorothy Bamberger 12, 13, 15, ***218***, ***219***, 220, 221, 247–251
Allen, Luke 189
American Smelting and Mining Company 31, 32
Anderson, G.H.P. 183
Anderson, Newton 180
Anderson, Paul 173
Archibald, Kenneth 171
Armengaud, Paul-Francois-Maurice 159, 161, 168, 202, 222
Arnold, Henry "Hap" 180, 186, 211
Arredondo y de Leon Barra, Juan Jose 56
Ashley, Sylvia 251
"The Asphalt War" 60–65
Ataturk, Mustafa Kemal 9, 141, 147, 204
Attenborough, David 194
Azzou, El-Mostafa 153

Bach, Jules James ***84***, 85, 93, 94, 107, 112
Baer, Paul F. 180
Baker, Carlos 8, 11, 12, 162
Baker, Newton 115
Bamberger, Clarence 12, 250
Bamberger, Dorothy *see* Allen, Dorothy Bamberger
Bamberger, Herman 73
Bamberger, Jacob 73, 218

Bamberger, Simon 73
Bankhead, Tallulah 181
Barrymore, Diana 192
Beaumont, Charles 85
Beaverbrook, Lord (Max Aitken) 179
Bebout, James D. 123
Beevor, Antony 160
Bergman, Ingrid 17
Berle, Adolf A., Jr. 175, 176
Besant, Annie 54
Bishop, William "Billie" 180
Bitmead, E.R. 189
Blake, Amanda 220
Blakeslee, Donald 195
Blum, Leon 226, 235
Boismaure, Charles 85
Bonaparte, Charles 56
Bonaparte, Napoleon 85
Booz, Oscar L. 49, 50
Borah, William 215
Bouillon, Henry Franklin 221
Bouligny, Edgar John 85, 86, 93, 95, 107, 112
Bowe, John 84, 102
Bowlby, Henry Lee 51
Brettell, Edward 194
Bridges, Harry 14
Brown, Constantine 180, 206, 212, 216
Brown, George A. 178
Brown Brothers investment bank 72
Bruce, David K.E. 17
Bruce, Nigel 192
Buffum, Thomas 150
Bullard, Robert Lee 120
Bullen, W. Graham ***151***
Burke, John 28
Burwell, Rose Marie 9
Butler, Smedley Darlington 72

275

Index

Cabrera, Manuel 69, 71
Cananea Consolidated Copper Company 55
Capdevielle, Ferdinand 85, 93
Capitano Juanita 55–57, 76, 77
Carstairs, James Stewart 83, *84*, 85, *86*
Casey, John Jacob *84*, 85, 95, 96, 107
Casmese, George 81, 83–*84*, 85–86, 112
Castro, Cipriano 58, 60–65
Castro, Demetrio 57
Chamberlain, Neville 209
Chapman, Victor 106
Charlemagne, Holy Roman emperor 238
Charles Scribner's Sons 9, 203, 205, 208, 213, 214, 216, 217
Charton, John 85
Charton, Louis 85
Chatkoff, Herman 85
Chevalier, Jacques 226
Chidester, Gene Ray 244
Churchill, Randolph 220
Churchill, Walter M. 182, 183, 186
Churchill, Winston 165, 174, 181, 191, 192, 198, 206, 209, 215–217
Clark, Bennett Champ 113
Clark, Champ 113
Clark, F. Lewis 41; *see also* Empire State Mining and Development Company
Clarke, Patricia Anne 242, 250, 268*n*6
Clemenceau, Georges 215
Cleveland, John Abell 5, 58, 62
Collins, Harry 85
Columbus, Christopher 146
Connelley, Joanne 251
Constantine I, King of Greece 142, 143
Coolidge, Calvin 198
Cooper, Gary 12, 17, 220
Cooper, Merian C. 6, 135–138
Cooper, Veronica "Rocky" 12, 220
Cousins, Shuyler *155*
Cowden, Eliot 106
Cowley, Malcolm 240
Coxey, Jacob 30
Craig, Charles 150
Creel, Enrique 56
Cronkhite, Adelbert 120, 127, 129
Crown Prince Wilhelm of Germany 99, 120
Crum, John 113, 123
Cummings, William L. 219
Custer, George Armstrong 20, 35

Daladier, Edouard 168, 174, 226
Daly, Louise 124
Davies, Norman Richard 135, 138
Daymond, Gregory A. "Gus" 188, 190
Dean, William 146, 147, 154
de Gaulle, Charles 135, 223, 224, 226
Delpeuch, George 85
Dempsey, Jack 220
de Rubio, Henry A.C. 113
Desmoulins, Camille 84

Diament-Berger, Ginette 242
Diament-Berger, Henri 242
Diaz, Adolfo 69, 71
Diaz, Felix 57
Diaz, Porfirio 52, 53, 56, 57
Donahue, Peter 21
Donovan, William J. "Will Bill" 196–199, 201
Dos Passos, John 10, 162
Douglas, Sholto 186, 190, 194
Doumergue, Gaston 222
Dowd, Dennis 85
Dreyfus, Alfred 77
Drummond, Gregory 190
Dufour, Emil 85
Duke of Connaught, Governor General of Canada 116
Dunn, William 190, 195
Duval, Robert C. 123

Eagle Squadron, R.A.F. 178–193
Earp, James 27
Earp, Wyatt 27
Eisenhower, Dwight 14, 173
Empire State Mining and Development Company 31, 41
Endicott, Willard O. 26, 27
Estrada, Jose Delores 71
Estrada, Juan Jose 67, 69–71
Everson, Kendall Winton 169–171

Faisal I, King of Syria 158, 263*n*2
Farago, Ladislas 162
A Farewell to Arms (by Hemingway) 8
Fauntleroy, Cedric E. 135
FBI (Federal Bureau of Investigation) 1, 5, 165, 167–173, 175
Ferdinand, King of Spain 146
Finucane, Francis 35
Flynn, John T. 142, 143
Foch, Ferdinand 90, 138, 141
For Whom the Bell Tolls (by Hemingway) 9, 11, 12
Ford, John 136
Foster, Addison C. 33, 34
Franco, Francisco 147, 148, 163, 164, 220, 235
Frankfurter, Felix 212
Franz Ferdinand, Archduke 79
Freeman, Wilfred 193

Ganson, Joseph 85
Gardiner, Ava 12
Geiger, William 192
Gellhorn, Martha 162
Genet, Edmund 101–103
George V, King of England 116
George VI, King of England 196
Gerow, Leonard 229, 231
Gibbons, Floyd 162
Glaoui, Thami El 200

Glarner, Andre 247
Glaudel, Colonel 88
Godskin, John 63
Goebbels, Joseph 211
Gomez, Juan Vicente 59, 62, 63, 65
Gonzales, Pedro N. 57
Goodbold, Frank (aka Ernest Hemingway O'Hare) 2, 13, 15, 158, 218, 238, 242, **243**, 244, **245**–248, 250n, 252
Goodbold, Raymonde Glarner 246–248, 269n29
Goodbold, Thomas 246–248, 269n29
Gouraud, Henri **155**
Grant, Ulysses S., III 49
Greene, Francis V. *see* New York and Bermudez Asphalt Company
Greene, William C. 55
Grundy, Francis. Bernard 95
Guggenheim family *see* American Smelting and Mining Company

Haas, Theodore 86
Haeffle, Louis 86
Hall, Bert 83. 86, 94, 106
Hall, Jon 192
Hall, William 187
Haller, Jozef 135
Hallinan, Vincent 14
Halsey, William F. 233
Hamilton, Horatio 60
Hanley, Kennedy J. 41
Harding, Warren G. 198
Harris, Walter Burton 76
Haugland, Vern 172
Hemingway, Ernest: books and short stories *see* specific titles; death 17, 252; Greco-Turkish War 5, 7, 8; as journalist 7, 159, 162; marriages *see* Gellhorn, Martha, Richardson, Hadley, Welsh, Mary; parents, relationship with 6, 7; Spanish Civil War 9–11, 160–163; Sweeny, friendship with 5, 6, 8–17, 144, 159, 163, 164, 216, 220, 249, 250; women, views on 6, 7, 9, 220
Henrys, Paul Prosper 135
Herbst, Josephine 162
Herrick, Myron T. 82, 83
Hill, Dudley 171, 172
Hitler, Adolf 165–168, 178, 185, 198, 199, 209, 210, 215, 223, 225
Hodges, Clyde Hamilton 169–171
Hoffecker, Charles 86
Holden, Lansing **151**
Hoover, J. Edgar 167, 175–177, 198, 199
Hopkins, Harry 212
Hotchner, A.E. 17
Hull, Cordell 201, 212, 229, 231, 233, 235
Hunt, Frazier 206, 213, 216, 239
Hutton, Barbara 182, 251

Isabella, Queen of Spain 146

Joffre, Joseph 90, 110–112
Johnson, William T. 130
Jones, Wesley L. 43, 47, 255n2

Karayinis, Nick 86
Kardec, Allan 54
Keegan, John 107, 108
Keller, Traugett Frank 51
Kellogg, Frank 152
Kennedy, Joseph P. 175, 179
Kennerly, Byron 173, 184
Keough, Vernon Charles "Shorty" 173–175, 180
Kershaw, Alex 174
Kerwood, Charles W. 150, **151**, **155**
Keynes, John Maynard 210
The Killers (movie based on Hemingway's short story) 12
Kimmel, Husband E. 229, 233, 234
King, David 86
King, Ernest J. 211
Kinross, Patrick 140
Kipling, Rudyard 152
Knickerbocker, H.R. 162
Knickerbocker Trust Company 35
Knight, Clayton 180, 188
Knox, Frank 231, 233
Knox, Philander 69
Kosciusko Squadron 6, 135, 136, 262n8

Lacouture, Jean 138
Lafayette Escadrille 106, 107
Lancaster, Burt 12
Land, Hildegarde 246
Landreaux, Fred 86
Lanham, Charles "Buck" 11, 12, 17
Lawrence (of Arabia), T.E. 145
Leahy, William 211, 212
Lebrun, Albert 222
Lechrone, Philip
Leigh-Mallory, Trafford 190, 192
Lemmon, Elizabeth 209
Lengel, Edward G. 121
Leroy-Besulieu, Pierre Paul 74
Lesser, Betsy Bamberger 218, 219
Liggett, Hunter 127
Linden, Robert J. 26
Linton, Raymond Aaron 51, 58, 62
Lloyd George, David 141, 165, 215
Lodge, Henry Cabot 215
Louis Philippe, King of France 82
Louis XIV, King of France 85
Lovelace, Thomas 63
Luczkow, Michael 180
Lyautey, Hubert 153, 200
Lyons, Leonard 17

MacArthur, Douglas 50, 213, 216, 256n31
MacKay, John W 22, 23
Mackin, James 36

Madero, Francisco 53–55, 57, 73
Madero, Gustavo 54
Madriz, Jose 71
Maghee, Torrey Borden 48, 255*n*17
Mahaffey, Birchie Oliver 51, 58, 62, 256*n*32
Malcolm, Kenneth 135
Mamedoff, Andrew 173–175, 180, 184, 188, 189
Marquez, S.V. 57
Marshall, George C. 200, 211, 228, 230–233
Martelli, C.F. 105
Martin, Frederick 229, 234
Matos, Manuel 61
Matthews, Herbert 162
Maximilian I of Mexico 21
McAllister, Thomas 56
McColpin, Carroll 190
McConnell, James 106
McCormick, Donald 1, 2, 8, 9, 41, 48, 63, 64, 66, 105–107, 131, 138, 139, 142, 143, 152, 156, 161, 163, 167
McGinnis, James 173, 184
McQueen, Steve 194
Meares, Stanley T. 189, 190
Meyers, Jeffrey 12
Mihajlovic, Draza 196
Mills, Albert L 47, 48, 50, 255*n*13
Mitchell, William "Billy" 228
Mitchell, Willie B. 126
Moffat, Thomas C. 69
Moomaw, Daniel Clovis 130
Moore, Richard A. 172, 173, 183
Moorhead, Alan 162
Morgenthau, Henry, Jr. 210
Morlae, Edward 86, 89, 93, 95, 101–103
Mott, C. Bentley 82
Mussolini, Benito 165, 168
Myers, Edward 138

Narvitz, Siegfried 86
Neville, Robert 162
New York and Bermudez Asphalt Company 58, 60, 61, 64, 65
Noe, Jack 86
Nogues, Charles 200

O'Brien, Hugh 220
O'Hare, Charles Sweeny 242, *243*, 244, *245*
O'Hare, Ernest Hemingway *see* Goodbold, Frank
O'Hare, Victor Edwin 242, 246, 247, 268*n*11
The Old Man and the Sea (by Hemingway) 13
"The Old Man at the Bridge" (by Hemingway) 8
Olinger, Achilles 86
Olson, Virgil Wilson 180
Omissi, David E. 159
One Man's Wars 1, 2, 8, 9, 10, 58, 63, 66, 131, 163

Orbison, Edwin 173
Ordonez, Antonio 17
Orlando, Vittorio 215

Paderewski, Ignacy Jan 137
Painleve, Paul 149, 150
Palmer, Walter Edwin, Jr. 169, 171
Paredes, Antonio 62, 65
Parker, Austin Gillette 150, *151*
Parsons, Edwin T "Ted" 171, 172
Patton, George S. 209
Paullet, Tony 86
Pearson, Drew 201, 206
Peck, Sedley 173
Penrose, Leo 172
Penrose, Paul E. 169, 172
Percy, Robert 86
Perkins, Max 2, 9, 10, 12, 162–164, 202, 204–206, 209, 209, 211–217, 221, 228
Pershing, John J. 90, 116
Petain, Philippe 90, 108, 153–155, 178, 200, 221–227
Peterson, Chesley Gordon 172, 173, 176, 183, 186, 187, 190, 185
Phelizot, Rene 83, 89, 93
Pierce, Waldo 9, 10, 253*n*12
Piles, Samuel 33, 34, 36
Pilsudski, Jozef 134, 136, 137
Pino Suarez, Jose Maria 57
Pollack, Granville A. 150, *151*, *155*
Porch, Douglas 145, 148, 149
Primo de Rivera y Orbaeja, Miguel 148
Prince, Norman 106
Powell, Peter 188

Quinlan, P.R. 61

Raney, William Scott 169–171
Reilly, Henry J. 137, 138, 166
Reynaud, Paul 221, 222
Reynolds, Michael 8, 9, 11, 12
Reynolds, Quentin 181
Rhodes, Richard 163, 164
Richardson, Hadley 7
Rockefeller, John D., Jr. 25, 31, 35, 37
Rockwell, Kiffin Yates 86, 97, 106
Rockwell, Paul Ayers 83, 85, 86, 88, 93, 97, 103–105, 107, 109, 112, 150, 152–154
Rogers, William B. 150
Rommel, Erwin 201, 267*n*14
Roosevelt, Franklin Delano 168, 176, 180, 183, 190, 192, 197–201, 206, 208, 209, 211, 213–2117, 228, 229, 232–234, 236, 239
Roosevelt, Theodore, Jr. 198
Roosevelt, Theodore "Teddy" 33, 60, 62, 64
Root, Elihu 55
Roscoe, Art 192
Rosenman, Samuel 212
Rubirosa, Porfiro 251
Rue, Larry 141

Sacasa, Roberto 67
Sanders, Hugh 186
Sargent, John 152
Satterlee, Dean 173
Scanlon, Bob 86
Scarborough, Ross 190
Scribner, Charles 7, 214; *see also* Charles Scribner's Sons
Seeckt, Hans von 165, 168
Seeger, Alan 85, 86, 101, 103, 109
Seeley, Hugh 179
Seldes, George 6
Sharp, William Graves 112
Sheridan, Philip 20, 49
Sheridan, Philip II 9, 12, 253n13
Shipman, Evan Biddle 9, 12, 253n13
Shor, Toots 17
Short, Walter 229, 231, 234
Silvestre, Manuel 147, 148
Smith, Homer 180
Somoza, Anastasio 72, 258n34
Soubiran, Robert 86, 107
Spaatz, Carl 192
Sparks, James V. 150, *155*, 156, 196, 263n34
Stack, Robert 193
Stalin, Joseph 192, 209, 210, 212, 239
Stark, Harold R. 200, 229, 232, 233
Stevens, Margaret 89
Stevenson, Adlai 14
Stimson, Henry 231, 233
Stone, Edward Mandell 86
Sussan, James *155*
Sweeny, Charles (Colonel's father) 19–21, *22*, 23–39, 41–43, 48, 52, 74, 106; Federal Mining and Smelting Company 31, 34, 54, 74; Sweeny Investment Company 35, 248
Sweeny, Charles F. (Colonel's son) 75, *77*, *156*, 157, 185, 241, 242, *243*, 249, 250, 252
Sweeny, Charles Francis (Colonel's nephew) 179, 182, 251
Sweeny, Charles Michael (The Colonel): Allen, Dorothy Bamberger, relationship with *220*–221; birth 25, 37; children *243*, *245* (*see also* Sweeny, Charles F.; Sweeny, Emeline Sophia; Sweeny, Patrick); death 252; Eagle Squadron 5, 178–179, *180*–183, 185, 186, 188, 189; education 38–51, 76; European civilization, views on 74, 77, 157, 159, 174; family background 6, 19–*22*, 23–36; father, relationship with 39, 40, 43, 48, 52, 106; Germany, attitude toward 76, 160, 165, 166, 167, 176, 178; Greco-Turkish War 5, 8, 141–144; health issues 15, *245*, 250, *251*; Hemingway, relationship with Ernest 5, 8–14, 17, 144, 159, 163, 164, 216, 220, 249, 250; Hemingway, relationship with Mary 13–17; Hoover, J. Edgar 167, 168, 175; as journalist 62, 63, 66, 67, 142, 159, 201; Lafayette Escadrille 106, 107; marriage 75, *77*; Mexico 52, 54–57, 203, 204; military

decorations 5, *6*, *80*, *82*, 93, *104*, 105, 131, *155*, *156*, 157, *159*, 204, 222, 260n53, 260n54; *Moment of Truth* 202–207; Nicaragua 5, 66, 70–72; *Pearl Harbor* 228–236; personality 72, 73, 163, 164; *Petain* 221–227; physical appearance 43; Polish-Soviet War 5, 133, 135–139, 204, 262n20; political views 159, 164, 176; public speaker 113, 237; race, views on 74, 152, 250; recruiting pilots 168–177; résumé for Scribner's 203–204; Rif War 5, 10, 149–*151*, 152–157, 204; Russia/Soviet Union, attitude toward 159; Spanish American War 40–42; Spanish Civil War 5, 9–11, 159–164, 204, 234, 235; State Department, relationship with 150–152, 164, 167, 168, 182, 185, 186, 201; Venezuela 58, 62, 63, 64; at West Point (academic record 1, 43, 46, 47; admission 42–43, *44*–*45*; cannon incident 5, 48, 50, 51; discipline record 46, 47; dismissal, first 47; dismissal, second 48; hazing controversy 44, 47–51; readmission 48; women, attitude toward 6, 9, 220; World War I in the Foreign Legion (Champagne Offensive 97–105; enlistment of American volunteers 81, *84*, *86*; promotions 93, 95, 97, 110, 203; tanks 86–89; training *107*, 109, *110*, 204; violating U.S. Neutrality Laws 82, 83; wounds 103–*105*, 106, 131, 260n50, 260n51, 261n65); World War I in the U.S. Army (brother's death 124; commendations 130, 131; commission controversy 112, 113; Meuse-Argonne Offensive *117*, 119–129; objections to training 113, 114; promotion to lieutenant colonel 131; service in 318th Infantry, 80th Division 114–131); *World Disorder/Revolution* 237–240
Sweeny, Emeline Agnes (Colonel's sister) *22*
Sweeny, Emeline Agnes O'Neil (Colonel's mother) 21, *22*, 24, 33, 35–37, 39, 73
Sweeny, Emeline Sophia (Colonel's daughter) 76, *77*, 185, 241–242, *243*, 244, *245*, 250
Sweeny, Eva Felicianne Vons (Colonel's wife) 75–*77*, 158, 185, 202, 241, 244, 245, 248–251
Sweeny, Frank Rockwood *22*, 35, 36
Sweeny, John (Colonel's grandfather) 19
Sweeny, Lillian (Colonel's sister) 21, *22*, 35
Sweeny, Maggie Swords (Colonel's father's first wife) 21, 35
Sweeny, Mary (Colonel's grandmother) 19
Sweeny, Mary Gertrude (Colonel's sister) *22*, 35–37, 154
Sweeny, Nicholas (Colonel's uncle) 20, 25, 37
Sweeny, Patrick (Colonel's son) 76, 185, 241, 249–251
Sweeny, Paul (Colonel's great-grandfather) 21
Sweeny, Robert (Colonel's brother) *22*, 25, 179, 182, 265n5
Sweeny, Robert (Colonel's nephew) 22, 35, 171, 179, 181–183, 251, 264n6, 245n19

Sweeny, Sarah (Colonel's aunt) 19
Sweeny, Sarah (Colonel's great-grandmother) 21
Sweeny, Sarsfield (Colonel's brother) **22**, 25, 35, 124

Talbot, Elizabeth **243**, **245**-247, 252
Talbot, Emeline **245**-247, 252
Talbot, Michele **243**, **245**-247, 252
Talbot, Nicole 2, **243**, **245**-247, 252
Talbot, Thyra 243, 247, 248
Talbot, Verden Lynn 242-244, 246-249, 269n26
Taylor, William E.G. 182, 183, 185-187
Thaw, William 83, **84**, **86**, 93, 94, 106
Thomas, Lowell 206
Thomason, John 266n9
Thurmond, Strom 14
Tierney, Gene 220
Tignor, W.F. 130
Tito, Josip Broz 196
Tobin, Eugene Quimby "Red" 173-175, 180, 190
Tojo, Hideki 22
Towle, Bertrand 86
Towle, Ellingwood 86
Trinkard, Charles 86, 107
Trotsky, Leon 78
Truman, Harry S 213, 239

Vanderbilt, Clarence 74
Vanderbilt, Mrs. Jacob 73, 74
Van Vorst, Rupert 86
Venizelos, Eleftherios 143
Viala, J.J. 171
Villa, Pancho 113

War in the Siegfried Line (by Hemingway) 11
Warner, Charles M. 61
Washington, George 73
Wayne, John 136
Weddle, Joseph Everett 172, 173
Weller, R.H. **151**
Wells, John C. 70
Welsh, Mary 12, 17, 254n41; relationship with Sweeny 13-17
West Point cadet "mutiny" 50-51
Weygand, Maxime 138, 139, 143, 174
Wheelock, John Hall 214
Whigham, Margaret 251, 269n44
White, Harry D. 210
Willoughby, Charles 146, 147, 262n4
Wilson, Woodrow 83, 215
Winant, John 190
Wintle, Alfred 159, 164, 263n6
Wise, Jennings 125
Woodhouse, Henry "Paddy" 187, 189
Wormuth, Francis D. 70, 71, 238
Worrilow, Ulysses 121

Yamamoto, Isoroku 232
York, Alvin C. 261n54
Young, Rush S. 115, 117, 118, 120, 122-125, 127, 129, 130

Zaharoff, Basil 142, 143
Zavala, Joaquin 67
Zeyala, Jose Santos 66-72
Zinn, Frederick 86, 107

www.ingramcontent.com/pod-product-compliance
Ingram Content Group UK Ltd.
Pitfield, Milton Keynes, MK11 3LW, UK
UKHW041929140426
5217IPUK00014B/379